THE RIGOR OF A CERTAIN INHUMANITY

Studies in Continental Thought

John Sallis, editor

Consulting Editors

THE RIGOR
OF A
CERTAIN
INHUMANITY
TOWARD A WIDER SUFFRAGE

JOHN LLEWELYN

Indiana University Press

Bloomington & Indianapolis

This book is a publication of

INDIANA UNIVERSITY PRESS
601 North Morton Street
Bloomington, IN 47404–3797 USA

iupress.indiana.edu

Telephone orders 800–842–6796
Fax orders 812–855–7931

♾ The paper used in this publication
meets the minimum requirements of
the American National Standard for
Information Sciences—Permanence
of Paper for Printed Library Materials,
ANSI Z39.48–1992.

*Manufactured in the
United States of America*

*Library of Congress
Cataloging-in-Publication Data*

Llewelyn, John.
  The rigor of a certain inhumanity :
toward a wider suffrage / John
Llewelyn.
    p. cm. — (Studies in Continental
thought)
  Includes bibliographical references
and index.
  ISBN 978-0-253-00326-3 (cloth : alk.
paper) — ISBN 978-0-253-00579-3 (pbk.
: alk. paper) — ISBN 978-0-253-00586-1
(electronic book) 1. Philosophical
anthropology. 2. Phenomenology.
3. Derrida, Jacques. 4. Lévinas,
Emmanuel. I. Title.
  BD450.L555 2012
  128—dc23

                              2012005092

1 2 3 4 5   17 16 15 14 13 12

For David Wood

*in friendship
and admiration*

it is perhaps more "worthy" of humanity
to maintain . . . the rigor of a certain inhumanity.

—Jacques Derrida

They will get it straight one day at the Sorbonne.
We shall return at twilight from the lecture
Pleased that the irrational is rational.

—Wallace Stevens

CONTENTS

ACKNOWLEDGMENTS

Chapters 1 and 2 are based on "Representation in Language," in Ananta Sukla, ed., *Art and Representation* (Westport, Conn.: Praeger, 2001), pp. 29–59; chapter 3 on "Close Reading, Distant Writing, and the Experience of Language," in Ananta Sukla, ed., *Art and Experience* (Westport, Conn.: Praeger, 2003), pp. 20–41; chapter 4 on the chapter in Welsh on Edmund Husserl in John Daniel and Walford L. Gealy, eds., *Hanes Athroniaeth y Gorllewin* (History of Western Philosophy) (Cardiff: University of Wales Press, 2009); chapter 6 on "Meanings Reserved, Re-served and Reduced," *The Southern Journal of Philosophy* XXXII, Spindel Conference 1993, Supp. vol., *Derrida's Interpretation of Husserl*, 1994, pp. 27–54; chapter 7 on "Approaches to (Quasi-) Theology Via Appresentation," *Research in Phenomenology* 39, no. 2, *Engaging the Religious* (Leiden: Brill, 2009), pp. 224–247; chapter 8 on "Am I Obsessed by Bobby? (Humanism of the Other Animal)," in Robert Bernasconi and Simon Critchley, eds., *Re-Reading Levinas* (Bloomington: Indiana University Press, 1991), pp. 234–245, adapted as chapter 3 of my *The Middle Voice of Ecological Conscience: A Chiasmic Reading of Responsibility in the Neighbourhood of Levinas, Heidegger and Others* (London: Macmillan; New York, St. Martins Press, 1991); chapter 9 on "Who or What or Whot," in J. Aaron Simmons and David Wood, eds., *Kierkegaard and Levinas: Ethics, Politics, and Religion* (Bloomington: Indiana University Press, 2008), pp. 69–81; chapter 10 on "Ecosophy, Sophophily and Philotheria," in Pierfrancesco Basile and Leemon B. McHenry, eds., *Consciousness, Reality and Value: Philosophical Essays in Honour of T. L. S. Sprigge* (Frankfurt am Main: Ontos, 2007), pp.

259–273; chapter 11 on "Pursuing Levinas and Ferry toward a Newer and More Democratic Ecological Order," in Peter Atterton and Matthew Calarco, eds., *Radicalizing Levinas* (Albany: State University of New York Press, 2010), pp. 95–111; chapter 12 on "Where to Cut: *Boucherie* and *Delikatessen*," *Research in Phenomenology* 40, no. 2, *The Non-human Animal* (Leiden: Brill, 2010), pp. 161–187; chapter 13 on the French text of endnote 22 to chapter 13 of my *Margins of Religion: Between Kierkegaard and Derrida* (Bloomington: Indiana University Press, 2009). I thank the editors and publishers for granting permission to adapt these items for publication here.

I am greatly indebted to Dee Mortensen, Angela Burton, Sarah Jacobi, Marvin Keenan, and Emma Young for their expertise in the editing of this book, to my brother Howard and my nephew Simon for rescuing me at times of crisis with the electronics, and to my wife Margaret, my brother David, and all other members of our families for their encouragement and cooperation. John Sallis and François Raffoul were *sine quibus non*.

THE RIGOR OF A
CERTAIN INHUMANITY

Introduction

How wide is our usual conception of what we call universal suffrage? The aim of this book is to show that that usual conception is not wide enough and that it is not wide enough because it does not do justice to what the book's title and one of its epigraphs calls "inhumanity." The envisaged widening of that common conception referred to in the book's subtitle is simultaneously a widening of our conceptions of the ethical and the political toward the ecological. The eco-logical. The envisaged progression starts in logic and the philosophy of logic—unless it is prevented from starting at all because philosophers have held too rigid a conception of logic's scope.

Because the widening of suffrage projected in this book culminates in chapters that owe not a little to the writings of Jacques Derrida, an apt way of illustrating the point I have just made about philosophers who have taken what I regard as a one-sided view of logic is to tell a short story that touches upon what some of those philosophers have said about him.

Among the philosophers just referred to I single out one who singled out me by sending a letter in which I was advised to steer clear of Derrida on the grounds that "Derrida's claim to understanding *any* logic [her emphasis] was a sham." I was flattered to receive this letter, because its sender is an eminent logician, one after whom a certain logical formula has been named and one whose work I greatly admire. It so happens that Willard van Orman Quine was a colleague of hers at her university in the United States. He was a co-signatory of a letter to the University of Cambridge, England, signed by her, requesting that Derrida not be awarded the honorary degree some dons there wanted him to receive. It so happens too that an article by Quine, whose room was put at Derrida's disposal when he was a visiting professor in America, was co-translated into French by the latter for publication in a Continental philosophical periodical. Treating of the limits of logical theory, Quine's article complains that philosophers have been too lax in their understanding of what counts as logic. Is it possible that when my correspondent informed me that Derrida did not have an understanding of *any* logic, she was being a wee bit too strict, understanding by logic the traditional formal logic, modal logic, non-standard logic and, generally, modern symbolic logic such as that based on Russell and Whitehead's *Principia Mathematica*? By that standard a considerable proportion of Sir Peter Strawson's *Introduction to Logical Theory* would not count as logic.

"Logic" is a word derived from the word "*logos.*" This Greek word means language or speech or word. What is *said* through the use of words falls under more or less abstract logic(s) of the sort studied by Quine and his colleague. But are not words entitled to a logic that treats of their use in the *saying* of them? And what about the relation between these logics, between the logic of what is said, propositional logic, and the logic of saying, the logic of proposing? What, in particular, about the relation between logics of the said ("propositions") in which impossibility is standardly opposed to possibility, and, on the other hand, logics of the phenomenology of language in which possibility implies or presupposes impossibility? How this can happen will be considered in the partly retrospective survey of this book given in its final chapter. Suffice it to say on this other sense of impossibility in these introductory paragraphs that if it is to be possible for me to really forgive someone in saying "I (hereby) forgive you," my forgiving must appear to me as being impossible in the sense that I cannot experience it as no more than an expression of my potentiality or power.

I (hereby) propose that we do not turn a key in a lock in a door that would close off *a priori* the second, third, and fourth of the spheres of language just listed from a study that would seek to give of them an account, a *logos* or a logic. For the study of the two adjacent fields I have marked out we could, of course, co-opt another word, perhaps the word "rhetoric" used by Aristotle, who supported this movement for a rigorous limitation of the term "logic" when at *De Interpretatione* 17a he wrote that nonpropositional sentences are of interest to rhetoric and poetics but not to logic and philosophy.

Or we could qualify the application of the noun "logic" to the two adjacent fields with the adjectives "formal" and "informal." Or instead of speaking of logical theory we could speak of the theory of speech acts. Such a study, such a study as was undertaken by John Austin and continued by John Searle, has already turned out to be as fruitful as the study, the "logy," of phenomena, the phenomenology of which Edmund Husserl outlined the method whose rigor was the topic of the first investigations in philosophical logic undertaken by Jacques Derrida and will be a topic of more than one of the chapters of the first part of this book. The questions for us today therefore are whether Derrida had some understanding of logic in that other sense of the word "logic" or its transliterations, and in what understanding of this word there could be an understanding of the chiasm in which things said, linguistic representations, are crossed by responsible addressings. For this crossing is not a hybridization. It is not an intermingling of kinds or genres or genders or ilks or sets of which there could be a theory, or of classes for which there could be a calculus. It is a crossing rather that might make it possible for us to represent, in the sense of stand up for, not only Jacques Derrida against the authoress of that letter to me about him or vice versa, but for both of them at the same time.

A crossing of a different kind is also hinted at in this book, the crossing of what the English call the English Channel (the name of the author of one of the texts discussed in part 2 is Ferry!). Communication and failure to communicate across that strip of water (not to mention the Atlantic) are subsumed under the distinction between the so-called Continental and so-called Analytic schools of philosophy. Any reader still inclined to equate that distinction with a rigidly antithetical opposition will soon learn from the following chapters that this inclination must be resisted. Among the signs that it must are the visit to Edmund Husserl in Germany made by one of the leaders of the Analytic movement, Gilbert Ryle, the return visit made by Husserl, the colloquium on that movement held at Royaument in France, and the presence and influence in Britain of Ludwig Wittgenstein.

Oblique to and subversive of that oversimplifying contrast is a distinction that frames this book in its entirety. I mean the distinction between two senses of representation. Associated with what I have described earlier as too narrow an idea of logic is the semantic idea of representation. That is the sense of representation that gets explicated in part 1. This first part of the present volume undertakes a representation of representation. But according to Wittgenstein's *Tractatus Logico-Philosophicus* a representation of representation is impossible. Hence the obligation to give some attention to his argument for taking that view, as is done in chapter 1, after reviewing some of the main notions about representation that philosophers have defended throughout the history of philosophy. Wittgenstein argues that, strictly and rigorously speaking, nothing can be said about representation. His grounds for saying this turn on his conception of logical form. However, his conception of logic in the *Tractatus* suffers from the restrictedness to which reference has been made above. Once we take into account the senses of logic passed over in silence by him, we learn that there are other and nonformal reasons—reasons to do with others, human or inhuman—why, when the scene is investigated with renewed and renewing rigor and with a wider angle of vision, representation does indeed call to be passed over in silence. Why this is so begins to emerge in part 1, but it is in part 2 that the implications for the "inhuman" are spelled out as far as spelling out in this context is possible. It is there that we learn more fully why the semantic sense of representation and the logic of the said treated in the first part of the book presuppose the ethico-political sense of representation and the logic of saying that is the thread running through the chapters in the book's second part. It is there, in the second part, that we learn that the presupposition just mentioned is the site of a tension that has to be endured (because it is duration itself) between, on the one hand, the rigor of universal law grounded in intuition according to the "principle of all principles" of Husserl's rigorous science, and, on the other hand, the tuition (from deponent, quasi-middle-voice, *tueor,* to regard, to keep in mind, to mind, to uphold—to represent in the sense of stand up for), deeper than intuition and principle, addressed to each of us by each existent in its exceptional singularity. It is there in part 2 that I apply the lessons I learn from Derrida and those we both learn from Levinas—though not without attempting to unlearn other lessons that the latter attempted to teach. The lesson of his that this book endeavors to unlearn is the one which would slight the in- or unhuman, even though the humanism which he favors in its stead is a humanism of the other human being, not a humanism of Enlightenment rationality centered on the individual's free will.

Enlightenment humanism belongs squarely within what Heidegger calls the age of the world picture. That is, the age of semantic representationism. It is the age of the Cartesian conscious subject over against an object or another subject à propos of which, condensing "a whole cloud of philosophy . . . into a droplet of grammar," the Wittgenstein of the *Philosophical Investigations* comments, "I can know what someone else is thinking, not what I am thinking. It is correct to say 'I know what you are thinking,' and wrong to say 'I know what I am thinking.'"[1] Thus through the lens of that drop of grammar do we see Cartesianism inverted. This Cartesianism is what is in the balance when the first chapter of part 2 of the present book treats of what in the fifth of his *Cartesian Meditations* Husserl calls appresentation.[2] This variation of representation is introduced by Husserl in his attempt to explain how we can know what another person is experiencing. I attempt to explain in chapter 7 how appresentation may play a role in the story of the alleged "theological turn in phenomenology." So with that chapter and its turn toward the divine the book makes a turn toward what its title calls a certain inhumanity.

To repeat, the first part of the book undertakes what John Austin calls a phenomenology of language. It takes the form here of a phenomenology of linguistic representation. In the second part what is at work is representation as something broadly ethico-political and indeed religious in a sense (articulated in my *Margins of Religion*[3]) that is not dependent on (or, however, incompatible with) some traditional notions of organized religion or of a God. Part 1 concentrates on the language of humanity (speculatively *humus-animus*, earth with soul or with mind or with reason). Part 2 concentrates on what could be called "an inhumanist turn in philosophy," starting in its first chapter with that alleged "theological turn in phenomenology," but going on in its second chapter to talk about a certain unconfined dog, before treating in succeeding chapters of other nonhuman animals, feline, ovine, bovine, vulpine, lupine, porcine, herpine, asinine, and other, and of the maltreatment of these.

The unhumanity to be considered in those chapters includes also plants, that category of life whose status is left under-investigated by Heidegger. By the time we reach the end of the last chapter we shall have learned something about the manifolded way it includes the inorganic. It includes all plants and the inorganic because it includes all existents. This is why I call the ethico-political ecology toward which the book progresses a blank or white ecology. It is blank ecology because its center of gravity is the notion of sheer existence. Existence, as Kant reminds us, is not a predicate. It is also independent of any predicates by which an existent may be characterized. Yet, because its existence is a good to each existent, its bare existence is enough to entitle it to a voice, a vote (*voix*), a say, a suffrage by which we human beings are elected as advocates charged to respond responsibly to it. To hear that voice is to hear what I have elsewhere called the call of ecological conscience. That call and the response to it is made in what, again following Derrida, I cautiously refer to as "something like the middle voice." I shall explain in chapter 12 why one must not omit these words "something like." Here at the beginning of this book and at the end of its introduction let me say about something like the middle voice only that this "let" is perhaps expressed in something like it, and that so too is or should be the standing-up-for of representation in the ethico-political sense which I invoke in articulating the issues treated in each of the chapters of part 2 and which is silently present, I maintain, behind the forms of semantic representation treated of in each of the chapters of part 1, namely, to count them down, the presence claimed to support representation in chapter 6, grammatical representation in chapter 5, phenomenology as logical re-presentation in chapter 4, representation as experience, experiment and habit in chapter 3, representation as worldview in chapter 2, and representation as idea in chapter 1, the chapter to which we now turn.

PART ONE

PHENOMENOLOGY
OF LANGUAGE

ONE

Ideologies

Old and new ways of ideas

Order may be conferred upon the following unchronologically arranged reminders of the history of thinking about linguistic representation if they are prefaced by the reminder that the word *Gegenstand,* so frequently used by Wittgenstein in the *Tractatus Logico-Philosophicus,* and that word's Latinate predecessor "object" bring with them the notion of something that is over against or cast in front and so stands in the way. A further complexity arises for us today from the fact that when the Scholastics, followed by Descartes and others, speak of the objective reality of an idea as distinct from its formal reality, objective means throwing before, projective. He says in the Preface added after the first edition of the *Meditations* that the formal reality of an idea is the idea as a psychological entity or operation "taken materially," meaning by this taken in abstraction from what the Scholastics, followed by Brentano and Husserl, call its intentionality. In a reply to Caterus, Descartes cites from himself a statement that anticipates a point upon which Husserl will insist and upon the interpretation of which will turn what one thinks about representation in language: "The idea is the thing itself conceived or thought in so far as it is objectively in the understanding." The star as observed by the astronomer through the "objective" lens of his telescope is not in his mind or in his eye or in his mind's eye in the manner in which it is in the sky. Only with respect to its formal (or "material") reality is the idea in the mind in the way that the star is in the sky. And as soon as our topic changes from that of the objective to the formal reality of the idea there results a compensating change in the idea of the mind that it occupies. The mind and its contents now become the topic of scientific study as when the astronomer's own experience of seeing the star gives way to a third-personal treatment of that experience as a case to be investigated by the science of optics.

Of course the word "contents" which I have just used repeats the ambiguity of the word "in." It encourages the thought just expressed that the occupation of the mind by ideas is like the occupation of space by the star, except that instead of occupying the dimensions of space and time, the idea occupies the temporal flow of consciousness. Like the star itself, the idea will still be a thing, but instead of being objectively observable in the modern sense of this adverb it will be observable only by the subject whose idea it is. This is the move that appears to be made by "the way of ideas" followed by classical empiricism. It is in order to counter this move that Husserl, echoing the sentence of which Descartes reminds Caterus, insists that when he says consciousness has the structure of *noēsis–noēma* or *cogito–cogitatum*, although the *noēma* is an *Objekt* it is not an entity additional to the *Gegenstand*—not additional to, for example, a spatio-temporal thing. It is nothing other than the thing itself in its appearing as the accusative of consciousness or as phenomenon.

The Husserlian "*noēma*" is not a freestanding psychological content (*Inhalt*) associated with other such contents by contiguity, resemblance, or causality. And if it can be called an idea it cannot be called inert, as Berkeley calls ideas of corporeal things. The hyphen Husserl inserts between "*noēsis*" and "*noēma*" indicates not a gap but a connection, one that can never be removed. A *noēma* is always animated (*beseelt*) by an act of *noēsis,* and *noēsis* is never without a *noēma*. But at least in the early writings, for example in the *Logical Investigations,* where some of the work done by the terms *noēsis* and *noēma* is performed by the terms *Sinn* and *Bedeutung* (though without the specific forces these terms are given by Frege), Husserl argues that, even where the topic is that of the meaning of linguistic signs, this animation need not in principle be the animation of the words of an empirical language.

Our interest here, however, is not the question of the dependence of meaning on empirical linguistic expression (though some aspects of this question will be treated in chapter 6). Our interest here is the question of the converse dependency. At this point of our historical but not strictly chronological tour of what philosophers have written about linguistic representation, having noted the medieval distinction between two ways of regarding ideas that is continued by Descartes, it is appropriate to ask how representation in language is construed by the philosopher who, while owing much to Descartes, is one of the founders of the so-called way of ideas.

Locke follows at least two ways of ideas. One of these will be signposted in the following section. He sets out on the more well-trodden way when in the first paragraph of the first chapter of Book Three of the *Essay Concerning Human Understanding*, writing "Of Words or Language in General," he distinguishes words understood as articulate sounds such as parrots may be trained to produce from words with what he counts as the further property that man can "make them stand as marks for the *Ideas* within his own Mind." Given this and many other statements to the same effect, it is not surprising that Locke should be held to subscribe not only to a representative theory of perception but to a representative theory of language. If on the representative theory of perception ideas are a screen between the mind and things in their real nature, the representative theory of language will simply add that these ideas get to be the meanings or conceptions denoted by words, and words will be general, signs of instances, if the "internal Conceptions" they name are general ideas. "Words in their primary or immediate Signification, stand for nothing, but the Ideas in the Mind of him that uses them." If to this be added mention of the distinction between writing and speech, it might seem that we have the seminal definition offered by Aristotle in *De Interpretatione* according to which "Words spoken are symbols or signs of affections or impressions of the soul; written words are the signs of words spoken." But Aristotle goes on to say: "As writing, so also is speech not the same for all races of men. But the mental affections themselves, of which these words are primarily signs, are the same for the whole of mankind, as are also the objects of which those affections are representations or likenesses, images, copies (*homoiōmata*)."[1] Aristotle declines to develop these thoughts. His excuse for not doing so there (assuming that the excuse he gives there has not been misplaced from another part of the text, as some scholars suggest) is that these thoughts have been treated in *De Anima*. In fact they seem to undergo no development there either. So on the evidence provided by this definition of words it is difficult to say whether the affections or impressions (*pathēmata*) are what Locke would call general ideas. That they are does not follow from Aristotle's statement that they are the same for the whole of mankind. They could be particulars in the mind that resemble particulars in the minds of others. Their serving to enable communication could be explicable by an account like that usually attributed to Berkeley. On that account an affection, although particular, could function as an archetype. The particular's capacity to represent particular things would be assured, so this story goes, thanks to the resemblance that other affections have to the original. The as it were lateral resemblance between *pathēmata* would be what enables them to function as likenesses representing things "vertically." One difficulty with this account relates to the ambiguity of the word *homoiōmata*. The lateral resemblance that is supposed to explain vertical representation itself supposes that one particular is a re-presentation of the other, even if it does not represent it. If everything resembles everything else in some respect over and above resembling it in virtue of its happening to represent the same thing, and if everything therefore re-presents everything else in the sense of repeating it, what is and what is not a re-presentation that counts for the purposes of linguistic representation remains unexplained. It remains unexplained even if the metaphorical use of the distinction between the lateral and the vertical is dropped and the things, Aristotle's *pragmata,* are analyzed phenomenalistically or subjectivistically as ordered clusters of *pathēmata.* This would still not meet the difficulty that communication would depend on a pre-established harmony between the affections of one soul and those of another. There would remain what Locke calls the secrecy of the reference my thought makes to yours, a secrecy no more surmountable than that which he ascribes to the real nature or the substance of things (*Essay,* III, II, 4).

Let us set aside the problem posed by the thought that everything resembles everything else in some respect. And let us allow that if one thing resembles another then it also re-presents it or re-presents the feature shared by itself and the other. Perhaps this does not amount to the one thing standing for the other. Perhaps we have at best a condition on the basis of which one thing may be made to stand for another, to signify or symbolize it—a condition on the basis of which one thing, even when regarded as a token (and not just because a token is a different *kind* of thing from a type), represents itself. We are still without an account of how one thing may be made to stand for another.

The account of this making that Aristotle goes on to give in *De Interpretatione* is centered on the significative function of words. So it raises the question whether anything is gained by having recourse to mental affections as intermediaries between words and the things they denote. Aristotle holds that the meaning of names or nouns (*onomata*) and nominalized verbs is due to convention. This cannot, however, be an unqualified endorsement of the position maintained in Plato's *Cratylus* by Hermogenes if the latter's view is that any correctness or incorrectness of naming is determined solely by custom or convention. Not if the correctness is determined also by the fact that the names tally with the mental affections of which Aristotle says they are signs and are the same for the whole of mankind. And of course this question concerning the meaning of names is paralleled by the question of the identity of the names themselves considered in isolation from their meaning. Barbarians and Greeks speak different dialects, vary their own pronunciation and form their letters in more or less discernibly different ways. Yet this does not prevent their using what at least members of their own respective communities would recognize across these variations as one and the same letter or word. Does this mean that there is a second affection common to the minds, a verbal impression that partners the semantic impression in virtue of which the word succeeds in naming the thing?

Further, in default of more than we have discovered so far to explain linguistic representation, and recalling Wittgenstein's statement in the *Tractatus* (3.1431) that the fact that tables and chairs are configured in a certain way can represent a state of affairs concerning other things, hence things like linguistic signs, there seems to be no reason why the thing could not serve as the name of a word and indeed of the intermediating mental affection, provided that between the latter and the thing a further intermediating mental affection be posited. Perhaps this is the wisdom concealed in the fact that the Hebrew "*davar*" can mean both word and thing or event, a fact that fits the Hasidic-Kabbalistic doctrine that the Torah existed before the Creation as a jumble of letters to be ordered by the events of which they will tell. This fact is mirrored in the fact that the Greek "*stoicheion*" can mean both letter and element, so the first element of a language, in Democritean atomism, and in Aristotle's comment in *De Generatione et Corruptione* 315b in connection with Democritus that tragedy and comedy come from the same letters.[2] When Philonous's protestation to Hylas in Berkeley's Third Dialogue that he is not for making things into ideas but for making ideas into things is conjoined with Berkeley's teaching that things are signs in the language of God to be deciphered by human beings, these signs are at one and the same time linguistic and natural, depending upon whether they be regarded theologically or as the subject matter of physical science.

Berkeley guarantees to names a correctness founded in nature because nature is founded in God. Ultimately this correctness depends on the undeceiving nature of God no less than does the reliability of the "lessons of nature" invoked in the Sixth Meditation by Descartes. The theological premise is not essential to the case, which, in opposition to the conventionalism of Hermogenes, Cratylus presents for his own claim, that the correctness of names is based on their etymology. That case is not destroyed by saying with Aquinas: "The etymology of a name is one thing, and the meaning of the name another. For etymology is determined by that from which the name is taken to signify something, while the meaning of the terms is determined by that which it is used to signify" (*Summa Theologiae* 11a, 11ae, 92, 1, and *ad* 2). While this is indeed a most salutary reminder that what I mean by a word may not be what my great-great-grandfather—or Adam—meant by that word, it simply denies without argument what Cratylus asserts. Cratylus's assertion amounts to the contention that the determination of what a name signifies is dependent upon the determination of the thing it originally named. The origin as understood by Cratylus would have a logical and epistemological force, but this would be secondary to its sense as historical beginning. Socrates provisionally agrees with Cratylus's thesis, but only because he makes the historical sense of origin secondary to its logical and epistemological force. He imagines a legislator or wordsmith—a forerunner of Berkeley's sign-writing God—who coins words in the light of the Forms or Ideas which, in the language of the altar, are partaken of, or, in the language of the stage, are imitated by the things of the world to which our words refer. So although Socrates appears to be agreeing with Cratylus's view that the correctness of names has a foundation in *phusis* and to that extent appears to be disagreeing with Hermogenes' view that this correctness is based on custom, rule, or law (*nomos*), he is in fact putting forward a third account in which the opposition between *phusis* and *nomos* is denied. To which we may be inclined to say that this is all well and Good, but that both the Cratylic and the Socratic postulates seem superfluous to any explanation of how we manage to get words to represent things correctly. We manage to do that without needing to carry out either etymological research or philosophical dialectic. And the needlessness of dialectic for this purpose remains even if that dialectic does not generate the infinite regress of ideas of ideas between the *eidos* or *idea* as Form and *idea* or *eidos* as thought, a regress analogous to the one to which we saw Locke's new way of ideas appears to lead.

Another idea of idea

If the old Platonic Way of Ideas and the Cratylic way of etymology both lead to dead ends as ways to explain how words represent, room is left open for consideration of Hermogenes' claim that the correctness of the application of words is a matter of customary use. Consideration of this may profitably begin with the reconsideration of Locke promised above, in particular of his statement to the Bishop of Worcester that "The New Way of ideas, and the old way of speaking intelligibly, was always and ever will be, the same thing,"[3] "a new history of an old thing: for I think it will not be doubted that men always performed the actions of thinking, reasoning, believing and knowing, just after the same manner that they do now."[4] Not unnaturally, some commentators see such remarks as an identification of ideas not with objects thought, as in the passages of Locke that support a representationalist reading of him, but with the thinking itself. It is noted by Richard Aaron, from whom the phrase "the thinking itself" is taken, that the interpretation of ideas not as objects thought but as the operations of thinking seems to be at variance with Locke's describing the ideas we have of these operations as ideas of reflection.[5]

Could Locke be saying that an idea is both the object thought and the thinking of it? He could say this if by reflective he means reflexive in the sense that there is self-consciousness without this consciousness having to be that of a subject posed over against itself as an object at the same time. Is this pre-reflective consciousness not what speaking and writing demand, though without demanding that one can never interrupt oneself with the observation that one had just said and/or thought such-and-such? Although statements cited from Locke in the section immediately preceding this one suggest that we observe objects that are internal to our own minds, an implication of private consultation is not compelled by the reference he makes to observations when he writes that "we make use of words both to record our own observations and to recount to others, and commonly also even to think upon things which we would consider again."[6] One's own observations are not bound to be observations of what is one's own in such a way that others may not share in their ownership when one's observations are recounted to them. Furthermore, the very expressions "idea" and "object of thought" for "whatever it is the mind can be employed about in thinking" may mean quite simply the topic of one's thinking. A topic may be a question as to what is the case, how something is done, when something happened, and so on. Questioning implies the engagement of the understanding. And, even where the topic is a physical object, its being a topic implies that it is also an object of thought. It is that for which a word "in its primary or immediate Signification" stands. Here "primary" is not of course equivalent to Locke's "simple," for ideas are also complex. Perhaps, adapting the Fregean way of distinguishing between "*Sinn*" and "*Bedeutung*" mentioned above, it could be said that the primary or immediate signification is what the word means, as distinguished from the physical or other thing to which the word refers.[7] Locke licenses Stillingfleet to substitute for the term "ideas" the terms "notions, or conceptions, or apprehensions,"[8] notwithstanding his own special use of the first of these expressions for "mixed modes," notions depending on stipulative definition or convention, for example perjury, sacrilege, and murder. If one allows oneself to imagine, in the manner suggested earlier, that the Platonic Idea may exist or subsist without being thought by a human intellect, and if one subscribes to the principle that there is nothing *in intellectu* that was not first *in sensu,* one may be inclined to imagine that sensory ideas may exist or subsist independently of being sensed. This inclination is discouraged by the synonyms for that idea proposed to Stillingfleet. They are expressions of the common speech of "countrymen" less likely to mislead a philosopher or a divine in this way than the word "idea" with its Platonic ancestors. However, it is precisely they and their Scholastic successors, substantial forms, that provoke Locke to make use of that word in order to bring it back down to earth and to its indissociability from the operations of *human* understanding, an indissociability that the equivalents offered to Stillingfleet wear more patently on their face.

If words in their primary and immediate significations stand for ideas or notions or conceptions or apprehensions, for what do words in their secondary or mediate significations stand? At least as regards words that are names of material substances one possible answer is real essences, real essences understood, however, not scholastically but mechanistically according to the atomistic hypotheses of Gassendi and Boyle. Saying, as Locke does, that we cannot know the true constitution of material or spiritual substances but only their nominal essences (*Essay* III, VI, 3–11) is another way of saying that the primary and immediate significations of words are based on agreement grounded in what we believe on the basis of experience. Hence, although Book Three, "Of Words," was not a part of Locke's original plan for the *Essay,* the word "Understanding" that figures in his title refers not just to "the" understanding or mind, but to understanding as opposed to misunderstanding. It is to that extent part of the tradition to which the treatises on method of Bacon, Descartes, and Spinoza belong and which culminates in Peirce's essay on how to make our ideas clear—or intelligible, as Locke says, picking up Stillingfleet's comment "but now, it seems, nothing is intelligible but what suits with the new way of ideas" (*Works* IV, 430).

Among the conditions Locke prescribes for the intelligibility of words is that they be joined up in sentences according to the rules of the grammar and that these sentences be joined in a coherent discourse. In the very last chapter of the *Essay,* after referring to practical science, *praktikē,* as one of "the three great Provinces of the intellectual World" and to Things (defined sufficiently generally to include spirits and their constitutions and operations) as the topic of natural philosophy, *phusikē,* he says that since Things other than the mind itself are not present to the understanding, it is "necessary that something else, as a Sign or Representation of the thing it considers, should be present to it: and these are *Ideas.*" So ideas are here included in addition to words within the subject matter of the science of signs he calls *semiotikē.* This is not as strange as it may seem, for in the final sentences of the work words are once again called "articulate sounds," and it will be recollected that the first sentences of its third book make it clear that articulate sounds do not for Locke include what they mean. An articulate sound when made by a parrot can be taken as a sign of something, but only if it expresses a notion, conception, or apprehension is it a linguistic sign or representation.

Forms of life

Locke's requirement for the intelligibility of words that they be linked with other words in sentences that are linked with other sentences in discourse anticipates Frege's statement that names make sense only in the context of a sentence or proposition, a statement that Wittgenstein endorses in the *Tractatus* (3.3). In the *Philosophical Investigations* this thesis broadens out into the claim that a word has meaning only in a form of life. This broadening is a broadening also of the Tractarian notions of pictorial, presentational, and representational form. It not only extends the conception of picture by reminding philosophers of the variety of things that may be meant by description (*PI* 24). It extends beyond the pictorial and descriptive conception of language, reminding us of all the non-representational activities in which words are used (*PI* 23), and so also reminding us that the subject matter of *semiotikē* is at the same time the subject matter of *praktikē,* as semioticians after Locke recognized when they distinguished semantics, syntactics, and pragmatics as the parts of semiotics that are concerned respectively with the relation of signs to meaning and truth, their relation to each other, and their relation to those by whom they are used.

It is because Heidegger too questions the pan-representationalist conception of language that he takes exception to the assumption a reading of Dilthey might reinforce, that the study of language would be at its widest and deepest when its topic becomes *Weltanschauungen*, worldviews. Compare Wittgenstein's self-interrogation "Is this a '*Weltanschauung*'?" (*PI* 122), where the single quote marks may be tantamount to a *sotto voce* "perish the thought," for although the question is asked about the surveyable representation of our uses of words that philosophy should aim to produce by discovering and inventing intermediate cases, the representation the *Philosophical Investigations* comes up with brings out that words are used to perform many functions other than representing or presenting views. If we continue to say that languages embody, express, or represent different views or theories of the world, let us understand that these views (*theōria*) are embodied, expressed, or represented in practices and that what, at its widest and deepest, semiotics is concerned with extends beyond an either/or of theory/practice to a theoretico-practical both/and.

Wittgenstein may have been aware of the irony that this extension is already under way in the passage from Augustine cited at the beginning of the *Philosophical Investigations* as an exemplar of the representationalist doctrine of language, of which the appropriateness for language quite generally is questioned throughout much of the rest of that book. Augustine writes:

> When they (my elders) named some object, and accordingly moved towards something, I saw this and I grasped that the thing was called by the sound they uttered when they meant to point it out. Their intention was shown by their bodily movements, as it were the natural language of all peoples: the expression of the face, the play of the eyes, the movement of the other parts of the body, and the tone of voice which expresses our state of mind in seeking, having, rejecting, or avoiding something. Thus, as I heard words repeatedly used in their proper places in various sentences, I gradually learnt to understand what objects they signified; and after I had trained my mouth to form these signs, I used them to express my own desires.

"In this picture of language," Wittgenstein writes, "we find the roots of the following idea: Every word has a meaning. This meaning is correlated with the word. It is the object for which the word stands." Language is not limited to such a system of communication as that which Augustine describes. In saying that a language that fits Augustine's description is a system, it may not be Wittgenstein's intention to concede that in Augustine's model the verticality of the *nomen–nominatum* model of meaning is supplemented by a horizontal relation among names and namers. But might not this horizontal or lateral dimension be implied in Augustine's assertion "as I heard words repeatedly used in their proper places in various sentences, I gradually learnt to understand what objects they signified"? Could not the phrase *verba in variis sententiis locis suis posita* be an acknowledgment that "Fido"–Fido nominalism or nomenclatism of the sort favored also by Hobbes is conditioned by a system of sentence-frames such that each name succeeds in naming its object only through its being substitutable for names that occupy places in various other sentences and not substitutable for others? So that, as Saussure writes, the positive power of a name, its function as a label imposed upon a thing, is constituted by the differences among its phonological, syntactic, and semantic "others": "in language there are only differences *without positive terms*" in so far as we consider the phonic or graphic type or signifier in isolation from the signified meaning.[9] Only when these mutually implicated aspects of a sign are taken together do we have positive terms and oppositions or distinctions between them. The positive meaning of signs understood in their signifying–signified totality will still be dependent on the positive meaning of other signs thus understood, as are, to employ the now familiar analogy employed by Saussure and Wittgenstein and others, the positive powers of the pieces in chess.

The infant Augustine's grasp of identity through difference subserves the expression of his own desires. His desires or wants (*voluntates*) are prescriptive of what he wants to say, what he means, whether this is what he refers to or names or intends (*meint*) or what he wants to enunciate or say about what he refers to or names or intends (*veut dire*). "Compare the grammar of 'meinen' and 'vouloir dire'" (*PI* 657).[10] The infant is more likely to express (*enuntiabam*) his desires by evincing them in the verbal and body language to which Augustine refers than by reporting or describing them. It is clear from what Augustine says that if there is description it is description for a particular use (*PI* 291), in this case, for example, to get someone to satisfy the child's hunger or thirst. His mastery of language at this stage between infancy and boyhood is the mastery of a fairly primitive form of life. But it is learned by the child's imitation of more mature people. This is why there is no room here for the objection that how the child learns the language is a matter of psychological genesis and therefore cannot be a logical norm for the analysis of the meaning of the terms he uses. See the citation from Aquinas made above in the section on old and new ways of ideas. The genesis is genea-logical. Norms are imbibed like the child imbibes its mother's milk. They are imbibed with it. In the first place the norms are the norms of a rudimentary form of life, a way of getting what one wants, in this case milk, which happens to be also what one needs. When the child wants to suck but no breast or bottle is ready to hand and to mouth, it feels that there is something radically wrong with its world, and expresses that feeling in what it would be premature to call words until it has reached the stage described in the sentences reproduced from Augustine. Even at that stage, when the bottle does not appear or the milk is not flowing freely and the child's world as a totality of facilities ready to hand or to mouth is detotalized through being interrupted by unreadiness to hand or to mouth, it may stretch credibility to suppose that now for the first time its world becomes a totality of facts or of things and materials present at hand representable by names and true or false descriptions.

Heidegger's analysis of the experience of confronting a broken hammer assumes a setting like that of a carpenter's or cobbler's workshop in which the question can arise how and with what the hammer can be mended or replaced. All that the child at the level of Augustine's analysis can do is express his loss in whatever words are at his disposal at that early stage of language acquisition, in the hope that in doing so he will acquire the nutritive goods of which he feels himself deprived. If he cannot suck at least upon his dummy, he will suck so to speak upon words. And indeed in due course he may experience a hunger for them and come to relish and value them for themselves in babble or in a more elaborately artful musico-literary form. His desires for bodily comfort, still met by the succulent succor of oral and aural words, through being catered to in the linguistic medium he shares with his elders, enable him to enter more deeply into the stormy society of human life, as Augustine goes on to say, and give him access to the more complex culturo-linguistic practices that in turn generate more and more complex desires, values, and ideals.

These values may include those of a scientific or philosophical representation of the world. Now linguistic representationalism, as we began to see above and are about to see confirmed now, is not confined to the kind that has words standing initially for private psychological experiences, the subjective idealist (idea-list) kind that, as we saw at the beginning of our discussion of Locke, many of his remarks seem to imply. Other remarks made by Locke imply a realism of a direct empirical kind that would enable him apparently to agree with Heidegger that in an assertion there is a pointing-out that "has in view the entity itself and not, let us say, a mere 'representation' (*Vorstellung*) of it—neither something 'merely represented' nor the psychical condition in which the person who makes the assertion 'represents' it" (*SZ* 154).[11] To cite but one of many statements to this effect made by Locke: "Thus, the idea of the sun, what is it but an aggregate of those several simple ideas, bright, hot, roundish, having a constant regular motion, at a certain distance from us, and perhaps some other: as he who thinks and discourses of the sun has been more or less accurate in observing those sensible qualities, ideas, or properties, which are in that thing which he calls the sun" (*Essay* II, XXIII, 6). But the natural philosophy for which Locke's philosophy of the understanding is intended to clear a path maintains that the sensible qualities in a physical thing are also in the mind. They require the involvement of mentality, not only because the lightness and warmth of the sun are, as Locke writes, "perceptions in me" (*Essay* II, VIII, 24), which seems to entail that the qualities of the sun are in two places at once, but because the place where the properties belong is intelligible and describable only through the idea of a conditional if/then. If the so-called secondary qualities of things are to be understood as consequences of hypothesized events or states among the atomic constituents of the world, then power or potentiality is part of the bright and warm world we inhabit. Locke's way of ideas is often seen as one that fuels the picture of the world as a picturable totality of things or facts represented by simple, compound, and complex ideas in turn representable by propositions and names. However, among ideas required to give the full picture are ones whose complexity can be expressed only in hypothetical statements that are not reducible to categoricals. Now it is true that these hypotheticals state causal connections. It is also true that these may arguably be analyzed as regular conjunctions in the manner of Hume. But what according to Hume is natural belief is indeed natural, and if it is an illusion, it is a transcendental illusion in the sense that it cannot be eradicated. For it remains at the root of all eradication if one's original way of inhabiting a world is not as a representer of things present at hand but as a seeker of solutions and a performer of tasks set by oneself and/or by a world which is an environment: an *Umwelt* that is an *Um-zu Welt*, a world of which the meaning (*Sinn*) is its being an oriented whole, what Heidegger calls a *Verweisungsganzheit*. In this totality it is the ready or unready to hand by which one is always already surrounded, before one is surrounded by a totality of representable objects or facts. Locke asserts that a great part of our complex ideas of things are ideas of their powers (*Essay* II, XXIII, 8). A great part of those powers are within the powers of those who live in the world. So Locke is beginning to understand the world as the lived world. In the world understood as the lived world the idea of correlation *as a rule* is dependent upon correlation *according to a rule* followed in pursuing an end, whether that of meeting a more or less simple bodily need or of explaining how the natural world works. For although the regularity of the conjunction of two kinds of event may not be a causal regularity, their being events implies a contextual *Umwelt* in the description of which counterfactually conditional truths cannot not be assumed, an assumption that need not exclude the possibility that some events are uncaused.

Even the objects that are the subject matter of a science are functions of the science's objective. Whether that objective be a technological application or knowledge for its own sake, the involvement in pursuing the objective is concealed by statements predicating properties of objects. The objectivity of the science itself is predicated upon the scientists' participation in the projectivity of a program of research which, like the less articulate project of the child to satisfy its humbler desires (and the scientist too must eat and drink in order to be able to carry on with his or her research), has the structure of a *Verweisungsganzheit*, a functional, operative totality defined by reference to our purposes. An object is defined by an objective, even and especially where the objective is at least partly defined by the steps taken to achieve it, as in playing a game, which may be a language-game, and more generally as in living a form of life. This telic structure, whether or not it depends on the innate forms of representation postulated by a Chomskian analysis of mastery of a *langue*,[12] is the deep structure of language in use, of *parole*. There is no screening (riddling, concealing, revealing) grammatical structure, however deep, the output of which is not itself screened by the acquired structures of rhetoric. As ethics is a part of politics, so grammar is a part of rhetoric. But rhetorical structures are unrepresentable if by representation is meant the naming of objects or the picturing of states of affairs. Involvement in a concern is a way of being rather than seeing, though it has its own mode of discernment which in *Being and Time* is called *Sicht*, sight, as in *Umsicht*, circumspection, *Vorsicht*, precaution, and indeed *Rücksicht*, consideration or solicitude such as one might show when one mends one's neighbors' shoes but refrains from doing so at night lest the hammering keep them awake (*SZ* §31).

The structure of the means–end involvements with feeding-bottles and hammers is not the same as that of the constating of a relationship between a cause and an effect. But it is very like the structure of involvement with the instrumentality of words. In both cases the mastery of skills is required. In both cases a mastery of tools presupposes the mastery of what is not a tool but an organ. In the case of hammering, the organ to be trained is the hand. In the case of speaking and suckling, the organ is the lips, the palate, the tongue (*la langue*); or, as Augustine says more generally, *edomito in eis signis ore*, his mouth had to be trained or accustomed to form these words.

As Heidegger says, the usual course is for words to accrue to meanings, significations, or references such as inform one's engagement in a task, rather than for meaning to be supplied to words considered as things present at hand (*SZ* 161). Nor for the most part and in the first place do words as sounds supplied with meanings normally get supplied to, for instance, sounds. If, as Philonous in Berkeley's First Dialogue maintains, the proper and proximate data of *the sense of hearing* are sounds rather than a vehicle in the street, it is the latter, the red juggernaut emitting pungent fumes from its exhaust, that is heard by *the person*, and it is this that originally gets named. "What we 'first' hear is never noises or complexes of sounds, but the creaking waggon, the motorcycle" (*SZ* 163). What gets given a name is what there is a point in naming. The point in naming something a coach or a car is given by the convenience of getting from one place to another more quickly or more comfortably than one can on one's own two feet. The point of calling what one has heard a sound is less clear, since it is a conceptual truth that the accusative of hearing is sound or its absence, and a conceptual truth of such simplicity seems not to need to be put into words. However, it is difficult to imagine how musicians would manage without names to distinguish sounds of different pitch. And the point for dogs of having different names for different smells might seem evident, if we decided that dogs do have names for things. This decision itself will turn on what point there would be in saying that they do. As does the point for us, whoever we may be, of having different names for different dogs, for different differences in general, in particular, and for having singular signs and signatures, and for having them not only for each other, however difficult for us to imagine or conceive that point may sometimes be.

Pictorial, presentational, and representational form

Throughout the entirety of this chapter so far we have assumed that we are able to have ideas about ideas and represent how language represents. Before bringing the chapter to an end we must ask whether in the light of Wittgenstein's challenging of this assumption we are entitled to make it.

We have been attempting to represent how language represents. Can that be done? At first blush it might seem that how language represents does not have to be represented in language if by language we mean words used in sentences as I am using them here now. It could be done by a diagram, thus: W → T. Or does this fail because we have to add that "W" represents a word, "T" represents a thing, and " → " represents the relation of representation, so that the original question recurs? Should we conclude that an attempted pictorial representation of linguistic representation demands a linguistic representation of pictorial representation? Or should we conclude that linguistic representation defies representation? It might be said, and Wittgenstein seems to have said or shown this in the *Tractatus,* that we should not oppose pictorial to linguistic representation, and that we should distinguish representation as saying from representation as showing or, to report Wittgenstein more faithfully, from showing itself, self-showing, *sich schauen.*

Wittgenstein argues that linguistic representation is ultimately pictorial representation, provided the latter be understood as a projective relation between the concatenations of logically proper names that make up elementary propositional facts and the objects or things arranged in other facts or possible states of affairs—in a *Sachverhalt,* a *möglicher Sachverhalt,* a *Sachlage,* or a *mögliche Sachlage,* as Wittgenstein variously says, leaving open a perplexingly wide range of options. I shall resist the temptation to embark upon the detailed analysis of the *Tractatus* without which we cannot begin to determine more precisely what these options are. I shall do no more than note that evidence can be produced from it and related works in support of more than one answer to the question whether Wittgenstein maintains in them that logically proper names are not all of the same logical form. Frege distinguishes saturated or complete terms from ones that are unsaturated or incomplete, a difference illustrated in common speech by that between "the star" and "shines." It would be possible for Wittgenstein to have this distinction marked in elementary propositions even though the names in them name only because of an interdependence.

Alternatively, it could be said that there is more than one way of being unsaturated. Two such ways are reflected in another Fregean distinction, that between reference and meaning or sense. According to proposition 3.203 of the *Tractatus*, "Der Name bedeutet den Gegenstand. Den Gegenstand ist seine Bedeutung."[13] If we follow Pears and McGuiness in translating this by "A name means an object. The object is its meaning," it may be complained that this fails to recognize the asymmetry of "meaning" and "means."[14] As Wittgenstein himself will later say, echoing Husserl, the meaning of a name remains when the object or person meant by it is destroyed or dies.[15] True, the asymmetry just mentioned is liable to be concealed by the phrase "what is meant," since this phrase can be used both of what a name means ("'Edinburgh' means 'Edwin's town'") and of what someone means by a name (the capital city of Scotland). Furthermore, in the second of these cases the name is the name of a place, whereas in the first it is the name of a name. In the perspicuous language that according to the *Tractatus* must underlie all language, these ambiguities would not obtain. In particular the ambiguity of meaning as between reference and sense would be precluded by the fact that the unit of meaning is the elementary proposition where no name is divorced from its use (*Gebrauch* 3.326, 6.211).

According to the Tractarian explanation of how elementary propositions represent states of affairs the meaning of each name would appear to be assimilated to a referent. For, as we saw, proposition 3.203 has names naming objects, *Gegenstände*. However, we have also seen that names may not all function in the same way, and that the objects they stand for may not all be of the same form. Wittgenstein tells us little more about them than that there must exist simple objects. The apparent irrelevance to his purposes of the question of the ontological status of these objects, the question whether they belong to the physical, the psychological, or some third realm, is one of the chief respects in which the theory of meaning advanced in the *Tractatus* differs from the earlier theories of linguistic representation to be rapidly surveyed in the following sections of this essay before attention is turned to some of Wittgenstein's later remarks about linguistic representation. However, this section cannot be brought to a close without noting an ambiguity in the reference made in its opening paragraph to the linguistic representation of pictorial representation. It is an ambiguity already present in the Greek "*logos*," hence one that will haunt the history of the thinking of what we are provisionally calling linguistic representation.

Some commentators maintain that the phrase "pictorial representation" conceals a distinction that in Wittgenstein's text is marked by the difference between *Form der Abbildung*, pictorial form or form of depiction, and *Form der Darstellung*. Is the latter to be called the form of representation, as most commentators and translators call it, or shall we call it the form of presentation, or does it make no difference which of these translations we choose? A decent treatment of this exegetical question is beyond the scope of this book. It must suffice merely to register the philosophical issues that are at stake in the choice between translating *Darstellung* as presentation or as representation. According to 2.22, "What a picture (re)presents (*darstellt*) it (re)presents (*darstellt*) independently of its truth or falsity, by means of its pictorial form." And the pictorial form of a picture is said in 2.15 to be the possibility of the structure of the picture, where the structure is the determinate way in which the elements of the picture are related to one another. But what about the relation between the logical picture—and all pictures are said at 2.182 to be logical ones—and what it pictures? It might seem that this question is addressed by the *Form der Darstellung* if that is understood as the form of representation, that is to say, if we equate *Darstellung* with *Vorstellung*. At 2.11 we are told that a picture *vorstellt*, represents a situation in logical space, namely the holding or not holding of states of affairs. The same verb is used at 2.15 to say "That the elements of a picture are related to one another in a determinate way represents (*vorstellt*) that things are related to one another in the same way."

A tidier way to distribute these terms, though one not always obviously supported by the text, is to understand *vorstellen* as representation and to understand representation as requiring both pictorial form, *Form der Abbildung*, and presentational form, *Form der Darstellung*. Pictorial form is equivalent to logical form and is what is common to the picture and reality. Pictorial form is also the form of reality. It is the possibility of structure. But the sense of a picture, hence of a proposition, is its actual structure and it is this which 2.221 says it presents (*darstellt*). The truth or falsity of a picture will depend on whether its sense corresponds with reality. Whether or not it does is contingent upon reality. But a further contingent factor is that of how the notation is to be interpreted, for example whether an arrow is to be taken to point to the left or to the right, or what relation convention stipulates in order "*that 'a'* stands to '*b*' in a certain relation says *that aRb*" (3.1432). According to this choice or convention the picture has one or another form of presentation, that is to say, form of presenting what it purports to be a picture of, and its correctness or truth or incorrectness or falsity will also depend upon this form of presentation. So whereas pictorial or logical form could be said to be an internal relation between the picturing and the pictured fact—as both facts they are both parts or aspects of reality—the form of presentation is externally related to the reality it enables the picture to represent truly or falsely. It may be presumed that this is why "A picture presents its subject from a position outside it," and presumed that "Its standpoint is its representational form (*Form der Darstellung*)" (2.173). It may also be surmised that this connects with the idea that in a book called *The World as I Found It* neither the author nor his will would be mentioned. In an important sense "There is no such thing as the subject that thinks or entertains ideas" (5.631). Given the right Wittgenstein confers on himself to employ discourse that is in his own terms strictly without sense as a ladder to bridge the gap between words and the world, it should be no surprise to find him using thought as a bridge between the discussion of pictures in general and of propositional pictures in particular. The transition is effected via the claim that all pictures are logical ones and that only what is logical is thinkable. One cannot think illogically. One can only think that one can think illogically.

Thinking the sense of a proposition is now said to be the way the propositional sign or sentence (*Satzzeichen*) functions as a projection of a possible situation in the world (3.11–3.13). There is a rule of projection by which the possible situation can be derived from the propositional sign, just as there is one that enables the musician to derive the symphony from the score and the technician to produce a disc from which the symphony and once more the score can be reproduced. This brings us finally to the crucial questions whether this projective thinking (which is not however "thinking out" as Pears and McGuinness translate the *Denken* of 3.11) is what some philosophers call intentionality and, if so, whether this intentionality is to be understood as requiring or as not requiring the performance of a mental act of willing, intending, meaning (*meinen*), or suchlike. Mercator's projection is a method for reading a map, a method, one among many, by which the map may be interpreted as a representation (*Vorstellung*) of the world. And Wittgenstein calls thinking the meaning of a proposition a method of projection. Perhaps other methods would be available here too; though it is to be noted that he refers to *Die Projektionsmethode* with the definite article and a singular noun.

It must be noted also that one speaks *about* or *of* (*von*) objects with the aid of names that deputize for or represent (*vertreten*) objects (3.221). If this is not intentionality, what is? On the other hand, names are the elements of the propositional picture, and although by 2.151–2.1515 a picture is said to be tied to reality and to touch it only through the relation of a name to its object, the consequent attachment of the picture, hence the proposition, to reality is said to be nothing other than "the possibility that things are related to one another in the same way as the elements of the picture." It may seem that the "vertical" relation of aboutness vanishes into a "horizontal" relation shared by the picture-proposition and reality. But it needs to be remembered that the shared relation is one among elements in the picture-proposition that name objects in the possible state of affairs. Yet again, names have meaning only in the context of a proposition (3.3). So there is interdependence, co-constitution, between what we may call the semantic and the syntactic relations. The pragmatic dimension of Wittgenstein's semiotics is introduced when the conjunction of the semantic/vertical and the syntactic/horizontal is brought under the term "use," as when we are told: "We use (*benützen*) the perceptible sign of a proposition (spoken or written, etc.) as a projection of a possible situation" (3.11) and the method of projection is thinking the propositional sense. The propositional sense is a thought of the form *that aRb,* and the thinking of it is thinking *that* "*a*" stands to "*b*" in a certain relation (3.1432). Thinking-that is inseparable from the intentionality of thinking-of. This is what Heidegger will call the ontological difference, the difference in sameness of beings and being, the difference between what is present and its presencing. But in due course we shall find that this difference is cut across by a certain non-intentionality which is not projective. Nor is it representative except in a sense of representation that is less semantic than ethical and political, a sense in which the intentionality of representation is in chiasmus with attention.

TWO

Worldviews

How ideas looked to the Greeks

Presented by Wittgenstein in the *Philosophical Investigations* is the idea that nominal, referential, and predicative representation presupposes a non-representational purpose or point (*Witz*).[1] Can the same be said of the closely related if not identical idea defended by Heidegger in *Being and Time* according to which the apophantic "as" of assertion or "judgment," for example the assertion "This hammer is too heavy," is a graft upon a hermeneutic "as," for example the experience of this hammer as too heavy expressed not by putting this finding into words but just by putting the hammer down and picking up one that is less heavy? Heidegger does claim to be giving an analysis of *Dasein* or human being as such, though he stresses that the starting point of that *existenzial* analysis is the concrete *existenziell* situation of inquiry in which he and his presumed reader are involved, the circumstance of philosophical questioning to which an ancient tradition says wonder gives rise. Wittgenstein describes imagined conceptual schemes in order to show that ones different from those with which we are familiar would be intelligible if certain very general facts of nature were imagined different (*PI* 230). Indeed, would not imagining the latter natural differences already be imagining the former conceptual ones? Such imaginings are designed to lead us away from

a philosophical conception that attributes a piston-rod rigidity to conceptual necessity. Apparently absolute freestanding necessity is conditioned by
historically relative circumstances. This holds for the necessity of Wittgenstein's own assumption that the so-called purely logical connections have
their roots in social practices. So-called "pure" logic is always already "applied." Pure logic is unemployed logic, so that the famed vacuity of the formal
relations that mathematical logic represents in its truth-tables is the vacation
of language, language on holiday (*PI* 38). Logical meaning or emptiness of
meaning, it could be said, is the offspring of rhetorical use. What that use is
can be shown only by describing actual or imaginary cases, as Wittgenstein
does in his later writings. So what I have just called an assumption is not an
assumption at all, for it is supported by the album of cases which those late
writings construct. To expect him, independently of the cases within which
we know our way about, to speculate whether it is parochial to say that representation lives on what is unrepresentable, is to expect him to join ranks with
the philosophers whose errings he puts down to their desire to philosophize
in a vacuum. The remarks on the alleged crystalline purity and hardness—
"rigor"—of the logical "must" made in the *Philosophical Investigations* are
paralleled in *Being and Time* by criticism of the notion of universal validity
(*Geltung*) and bindingness revived by Lotze (*SZ* 155) but going back at least
to the *Organon* of Aristotle in which *logos* came into the philosophical ken
of the Greeks primarily as assertion, and assertion is regarded as the primary locus of truth. It is important to observe that this is a statement about
philosophy. Otherwise one will find it puzzling that Heidegger, especially in
his work after *Being and Time,* can explore the Greek thinking of *logos,* for
example the poetic thinking of *logos* in Heraclitus, for clues as to how today
there could be a beginning of a kind of thinking other than that for which
Aristotelian logic and its modern successors provide the norms.

Where in order to expose philosophical pretentions Wittgenstein describes forms of life that make no explicit philosophical pretentions, Heidegger describes epochs in the history of philosophical thinking of being.
Most relevant to our purposes is his claim that it is only in modern philosophy that thinking is identified with representation.

In the essay titled "The Age of the World Picture" Heidegger says that the
word and the concept of representation (*Vorstellen*) is worn out (*abgenutzt*).[2]
In order to grasp fully the modern essence of representedness, he says, we
must trace the original power of naming that the word has lost. How far
back must one go? To the beginning of the modern age or beyond? Is there
an essence of representedness that is not modern, a representedness that does
not have as its center subjectivity as understood by Descartes and Locke? If

the essence of modern representativeness can be expressed, as Heidegger expresses it, by saying that it makes man the measure of all things, has he not conceded that it is the same ancient essence that Protagoras expressed? By no means. For what is asserted in the sophistic thesis attributed to Protagoras at *Theaetetus* 152 is, in Plato's words, that "any given thing" is to me as it appears to me, and to you such as it appears to you, "you and I being men." But the sophist is speaking from the same basis of *sophia* as Heraclitus and Parmenides, namely the basis of presencing and truth as unconcealment. The measure of things is how human being accommodates itself to being. On the Cartesian account of the I that thinks, man requires things to accommodate themselves to him. Greek man's belonging within a horizon of un-concealment (*a-lētheia*) lets that which is absent and that which is present be, allowing concealment (*lēthē*) to be if there is to be clearing (*Lichtung*). Cartesian man presumes to decide for himself what will be represented in the light of his understanding. Descartes does not deny that human *comprehension* of God is limited, but our *conception* of God's nature is according to him certain enough to enable man to have clear and distinct ideas of the natural world. The modesty of the Greek's relationship to the cosmos is expressed as the modesty with which he regards his relationship to the gods, as when Protagoras says, "I am surely not in a position to have in sight anything regarding the gods, neither that they are nor that they are not, nor how they are in their visible aspect."[3] This citation raises another question about how the Greeks see the world and how it is represented by the Cartesian. For the phrase "visible aspect" translates the Greek word "*idea*." How can this not be a progenitor of Descartes's Latin "*idea*" and hence already the seed of modern representation? Heidegger tells us that it is both. The aspect or view for which Plato's word is *eidos* "is the presupposition, destined far in advance and long ruling indirectly in concealment, for the world's having to become a picture."[4] This does not however mean that it is already a world picture or representation. For the aspect or view of a thing for the Greeks is more the thing's looking to man, with the full ambiguity of the word "looking" (*anschauen*), than its being the subject of and subjected to man's look.[5] It is not the *Weltanschauung* first named by Kant in 1790 in §26 of the third *Critique*. Man's worldview is not a passive registration, but active world-viewing, viewing of which the world is object as world picture and where man views himself as the *subjectum* and center, capturing the world in the concepts he imposes upon it.

In the essay on "Science and Reflection" published sixteen year after "The Age of the World Picture," a reference to the scene or stage is implicit in the reference again made to what Plato names "*eidos*," here connected with "*theōrein*," hence with theater and theory. Without taking back what he said in the earlier essay about *eidos* having the sense of man being looked to, Heidegger stresses here that *theōrein* is to look at something with close attention or heed. So, again, it is by no means mere passivity. On the contrary—or higher than contrariety—it is for the Greeks the highest form of doing.[6] So it must be distinguished from the entrapment implied by the viewing (*Betrachtung*) of modern scientific theorizing. Greek *epistēme* is not science. Greek "*logos*," as gathering, "*legein*," is not language that represents. Epistemology—*épistémologie*, the philosophy of science—is a modern invention, despite its ancient Greek name.

Yet modern idea, theory, and language as representation are, Heidegger allows, haunted by *eidos, theōrein,* and *logos*. And again and again he describes how the senses of these and other terms employed in the modern age of the world picture are transformations of the senses of the Greek via the Latin "*idea, contemplari*," meaning to divide and inspect, and so on.

Language and the very idea of a conceptual scheme

Heidegger's etymological meditations, which are not to be mistaken for lexicographical antiquarianism, could make a big difference to how we see the area of the debate about representation in language that treats of what the title of a seminal essay by Donald Davidson calls "the Very Idea of a Conceptual Scheme."[7] The idea in question is most familiar in the special version known as the Sapir-Whorf hypothesis, one statement of which runs as follows:

> Formulation of ideas is not an independent process, strictly rational
> in the old sense, but is part of a particular grammar, and differs, from
> slightly to greatly, between different grammars. We dissect nature along
> lines laid down by our native languages. . . . We cut nature up, organize
> it into concepts, and ascribe significances as we do, largely because we
> are parties to an agreement to organize it in this way—an agreement that
> holds throughout our speech community and is codified in the patterns
> of language. The agreement is, of course, an implicit and unstated one,
> BUT ITS TERMS ARE ABSOLUTELY OBLIGATORY; we cannot talk at all
> except by subscribing to the organization and classification of data which
> the agreement decrees.[8]

Whorf goes on to say that this control thesis, as we may call it, holds not only for languages like Greek, Hebrew, English, Hopi, Chinese, etc., but for sublanguages of which he cites as an example the language of Western scientific thought. Would not this be paradigmatic of a conceptual scheme, and would we not have to exclude as illustrations of the control thesis at least Ancient Greek if, as Heidegger says, "The Greeks in a unique way thought out of their language, i.e. received from it their human existence,"[9] and if the description he gives of that outlined above is faithful to it? For that description is worlds apart from the description he gives of a language like the language of modern science, of which it could be said that it expresses or imposes a conceptual scheme. The very idea of a conceptual scheme, the very idea of a concept, a *Begriff*, and the very idea of an idea in its Cartesian and Lockean sense of a representation, belong to the age and language of the worldview that pictures the world as a world picture, something taken like a snapshot taken by a camera.[10] Hence, if one accepts what Heidegger says about the world as representation and about languages in this age of representation, one must also accept that any discussion of the incommensurability of two or more languages which impose different conceptual schemes is limited to languages that belong to this modern age. The age of representation, *Vor-stellung*, is the age of world picture, and the age of world picture is the age of *Ge-stell*, of setting securely within a frame, of set-up, one could even say of frame-up, for a conceptual scheme is a conspiratorial scheming in which man inquisitions nature and himself, puts them both to the test.

Control

Whorf and Sapir present an argument for ideological stalemate and absolute linguistic relativity. That argument falls into two parts, defense of a thesis of absolute incommensurabality and defense of a thesis of control. Their argument seems to be that each of these theses supports the other. Let us first examine the thesis concerning control. Whorf writes:

> What we call "scientific thought" is a specialization of the western Indo-European type of language, which has developed not only a set of different dialectics, but actually a set of different dialects. THESE DIALECTS ARE NOW BECOMING MUTUALLY UNINTELLIGIBLE. The term "space," for instance, does not and CANNOT mean the same thing to a psychologist as to a physicist. Even if psychologists should firmly resolve, come hell or high water, to use "space" only with the physicist's meaning, they could not do so, any more than Englishmen could use in English the word "sentiment" in the meanings which the similarly spelled but functionally different French utterance *le sentiment* has in its native French.[11]

What does Whorf mean by "inexorable laws of pattern" and "ordained pattern-systems"? What constitutes the pattern-system of a language? Its components, according to Whorf, are of two kinds: overt categories (or phe-notypes) and covert categories (or cryptotypes). The former are identifiable by lexical, morphological, or syntactic features such as the suffix "-s" to mark the plural in English, the morpheme "can" or "could" to mark a certain ver-bal modality, and certain signs to mark the middle voice in Sanskrit and Greek.[12] The covert category under which a word may fall is not identifiable by a formal mark, but is determined by what Whorf calls a "reactance," as the middle voice is determined in most languages other than Sanskrit or Greek. Some of the things Whorf says about cryptotypes are cryptic; for example, a cryptotype is described as a "submerged, subtle and elusive meaning, corre-sponding to no actual word, yet shown by linguistic analysis to be function-ally important in the grammar."[13] But it becomes apparent from the examples he gives that to exhibit the reactance of a covert category is to exhibit which sentence-frames words of that category cannot fill. To adopt a crude meta-phor, the reactance is the reaction or response a word gives to the stimulus of being placed in this or that linguistic environment, the word's capacity to indulge in this rather than that type of logical behavior. Take, for instance, the concept of gender. This is an overt category in Latin, but a covert one in English.[14] Such a concept is "as definable and in its way as definite as a verbal concept like 'female' or 'feminine,'" says Whorf, "but is of a very different kind; it is not the analog of a word but of a rapport-system."[15] Covert catego-ries "are not like individual sentences but like SCHEMES of sentences and designs of sentence structure."[16] Thus, in putting the English particle "up" (meaning completely, to a finish) through the hoops in order to display its reactance, "we don't say 'spread it up, waste it up, spend it up, scatter it up.'"[17] Again, "in English, intransitive verbs form a covert category marked by lack of the participle and the passive and causative voices; we cannot substitute a verb of this class (e.g. 'go, lie, sit, rise, gleam, sleep, arrive, appear, rejoice') into such sentences as 'It was cooked, It was being cooked, I had it cooked to order.'"[18] It should be noted, however, that Whorf's notion of categories treats not only of what words can fill a gap in a given sentence-frame. It treats also—and in this it is wider than the notion invoked in Gilbert Ryle's concept of category-mistake—of what word-parts or morphemes can fill a gap in a given word-frame and what word-parts can be affixed to a given word in order to modify its meaning. For example, we say "unhook" but not "unrejoice" or "unsleep."

Whorf's statements about overt and covert categories can be translated respectively into statements about plain grammar or syntax and statements about logical grammar or syntax. If we subscribe to the practice followed among many philosophers of using the word "grammar" to cover both of these, this translation is authorized by the parenthetical phrase in Whorf's statement that "the background linguistic system (in other words, the grammar) of each language is not merely a reproducing instrument for voicing ideas but rather is itself the shaper of ideas, the program and guide for the individual's mental activity, for his analysis of impressions, for his synthesis of his mental stock in trade."[19] We can see too that it is important that Whorf should equate what he variously calls the "background linguistic system," "pattern-system," and "rapport-system" with grammar, since it is one of his chief contentions that this system determines how we see the world. If we take seriously his statements that the pattern-system is "sensed rather than comprehended" and that "awareness of it has an intuitive quality,"[20] it may appear as though he is saying that our way of seeing determines our grammar rather than vice versa. This appearance is false. That he escapes this Scylla of inconsistency can be shown by reminding ourselves that the tint and focal point of the lenses in our spectacles determine the visual sensations we experience even when we do not notice that we are wearing spectacles. This does not mean that it is only the world seen through the spectacles that is sensed or intuited, never the spectacles or the difference they make to our sensations as compared to seeing without them.

However, what about the Charybdis upon which we can take a bearing with the assistance of the following statement in Kant's *Prolegomena to Any Future Metaphysics That Will Be Able to Present Itself as a Science*?

> To seek out from ordinary knowledge the concepts which are not grounded on any particular experience and none the less occur in all knowledge by experience, of which they constitute as it were the mere form of connection, presupposes no greater reflection or more insight than to seek out from a language rules of the real use of words in general and thus to collect the elements for a grammar (in fact both enquiries are very closely related to each other).[21]

Whorf's argument comes to grief because it follows from what he says not just that both of these enquiries are very closely related to each other, but that they are one and the same enquiry.

To illustrate this, consider the concept attributed to the Hopi ideology which Whorf calls "latering" or "durating." The Indo-European ideology (*pace* Bergson) does not contain this, Whorf says, but contains instead what he refers to as Newtonian time and describes as an objectified, spatialized continuum. The Indo-European (or "Standard Average European") ideology "tends to see existence through a binomial formula that expresses any existence as a spatial form plus a spatial formless continuum. . . ."[22] Like Hopi latering, the Newtonian concepts of time, space, and matter are "recepts" from language: "that is where Newton got them."[23] But this presents Whorf with a dilemma. Are all the concepts of one's ideology linguistic? If they are, then of course the ideology will be tied to language, but in a manner that renders Whorf's thesis trivial. If ideology is defined as an aspect of language, then it is no wonder that the "bond" between the two is "unbreakable,"[24] for it is one of tautological necessity. Whorf himself admits as much when he says that "it will be found that it is not possible to define 'event, thing, object, relationship,' and so on, from nature, but that to define them always involves a circuitous return to the grammatical categories of the definer's language."[25] As Wittgenstein says at the end of the *Tractatus*, "What *can* be shown *cannot* be said."[26]

Is Whorf any better off if he denies that all the concepts of one's ideology are linguistic? In case some of us should want to say straight off that such a denial would be self-contradictory, we should rephrase the question, substituting "idea" or "thinking" for "concept," or else be clear that this last term is being used in a sense wide enough to cover, for example, visual, auditory, motor, or kinesthetic images. Note too that in order for Whorf to be able to escape the first horn of the dilemma, namely, the trivializing of his thesis, these images would have to be other than images simply of *words*. Thus Sapir would be gored by that horn because he limits thinking to what is either primarily or parasitically verbal. Whorf is willing to allow, however, not only that linguistic thinking may be neither verbal nor linguistic,[27] but also that linguistic thinking need not use words. This, according to Whorf, is precisely how it is with the logico-grammatical categories, which need not be verbalized. So he can answer the charge made against him by Max Black that he commits the "linguist's fallacy" of imputing his own sophisticated attitudes to the speakers he is studying. "An uncultivated Choctaw can as easily as the most skilled litterateur contrast the tenses or the genders of two experiences, though he has never heard of any WORDS like 'tense' or 'gender' for such contrasts."[28] Ability to make the contrast is shown not by one's being able to apply correctly the classificatory labels approved by, say, the Linguistic Society of America, but by one's knowing how to speak.

To return to the second horn of the dilemma and to put a finer point on it: granted that all concepts of an ideology need not be linguistic, how can we test the thesis that this nonlinguistic segment of the ideology is "controlled" by the "laws of pattern" of the language one speaks? The thesis that this control does operate cannot be tested, and in so far as this "control thesis" is what is advanced by the so-called Sapir-Whorf hypothesis, this latter is not a hypothesis at all. For to test it, it would have to be logically possible to come up with a counter instance; it would have to be possible for one to discover that a concept which a person possessed nonverbally was one that his "background linguistic system," the logical grammar of his language, prevented his having verbally. But this is not a conceivable test situation.

Let us suppose that the nonverbal thinking is a use of images or a nonverbal performance such as the drawing of a certain species of animal on a cave wall or the repeatable selection of the appropriate tool to do a particular job. Then, what would it be like to come across a drawing by a speaker of a certain language showing an animal with properties that the logical grammar of that language prohibited one from predicating of it? Or again, what would it be like to be able to pick out nonverbally, for example by holding it up or pointing to it, an instance of an x which was F, where according to one's language neither the affirmation nor the denial that some x's are F makes sense? Judging by what Whorf—and, come to that, Bertrand Russell —says about the alleged "binomial" form-content formula of Indo-European languages, it will be impossible in any of these languages to say "The ammonia took the tablecloth out of the color." Now we are trying to decide what would have to hold for it to be logically possible to discover a case of nonverbal thinking corresponding to the thought that would be verbalized as "The ammonia took the tablecloth out of the color." For this to be possible we should have to be able to compare the verbal and the nonverbal pieces of thinking. Surely, this comparing would have to be done in a *language*. But on the supposition that the Indo-European language we are considering is English, the comparing could be done in English, for, in order for a comparison to be made, the image or nonverbal performance would have to be translated into verbal terms, and if these were terms of English *we could not fail* to find that the two versions obeyed the logico-grammatical rules of English—or, more accurately, there could no longer be two versions, for the supposed nonverbal version would have become the allowable verbal version, "The ammonia took the color out of the tablecloth." Hence the comparative testing would have to be done in a language whose "laws of pattern" admitted statements of the form "The ammonia took the color out of the tablecloth." The logical grammar of the tester's language might admit both statements of that form and ones of the form "The ammonia took the tablecloth out of the color." Let us suppose that this is so of Finnish and that the testing is being attempted in this language. In that case it would seem that the experiment could now go ahead with neither the positive nor the negative outcome being logically entailed. The snag here is that what is up for examination is no longer the nonverbal thinking of the Indo-European subject, but a piece of the Finnish experimenter's own verbal thinking—and the dice are loaded once again.

Incommensurability

To the extent, then, that it is the control thesis that is advanced by the so-called Sapir-Whorf hypothesis, the latter states not a hypothesis but a tautology. It therefore does not serve as support for the empirical thesis that this so-called hypothesis also advances, the thesis of incommensurability or ideological stalemate which Sapir formulates as follows:

> Inasmuch as languages differ very widely in their systematization of fundamental concepts, they tend to be only loosely equivalent to each other as symbolic devices, and are, as a matter of fact, incommensurable in the sense in which two systems of points in a plane are, on the whole, incommensurable to each other if they are plotted out with reference to different systems of coordinates.[29]

Whorf illustrates this by attempting to show how physics might have to be reconstructed for it to be compatible with Hopi ideology, which, Whorf would give us to understand, lacks the limiting presupposition that there is such a thing as dimensional time. He says that the nearest Hopi gets to the English terms "speed" and "rapid" is a term meaning *intense* or *very* that is used with verbs of motion. Therefore a Hopi transcription of the "V," standing for "velocity," of physics would have to be replaced, perhaps, by "I" for "intensity." Having suggested other changes that might consequently have to be made, he infers:

> A scientist from another culture that used time and velocity would have *great* difficulty in getting us to understand these concepts. We should talk about the intensity of a chemical reaction; he would speak of its velocity or rate, which words we should at first think were simply words for intensity in his language. Likewise, he at first would think that intensity was simply our word for velocity. At first we should agree, later we should begin to disagree, and it might dawn upon both sides that different systems of rationalization were being used. He would find it *very hard* to make us understand what he really meant by velocity of a chemical reaction. WE should have no words that would fit.[30]

I have italicized expressions in this passage which betray that the control referred to in the argument for linguistic relativity is not after all "unbreakable," "invariable," "inexorable," or "absolute." They indicate that what Whorf's essays in comparative linguistics bring out is not that the speaker of Hopi and the speaker of German, for example, are confined to disparate ideological universes, but that there are some concepts that the Hopi language expresses with *greater facility* and *frequency* than the German, and others which German allows to be expressed more readily than Hopi. Ancient Greek and Sanskrit and Icelandic and Bangla, because some of their verbs have phenotypical markers of the middle voice, may be able to express this voice with greater facility than do Latin or German or English. But, as we have noted, Latin expresses something like it through deponent verbs, and something like it may be expressed, if less frequently and less easily, through the verb or other parts of speech in German and English.

I conclude that although an argument for relative linguistic relativity may be tenable, the argument that Whorf and Sapir produce for absolute linguistic relativity and permanent ideological stalemate is not. This argument appeals to two theses, one about control and the other about incommensurability, the latter being an empirical thesis, and each thesis purporting to support the other. I have argued that the control thesis is either trivially true or untestable.

We can't find our feet with them

However, the demand for strict empirical testability is very much a child of its time, the age of modern science in which things are put to the test, the age of the principle of verification and falsification. Because that principle does not pass its own test, and because it is to misconceive its status to require that it should, perhaps the control thesis is not damned by its untestability. "Not to know of what things one should demand demonstration, and of what one should not, argues want of education," Aristotle observes at *Metaphysics* 1006a. This is a piece of advice of which we shall have further occasion to remind ourselves below.

It is not clear that any breakdown of interlingual communication that is alleged to be consequential upon differences of conceptual scheme can be put down either to an in principle explicable verbal misunderstanding or idiosyncrasy or to difference of belief. For if there can be belief only where there can be doubt, it is odd to say either that there is a difference of conceptual frame or that there is a difference of belief in, for instance, some of the circumstances Wittgenstein may have in mind when he speaks of how sometimes we are not able to find our feet with people—*nicht in sie finden,* literally, not able to find ourselves in them, not able to understand them. This may be because we have not mastered their language.

> The Chinese concept of *yu/wu* excludes all senses of English "being"
> except the existential, but overlaps English "having." Thinking in terms
> of Being, we start from an object which on the one hand *is, exists,* on

the other hand *has* properties. Thinking in terms of *yu*, we start from an environment which we may or may not determine as "the world," which has, within which there is, the object; arriving at the object we find that it has, that within it there are, form and colour.... An English learner of Chinese takes a little time to rid himself of the impression that there is something missing from such a sentence as (MAN) NATURE GOOD "Human nature (is) good." If I say "The rose red" or "He in Paris," have I not left out the relationship between the rose and the colour, the man and the place—a relationship which is exactly defined by the splendidly unambiguous word "is"? No, for "the red rose" and "the man in Paris" are no more ambiguous than "the rose which is red" and "the man who is in Paris." But these phrases do not pretend to be sentences. "The rose red" needs a verb, not to show how redness is related to the rose, but to assert the redness; for it is a rule of English that there is no sentence without a verb.[31]

We feel the speakers of Chinese to be alien in this sense because we have not mastered their language. But we may feel people alien to us because, although we have gone a long way toward mastering their language, we are at sea with their traditions (*PI* 223). The traditions or customs are part of the activity, the form of life of which *speaking* a language forms a part (*PI* 23). Hence for the expression "conceptual scheme" we could substitute the expression "form of life" or "form of language" if talk of conceptual schemes limits the discussion of their alleged incommensurability to the age of representation as strictly defined by Heidegger. In doing this we would be extending the scope of the discussion of this problem to take in historically earlier ages or ages that, although historically contemporary, do not belong to the *Zeit des Weltbildes*—maybe precisely because their *Zeit*, their temporality, is different, as Whorf argues that Hopi temporality is. Or we could speak with Husserl of a lifeworld, *Lebenswelt*, the expression that may have been in Heidegger's thoughts when he wrote that the word "world" can be understood as "that 'wherein' a factical Dasein as such can be said to 'live'" (*SZ* 65). So could we speak of the incommensurability or otherwise of worlds understood in this sense? No harm will come if in discussing what Davidson writes on this problem we continue to use the expression "conceptual frame," which he employs without intending the restriction that is imposed upon its use by Heidegger's definition. And provided we do not forget the restriction Heidegger puts on the scope of "representation," we may use that term more generally without too much risk. Heidegger is himself committed to using the German equivalent of that word (*Vorstellung*) even in describing the world of the Greeks. But with this word "world" there is a greater risk of confusion. For in the course of his essay Davidson remarks, "there is at most one world."[32] That there are at least two worlds in the sense in which Heidegger proposes to use the word "world" is apparently implied by his statement that "'world' may stand for the 'public' we-world, or one's 'own' closest (domestic) environment." Yet Heidegger says also that although *Dasein* or *Da-sein* is always the being-here-or-there of an I, always *jemeinig* (compare "I am my world" and "the world is my world," *Tractatus* 5.63, 5.641), it is also a being-here-or-there-with-others, *Mitdasein* (*SZ* 41–43, 123). This implies that the we-world and one's own world are one world, though not that the "we" of my world embraces everyone. On the other hand, Davidson's remark that there is at most one world is made in connection with the statement Strawson makes in *The Bounds of Sense* that "It is possible to imagine kinds of worlds very different from the world as we know it," so, Davidson concludes, these pluralities are metaphorical or merely imagined.[33] That is to say, Heidegger and Davidson each admits in some sense, literal or metaphorical, both a unity and a plurality of worlds. Heidegger, further, admits a plurality of pluralities. There is the plurality of my world being my world and your world being yours—which does not mean that we do not inhabit a common world. There is also the plurality of worlds, stressed in his writings after *Being and Time,* consisting in the fact that our common world is the world of the world picture, whereas the common world of, for example, the Greeks, was not. Heidegger, we noted, pays homage to Husserl's notion of the *Lebenswelt,* the lifeworld or the lived world. The world that is lived is the world of the human being defined by Aristotle as animal endowed with reason or language, *zōon logon echon.* The world is, in Old English, "*wer-eld, wer-old, wer-alt.*" Compare German "*Alt*" as in Schelling's title *System der Weltalter, The Ages of the World.* Compare also "aliment," from Latin "*alere,*" to feed, nourish, grow in strength. The world is the age of man. The homage Heidegger pays to Husserl's phenomenology of *Lebenswelt* is qualified by his concern to show that the classical Aristotelian notion of the human being is subordinate to that of the being whose being is to be somewhere or to be the where, *être le là, Da-sein,* a being that Heidegger would have us understand not primarily in terms of animality or life plus reason or language. Man's being-in-the-world is as such articulated by language, *Rede.* This suggests the metaphor of the world as a text to be read, the metaphor of the book of the world employed by Berkeley and others. But this metaphor is misleading if it leaves us with the idea of a world over against us like a book. One's living the world or, better, existing it, one's verbally and transitively be-ing the world, is in both the narrower and the wider sense of the word "verbal," verb-al and wordly, one's verbally worldly being. Here is the wider truth embracing the *Tractatus* doctrine that statements and states of affairs have logical form in common, the wider truth which Heidegger elicits from the statement made in Parmenides' Fragment 5 that being and thinking are the same, *to gar auto noein te kai einai.* Wittgenstein's *Tractatus* doctrine that the analysis both of propositional symbols and of their sense contains the notion of the fact that so-and-so is the case is a corollary of what at that time he would have been inclined to regard as the strictly unsayable superfact that if the being of the world is loaded with language, the being of language is no less loaded with the world. Both the *Tractatus* and the *Philosophical Investigations* teach that there is no unstructured world. The *Tractatus* would like to say that in the beginning the world is structured by the *logos*. The *Philosophical Investigations* seeks to show that in the beginning was the deed, though among deeds are those performed by words. *Worte sind auch Taten,* "Words are at the same time deeds" (*PI* 546). One could say that there is a certain commonness of logical form shared by Wittgenstein's earlier and later work, and by both of them and Heidegger's analysis of being-in-the-world.

Hence, if Heidegger's analysis of being-in-the-world is to be illustrated by the metaphor of the reading of a book, this last "of" must be interpreted speculatively, both as a subjective and as an objective genitive—though Heidegger would say that the grammarian's terms "subjective" and "objective" really belong to the age of the world picture. As does Berkeley's use of the metaphor of the world as book. As do the words of the text (*Wörter*) until brought alive as words of speech (*Worte*). As does the world of physical or human nature investigated by the sciences. As therefore does the one world of Davidson, if that is understood as the world as investigated by the sciences. Whether that is how his "at most one world" is to be understood is not crucial to the question he is concerned with in his essay "On the Very Idea of a Conceptual Scheme," the question we are concerned with here. Indeed, if by the world that is the object investigated by science is meant an entity, Davidson is for doing without it. That is a world well lost.[34] According to him, whether understood as the totality of things or as the totality of facts, the world no more needs to be posited as that which the conceptual schemes of language as a whole represent than things or facts need be posited as that which particular sentences truly or falsely represent. "The sentence 'My skin is warm' is true if and only if my skin is warm. Here there is no reference to a fact, a world, an experience, or a piece of evidence."[35] *A fortiori,* the idea of a theory-neutral referent that conceptual schemes fit or fail to fit goes by the board, and with it goes the very idea of a conceptual scheme that Davidson says depends on it. The same holds for the idea of a neutral world organized by a conceptual scheme. And for the same reason, not because it is nonsense to talk of organizing a single thing; this is not nonsense if what is meant by it is that structure is introduced into what would otherwise be an amorphous mass.

Davidson concludes that there is no more to the idea of a conceptual scheme than there is to the idea of truth as formulated by Tarski's Convention T, according to which, as formulated by Davidson, an adequate theory of truth for a language L entails for every sentence s of L a theorem of the form "s is true if and only if p," where "s" is replaced by a description of s and "p" by s itself, if L is English, or by a translation of s into English, if L is not English. Suppose we agree that Convention T "embodies our best intuition as to how the concept of truth is used," at least for the truth of assertive sentences, whatever our intuitions may be regarding the notion of truth as unconcealing which Heidegger attributes to the Greeks. Then, Davidson says, "there does not seem to be much hope for a test that a conceptual scheme is radically different from ours if that test depends on the assumption that we can divorce the notion of truth from that of translation." And this divorce is what the notion of incommensurable linguistico-conceptual schemes assumes. It assumes that the incommensurability of two languages is a total or partial untranslatability which is consistent with the falsity or truth of statements made in them being determined either by reference to a theory-neutral reality or experience which the linguistic scheme does or does not fit, organize, or represent (or, if there are purely conceptual truths, by reference to a "fixed stock of meanings").

The case for the unintelligibility of the idea of radically different conceptual schemes can be made more directly. I argued above that this idea is either untestable or uninterestingly, because trivially, true. Here now is a quick argument for the claim to coherence of the notion of incommensurability being necessarily false, once granted that Davidson is right to hold that this claim requires a "ground for comparison," "a single space within which each scheme has a position and provides a point of view." The argument is simply that comparability cannot be a requirement for incomparability. However, this argument is too quick if incomparability does not entail incommensurability. Perhaps we have to distinguish levels, that of the linguistic schemes being compared and that of the point of view of the comparer. If that putative point of view is unstructured by any language, it is difficult to understand how it could be a point from which to make comparisons. If it is structured by a language it will be either another particular perspective that has to be compared or a linguistic scheme common to all perspectives. In either case, given that Convention T is accepted, it is more natural to attribute at least a partial failure of comprehension, one not so radical that we wonder even whether the other party is speaking a language, to difference of belief (assuming the absence of malapropism for which we would usually be ready to make charitable allowance). Davidson concedes that no principle or evidence compels us to put down a failure in understanding to a difference of beliefs rather than of concepts. He just does not see that anything is gained by explaining it in terms of the latter rather than in terms of the former, given acceptance of Convention T.

Is there nothing to be gained at all by this? It seems to me that we do need to mark the distinction between on the one hand true and false sentences, whether their truth be believed, wondered about, hoped for, something one tries to bring about, etc., and on the other hand principles assumed or presupposed by such true sentences, principles of which the principality consists in the fact that although the question of their truth may be raised when there is a breakdown in understanding, that question is not otherwise raised. They are constitutive of the language, language game, form of life or of the *L* in which in the formulation of Tarski's Convention T a sentence is true. R. G. Collingwood marks this distinction by contrasting absolute and relative presuppositions.[36] The latter are true or false propositions, the former are not. This distinction is masked by speaking of sentences rather than of propositions or statements, a practice aided and abetted by the fact that *Satz* can mean either. For one thing, talking of the truth of sentences neglects the differences between interrogative, imperative, and indicative sentences—as when the propositional calculus is called the sentential calculus, a practice foreshadowed by Aristotle's judgment made at *De Interpretatione* 17a and cited in our introduction that nonpropositional sentences are of interest to rhetoric and poetics but not to logic and philosophy. Talk of the truth of sentences also assumes that no grammatically interrogative sentence, for example, can be used to make a true or false statement.

The distinction between absolute and relative presuppositions is one of function, one that is well marked by distinguishing true or false statements from conceptual schemes, practices, or forms of life. A language-game *L* is *spoken*. And just as one has to have learned to find one's way about a scene before one can point to things or call them by their name, so before one can say something that represents what one believes is the case one has to have learned how this is done. And this, the "form of representation," is concealed when one attempts to represent it by saying of it what is the case. It cannot be said, for it shows itself only. It shows itself in language in use, most of all when one is using it oneself in conversation with someone who belongs to the same tradition. In paragraph 435 of the *Philosophical Investigations* Wittgenstein writes: "If it is asked: 'how do sentences manage to represent?'—the answer might be: 'Don't you know? You certainly see it, when you use them.' For nothing is concealed." That is to say, although Wittgenstein bids us "don't think, but look!" (*PI* 66), since what a sentence means and how it represents is a matter of how words are customarily used and what people who use them go on to do, there is no *seeing* how sentences represent, no *Sicht*, as Heidegger would say, that does not consist in *using* at least some of them in their customary way. Only in using sentences can you tell how they represent. If representation is telling in words how things stand, then how sentences represent cannot be represented. The *Vorstellung*, the representation, of this is its *Verstellung*, its dissembling. This is why Tractarian representation as pretending to state superfacts gives way in the *Philosophical Investigations* to representation as presentation, as performance, as on a stage, in the hope that we will identify with the *dramatis personae*, become actors, speech actors for whom the dependence of the apophantic "as" upon the hermeneutic "as" *and vice versa* becomes once more alive. Wittgenstein invites his reader to imitate the actor on the stage, to imitate the imitator, to become temporarily a re-enactor in order to re-enter "real life." The quotation marks here mark a crossing of a proscenium arch in both directions. Re-enactment understood in terms of it may be a clue to what R. G. Collingwood means when he writes of the historian's re-enactment of the past. In this re-enactment historiography as chronological narrative is refreshed by history as *Geschichte*, that is to say *Geschehen*, that is to say effective happening. This holds for the history of philosophy, in which philosophy earns the title of philosophy "in effect," philosophy *en effet*, given to it by Derrida.

Sending on representation

Derrida points out in "Sending: On Representation" that nevertheless the form of representation, the very idea of linguistic representation in the time of representation, is said even by Heidegger to be represented. For Heidegger says that it is *vorgestellt* by the Platonic idea or form.[37] Heidegger brings himself to admit too that our idea of the truth of a proposition is anticipated, put before us, *vor-gestellt*, in Platonic *orthotēs*, that is, in rightness, correctness, or (*pace* Davidson) fittingness, despite Heidegger's insistence elsewhere that for the Greeks truth is literally *a-lētheia*, un-concealing.[38] The Greeks already had the experience of truth as correctness concealing truth as unconcealing. It is difficult for us not to think of this already historiographically, especially when our time of world picture, our world as will and representation, is described by Heidegger's translators as an age. This encourages us to think of the medieval, the Roman, and the Greek as ages that occurred earlier than ours in dated chronological time. This itself is an event of concealing. Chronological history and historiography, *Historie*, conceals history as *Geschichte*, history as existed or lived. The latter, Heidegger tells us, is a happening (*Geschehen*) of *Geschick*, of communal dispensation, mission, sending, *envoi*, or, most ominous of all, destiny, and, in the broadest possible sense of *polis*, political fate. Without pausing to consider what this thinking of destiny portends for Heidegger's personal political destiny, let us note simply that the ambiguity of history as between a series of events or their description and "existed," existential, inhabited, or operative history, *Wirkungsgeschichte*, as Gadamer would say,[39] is reflected in the ambiguity of Heidegger's *Vorstellung*. On the one hand the word means representation or just presentation, like that of a performance on a stage. On the other hand it means pre-sent (with a hyphen), sent before in time. If this pre-sending or pro-position can be understood in its participated-in occurring, *geschichtlich*, rather than simply historiographically, *historisch*, if it can be understood nonpropositionally, it will not be to an inconsistency in Heidegger to which Derrida will be pointing or intending to point. That Heidegger himself is intending to point to a duplicity of representation "itself" is indirectly confirmed by the resilience, as it seems to me, with which he responds when scholars make the observation that for the Greeks truth is both *orthotēs*, correctness, and *a-lētheia*, the privation of concealment or of forgetting, that is to say, recollection, *anamnēsis*. Truth is the locus of a *Zweideutigkeit*, an ambiguity, perhaps a chiasm, a crisscrossing, in which truth as the straight and true twenty-twenty vision of orthodoxy is darkened by the shadow it itself casts over truth as withdrawal from hiding. This very hiding is at one and the same time effected and hidden by truth as propositional representation. Similarly, *Vorstellung* as propositional representation hides *Vor-stellung* as pro- or pre-position. But it does so because *Vor-stellung* predestines *Vorstellung*. The originality of the former, its status as "origin" of propositional representation, is already relegated to a second place, displaced to the place of propositional placing, of language as representation, while (*weil*) and because (*weil*) it is this "originally" secondary representation's (p)representation. The original is secondarized and the secondary is originarized. The not yet is the already and vice versa.

This interdependence, which is not a biconditionality simply of grounding, but at the same time an ungrounding, is writ large in the interdependence of metaphysics, which is typically foundational, and the a-metaphysical, whether the latter be the experience of early Greek thinkers like Parmenides or of the task of thinking at the end of metaphysics. Parmenides named *alētheia* in his poem, but he did not *think* it as *a-lētheia*. And the moment Plato begins to think of being as idea or form there comes to pass a concealing of being as such. Yet it is thanks to the history of this concealment beginning with Plato that there can be a chance for another beginning at the end of metaphysics. Already, "*alētheia* as opening of presence and presenting in thinking and saying originally comes under the perspective of *homoiōsis* and *adaequatio*, that is, the perspective of adequation in the sense of the correspondence of representing with what is present."[40] But if truth (*Wahrheit*) as *mimēsis*, as likeness and as correspondence, shelters and preserves (*bewahrt*) the unconcealment of being as such, then the task of thinking at the end of metaphysics will be dia-lectical in the sense that it must pass through (*dia*) metaphysics. Its task (*Aufgabe*) will be a giving of itself up to metaphysics, a surrender (*Aufgabe*). The task will not be to negate metaphysics, for the dialectic of negation or cancellation preserves metaphysics at the expense of leaving concealed what metaphysics preserves, namely the thinking of being as such, of presencing that is other than the presencing only of some represented thing. The task at the end of metaphysics will be that of a setting over (*Übersetzung*) of the translation (*Über*setzung) of the truth of being as a being, entity, thing, fact, state of affairs, process, or event (*idea, energeia, hypokeimenon, subjectum, actualitas, certitudo, vis,* Objectivity, freedom, will, Representation as conceptual scheme, frame, or *Ge-stell*) toward a thinking that precisely in letting metaphysics be as metaphysics lets be the concealing/unconcealing of truth. Setting over and getting over, *Überwindung*, not in the sense of triumphal overcoming, but in the sense of learning to live with it, as one twists free from and ceases to be overwhelmed by (*verwindet*) an illness in making adjustments for and coming to grips with it.[41]

Could Tarski's and Davidson's proposal that we think of truth in language otherwise than as conceptual framework or correspondence to something presented be a step forward beyond the time of world as picture or pictured and of language as constative representation without being at the same time a step back to metaphysics? Could there be representation as the performance enacted in the *Philosophical Investigations* without representation as the propositions of the *Tractatus Logico-Philosophicus*—and not only because the former as therapy presupposes the disease, but because philosophical therapy is homeopathy? The break with the proposition (*Satz*) is a leap (*Satz*) that uses the proposition as its springboard, its ground. It is a *Satz vom Grund*. The moment of the break is the moment when that with which one breaks becomes objectified. This moment of alienation, the moment in which the thought occurs to us that we have been in error, is at the same time the moment, *Augenblick,* of a return to the non-thetic inhabiting of language that is the source of the objectivating thesis itself, the return the later Wittgenstein and the later Heidegger would have the reader make when they practice a style of writing that would enable the hermeneutic "as" both to appear as and to disappear as the apophantic "as." This is a return to origin not as some "crystalline purity" of logic (*PI* 108) but as the "rough ground" of daily practice (*PI* 107). The *Augenblick* of origination is the moment when the move forward to another style of thinking represents as alien the ground which it is leaving behind. No longer that on which one stands, that ground becomes visible for the first time, as the perch it has left becomes visible to the owl of Minerva that has just taken wing. A concept that was once one's home is now no longer inhabited, but viewed, pictured, represented from outside. No longer an operatively *geschichtlich* motive, but an explanatory *historisch* cause, no longer an absolute but a relative presupposition, it is seen as one of those *Vorstellungen* that in Hegel's science of logic and science of the experience of consciousness precede every phenomenological elevation—and, above all, the elevation in which the understanding (*Verstand*) disappears into reason (*Vernunft*)—and that in Kuhn's and Bachelard's logic of science precede every epistemological break. Now "only" a propositionally representable presupposition, but still the presupposition of what is not thus representable yet.

This process is not a dialectic of determinate negation if what is not yet propositionally representable is as such incommensurable with that by which only from the point of view of a time in the future it can appear to us to have been sent, a time when what was not yet propositionally representable to us has become so. By that time what was not propositionally representable will have become for us both propositionally representable and commensurable with its superseded *Vorstellung*—which does not however mean that the superseded and superseding representations are mutually necessarily consistent by the standard of the principle of noncontradiction. We shall have learned that the -ability of the commensur-ability demanded by interlinguistic translation has moved to a "can" qualified by an "if" stating conditions that can now be fulfilled from a "could" qualified by an "if" stating conditions that could be fulfilled only given that "certain very general facts of nature" were different and/or that a certain "fixed stock of meanings," a certain *Ge-stell*,[42] were to become unfixed. Meantime, the future of the world looks uncertain. And rather than my being able to represent it propositionally, it looks as though the world looks at me, like an alien with whom I am in a conversation, which is possible not, as Quine writes unwittingly echoing Husserl and Merleau-Ponty, "because we are bound to adapt any alien pattern to our own in the very process of understanding or translating alien sentences,"[43] but because we are bound at the same time to adapt ours to his. To have an open conversation with another is to be open to a conversion. How else will we ever learn about the other, whether the other be another human being or the human and natural world? How else will we ever learn about ourselves? "He who knows no foreign languages knows nothing about his own," "Wer keine fremde Sprache kennt, weiss nichts von seiner eigenen." This dictum, versions of which are attributed to Goethe, does not beg the question of the incommensurability of other linguistic patterns of representation. The only way to gain evidence that our languages cannot be made commensurable is to behave as if they can. And that is the only way to gain evidence that in the case of the intransitivity of commensurability (meaning that from language L1's being commensurable with L2 and L2's being commensurable with L3, it does not follow that L1 is commensurable with L3), when the other appears to say that he can understand, interpret, or translate a third language that appears to be a closed book to us, he does not understand "understand," interpret "interpret," or translate "translate" in the way that we do.

The only way to open the book of nature is to open our eyes to the possibility that, whether or not we "demand that nature open up its eyes" and that "we talk with animals, plants, and rocks,"[44] there is a sense in which the eyes of nature are already open and upon us. Perhaps what Gadamer says of every assimilation of tradition (and tradition is traducement and translation) holds for every assimilation of the language in which that book is composed. It is "the experience of a 'view' of the object itself,"[45] where "view" translates *"Ansicht,"* and *"Ansicht"* is not just the representation that the investigator asserts regarding the object, but the object asserting itself,[46] as though the object were lodging an objection against being regarded as no more than an object, asking to be regarded with regard instead merely as the subjected subject of an asserted and enserfing representation: given a say, suffered to have suffrage, granted a voice and a vote; asking to be represented in the political sense.

THREE

The Experience of Language

Isness

How close does the experience of language let reading get? How close is close reading? Taking close reading as its point of departure, this chapter will then widen its focus in order to consider the experience of language with some reference to art, interpretation, and what we are now accustomed to calling archi-writing. This last will also be called telescripture, written in the lower case, so that through its first and second syllables, derived not from "*telos*," end, but from "*tēle*," distant, far, and through the allusion to uppercase (Holy) Scripture which its third and fourth syllables make, we do not underestimate the theological and religious depths and heights to which its forces reach.

What are the principles of close reading? Principles are practical or methodological and theoretical or logical. The principles of close reading are either rules for doing close reading or the conditions of the possibility of close reading. If the methodological rules are going to be good guides for conducting close reading, our formulation of those rules had better be guided by our knowledge of the logical foundations. But do close reading and interpretation more generally have any logical foundations?

In its technical sense the expression "close reading" is chiefly used of literary texts and of the approach to them advocated by the school of New Criticism active mainly in the 1930s and 1940s in the United States, as well as in Great Britain. Based on the title of John Crowe Ransom's book *The New Criticism* (1941), the label New Criticism is applied to the disparate family of poets and critics that includes Ransom himself, Robert Penn Warren, Allen Tate, Cleanth Brooks, W. K. Wimsatt, and Monroe Beardsley. These writers recognized an affiliation with what was being performed at Cambridge, England, by I. A. Richards under the name of practical criticism, the title of the book he had published in 1924. A key idea shared by these authors, along with F. R. Leavis and T. S. Eliot, is that a text, whether it be a poem, a play, or a novel, is to be read independently of its social, biographical, and historical context. What matters primarily are "the words on the page." The author's intentions and the affect or other effect the words have on the reader are irrelevant to the work as a work of art. What the work asks for is a close reading of the text in itself and of the more or less complex internal interrelationships of its parts. Like the well-wrought urn of Donne's poem "The Canonization" and of the title of the study by Cleanth Brooks, what is paramount is the ontology of the work. The business of the text is its isness. Hence the slogan that "a poem should not mean, but be." The paradigm of the work of art is the poem. Frank Kermode will say later that "the image is" and that "Poetry, by virtue of the image is."[1] (We shall come back to images below.) Kermode goes on to say that "prose merely describes." For the New Critical close reader, for whom the paradigm of the work of literature is the poem, even if the work is written in prose, paraphrase is a heresy and what is called a translation is at best a new work of art.

What can close reading thus described have to do with the study of Holy Scripture? It may seem that it poses a threat. For if paraphrase is a heresy according to New Criticism, is this not because New Criticism is a heresy according to Scripture, namely the heresy of idolatry? In his review of New Criticism in *Anatomy of Criticism* (1957), Northrop Frye speaks with some justification of the "vaguely sacramental" character of the movement, of its members belonging to an élite "ritual masonic" "mandarin caste," a revival of the movement that preached art for the sake of art.[2] How can it be possible, therefore, for Lyle M. Eslinger to write a book titled *Kingship of God in Crisis*, give it the subtitle *A Close Reading of 1 Samuel 1–12*, and tell his readers that he means the words "Close Reading" to be understood in the way intended by New Criticism?[3]

One response to this question would be to say that the biblical text is literature in the sense of letters in the sense that there are two letters in the word "in," adding perhaps that where the letters thus understood are those of the Hebrew alefbeth they may correspond to numbers in the Kabbalah and elsewhere. It could then be said of the Hebrew Bible, as the New Critics say of the poem, that it *is,* adding that its ontology is not apart from cosmo-theology but identical with it. A second and less drastic response would be to distinguish literature from literary criteria. New Critical close reading takes the standard of excellence of a text to be how well it combines complexity of structure with coherence. This literary standard is what Eslinger calls unity. I shall not presume to judge and cannot claim always even to follow the case he makes out for this unity of 1 Samuel 1–12. I limit myself to reporting or reminding my reader that what Eslinger does is to divide the chapters into two groups, chapters 1–7 and 8–12, then to argue for a series of correspondences between these two groups, the second group either simply repeating an event or state recorded in the first, or resolving a strain or ambiguity mentioned there. Having detailed ten such correspondences he observes:

> Until the suggested unity of the narrative and the supporting evidence thereto is refuted, any further suggestions about the socio-historical settings . . . must be regarded as unnecessarily complex, both as hypotheses and as explanations of the data. Literary explanations of the narrative are inherently stronger because they are primarily descriptive and so subject to refutation; a holistic literary approach eliminates the undesirable multiplication of historical assumptions, and its conclusions can be accepted or rejected as they agree or disagree with the text. The literary approach is a way out of the proliferation of studies whose conclusions cannot be compared because they depend on varying, non-verifiable hypotheses and assumptions.[4]

This is reminiscent of the view of the New Critical close reader that the author's intentions are not relevant to the appraisal of a piece of literature for the reason that we often do not know who the author was. This reason is a bad one. We do not need to know who the author was in order to get some grip on what he or she intended. But, staying with Eslinger, it is noteworthy that whereas the correspondence between the two groups of chapters described by him is internal, as are the correspondences the New Critical close reader considers to be the only ones relevant to a literary work, Eslinger does not dismiss as irrelevant a certain correspondence between verses 1–12 of Samuel chapter 1 and something outside them, namely their theological import. However, this does not amount to a return to a nonliterary criterion. It means only that the literary criterion must be extended, extended to other scriptural texts. As he explains,

The theological implications of these chapters, especially as regards the characterization of God, suggest that 1 Sam 1–12 is more comparable to a book like Job than has previously been accepted. It would, of course, be question-begging to suggest that these theological implications reveal the perversity of my reading when viewed in the wider context of the known theology of the deuteronomistic history. A close reading of the remainder of the deuteronomistic history is necessary to evaluate a close reading of 1 Sam 1–12.[5]

From this it appears that on the traditional philosophical question as to the criterion of truth, Eslinger is among those who take coherence with comprehensiveness to be sufficient. But a criterion of truth is not truth. Eslinger's limitation to coherence and comprehensiveness as a criterion of truth, that is to say, his restricting himself to the criteria of intra-textual and inter-textual correspondence, does not prevent him or us regarding truth as extra-textual correspondence. He and we are still free to think of the truth of sentences as a "realist" correspondence between text and what is outside text. Is that freedom denied by Derrida's controversial remark "*Il n'y a pas de hors-texte*"?

What does this text of Derrida's mean? As is not uncommon with Derrida, this frequently cited sentence is not as simple as it seems. We learn this when we put it in the context of C. S. Peirce's interpretation of the word "sign," cited and adapted by Derrida, according to which a sign is "Anything [called by Peirce the *representamen*] which determines something else (its interpretant) to refer to an object to which [it] itself refers (its object) in the same way, the interpretant becoming in turn a sign, and so on *ad infinitum*."[6] It is clear from this that Peirce is an ontological realist of some sort. There are referents, objects. But once we think of objects we are launched into an infinite progress. For, "We think only in signs."[7] A sign denotes a kind of thing and is itself a kind of thing. So Peirce could be a nominalist if nominalism is understood as the doctrine that generals are words without its being the case, *pace* Ockham, that words are nothing but individuals. Generality is the repeatability of words, their iterability, as Derrida says, with *iter* having the sense both of "again" and of "travel," from the Sanskrit "*itara*," other.[8] Words make up a text and text has a texture, a weft and a warp in more than one sense of the word "warp"—though Derrida is chary of this metaphor because of the suggestion of homespun naturalness conveyed by the term "textile" compared with the artifactuality of sewing (*couture*).[9] A word in a given text is necessarily repeatable in another context somewhere further along the road. With a change of context the text inevitably changes, since a text is a context of its context, granted the eventuality of a switch between figure and ground. So iteration is alteration. This is what is meant by that so often misinterpreted—warped—string of words "Il n'y a pas de hors-texte." In Derrida's text (*Of Grammology*)[10] these words are not put together in order to make a metaphysical claim to the effect that there are no objects or subjects, only text, only words, words, and still more words. To translate Derrida's words by "There is nothing outside the text" is to mistranslate it. In English the French says "There is nothing without text" and in Scots it says "There is nothing outwith text." The outsideness is with insideness and vice versa, both with and without at one and the same time. Derrida does not say "Il n'y a rien hors le texte," or "Il n'y a rien hors du texte." He does not say that there is nothing outside the text. He says that there is nothing outside text, or without text, or without context, there is no textlessness, broadening Frege's and Wittgenstein's statement that a name has meaning only in the context of a sentence.

Further, perhaps in the "il y a" of "Il n'y a pas de hors text" we should hear a resonance of the "there is" of Heidegger's "'there is' being," "es gibt' Sein." Heidegger tells readers of *Being and Time* that there is being only where there is what he calls "*Dasein*," which is the way of being of human beings, beings open to understanding and truth, beings with a sense of what it is to be in that it matters for such beings how they fill the time of their being. Lest this be heard as an assertion of metaphysical idealism, it should be noted parenthetically that Heidegger stresses that to say there is no being without *Dasein* does not mean there cannot be unDaseinish beings like rocks and glaciers in an age where there is no *Dasein*. What it does mean is that Daseinish beings have a sense of what it is to be, *sein,* as is marked by the word *Dasein* which Heidegger usually uses in preference to the word "*Mensch,*" meaning "man" or "mankind." Now suppose we give being a linguistic turn, and say of text or textuality or web—at least the artifactual www dot—what Heidegger says of being. Already in *Being and Time* one of *Dasein*'s fundamental ways of being is linguisticality. Heidegger's word is "*Rede,*" which sounds like English "read," though "*reden*" can mean to speak—especially however to make a speech, and some speeches or orations, like papers, are often read from a written text. Liddell and Scott give "to recite what is written" as a possible sense of Greek "*legein,*" and it is "*legein*" and "*logos*" that Heidegger's "*Rede*" is meant to translate. Given that so many of the other classical texts cited under "*legein*" by Liddell and Scott exemplify oral communication, we may infer that Heidegger's "*Rede*" as a translation of "*legein*" denotes a "common root" of the written and spoken word. It is the way what we call the human being has of collecting, colligating, articulating, or interpreting a world, independently of whether this articulation or interpretation is expressed in writing or in speaking. But if Heidegger's "*Rede*" is a recuperation of "*logos endiathetos,*" the mental word, as distinguished by Philo from "*logos pro-phorikos,*" the uttered word,[11] it is also his reading of the Latin "*ratio,*" to which it is related etymologically, as it is presumably again to "*ratus*" and "*rhetos,*" reckoned. "*Ratio*" collects one sense of "*logos*" as "the power of the mind" (Liddell and Scott), the capacity to construe, to construct, to collect, *co-legere,* to read together, to set side-by-side, as we have been reading together in close proximity a few words from different languages in order to show that it is not a long step from saying with Heidegger that *Dasein*'s way of being is to be articulatingly or interpretatively to saying with Derrida that *Dasein*'s or "*Dasein*'s" way of being is textuality. Since being is not without or outwith that kind of being that Heidegger calls *Da-sein,* it follows that the being of any entity is inseparable from what Derrida calls textuality. Derrida's *Da-sein* is a *Da*-reader. Except that allowance must be made for the qualms he would have—as Heidegger himself came to have—over using *Dasein* as a term of fundamental ontology, in particular because he would insist that the *Da* of *Da-sein,* the "somewhere" or "here or there" of being-there, must be supplemented with a *fort,* a being elsewhere more disruptive than the "there" of Heidegger's *Da,* so disruptive that foundations are destabilized and construction de-construed. Having touched on this forthness or displacement of the place into which reading as *Rede* collects and recollects itself, let us now ask again: how close can close reading get?

Thisness

More specifically, how close does the experience of language let close reading get? The phrase "experience of language" is to be understood not only in its objective genitivity as the experience someone may have of language, but also in its subjective genitivity, as language's experience. Although these two genitivities are interdependent, I want to attend first to the sense in which we may say of a language as we say of a human being that it embodies a degree of experience rather as we may say of people that they are experienced or wise. As people may become wise through experience, so in the course of its history and travail and travel (*fahren*) a language acquires experience (*Erfahrung*) and a degree of what we may provisionally call wisdom. Indeed, the experience of language contributes to the experience of people and of a people, though it is arguable that just as not all people grow wiser as they grow older, so too in the course of the history of a language the language may become less sensitive. For, like people, languages are liable to *Verfallenheit;* they have a propensity to fall, though in their fallen state they may retain a potentiality for being salvaged, if not a potentiality for salvation understood as being made whole.

Taking the words "experience of language" in this sense, illustrations of which will be given in what follows, how close, for the third time of asking, does the experience of language let close reading get?

The answer to this question, put in the way it would be put by Peirce, is that reading can never be so close that what is read is a generality or an individual unmediated by words or other signs. Put in the way it would be put by Derrida, the answer is that reading can never get so close to meaning as to be fully present to it and to itself. My meaning what I read or write or say is never entirely mine, notwithstanding that, as Hegel is pleased to observe, the word "*Meinung*" invites us to equate meaning with making *mein*, making mine, "mining." This does not mean that we cannot mean what we say. It means that we are always, necessarily, not accidentally, liable to say more than we mean or otherwise other than we mean. In his interpretation of one version of the dream of semantic *parousia,* the version according to which it is when we purport to indicate a sensory datum with the word "This" that we most faithfully read how reality is, Hegel asks its proponent to write this word down. Immediately, with the moment of writing having slipped from the present into the past, the word "This" has to be replaced by the word "That," and vice versa, and the "Now" of that moment has become a "Then," and vice versa. A further moment's reflection suffices to make us realize that the spoken word suffers the same fate. The closeness that speaking may seem to promise is prevented by a distancing, a temporal deferral to a time when the speaker is no longer present, when he or she is in the same position as a writer, all writing being testamentary in that it is addressed to, among others, readers who come after the writer's death, that is to say, after the death of the first reader, and after the death of other readers, after the death of the other. Likewise for any thinking that is supposed capable of being conducted without any direct or indirect dependence on written or spoken signs, such as was supposed to be possible at least in principle by Plato, Augustine, and Husserl. Plato already begins to disturb this dream of a pure thought-language when, having described thinking as the conversation the soul has with itself, he compares the Forms or Ideas that are the objects of that thinking to marks inscribed on the tablet of the mind.

Whether what signs signify are conceived as individual or as general, a *signum–signatum,* "Fido"–Fido foundation for linguistic meaning is supposed in the semiotics of the three thinkers just named and of many other theoreticians, notwithstanding their acknowledgment of the need to supplement this account of the alleged foundation with an account of how the *signata* are connected. In Saussure's *Course of General Linguistics* (1915)[12] the order of priority is not simply reversed. Rather, connectedness, whether by sameness or difference, what Plato calls "*symplokē*," intertwining, and what medieval logicians call syncategorematic expressions, e.g., "if," "and," and "or," are held to be constitutive of even nominal, categorematic, deictic, and other purportedly freestanding expressions. This structuralism, as Saussure's readers came to call it, maintains that, with the exception of onomatopoeic words, the importance of which Saussure argues is marginal, the meaning of a sign is not anything positive or posited. Rather is it a sign's differences from other signs, as illustrated by the fact that while the signs "red" and "blue" may fill the space in "The sky is ___," the sign "because" normally will not. On Saussure's differentialist account of meaning the meaning of a sign is the product of relations of differences among marks or sounds, what he calls the signifier, and differences among signifieds, where the signified is the concept, connotation, or meaning, the semantic object or objective, the "internal accusative" thanks to which the sign may refer to the object as understood in Peirce's definition of a sign.

This object may happen to be the "internal object" externalized by being regarded as a referent. That is to say, the referent may happen to be another semantic object. It is this again when someone says "I do not approve of a statement like that." Umberto Eco offers this as an example of that sort of sign which Peirce calls an index, and he offers it because, as he expresses it, he is "eager to challenge Peirce's idea that in order to be understood as signs indices must be connected to the object they designate."[13] Peirce distinguishes indices from icons and symbols. A symbol could not function as a sign, could not have a particular signification, he says, unless it had an interpretant, that is, unless it can be interpreted, translated, or otherwise glossed. And whereas an icon can still be significant even if its object does not exist (for example a pencil stroke standing for a geometrical line), this is not how it is with an index. "An index is a sign which would, at once, lose the character which makes it a sign if its object were removed, but would not lose that character if there were no interpretant."[14] Eco counters this with the example cited earlier, "I do not approve of a statement like that," of which he says that even where nobody has recently made a statement the indexical expression or shifter "that" retains its meaning. The hearers will be puzzled by what the speaker has said, and try to recollect to what statement he can be referring. In other words they will take the speaker to have presupposed "I am naming through the shifter something which is not there, and which preceded the present statement." From this Eco concludes that the meaning of the indexical "this" "is understood even if the presupposed event or thing does not exist and never has existed.[15] Allow me to say of Eco's statement, echoing him, "I do not approve of a statement like that." I doubt whether Eco's statement, in the circumstances in which he envisages it made, is a counter-instance to what Peirce actually says. That it is not is suggested also by Eco's taking the possibility of telling a lie as further proof that what Peirce says is wrong. Eco says that "a lie is made possible by the fact that sign-vehicles always convey a content, even when there is no testable referent." But what I take Peirce to mean is that if there were no object to be referred to, a putatively indexical sign, unlike an iconic sign, would lack the character that would make it an indexical sign. He is concerned not only with signification in general, but with marking the differences between the three kinds of sign, iconic, indexical, and what he calls symbolic. Take as a clue what he says about an iconic sign. "An Icon is a sign which refers to the Object that it denotes merely by virtue of characters of its own, and which it possesses, just the same, whether any such Object actually exists or not. It is true that unless there really is such an Object, the Icon does not act as a sign; but this has nothing to do with its character as a sign."[16] This seems to conflict with the case of the stroke penciled on a piece of paper as representing a geometrical line. Of this iconic sign he says that it "would possess the character which renders it significant, even though its object had no existence."[17] If what he means by the geometrical line having no existence is that it does not exist in the way that marks on paper do, but is a theoretical entity of which we might say that it only subsists, then there is no conflict. In this case the iconic sign, the mark on the paper, does have an Object (upper case O) in the sense he says is required for the icon to act as a sign, taking him to mean by this acting specifically as an iconic sign. A sign would not act as an iconic sign if it purported to stand for a round square. But we should still understand that it purported to stand for something; we should still understand what is required for a sign to function iconically. Unless we did we would not be able to say that it fails to function iconically because round squares do not exist in any possible world or, in his phrase, in any "mode of existence."[18] This understanding is the understanding of the concept of the iconic, and a concept for Peirce is a symbol.

Return now to the case of the indexical sign, and to Eco's claim against Peirce that in the assertion "I do not approve of a statement like that" the word "that" still functions indexically when no statement was recently made. On my reading of Peirce the signification that would survive the nonexistence of a referent for "that" in Eco's purported counter-case is not the indexical signification. It is the symbolic signification that a sentence must have if it is to puzzle or deceive the hearer or reader. We have shifted in these two cases from the indexical and iconic sign of an object to the sign of a concept, reversing the order of the paradoxical shift we make according to Frege from concept to object when we move from the sign "horse" to the sign "the concept horse."[19] Eco's reading takes Peirce to be equating indication with reference. My reading takes Peirce to be distinguishing these. That he is is evident from his definition of a sign in general, which implies that signs of any kind refer. But both my reading of Peirce on this point and Eco's are supported by Peirce's concession that "it would be difficult if not impossible, to instance an absolutely pure index, or to find any sign absolutely devoid of the indexical quality."[20] Only a closer reading of what Peirce writes on this matter here and elsewhere will settle whether I am reading him more closely than Eco.

Peirce is not easy to read. He demands to be read closely. For instance, it is not easy to be sure that one has interpreted correctly what he says about the interpretant. It is worth noting that according to Wittgenstein it is only if a text demands close reading, only if it is difficult, like Peirce's, only if it is problematic or obscure or foreign that it can be interpreted. Where we understand something straight off there is no room for interpretation (*Deutung*) in what Wittgenstein regards as the ordinary use of the word. So, despite his admiration for Peirce, he would question from the start Peirce's statement that every sign has an interpretant, if that means that we interpret every sign we understand. Setting aside such cases of interpretation as Brendel's interpretation of Schubert's sonata D. 664 or Orson Welles's interpretation of Othello, to interpret, on Wittgenstein's interpretation, is to consider hypotheses or compare one rule for reading with another, for instance as factual or as fictive. To interpret is to think in the sense of doing something. It is not to see what is meant at once, where seeing is a state or condition (*Zustand*), not a deed. To interpret is, in words that only seem to say something different from what has just been said, not to follow a rule blindly.[21]

Firstness and secondness

Having warned against some of the dangers exposed in attempting to answer the question as to how close the experience of language lets close reading get, I now turn to another temptation that some readers of Peirce and Derrida have found themselves unable to resist. I have in mind the inference that because the interpretants, glosses, translations, or iterations of a sign token are not a finite class, no interpretation is barred and reading is ungoverned free play. Two formal points call to be made about this inference. First, to exclude certain items from being counted does not exclude there being an infinite series of items to be counted. For example, there is an infinite series both of even numbers and of even and odd numbers taken together. Second, the very idea of an infinite class implies certain restrictions, a certain finiteness that needs to be mentioned if one is to refer to deconstruction's "endless slither of signifers," as Frank Kermode does in his essay "The Bible As It Was."[22] Foucault reproduces a celebrated passage from Borges in the preface to the former's *Les mots et les choses,* a title we may think is somewhat one-sidedly glossed (following what we are told was Foucault's own first preference) as *The Order of Things* by its anonymous translator, unless we agree that words can be classed among things. Do things simply as things form a class or an order? That is the question raised by the title of the radio program "The Ghost of Federico García Lorca—Which Can also Be Used as a Table" and, more famously, by the passage from Borges of which Foucault says:

> This book first arose out of a passage in Borges, out of the laughter that shattered, as I read the passage, all the landmarks of my thought—our thought, the thought that bears the stamp of our age and our geography— breaking up all the ordered surfaces and all the planes with which we are accustomed to tame the wild profusion of existing things, and continuing long afterwards to disturb and threaten with collapse our age-old distinction between the Same and the Other. The passage quotes [and I quote] a "certain Chinese encyclopaedia" in which it is written that "animals are divided into: (a) belonging to the Emperor, (b) embalmed, (c) tame, (d) sucking pigs, (e) sirens, (f) fabulous, (g) stray dogs, (h) included in the present classification, (i) frenzied, (j) innumerable, (k) drawn with a very fine camelhair brush, (l) et cetera, (m) having just broken the water pitcher, (n) that from a long way off look like flies."

It is as though this classification is too long a way off from us to count as a classification—unless we admit the paradox of a class of things that are unclassifiable. As Foucault goes on to comment, "In the wonderment of this taxonomy, the thing we apprehend in one great leap, the thing that, by means of a fable, is demonstrated as the exotic charm of another system of thought, is the limitation of our own, the stark impossibility of thinking that."[23] But what the fable would show or imply if we could get its drift is that it too has a limitation of its own, however difficult it may be for us to find a footing in it. Our difficulty is that of grasping not the sense or reference of the items in the list, not how to gloss each of them word for word, word for thing, thing for word, thing for thing. Our difficulty is one of grasping the point. On the one hand Borges stirs in us a sense of wonderment. But part of that wonderment regarding this cluster of properties—not all of which (e.g. "included in the present classification" and "et cetera") belong to what we would consider to be the same logical level or ontological category—is wondering what purpose can be served by this grouping (a grouping which is a groping like that marked by a tendency in British English nowadays to pronounce "wonder" as "wander"). A language, and that means a classification, is, as Wittgenstein and Heidegger among many others have reminded us, a form of life. So, although the wonderment of which Foucault writes is aroused by the defamiliarization and distancing of the text from everyday life promoted, in the wake of Russian Formalism, by the New Critics, try as we may with them to peer closely at the words on the page and to isolate them from our and others' social, historical, economic, religious, etc. cultures, the latter are, as it were, the aqueous fluid of the eyes by which the words on the page are read. The words on the page say to us, with Emerson's sphynx, "Of thine eye I am eyebeam," where this last word has the wonderful ambiguity we expect of a saying of a sphynx, leaving us oscillating between insight and blindness, between a beam of light, a light to the Gentiles perhaps, and the beam that I am called to remove from my own eye before I attempt to remove the one in my brother's.

Without remarking on the ambiguity of its last word, Peirce uses Emerson's line to encapsulate the thought that a symbol lights the way for other symbols. What Peirce says and the cadences of the sentences in which he says it are both reminiscent of the paragraph (34) of *Being and Time* in which Heidegger says that it is wrong to think that word-things have significations added on to them. On the contrary, "words grow on meanings," *Den Bedeutungen wachsen Worte zu.*[24] We are in the vicinity of the metaphor (or catachresis) of grafting brought freely into play, but not without license, in at least two senses of that word "license," in Derrida's speculations on classification in *Glas.* Not without license in two senses because, although Derrida is quick to celebrate with Borges and Foucault and Joyce, etc., the wonder that the proliferation of meanings excites, he is only a little less quick to stress that this displacement takes place before the law. No doubt after it too. But not without (the) law. And some of his reasons for saying this are the same, if also different from, things he and we read in Peirce, things we have already touched on, and which can be fleshed out if we now read the paragraph in Peirce that strikes the ear like a pre-echo of the paragraph in which Heidegger writes that "words grow on meanings."

> Symbols grow. They come into being by development out of other signs, particularly from icons, or from mixed signs partaking of the nature of icons and symbols. We think only in signs. These mental signs are of mixed nature; the symbol-parts of them are called concepts. If a man makes a new symbol, it is by thoughts involving concepts. So it is only out of symbols that a new symbol can grow. "Omne symbolum de symbolo."

> A symbol, once in being, spreads among the peoples. In use and in experience, its meaning grows. Such words as force, law, wealth, marriage, bear for us very different meanings from those they bore to our barbarous ancestors. The symbol may, with Emerson's sphynx, say to man, "Of thine eye I am eyebeam."[25]

Why does Peirce say that symbols grow by development particularly from iconic signs? An icon for him is a sign that signifies an idea that may be the predicate of an assertion. It is indispensable for direct communication of an idea. Indirect communication is parasitic upon the direct communication of an idea by an icon or set of icons.[26] This is why Peirce says that the representative quality of an icon is its firstness. Notwithstanding his saying that an icon signifies an idea, he says too that it is an idea: "A sign by Firstness is an image of its object and, more strictly speaking, can only be an idea."[27] So much for "more strictly speaking." "But," he goes on to say, writing still more closely, "most strictly speaking, even an idea, except in the sense of a possibility, or Firstness [that is, in the sense of a predicate or universal quality], cannot be an Icon." He is not saying first that an iconic sign is an idea and then contradicting himself by saying that an idea cannot be an iconic sign. He is saying perfectly consistently that an idea can be an icon and therefore an icon can be an idea, but as soon as we move from the iconic idea to the interpreting idea (the "interpretant"), as we must be able to do by definition with any sign whatsoever, we have left iconography. We have left the icon because the icon functions as an image; it represents its object "mainly by similarity."[28] We are removed from its firstness when that first qualitative (one-place) predicate is interpreted by the idea of what is contrasted with it. The contrasted idea and sign is motivated by the first idea. We have now what Peirce calls secondness. Firstness is of quality, so Peirce calls its sign a qualisign. Where a qualisign represents (re-presents) a feeling or impression passively suffered, secondness is the experience of being impressed and interrupted by the occurrence of an object in the "literal" sense of ob-ject, something thrown in my way, opposed to, resisting, or contrasted with me. It is represented by a "Sign by Contrast." Peirce calls this a sinsign, because what it signifies occurs only one single time (*sin, semel*). One of his examples (though not one that illustrates obviously the experience of an object opposed to the experiencing subject) is the singleness of the replica (token) of the word "the" as distinguished from the word "the" taken as a type, as the same word reiterated in its replicas or tokens. Other examples might be the traditionally secondarized terms of oppositions like writing as opposed to speaking to which deconstruction would do greater justice. Or, if such terms are too conceptual for the indexicality that marks secondness according to Peirce, perhaps secondness would be better exemplified by the way the opposed terms are both "effects" or indications of tele-scripture.

So much for firstness and secondness. What is thirdness?

Thirdness

As firstness stands to possibility and iconicity, and as secondness stands to existence and indexicality, so thirdness stands to law, conceptuality, or symbolicality. However, Peirce distinguishes orders of thirdness. By his definition of a sign all signs partake of thirdness because all sign relations are triadic. Iconicity, indexicality, and symbolicality are all relations among an object, a representation (*representamen*), and an interpretant. But thirdness, as the conceptual or symbolic, is distinguished from the iconic and the indexical which it brings together. One could risk saying that the conceptual or symbolic is an incomplete symbol in that it collects together qualities that are capable of belonging to an existent object.

We are now in a position to answer the question why Peirce says that symbols grow by development particularly from iconic signs. An index is a sign of an object, whereas an icon is the sign of a felt or impressed quality. It is the quality, not the object which may have the quality, that is generalized in the concept. A symbol brings with it implications of what, having said something, one would be expected to say further, on pain of not being understood. It turns on a conditionality grounded in a convention, a law. A symbol is a legisign. So it is a type, as opposed to a token, but it is more than that.[29] It is a disposition, what one would be expected to say if a certain condition holds. The *sym* (*syn*), that is to say the togetherness of sym-bolism, is this connection of the if/then that is expressed in habitual behavior. Peirce uses the term "habit" not only of human conduct but also of the behavior patterns of non-human animals and even of the laws of physics or chemistry, for instance the regularities with which lithium behaves under certain specified conditions. Whatever one may say of so-called habits and laws of the inorganic world, human habituality on Peirce's analysis of it is not a must-be but a would-be. Habit allows for the chance that what would normally be expected fails to occur. Peirce is a tychist. His tychism is manifest in the paragraph cited earlier on the growth of symbols, where he notes that "such words as force, law, wealth, marriage, bear for us very different meanings from those they bore to our barbarous ancestors." Like other human behavior, the human handling of symbols is adaptive. The interpretant, it will be recalled, is a sign of an object that is substituted for another sign referring to the same object, whether that substitution articulates a meaning or changes it. Even where chance intervenes in the change, it is not "mere chance" but chance geared to purpose. Peirce is a pragmaticist, pragmaticism being the term he employs in order to keep at arm's length the pragmatism of, for example, William James, understood as the doctrine that, to state it crudely, truth is "what works." At arm's length too would be the pragmatism of Richard Rorty, who finds the notion of purpose "pretty embarrassing."[30] Purpose or point or teleology, that is to say thirdness,[31] is no less the context for growth of meaning than it is for the interpretation of a sign whose meaning is being spelled out.

Note that thirdness here applies to the will. That the will is involved even with the logical or semantic interpretation of a sign is indicated by the fact that in French to mean is *vouloir dire,* a topic to which we shall return in chapter 6. The will is more directly engaged by imperative signs like "Ground arms!" which have what Peirce calls an energetic interpretant that is manifested by a muscular or mental effort. A sign may also have an emotional interpretant, for instance the feelings conveyed by a piece of music.[32]

What Peirce says about the case where meaning is conserved is relevant to our question as to how close the experience of language lets close reading get. For he presents us with the problem of reconciling his assertion that the interpretant of a sign is a sign that becomes "in turn a sign, and so on *ad infinitum*" with his assertion that one may reach "the entire general intended interpretant,"[33] the "very meaning,"[34] an "adequate ultimate interpretation."[35] The solution of this problem lies in recognizing that all these phrases refer not to a sign, but to a habit.

> I do not deny that a concept, proposition, or argument may be a logical interpretant. I only insist that it cannot be the final logical interpretant, for the reason that it is itself a sign of that very kind that has itself a logical interpretant. . . . The concept which is a logical interpretant is only imperfectly so. It somewhat partakes of the nature of a verbal definition, and is as inferior to the habit, and much in the same way, as a verbal definition is inferior to the real definition. The deliberately formed, self-analyzing habit—self-analyzing because formed by the aid of the analysis of the exercises that nourished it—is the living definition, the veritable and final logical interpretation. Consequently, the most perfect account of a concept that words can convey will consist in a description of the habit which that concept is calculated to produce. But how otherwise can a habit be described than by a description of the kind of action to which it gives rise, with the specification of the conditions and of the motive?[36]

Consider first this reference to a description of a habit or of the kind of action to which it gives rise under certain conditions. Does this undermine our claim that the ultimate interpretant is a habit, not a sign? I think not. Not if a description is a proposition. For Peirce says that although a proposition may be a logical interpretant, therefore a sign, in the first sentence of this passage he denies that a proposition can be a final logical interpretant.

Consider next Peirce's reference here to a self-analyzing habit. To say that a habit is self-analyzing is to say that it is self-critical, because it has learned by experience that it must remain open to the possibility of change. Its ultimacy or finality must be understood in a way that allows it to be provisional. This way of understanding the ultimacy of a habit is met by Peirce's doctrine that signs can be substituted for signs potentially *ad infinitum*. Another way of saying this is to say that interpretation is a disposition of imagination to construct and construe, to read schemas that interpret percepts and concepts in terms of each other, the art or skill or gift of judgment in the sense of a habitual practical or theoretical or practico-theoretical tact. Peirce's mature view of a habit as the "adequate ultimate interpretant" is that this is a habit of changing habit. But how, it will be asked, can this metahabituality be ultimate given that a change of habit is not to be made for the sake of change, but in order better to achieve a specific purpose? Would it not be this purpose rather than the habit that is ultimate? However, although the particular purpose would in a sense be ultimate, it would not be an adequate ultimate interpretant. It would not be this because it would be neither an interpretant nor adequate. For example, to describe what happened in Manhattan on September 11, 2001 CE as the Destruction of the Temple of Trade is to interpret that event. However, the reason for putting that interpretation upon it—say, to suggest that Mammon has become our God—is not an interpretation. Moreover, that reason or any other reason would fall far short of the comprehensiveness of the capacity of a habit to change habits on the part of the individual—and it would fall short at the trans-individual level of the comprehensiveness of what in *The Problem of Christianity*, adapting Peirce, Josiah Royce calls a "community of interpretation."

Nunc distans

Still keeping in mind the question of close reading, let us now sew on to what has been said above about Peirce some further observations about Derrida.

It will be recalled that Derrida cites and applauds Peirce's definition of the sign as infinitely interpretable. We have shown how for Peirce this does not open the floodgates to any and every reading of a text. At the very least some readings will be set aside because they fail to survive the auto- and hetero-criticism intrinsic to the ultimate interpretation which for Peirce, we have now seen, is not an ultimate sign, but a habit with regard to signs. Despite what may be the case with ground-level habits, the acquisition of this meta-habit marks not a diminution but an increase of self-criticality and self-exposure to criticism by whatever interpretive society is relevant—the community of chemists or biologists or lay persons. It is therefore difficult to see why Eco says that we have here in Peirce "something that cannot find a place within the [Derridean] deconstructive framework,"[37] namely the extralinguistic or extratextual full stop that Derrida calls a transcendental signified. A habit, a disposition, is just not of the category of that to which could belong the kind of presence a transcendentally signified entity is envisaged as having. This, therefore, is not the point at which Derrida diverges from Peirce.

The point at which Derrida diverges from Peirce, the point at which deconstruction gets grafted on to semiotics and refuses to be assimilated to pragmaticism,[38] is the point at which construction or construal gives way to deconstruction—the point, furthermore, at which, in the light of my passing reference to the imagination, one should have to ask whether the imagination is not only constructive but also deconstructive, either by turns or at one and the very same yet differant (sic), deferring moment. The point of Derrida's divergence from Peirce lies elsewhere. Although agreeing with Peirce on the polysemic productivity of meanings, and although no less insistent than he is that this productivity is limited by the grammatical and other socially instituted habits without which one could not form certain purposes or say what one wants to say, Derrida goes a step further in shaking our confidence in the stability of meaning and intention, that is to say of wanting to say, *vouloir dire*. In this, incidentally, and perhaps to the surprise of some of Derrida's readers, Derrida is closer to Hegel than Peirce. Like Hegel, Derrida brings out how certain writers (Plato, Kant, Condillac, Rousseau, Nietzsche, Husserl, Heidegger, Saussure, Foucault, Lévi-Strauss, Freud, Lacan, Hegel, and Derrida himself) say something other than what they intend. In order to do this he must read their texts with respect for the apparatus and recognition of the methodologies of literary and/or historical scholarship. "Without this recognition and this respect, critical production would risk developing in any direction at all and authorize itself to say almost anything."[39]

"But," Derrida immediately adds, "this indispensable guardrail has always only protected, it has never opened, a reading." While what Derrida refers to as his "principles of reading" demands that reading be close in the sense that it will "recognize all [the] classical exigencies" and "require all the instruments of traditional criticism," the principles are ones that have been instituted, not ones that have been intuited, like those invoked by the "principle of all principles" which purport to constitute the bedrock of Husserlian phenomenology. And what is instituted or constructed can be de-instituted and de-constructed. On a closer reading a text may deconstruct itself, open itself, and open itself not only to a fuller meaning, but to a certain unfullness, to an exteriority that cannot be described in the geometry of the opposition between the inside and the outside, or indeed in terms of any of the other oppositions of classical, classifying philosophy or theory of literary genres, for instance that of the sacred text as opposed to the profane or of *logos endiathetos* as opposed to *logos prophorikos*. Whatever is opened, published, made visible, made plain, made profane, or interpreted ("-*pretis*," cognate with Sanskrit "*prath*," spread abroad, as "*logos spermatikos*") is so thanks to the at least momentarily secret and at least in that sense sacred invisible frame: the ground—or unground—that goes without saying. Yet at the same time this opening is an opening in the sense of an inauguration, an overture, *ouverture*, in that it makes these oppositions possible. It makes them possible, however, as effects rather than causes or grounds, without these effects being the effects of a foundational first or second cause or ground. And if ground be taken in the sense of background as distinguished from the figure raised as a theatrical effect against it, the figure in focus will owe its figure to the ground that is not in focus, because, to reiterate, a context is quasi-internal to a text.

Consider again the case of the sign, in particular the case of the sign in Derrida's close reading of Saussure. Let us say in scare quotes that the case of the sign is a case in the "etymological" sense of the term. It is a *casus*, a fall. But it is at the same time a rising, a resurrection, and a resource. It is a resource or springing, however, that is without a source, if by source is meant a first origin. Re-source is as close as one gets to a source. Secondness is where we begin. And Derrida would probably say this too if "secondness" is taken in Peirce's technical sense. Peircean firstness, Derrida would probably say, is only an effect of secondness, an effect of a certain relation of production without first cause, production that is the production of meaning only because it is indexical, as Peirce would say, indicative, as Derrida would say, where indication imports the empirical signifying element that Husserl says is in principle excludable from the expression of signified meaning. A deconstructive close reading makes it difficult to count even up to two, for at the anarchic unground beneath principial effects there is no simple opposition between first and second, one and two. Likewise, the structuralist construction—the construing together—of the signifier and the signified as an opposition of terms constitutive of the sign turns out on a close reading of Saussure's (or Saussure's students') sentences to be a simple opposition of terms only on the surface. This opposition depends upon an interlacing of forces that are non-terminating because, to make the point in the manner it is made in Derrida's adaptation of Peirce, the signified is always already in the position of the signifier.[40] The signified is the meaning aspect of the sign as distinguished from the aspect of the sign as a phoneme or grapheme—or cheironomeme or morphazememe, as we could call the nodes of the semiotics of gesture, to mention only one of the many other varieties of semiotics for which Saussure took the semiotics of language as the model and which Lévi-Strauss, Roland Barthes, and others developed further. But while, on the one hand, there is no signified semantic meaning unless this meaning can be put in words, that is to say, said through recourse to different signifying marks or sounds—or through the same ones repeated in limiting cases like *eheyeh asher eheyeh* (Exodus 3:14), to which there is no like—on the other hand, the same phoneme or grapheme, etc., which is the signifying aspect of the sign, is already endowed with syntactic and grammatical meaning. To say that it functions as a signifier is to say that it is a sound or mark employed as belonging to a syntactic and grammatical system. The "as" of the phrase "as belonging to" implies the "if" of hypotheticality, of what one would be expected to say given a specified condition. And this "if" implies a stretch of time beyond the present. Indeed, it depresences the present by importing into it an always already pastness and an always already futureness. For human beings linguistic meaning is discursive, *cursus*, running, passage. But human beings are inclined to fall under the spell of a certain theological idea of linguistic meaning according to which a signifier is face to face with its signified in a totally present *nunc stans*. This idea is exemplified by the New Critical conception of the poem as a self-contained verbal icon. And it is exemplified by Saussure's conception of language as a synchronic system in which signification is defined by difference, as chess is constituted by the different powers of its pieces rather than by any positive nonrelational properties of the pieces, for instance their color.

Despite the emphasis Saussure puts on the primacy of difference over what he calls the positive, and despite his appeal to what remains constant through the various ways of writing a particular letter of the alphabet to illustrate how systematic differentiation makes possible spoken language (*langue,* tongue), even he occasionally forgets the distancing differentiation typified in writing where the author is removed from the text. Even Saussure occasionally reverts to "phonologism," that is, to the supposition that the key to the understanding (*entendre*) of linguistic meaning is hearing (*entendre*) oneself speak where there is supposedly no distance between what the inner ear hears/understands and what the inner mouth utters.

This phonocentrism is also a logocentrism, that is, it presumes that the author is in full control of the meaning present to her or his mind or/and that the meaning, like some despotic Upper Case Author, is in full control of the would-be lowercase author and his authorial intentions.

Now if the human condition is one in which the presence of the present is interrupted by the past and the future, past and future presents too interfere with each other. This is why the phrase "etymological sense of the word" was used above with signaled caution. The phrase suggests that we may start with the meaning a word has now for us and track back through the history of its use to its first true root meaning. Is that not what etymological dictionaries aim to do? But when we read in square brackets in the OED that our word "case" derives via Middle English and Old French from the Latin *casus* and that that noun is cognate with the verb *cadere,* to fall, we now have to ask what sense of "fall" is intended. Although we may demonstrate what "fall" means by, say, pointing to the rain, we must also say something if we are to explain that we mean the falling, not the rain that falls or its wetness, and so on. And the addressee must already understand the point of the pointing. As Wittgenstein has helped us understand, pointing is already a fairly sophisticated speech act, a work of language, a move in a language-game where language is a form of life or a way of being in the world. Speech acts can be performed in writing, as I now, at the time of writing, am performing a constative speech act in writing if I state in my text that the topic of this paragraph in my text is etymology. The topic of this text is reading, therefore textuality, the textuality of texts the close reading of which is not closed reading but is facilitated largely by other texts whose authors have left the scene. To say that language is a form of life is to say at least that the meanings of isolated words can be grasped only in the context of their uses in speech or in writing, as spoken *Worte* or as written *Wörter.* Some texts purport to be both written *Wörter* and spoken *Worte,* notably Holy Scriptures that purport to express and not only to report the word—*davar* or *logos*—of God. In reading uppercase Holy Scripture the otherwise dead letter is reinvested with life. That means at the very least that, like the reading of lowercase scriptures quite generally, the written word is animated by the life of the form of life in which the reader is more or less at home. That form of life might be one in which all communication is carried out in writing, in which case every reader would be a writer. But the writing would be the medium in which the reader would be more or less at home. The sender and recipient of the messages would share a point of view. They would agree on the point of their exchange.

Now the point of their exchange might be that of philologists, to reach a scientific conclusion about the etymology of a certain word and what a word meant for the ancient community that used it. The philologists are interested in a question that is historical in the sense in which Heidegger, Bultmann, Gadamer, etc. use the word "*historisch*" to refer to objectified chronology. But, as these authors maintain, that interest in objectified historical textual scholarship arises out of the scholars' historicity, their *Geschichtlichkeit*, that is to say, it is supported and animated by the contemporary "community of interpretation" to which they belong without their usually reflecting upon it, and which defines more or less the shape of the future they imagine for themselves. In this way their scholarly interest in the past, for example in the meaning of a word on the page of a document written in a so-called dead language, is engaged with their unscholarly, lay, usually unreflectively lived interest in the future. And that future includes the possible uses to which may be put the word they use to translate the Latin word *casus,* namely the English word "fall."

So much by way of a simple illustration of how the present and the past and the future are involved linguistically with each other. It may be objected that a people can be interested in what a word means for them now independently of what it meant for their grandparents or what it will mean for their grandchildren, and that it is woolly-headed to suppose that what it meant for their grandparents is inseparable from what it means for them now or will mean for their grandchildren, and that what it will mean for their grandchildren is inseparable from what it means for them now or meant for their grandparents. This denial of temporal overlap may or may not be correct. But if it is correct it is because in making it time is conceived as a straight line, and history as *Historie.* The denial of temporal overlap is undermined once it is granted that the view of time as a straight line is an abstraction from our concrete lived experience of the geometry of time and therefore the experience of language is that of a circle or, better, a spiral. This may be a spiral upward or a spiral downward, depending on whether the interpretation of a term is imaginative or unimaginative. In either case (assuming a movement up can be a case, a *casus*, a fall, perhaps as when somebody falls upstairs), to interpret is to imagine, in a sense of imagine, however, that is not opposed to true experience. This, up to a certain point, is the sense in which Husserl says that imagination (*Phantasie*) is the essence of phenomenology.[41] To imagine is at least to ask What if? And that question can be asked of the past, of the present, or of the future. But the temporality of the imagination in Husserl's sense partakes of the structure it has in Kant's, though the latter's word for the imagination is usually "*Einbildungskraft,*" not "*Phantasie.*" In both transcendental phenomenology and transcendental idealism imagination requires that time—and therefore space—be a continuum, and that things in that continuum be constructed. On both accounts the temporality of imagination is such as to allow for construction or construal. Now if imagination is to figure in Derrida's reading of Peirce's semiotics it must admit deconstruction into construction and construal. Imagination will "itself" have to be so construed and deconstrued that, no matter how close to the elicitation of a coherent and comprehensive narrative close reading an interpretation would appear to get, that would be the story or history of an effect. The oppositions of felicity and infelicity and of fidelity and infidelity to the facts and to the text under interpretation would be but effects of a happening that goes on under the interpretation or reading, or, unnoticed, through the interpretation or reading. "Writing" is one of Derrida's names (though strictly speaking it cannot be a name, not even the name of a name) for what goes on in this space of the spacing that disrupts the continuum of time, and for this spacing he sometimes borrows from the *Timaeus* the unterminating term *"chōra"* which Plato uses of the illegitimate matrix, the motherly though not therefore necessarily female space in which takes place creation.[42] "Writing" as thus employed in the rewriting and rereading of the imagination is not writing as opposed to speaking, as one might be led to think by the gloss given in a chapter in which W. J. T. Mitchell observes that whereas in *The Interpretation of Dreams* Freud outlines a science of psychoanalysis of the "laws of expression" which elicits a verbal message from a supposedly "natural" but in fact deceptive pictorial surface, in Wittgenstein's *Tractatus Logico-Philosophicus* logical analysis runs in the opposite direction, from the supposedly natural verbal surface of everyday language to underlying logico-pictorial structures. Mitchell proposes that

> Perhaps the redemption of the imagination lies in accepting the fact that we create much of our world out of the dialogue between verbal and pictorial representations, and that our task is not to renounce this dialogue in favor of a direct assault on nature but to see that nature already informs both sides of the conversation.[43]

While this proposal for attaining a "redemption of the imagination" is to be applauded, not least for the prospects it opens on to the work of imagination in the work of art, it has to be noted that it does not cut more deeply than the opposition between pictures and predicates. The reference to "the dialogue between verbal and pictorial representation" is a reference to a symmetrical dialectical relationship. And the reference to this relationship as one between kinds of representation betrays no suspicion that representation may be a product of an unrepresentable. In the deconstructive rereading of the imagination redemption would be bought at the price of an unfounding of both pictoriality and verbal predicativity, of representation and of symmetry. That is, imagination would not be redeemed without a loss of security.

> Derrida reinstates the ancient figure of the world as text (a figure which, in Renaissance poetics, made nature itself a system of hieroglyphics), but with a new twist. Since the author of this text is no longer with us, or has lost his authority, there is no foundation for the sign, no way of stopping the endless chain of signification.[44]

However, even if the author is "with us," and even if we are being spoken to, "writing" in Derrida's rewritten and reread quasi-interpretation of archi- or telescripture prior to the book is prephenomenologically, preontologically, and choratically "there." It is there, however, in a sense that is prior to the sense conveyed by the Latin and French "*est*," and prior to the isness attributed to the work of art by the New Critics. This sense of being there is better conveyed by "*reste*," meaning among other things a remnant, a remainder, and therefore a reminder or trace. But "*reste*" is also the verb cognate with these nouns. In it can be read the *est* of the verb to be, but also the re- of the re-petition and re-source with which everything starts, as Peirce's sign is always already the sign of a sign. The sign is always resigned. Signification is always resignification, a formula that includes but extends beyond the scope of Norman Kemp Smith's apothegm, commenting on Kant, that all cognition is recognition. What interests deconstruction is writing thus reinscribed as repetition and therefore as unoriginal re-source of the simple opposition of writing and speaking made throughout the history of reflection on language and thought from at least as early as that other text of Plato, the *Phaedrus*. If Derrida reinstates the ancient figure of the world as text, he does so by desystematizing that figure, and to do this—or rather to let us learn how system undoes itself—he must not stop, as the just cited gloss does, at the stage of dialectical neutrality. Nor must he stop at the stage of reversing the order of priority given to speech over writing in another ancient figuration. He must move on to the further stage of intervention where the paleonyms, here "writing" and "reading," are not opposed to speech but grafted on to it in order to indicate that the opposition is not fundamental, not inscribed on tablets of stone or stane, the material to the name of which it is sometimes said we owe the ontological lexicon of stance, substance, standing, understanding, sistence, existence, *histemi, histine* and so on, whether or not this etymology results from an alleged confusion in the course of the experience of language, a slip of the tongue, a lapse from wisdom into error.

Deconstruction

Deconstruction calls into question the credentials of classical metaphysical oppositions. But they are called into question by what makes them possible as theatrical, that is to say artful effects, and, allowance being made for the strange identity of deconstruction's itselfness, they in turn are necessary to the work of deconstruction itself. The "other side" of Derrida's extrapolation of Peirce is that no more than the rest of us can Derrida get by without these oppositions, for instance the opposition between protection and opening and between signifier and signified. Indeed, his extrapolation exploits the opposition between signifier and signified, which is not articulated in Peirce's definition of the sign, in order to shake the assumption that the signifier is an epiphenomenon of the signified and to advance the hypothesis that the movement in which what is signified becomes a sign according to Peirce's formula is a movement of tracing indicated better by the signifier than by the signified, though the latter is not immune to its force.

Another indispensable opposition to which it is high time we turned is the one Derrida himself draws between polysemy and dissemination.[45] Much of what has been said in this chapter, especially what has been said here in the context of Peirce's account of signs, will have seemed to be about polysemy, that is to say, about the multiplication of meanings such as is pursued by the infinite midrashic imagination. But even the infinite midrashic imagination is logocentric if the Augustinian response to the commandment "Be fruitful and multiply" (Genesis 1:22, 28) is an open-ended catena of exegeses of an original founding revelation vouchsafed on Sinai.[46] For "there is no foundation for the sign," not only because there is "no way of stopping the endless chain of signification." There is no foundation for the sign because semiology is an effect of the dissemiology that intruded upon our reflections when we linked on to Peirce's account of the sign and of the interpretant the catena of Derridian signifers—deconstruction, *différance,* supplement, trace, remainder, archi-scripture, and so on. At that moment we passed from an emphasis upon questions of interpretation or hermeneutics, whether it be of the spoken word with its phonemes or the written word with its graphemes and units of reading which we might call anagnosemes, *anagnōsis* meaning a reading but also knowing again or recognition, so that the prefix "ana-" is a symptom of the ancient tradition of regarding the written and read word as secondary to the spoken. From that moment on the emphasis was placed on the manner in which into all these memes of semiotics, and the sememe itself, the unit we call a sign, with its inbuilt construing of a signifying sound or mark opposed to a signified meaning, there intervenes the disseme. The disseme would be the disunifying force of dissemination. Dissemination is not simply the history of the development of meaning toward increased richness or poverty by metaphor, analogy, and etymology, whether the etymology be deemed true or false. Dissemination would be the de-signing of the sign, de-signation of designation, outwith which there would be no opposition of the literal and the metaphorical, the true and the false, wisdom and stupidity, the same and the other. And without the possibility of making these oppositions there could be no experience whatsoever. Not if experience is the acquisition of wisdom as the remembering of lessons learned in the past so that they are readily available for future eventualities, wisdom such as we owe to the experience of language, wisdom such as we obtain by close reading thanks to the distance reading, the grace of the teletext traced like a watermark on the pages we read, for example the pages of the chapter you have now finished reading—except for a brief postscript.

Experience

To what has been written above concerning the experience of language must be added an indication of how that experience may be reread following a hint given at the beginning of the second section of this chapter. In this imaginable postreading the experience of language interpreted as language's *Erfahrung*—the experience, learning, wisdom, and cunning acquired by language through its having travelled so far—becomes what is experienced in the sense of what is *erlebt* by the speaker or writer. It becomes the object of an *Erlebnis*. The objecthood of this object may be that of scientific investigation. In this case the travel and travail of language's experience are regarded as having taken place in chronological time, the time of *Historie*. But if within the same temporality the etymological wanderings of language are allowed to strike us with wonder, the artifact of language gets regarded as a huge work of art. Huge to the degree that language is regarded as the web of languages whose crossings are commemorated in those entries that dictionaries put between square brackets. Astonishment at the inventiveness and humor of the leaps and bounds and bindings recollected there is not foreign to the scientific study of language. The work of science quite generally does not exclude the aesthetic responsiveness called for and called forth by the work of art. Without this aesthetic sensibility science does not begin to work. For without it science is without imagination and therefore incapable of becoming experience in that further sense of the word conveyed by the Latin "*experientia*" and still very alive in the French. *Expérience* is experiment. And it is to experience as experiment that the work of art moves when it is no longer passive undergoing but active going over (*Übergehen*), putting over (*Übersetzung*), translation (*Übersetzung*), as the work of art is for its maker and its re-creative recipient. The genius, wisdom, and cunning of language allow the experience of language to be at one and the same time *épreuve* as passive suffering and *épreuve* as active test. This is precisely what Peirce is saying when he writes of the habit of dehabitualization. The artfulness of the experience of language is art as work of imagination that is both made work and work in the making. But telescriptural imagination is also an unmaking and an undoing. It unmakes and undoes simple oppositions, such oppositions as that of script to voice and of science to art. It calls into question the fundamentality of the phenomenological imagination. Whereas the variations in imagination that essentialist phenomenology performs have in view the *telos* of an invariant essence, the telescriptural imagination distances itself from teleology, essence, and distinct division, not because their alleged fundamentality can be derived from something more fundamental, but because it is no more than alleged, an illusion. It is a transcendental illusion. That is to say, it is an illusion that will persist despite the recognition that it is quasi-transcendentally conditioned by anarchic scripture. This is why Philo is writing about interpretation and meaning, not dissemination and force when he writes of Abraham that

> He wishes you to think of God who cannot be shown, as severing through the Severer of all things, that is his Word, the whole succession of things material and immaterial whose natures appear to us to be knitted together and united. That severing Word whetted to an edge of utmost sharpness never ceases to divide. . . . So it divided . . . the soul into rational and non-rational, speech into true and false, sense into presentations where the object is real and apprehended, and presentations where it is not.[47]

Imagination is the locus in which no division is made between presentations where the object is real and apprehended, and presentations where it is not. In that place sharp, clear, and distinct divisions between opposites are made, either by the phenomenologist who asseverates, albeit outwith the field of natural and metaphysical factuality, or by the Severer, the visible and audible Logos whom the invisible God appoints to set the forms of created things "opposite each other." But "The birds He left undivided, for incorporeal and divine forms of knowledge cannot be divided into conflicting opposites." The birds here referred to are the pigeon and the turtledove of Genesis 15:9: the pigeon that feeds on the earth and represents human reason, but also and especially the dove that differs from the pigeon as the genus differs from the species and as the archetype differs from the copy. The dove soars and loves secrecy. It symbolizes distance. But its distance, as too the distance of the *telos* Hegel calls absolute knowledge, is haunted by the distance spelled out in telescripture. Telescripture is what takes one's breath away, dispirits the spirit of God's spell. When in the experience of a sudden fright one's breath is, as we say paradoxically, taken away, there occurs a sharp intake of breath. This, for instance the first breath drawn by the child surprised by its birth, is a necessary condition for breathing out, a necessary condition for our doubly genitive experience of language's experience right up until, unsurprised by death, we are uttered by the purely consonantal and consequently, like YHWH, unvocalizable subscript "*gl*," a glottal stop that, not yet itself a word, is yet a fragment of the word "*glas*," meaning death-knell and voice or vowel, the vowel "*a*" that as aleph enables the pronunciation of the consonants of the Hebrew alphabet and the choice between utterance and consignment to silence. The distance of the telescript is the distance that defers death by being inscription waiting for the next breath. It is what leaves us open-mouthed when we read a holy scripture and when we ascribe to the so-called secular text the secret sacredness of a verbal icon. It is what, when we are faced by any work of art, leaves us with a sense of its essential incompleteness, a sense of unending, so that the literary work of art is not in its isness and thisness all there on the page.

FOUR

Phenomenology as Rigorous Science

Constitutional objectivity and intentionality

As a student of mathematics at Berlin, Husserl became acquainted with Karl Weierstrass and his project for founding mathematical analysis on the concept of number. Not without finding Weierstrass guilty of a certain naïve empiricism, Husserl himself aimed to further this program in the dissertation *On the Concept of Number* (1887) which he went on to compose at Halle under the direction of Carl Stumpf, a former student of Brentano, and which became integrated into his *Philosophy of Arithmetic* (1891).[1] In these works Husserl demonstrates that numbers belong to a continuum that presupposes a mental act of collecting. It is not surprising that Frege criticized the *Philosophy of Arithmetic* for its psychologism. Without fully accepting Frege's criticism, Husserl henceforth stressed the objectivity of the fundamental concepts of mathematics and logic. The mental act of collecting, for example, was not a subjective operation; it was conducted according to "rigorous laws," as will be what Husserl will call his "philosophy as rigorous science." This philosophical science will steer a course between the naïve empiricism he finds in Weierstrass, the naïve Platonism he finds in Bernard Bolzano's *Theory of*

Science, and the naïve psychologism he finds in *Psychology from an Empirical Standpoint* and other works of Franz Brentano whose classes he had attended at the University of Vienna.

It is nevertheless by the writings of these three heroes that Husserl will be spurred toward the discovery of two of the main ingredients of his rigorous philosophical science: constituted objectivity and intentionality. Crucial to the latter is Brentano's thesis that what distinguishes mental phenomena from physical ones is the former's intentionality. All mental phenomena refer to what Scholastic philosophers call "inexistent" objects, objects of consciousness whose reality is "objective" in the sense still maintained by Descartes in opposition to what he and the Scholastics call "formal objectivity," that is to say, independent reality such as is possessed by things in the natural world, by psychological phenomena or by the ideal entities of mathematics and logic. "In presentation something is presented, in judgement something is affirmed or denied, in love loved, in hate hated, in desire desired, and so on."[2] This directedness of mental states will become a principle of the science of phenomenology that is yet to be born. Although the word *Phänomenologie* is used already in the eighteenth century by J. H. Lambert and Kant, and in English in William Hamilton's *Lectures on Metaphysics* dating from the late 1830s (though not published until 1858), it begins to get the sense it will have for Husserl only when it is used of the "descriptive psychology" discussed in lectures delivered by Brentano in 1888–1889.

In Husserl's conception of phenomenology constituted objectivity and intentionality are inseparable. For by constitution of an object Husserl means not its creation, but its self-manifestation.[3] In this sense even an object in space may be constituted. However, before focusing on such objects in lectures of 1907 published under the title *Thing and Space,* Husserl conducts an intensive and detailed campaign against psychologism in the *Prolegomena to Pure Logic* which forms the first part of the *Logical Investigations* (1901). The first of these titles and the term "pure" that occurs in many of the titles and subtitles of the six Investigations inevitably raise the question of the relationship between the philosophical method followed by Husserl here and that followed by Kant in the *Critique of Pure Reason.* While expressing the highest admiration for the work of Kant and declaring in his lectures on *First Philosophy* (1923–1924) that it is from him that he borrows the word "transcendental," Husserl maintains that transcendental arguments regressing from facts to the conditions of their possibility need to be founded on pure intuition of evidence, *Wesenschau.* Several of the transcendental arguments developed by Kant take as their starting point certain facts about time. But Kant does not pause to consider whether his or Newton's or Leibniz's notions of time are abstractions from a quite different experience of temporality, the "inner" or (better, see below) "intimate" temporality examined in Husserl's *Lectures on the Phenomenology of Internal Time Consciousness* of 1904–1905, edited (with additions made between 1905 and 1910) by his assistant Martin Heidegger in 1928.

These lectures on time take forward the reflections on the continuum begun in Husserl's earlier studies of number. They bring out another difference between Husserl and Kant. Kant links temporality with schematism and links schematism with imagination (as too will Heidegger in his *Kant and the Problem of Metaphysics*). Recollection, for instance, is for Kant dependent on imagination. Husserl insists that a distinction be made between, on the one hand, recollection (a variety of the collection that plays a part in Husserl's theory of number) and, on the other hand, retention of the immediate past, which is not a function of imagination but is a moment of a present perception in the way that a comet is accompanied by its tail. This distinction between primary and secondary remembrance corresponds to the distinction between protention and expectation, where, like retention, protention is a halo of a present sensation and where expectation or anticipation is the reversed memory, *Erinnerung* (literally, interiorizing), that Husserl calls "*Vorerinnerung.*" And analogues of these temporal imbrications hold for our experience of objects presented in space. We "see" the back of the wardrobe which is against the wall and the strip of the carpet that is hidden under the wardrobe. These shadowed aspects (*Abschattungen*) are among the many phenomena hitherto neglected by philosophers. They are among the phenomena that reveal themselves when we respond to Husserl's clarion call to go "back to the things themselves!"—"zu den Sachen selbst!" Hence "associationist" philosophers and psychologists are mistaken if they take the stream of consciousness to be a chain of discrete items in which one item suggests the next. Consciousness, which, we have seen, is according to Husserl always consciousness *of* something, that is to say, intentional, is also such that "everything new reacts on the old; its forward-moving intention is fulfilled and determined thereby, and this gives the reproduction a definite coloring. An *a priori*, necessary retroaction is thus revealed here."[4] On the other hand, the horizon of recollection is directed toward the future of what is recollected. We recollect what was protended albeit in a not yet then fulfilled intention.[5] A corollary of this is that intentionality is twofold. There is a so-to-speak lateral intentionality between the so-to-speak vertical intentionalities between constituting and what is constituted.

We thus come back to the question of constitution defined earlier as the self-manifestation of the object. The object is given, but its givenness is constituted. What does the constituting? Absolute subjectivity. Why absolute? Because the subjectivity is a temporal flux, hence an alteration, but an alteration that is not the alteration of an object, for instance a thinking thing such as is identified with the ego by Descartes.

> We can only say that this flux is something which we name after what is constituted, but it is nothing temporally "Objective." It is absolute subjectivity and has the absolute properties of something to be denoted metaphysically as "flux," as a point of actuality, primal source-point, that from which springs the "now," and so on. In the lived experience of actuality, we have the primal source-point and a continuity of moments of reverberation. For all this names are lacking.[6]

There is no object there to be named, any more than the temporality that according to Heidegger is the truth of Dasein's being-there is an entity. For Husserl the phrase "consciousness of time" expresses a double genitive. This is why the German "*innere*" of the title of his lectures on time is better translated not by "inner" or "internal," which suggest that time is contained in consciousness, but by "intimate."[7] Neither absolutely and cosmically objective, as time is for Newton, nor a mental content, time as described phenomenologically is the origin of space.

Reduction

By phenomenological description is meant here not the narrative of the psychological events that take place in the biography of a particular person. The absolute subjectivity of the temporal flux has its own objectivity. Somewhat as Nietzsche records the turning point in his intellectual career that took place at Sils Maria in the Upper Engadine, Husserl records that in 1905, the second year of the lectures on time, while on holiday at Seefeld in the Tyrol, he was first struck by the idea of the transcendental phenomenological reduction—re-duction, leading back—that would put on firmer ground the intentional analyses undertaken in the Logical Investigations. But this insight is not developed until two years later in lectures on the Thing. It can fairly be said that the insight owes much to Descartes's systematic suspension of belief in anything for the existence of which the evidence is not clear and distinct. The difference is that in the Husserlian reduction all questions of existential belief are put and remain under suspension (*epochē*) and all matters of empirical or metaphysical fact or causal explanation set aside. We bracket off what interests us when we are engaged in the world in what Husserl refers to as the general thesis of natural positing, which is a general thesis about thesis, about positing. Although the term *"natürliche Einstellung"* is commonly translated into English as "natural attitude" or "natural standpoint," what Husserl means by it is not an attitude or standpoint or position understood as one of a multiplicity of ways of viewing the world that might be formulated in a scientific or metaphysical theory. It is a thesis or positing that is natural to us all, general. So the natural here must not be understood as naturalistic. In §29 of *Ideas: General Introduction to Pure Phenomenology* (1913) he writes that despite the variety of ways in which we apprehend our surroundings, "we come to understandings with our neighbours, and set up in common an objective spatio-temporal actuality as the world that exists about us all and to which we ourselves belong despite individual differences." This common setting is taken for granted, so that in reflecting on it as we are doing here we have already begun to exit from it. We have already begun to adopt with regard to it the transcendental phenomenological standpoint that neutralizes any claim to existence or nonexistence. In *Ideas I* (§49) Husserl goes as far as to say that even if the entire empirical world were destroyed the field of phenomenological consciousness would remain. In other words, rather as he had said that the temporal flow of absolute subjectivity is not predicated of any object, the subject that constitutes phenomenological objectivity is not a particular human subject or psyche, but an ego in general. Hence one might well ask whether in *Ideas I* Husserl adopts a metaphysical position, namely that of transcendental idealism. This would appear to be inconsistent with the neutralizing of questions of existence that the phenomenological reduction is supposed to require.

Among the developments that Husserl's reduction will undergo are its restrictions to the eidetic and to the egological. The reduction is to concern itself with the *eidos,* the essence, the as such. This is the invariant to be found by imagining various fictive possibilities. In case this reference to imagined fictions leads us to think of the way Husserl's Viennese neighbor Wittgenstein has recourse in his later philosophizing to inventing cases, it should be noted in passing that Wittgenstein's reason for doing this is to show that the cases falling under a concept may have nothing in common other than their falling under the same concept. Husserl could be one of the philosophers Wittgenstein has in mind when he resorts to fictional cases. Husserl's fictions are directed at revealing what is common, essences. The essences to be discovered in this way include the general form or essence of the ego. This means that there can be a phenomenology that concentrates on the constituting *cogito* or the *noēsis,* and a phenomenology that concentrates on the constituted, the *cogitatum* or the *noēma.* However, the thesis of the intentionality of all consciousness means that the topic of phenomenology is the complex *noēsis–noēma,* the *noēma* being the intentional object of the *noēsis,* neither external to it in the manner of a Kantian thing-in-itself nor internal to it in the manner of a Cartesian idea in its "formal reality," that is, as a psychological entity or event. It is only in this sense that one can legitimately interpret the words Husserl cites with approval from Augustine: "Noli foras ire, in te redi, in interiore homine habitat veritas," "Do not go out; enter into yourself, in human interiority dwells truth."[8]

One way to avoid misinterpreting Husserl's reading of this citation is to say that his phenomenology is a science of meaning. But we avoid misinterpretation only if we agree with Husserl (and Wittgenstein) that meaning is not a mental picture or any other psychological entity or event that may happen to be or to take place as it were in the theater of an actor's or spectator's mind. Husserl and Wittgenstein are in agreement too that meanings are not physical or other thought-independent objects. In the *Logical Investigations* Husserl uses the word "*Sinn*" almost synonymously with "*Bedeutung,*" the former standing for meaning quite generally, for instance in the field of perception, the latter for the meaning of an expression. He does not follow Frege in, as usually interpreted, reserving "*Sinn*" for "meaning" and reserving "*Bedeutung*" for "reference." He is nevertheless as insistent as Frege and Wittgenstein are that meaning and referent must not be confused.[9] This holds for meaning in any area of intentionality, whether that of perception, of imagination, or of linguistic signification, this last being the topic treated most closely in the first Investigation. Before saying something about this significative and expressive meaning, something must be said about a question we have passed over in silence, one about which Husserl's readers may well think that Husserl himself should have been more explicit.

Transcendental phenomenological idealism is more fundamental than transcendental Critical idealism, but it can be shown to be consistent with a transcendental phenomenological realism by a move analogous to that which allows Kant to argue for the compatibility of transcendental Critical idealism with empirical realism. Kant argues that we can have knowledge of real things in space despite or because of the fact that space is originally a transcendental form of aesthetic intuition. Analogously, as was remarked above, Husserl can say that the independence of external things in space is itself constituted. As for the idea of allegedly unconstituted entities, Husserl says with Berkeley, though for different reasons, that that idea is absurd. It is in light of this category of constituted empirical externality that Husserl can answer the following question. After I have, following Augustine's injunction, entered into myself, must I then go back out? That is to say, after performing the reduction, must I return to the natural standpoint? This is not what at least the Husserl of *Ideas I* would lead us to believe. But this is because a philosopher carrying out the phenomenological reduction remains an ordinary human being, so that although with regard to his subject matter he disconnects himself from the natural standpoint, he does this without ceasing to be an ordinary human being who won't survive long and indeed won't be able to write down his philosophical findings unless he remains in the natural standpoint with regard to, for example, the existence of the pencil he holds in his hand. But because the phenomenological reduction is universal and because the thesis of the natural standpoint is general, the very pencil Husserl is using to describe the phenomenological landscape is part of that landscape—like the back of the wardrobe. No vicious infinite regress or circle is implied in the infinitude of the agenda that phenomenology seems about to threaten or promise.

Meaningfulness and purity

A further question regarding externality is provoked by what Husserl says about what in the first Investigation he calls expressive meaning. It is a question posed in the studies of Husserl conducted in some of the earliest publications of Jacques Derrida.[10] Derrida elicits difficulties relating to Husserl's ideal of purity and meaningfulness. Can meaning be full? Can it be pure? Derrida's negative answers to these questions are not meant or intended to undermine the notion of meaning or intention. They challenge Husserl's conception of the *telos* of meaning as an ideal plenitude free from spatial separation. Allowing for Husserl's equation of the eternal with the omnitemporal, Derrida's challenge is akin to the one he directs at the Platonic doctrine that the mind may be immediately present to a Form or Idea. As applied to the sphere of language, both the Husserlian and the Platonic teachings are phonological. Language for them is spoken language, even though the speaking may be that of the soul's dialogue with itself. According to this model it might seem that the speaker is in auto-affective immediate contact with what he means, uninterrupted by any interval such as may separate the writer from the meaning of what he writes. Derrida maintains against this privileging of spoken language (see Plato's *Phaedrus*, 275f.) that the latter is no less characterized by spacing than is writing. It depends on there being spaces between words, on the auditory equivalent of punctuation marks, and what is said is distanced from the speaker and hearer the moment it is pronounced. So like a written text the spoken word is exposed to the contingencies that changes of context may or do bring. Derrida therefore coins the term "archi-writing" for the generally graphic character that is common to speech and writing as these terms are ordinarily opposed to each other. Without archi-writing, he holds, this ordinary distinction could not be made. Husserl maintains in the first Investigation that what he there calls expressive meaning, signified concepts or ideas, belong to a realm of temporality in principle pure of spatial distancing, and only contingently reliant upon the acoustic or graphic aspect of signs. Derrida maintains that the latter are necessary conditions of linguistic meaning. It is as though Derrida were saying to Augustine that if the truth dwells within human interiority, so does a certain exteriority. If Derrida's argument is valid it will be a stumbling block for a project of a pure phenomenology like Husserl's.

Not in me, but among us

Derrida translated into French and wrote an introduction to the essay "On the Origin of Geometry" that was published as an appendix to *The Crisis of European Sciences and Transcendental Phenomenology* of 1936. The subtitle of this work is *An Introduction to Phenomenological Philosophy.* Husserl spent his life writing what he considered to be introductions, programs, and new beginnings for phenomenology. He used up more space writing and rewriting programs for phenomenology than actually carrying out phenomenological descriptions. On his deathbed he bewailed that he had at last achieved a glimpse of the promised land of pure phenomenology but was to be denied the opportunity to set his foot upon it. One may fancy that, as Corot expressed the hope that in heaven there would be paintbrushes, *pinceaux,* Husserl may have harbored the hope that in heaven there would be pencils, at least in their eidetically reduced formality. In the *Crisis* a new beginning is made toward the new phase of phenomenology announced in *Formal and Transcendental Logic* of 1929 and in lectures delivered in Amsterdam and Paris that culminated in 1931 in the *Cartesian Meditations,* which are subtitled once again *An Introduction to Phenomenology.* The first of these books takes up once more some of the problems treated in the *Logical Investigations,* including those bearing on the theory of signs treated in the first and fourth Investigation, though these pick up again a preoccupation of his earliest work in that an essay of 1890 is titled "On the Logic of Signs (Semiotic)" and in a letter to Stumpf of perhaps the same year he writes that formal logic is a technique or art of signs (*Kunst der Zeichen*).

In *Formal and Transcendental Logic* there is a section on "the illusion of transcendental solipsism" in which the author observes: "The world is continually there for us; but in the first place it is there for *me*. This fact too is there for me; otherwise there could be no sense for me in which the world is there for *us*, there as one and the same, and as a world having a particular sense—not a sense to be 'postulated' as such and such . . . , but a sense to be explicated . . . out of experience itself."[11] The "onward march" of this "concrete explication" proceeds in the fifth Meditation of the roughly contemporary *Cartesian Meditations*. There, intersubjectivity is shown to be an articulation of the monadologically reduced ego. Although Husserl is willing to use the term empathy (*Einfühlung*) to describe intersubjectivity, he denies that intersubjectivity is manifested through empathy understood as a method that projects me imaginatively into the mind of another person. He also denies that this manifestation is based on an analogical argument from the perception of my own physical body (*Körper*) and comparison with that of another, which would assume I can already distinguish human beings from nonhuman ones. It is based rather on the experience of the other's lived body (*Leib*). Somewhat as the sensory perception of the note of a melody includes a retention of its immediate predecessors (its *Abschattungen*), so the experience of another human being as such comes coupled with appresentations (*Paarungen*). The vital difference is that whereas the note co-presented in the note I am hearing now was once presented, "the *co-existence* (*Mit-dasein*) of a concrete subjectivity, . . . [is] co-present with a bodiliness that is experienced originally and harmoniously in my own sphere of consciousness; and [yet], on the other hand, not present for me *originaliter* the way my own subjectivity is [present] in its original relation to my corporeality."[12] So long as we do not confuse pure phenomenological immanence with private psychological immanence—which is, as Husserl says, *reel* as opposed to the reality of *real* objects in space—we can grasp that our experience of the objectivity of things in space is inseparable from the experience of intersubjectivity. The objectivity of our world *is* its intersubjectivity, its being *our* world.

Note here in passing that Husserl's description of mundane cohabitation and "flesh" is furthered with great subtlety in Maurice Merleau-Ponty's *Phenomenology of Perception*. See in particular the section titled "Other People and the Human World." See also his *The Visible and the Invisible*.[13] Merleau-Ponty has written with insight too on the manuscripts in which Husserl treats the closely related topic of the earth regarded not as the subject matter of natural science but as the phenomenologically more Ptolemaic than Copernican zero point that remains our absolute unmoving base even when we move on it or visit other planets or imagine ourselves in worlds different from our own.

[I]f we vary our factual world in free fantasy, carrying it over into random conceivable worlds, we are implicitly varying ourselves whose environment the world is; in each case we change ourselves into a possible subjectivity, whose environment would always have to be the world that was thought of, as a world of its [the subjectivity's] possible experiences, possible theoretical evidences, possible practical life. But obviously this variation leaves untouched the pure ideal worlds of the kind which have their existence in eidetic universality, which in their essence are invariable.[14]

What Husserl refers to as the Copernican Revolution brought about by transcendental phenomenology is a phenomenologizing of Ptolemaic cosmology and of the epistemological version of the Copernican Revolution brought about by Kant and sustained by the neo-Kantians. The latter, for instance Hans Natorp, were as uncomfortable as Husserl with the Kantian thing-in-itself, but in their haste to do away with this they swung too far in the direction of an extreme "positivistic" idealism through failure to distinguish transcendental phenomenological constitution from creative productivity.

No less worthy of mention at this stage is the response of Emmanuel Levinas, another distinguished student of Husserl, to the fifth Cartesian Meditation. Indeed, Levinas is the author of the French translation of that Meditation. Husserl's account of human relationship is cast in terms of consciousness. Further, although he insists that the consciousness another person has of his or her own body is only "appresented," not directly presented, he stresses the respect in which the relationship is one of fusion. Levinas attempts to persuade readers of *Totality and Infinity* and *Otherwise than Being or Beyond Essence* that a certain fission and apartness is prior to fusion and being-with, that this relationship of all relationships is not symmetrical, but a dissymmetry in which my intentional consciousness of the other person is conditioned by an absolute and unique responsibility to the singular other without which moralities such as those founded on the moral law as in Kant or on mutual sympathy as in Adam Smith would be the worst possible violence. This recourse to a "reversed intentionality" is a recourse to what is "beyond essence," beyond the eidetic, and beyond consciousness. It is therefore a radical revision of pure "Cartesian" phenomenology as conceived by Husserl. Nevertheless, it owes much to the phenomenological descriptions carried out by Husserl, for instance to his descriptions of "passive synthesis."

Husserl's *Analyses Concerning Passive Synthesis* are comprised of lectures and papers composed between 1918 and 1926. In them Husserl says it is as though affective rays radiated from the object. He speaks of a self-givenness where the self in question is that not only of the noetic subject but also that of the intended noematic object. "Sensible data (and thus data in general) send, as it were, affective rays of force towards the ego pole. . . ."[15] He speaks of the affective allure or attraction (*Reizwirkung*) that an object exercises on a subject. If note be taken of the phrase "as it were" and if the phrase "data in general" be understood to include other human beings, an opening is offered for Levinas to interpret the word "affectivity," which he too uses, in a broadly and deeply ethical sense. We should also have to bear in mind that a *Reiz* can be not only the agreeably charming, but a discomforting itch, and that affectivity must not be taken to exclude rationality as this might be expressed by other human beings in words or in their eyes.

Lifeworld, history, and teleology

Amplifying the reflections on the themes of society and culture pursued at the end of the fifth Meditation, Husserl writes in *The Crisis of European Science and Transcendental Phenomenology* about history and what, borrowing the term from Richard Avenarius's *Critique of Pure Experience,* he calls the "*Lebenswelt.*" What does Husserl mean by this last term, usually translated as "lifeworld"? It may help to get clear about this if we ask how it relates to his special concept of "earth" referred to a few paragraphs ago, and to the earlier-mentioned notion of the world as inhabited in the *natürliche Einstellung.* This last notion of an environment unreflectively taken for granted by all has in common with Husserl's notion of earth the idea that it does not move and that it is an absolute zero-point of orientation in relation to mutually competitive particular worldviews. Against the background of this naturally assumed and unreflected-upon universal horizon modern science typified above all by the science of Galileo has imposed the artificial and technical structures of mathematics and mathematical physics. Intermediate between these mathematico-scientific theories and the unquestioned assumption of a common world is the history of concretely lived and changing experiences out of which the mathematico-scientific theories have emerged. In the course of that history the structures of modern mathematical science have become more and more remotely separated from the original experiences to which they owe their validity and applicability. So there is a crisis concerning foundations, for instance concerning the foundations of geometry treated in an appendix to the *Crisis* under the heading "The Origin of Geometry." The sciences are threatened by relativism and their objective validity by logical paradoxes. This is the crisis of European sciences which transcendental phenomenology can resolve, Husserl believes, by turning its attention to describing and making explicit the experience of the so-called life-world, the

Lebenswelt that has hitherto been lived through only implicitly within a universal unthematic horizon. To say that this horizon is universal is to say that it is the omnitemporally given. It is therefore (to borrow an adjective from the title of one of Merleau-Ponty's books) the invisible prepredicative context of any prescientific or scientific way of living in the world (*Weltleben*).[16] Husserl's turn to history is a concomitant of his turn from static to dynamic or genetic phenomenology. The latter is a phenomenological parallel to developmental psychology. It ranges over the time between childhood and maturity. And it is an aspect of passive genesis understood now not only in terms of a relation between the ego and the object over against it, but in terms of the growth of a subject from a condition in which it begins to learn to perceive physical things, to the condition in which its perception of its environment is thickened through the acquisition of an understanding of and engagement in social, cultural, and historical institutions more complex than those already engaged in its beginning toward finding its way about among tangible, audible, and visible things. Meditating on these genealogical phenomena, the phenomenologist discovers "intentional references leading back to a 'history' and accordingly making these phenomena knowable as formations subsequent to other, essentially antecedent formations . . . eidetic laws governing a passive forming of perpetually new syntheses (a forming that, in part, lies prior to all activity and, in part, takes in all activity itself)."[17] History and the human sciences were already topics in *Ideas II,* a manuscript of which was available in 1912. If in the treatment of these topics in the *Crisis* Husserl is consciously or subconsciously responding to Heidegger's treatment of them in *Being and Time,* he is also returning to a topic he had taken up well before the late 1920s. Both he and Heidegger are responding to Wilhelm Dilthey, of whom Husserl writes that he is "a man gifted with the intuition of genius," who first recognized the distinction between the natural and human sciences, but who failed to see that what an understanding of the world of spirit requires is not only a new psychology that would be descriptive rather than hypothetico-deductive, but a transcendental phenomenology.[18]

The turn to history is a turn to teleology. It is comparable to Kant's turn to that subject in "What is Enlightenment?" and "What is Orientation in Thinking?" It is the ambitious claim that philosophy as transcendental phenomenology is the only way to meet "the 'crisis of European existence' talked about so much today," today being the time at which Husserl referred to this crisis in the course of the so-called Vienna Lecture delivered in the year of the completion of his *Crisis of European Sciences* and published as an appendix of that book. Put bluntly, the crisis arises from a failure to see beyond the naturalistic to the natural. The way out of this crisis passes beyond the scientific attitude according to which both the physical and the psychological realms are viewed as realms of objects over against us. We have seen that the "objectivity" of transcendental phenomenology is not that of allegedly mind-independent physical objects or events, *res extensa,* opposed to a *res cogitans,* or of the latter dualistically opposed to the former. It is the omnitemporal objectivity of intentional, that is to say noetic–noematic, constitution. This constitution was overlooked both in Kant's and in Dilthey's reflections on history and teleology. On the one hand, in *Experience and Judgment* Husserl writes that a more profound transcendentalism will be a phenomenologically descriptive genealogy that goes back to the prepredicative *doxa* on which exact science, *epistēmē,* is founded.[19] On the other hand, already in *Formal and Transcendental Logic* he writes that "Thanks to evidence, the life of consciousness has an all-pervasive teleological structure, a pointedness toward 'reason' and even a pervasive tendency toward it—that is: toward the discovery of correctness (and, at the same time, toward the lasting acquisition of correctness) and toward the cancelling of incorrectness (thereby ending their acceptance as acquired possessions)."[20]

Positivism and *philosophia perennis*

The mention of evidence at the beginning of the sentence just cited should be put in the context of the positivism that had been dominant in the nineteenth century, for instance the positivism of Auguste Comte, and the logical positivism that was all the rage in Vienna and elsewhere at the time when that sentence was being written. The evidence to which Husserl is referring cannot be the empirical evidence on which according to logical positivism literal synthetic *a posteriori* statements of fact rely for their meaningfulness. What Husserl considers to be "the principle of all principles" for phenomenology is not the equivalent of the positivist principle of verifiability. Put baldly, the latter principle affirms that the meaning of a proposition is the method of its empirical verification or falsification. Husserl's principle affirms more broadly that "Immediate 'seeing' ('*Sehen*'), not merely the sensory seeing of experience, but seeing in general as primordial dator consciousness of any kind whatsoever, is the ultimate source of justification of all rational statements."[21] The evidence to which Husserl refers in the sentence cited at the end of the last paragraph cannot be simply empirical evidence. But nor can it be simply the self-evidence of analytic *a priori* statements. The evidence of which Husserl writes is that of synthetic *a priori* statements, "material" *a priori* statements as they are called in an article by the Viennese logical positivist Moritz

Schlick in which their possibility is called into question.[22] However, Husserl is thinking not only of statements. He is speaking primarily of perceptions on which statements may be based. Yet based not infallibly. Rather, as the logical empiricist underlines the fallibility of statements reporting observations, the Husserlian phenomenologist allows that "in a certain category of intuitions (those of sensory experience would fit the suggestion), seeing in its very essence is 'imperfect'; it can as a matter of principle be strengthened or weakened."[23] This metastatement about verifiability and falsifiability is itself an example of a phenomenological insight. To describe closely how confirmation differs from disconfirmation is one of the tasks of phenomenology.

Since Husserl is speaking of the primacy that perception has over conception, his method of doing philosophy is not conceptual analysis. Admittedly, there is an analogy between, on the one hand, the way in which in his later work Wittgenstein resolves philosophical problems by reminding us how we learned to use the expressions in terms of which the problem is posed and, on the other hand, Husserl's method of going back, in his later work, to the concrete lifeworld (remember Wittgenstein's remark that to imagine a language is to imagine a form of life) or, in his earlier work, to the intuition of formal objectivities. Here, intuition is not the passive reception of empirical sense-data. Nor is it the passive reception of Platonic or Cartesian rational ideas. It is the intuition of meanings, where meanings are the undivorcable noematic partners of noetic acts. This is another way of saying, as was said above, that the intentional objectivities investigated and described by transcendental phenomenology are constituted. The objectivities are data that are not taken unreflectively to be self-evident. Through transcendental phenomenological reduction they are enabled to manifest themselves as they are without prejudice or metaphysical presupposition. The activity/passivity involved in intuition thus understood is something like what is expressed in the grammatical middle voice of Greek and Sanskrit. It heralds what Heidegger will call letting-be, *seinlassen*. In this letting-be being, *Sein* as such, is let be by *Da-sein* and thereby by being as voiced by *Da-sein*, voiced medially.

Mention has just been made of prejudice. This offers a cue to note in passing that another challenge to Husserl is made by Hans-Georg Gadamer when in his *Truth and Method* he questions whether philosophy can be without presuppositions, prejudices understood neutrally as pre-judgments. But, as indicated a moment ago, when Husserl speaks of the science of transcendental phenomenology not making any presuppositions, he does not mean that it must avoid speaking of conditions of possibility. He means that such conditions must not include presup-positions as pro-positions affirming (or denying) existence, whether empirical or mathematical or metaphysical or other. Any empirical actuality is only an incidental example (*Beispiel*) from which by variation in imagination not yet phenomenological sciences like eidetic psychology and, on the other hand, transcendental phenomenology seek the invariant core of the variants.

We have hit here upon a distinction that Husserl insists we do not overlook. Locke and Hume are, with Descartes, inspirers of psychological phenomenology and transcendental phenomenology. Hume's "brilliant *Treatise*," he says in his *Encyclopaedia Britannica* article on Phenomenology, "is nothing less than the first attempt at a phenomenological transcendental philosophy."[24] It is this because of its "fictionalism," that is to say, its rejection of metaphysical causes and persisting things in themselves. However, it and Locke's "noteworthy and fundamental work" are not fundamental enough. This is because they remain psychologically positivistic. They fail to reach as far as the pure eidetic psychology and the still more fundamental stage of pure transcendental phenomenology.

Husserl's thoughts on this and some of the other matters touched on in our last few paragraphs are summed up in *Ideas I* as follows:

> If by "*Positivism*" we are to mean the absolute unbiased grounding of all science on what is "positive," i.e., on what can be primarily apprehended, then it is *we* who are the genuine positivists. In fact we permit *no* authority to deprive us of the right of recognizing all kinds of intuition as equally valuable sources for the justification of knowledge, not even that of "modern natural science." When it is really natural science that speaks, we listen willingly and as disciples. But the language of the natural scientists is not always that of natural science itself, and is assuredly *not* so when they speak of "natural philosophy" and the "theory of knowledge of natural science." And it is above all not so when they would have us believe that general truisms such as all axioms express (propositions such as $a + 1 = 1 + a$, that a judgement cannot be coloured, that of every two sounds that differ in quality one is lower and the other higher, that a perception *in itself* is a perception of something, and the like) are expressive of facts of experience, whereas we know in the *fullness of insight* that propositions of this type bring to developed expression data of eidetic intuition. But just on this account it is clear to us that "positivists" confuse at one time the cardinal distinctions between types of intuition, and at another, though they see them as opposed types, are yet *not willing*, being bound by their prejudices, to recognize more than one of these as valid, or indeed even as present at all.[25]

Transcendental phenomenology is then the true empiricism because it alone goes back "to the things themselves." But it is at the same time the true rationalism: "it overcomes narrow, dogmatic rationalism by means of the most universal rationalism, that of eidetic research related in a unified way to transcendental subjectivity, ego-consciousness and conscious objectivity."[26] Just as the antithesis between dogmatic empiricism and dogmatic rationalism is superseded, so too are other traditional antitheses: those of subjectivism and objectivism, idealism and realism, ontologism and transcendentalism, psychologism and anti-psychologism, positivism and metaphysics, between an efficient causal interpretation of the world and a teleological one describing motivations. Thus is metaphysical subjectivism overcome by transcendental subjectivism, and pluralistic relativism of idiosyncratic worldviews is overcome by transcendental relativism, "the most radical relativity, the relatedness of transcendental subjectivity to itself."[27] Husserl goes as far as to say that it is because transcendental subjectivity is the absolute origin of intentional constitution that the world must be conceived teleologically. But if intentional constitution and the intentional phenomenology that describes it have this origin, it is not teleological in the sense that the path of phenomenology has an end conceived as a destination at which it may arrive. "In the manner of true science this path is endless. Accordingly, phenomenology demands that the phenomenologist forswear the idea of a philosophic system and yet as a humble worker in community with others, live for a *philosophia perennis.*"

Some of those philosophers Husserl expected to be co-workers proved to be less humble than he would have wished. For instance his assistant Martin Heidegger, whose *Being and Time* first appeared in the *Jahrbuch für Philosophie und phänomenologische Forschung* of which Husserl himself had been one of the founders. That neither Husserl nor his assistant was humble enough to work in community with the other can be judged from the latter's comments on the former's draft for the *Encyclopaedia Britannica* article and by Husserl's comments on *Being and Time* and *Kant and the Problem of Metaphysics.* In the earlier of these books, alluding to the Platonic declaration that philosophy begins in wonder, Heidegger proclaims that the wonder of all wonders is that there is something rather than nothing. Although Husserl's phenomenology is the science of how the phenomena described are, their *Seinssinn,* the latter is according to him inseparable from consciousness. He cannot understand why his former friend and pupil makes being, *Sein,* more fundamental than consciousness, *Bewusst-sein,* and why subjectivity should have to be understood as *Da-sein,* being-there. It is plainly his pupil's view of the wonder of all wonders which he is challenging when he writes that most wondrous of all is the way the subject can be regarded doubly as the subject matter of psychology and as the transcendental phenomenological ego.

The transcendental ego is the topic of Sartre's *The Transcendence of the Ego* (1936), in which the author shows himself to be no less willing than Heidegger to work against rather than with the father of phenomenology. For Sartre's title can be read in two ways. It refers to the transcendental ego as treated by Husserl, and it announces that that ego as treated by Husserl is transcended. Sartre argues that what Husserl calls the transcendental ego is transcended by being shown to be not transcendental, but transcendent. When reflected on, as in the practice of phenomenological reduction, it is over against us. And the unity of our experience is afforded by the synchronic and diachronic passive intentionalities among the things of the outside world, which now include the me. Likewise, when not reflected on, the unity of consciousness is that of, for example, the items collected together when I count them, or of the streetcar-having-to-be-overtaken. In neither case is there need for a transcendental I. Husserl himself, Sartre implies, was ready to accept this at the time of the *Logical Investigations*. But in the arguably "idealist" *Ideas* and the *Cartesian Meditations* he could not face the fact that the only I phenomenology demands is the "impure" and impersonal psychological and psycho-physical *me*. "Like Husserl, we are persuaded that our psychic and psycho-physical me is a transcendent object which must fall before the *epochē*. But we raise the following question: . . . Need one double it with a transcendental *I*, a structure of absolute consciousness?"[28] "All the results of phenomenology begin to crumble if the *I* is not, by the same token as the world, a relative existence, that is to say, an object for consciousness."[29] With the reduction of the supposedly reducing transcendental phenomenological I itself the opportunity is lost for the later Husserl to be struck by wonder at the thought that this transcendental phenomenological I can be in parallel with the I of eidetic psychology. But with that reduction of the supposedly reducing transcendental phenomenological I the opportunity is found for Sartre to express as follows his wonder at the way in which at least the earlier Husserl gives us back the world:

> Husserl has restored to things their horror and charm. He has restored to us the world of artists and prophets: frightening, hostile, dangerous, with its havens of mercy and love. He has cleared the way for a new treatise on the passions which would be inspired by this simple truth, so utterly ignored by the refined among us: if we love a woman, it is because she is lovable. We are delivered from Proust. We are likewise delivered from the "internal life": in vain would we seek the caresses and fondlings of our intimate selves, like Amiel or like a child who kisses his own shoulder, since everything is finally outside, everything, even ourselves. Outside, in the world, among others. It is not in some hiding-place that we will discover ourselves; it is on the road, in the town, in the midst of the crowd, a thing among others, a man among men.[30]

Thus in Sartre's hands does transcendental phenomenological idealism become transcendent existential realism. But in preferring the Husserl of the *Logical Investigations* to the Husserl of *Ideas* Sartre is in the lineage of the Husserlians of Göttingen, for instance the Polish philosopher Roman Ingarden, whose work has been described as "a sustained effort to break the deadlock in the perennial controversy between idealism and realism."[31] The perenniality of this controversy is somewhat less comprehensive than the perenniality that Husserl must have had in mind when he made the statement cited above that the phenomenologist must live for a *philosophia perennis*. For the phenomenologist, like others on the road, in the town, in the midst of the crowd, is bound sooner or later to become occupied by questions of representation that are not purely ontological and epistemological but also ethical and political. One response to the clarion call Husserl sounds in that statement about a *philosophia perennis* is what we might call Derrida's *respublica perennis*, provided the adjective in this appellation is not taken in the sense of perpetual, not even in the sense of perpetual peace, but in the quasi-reversed sense of the adjective "futural," "*à venir*," as used by Derrida to qualify a certain democracy the rigor of which calls to be attended to later in this book.

FIVE

Pure Grammar

A turning point in the development of logic

What is the idea of pure grammar to which the title of Husserl's fourth Investigation refers? What is the idea of a grammar of pure logic to which §14 of that Investigation refers? What is the logic of this grammar? What is the grammar of this logic? And what is the philosophical significance of his idea of pure logical grammar? I shall begin to try to answer these questions by way of the answer Husserl himself gives from a historical point of view to the last of them, explaining what part he sees this answer contributing to philosophy. I shall focus upon the development of logic.

The Development of Logic is the title of a large book by William and Martha Kneale in which one will search in vain through its 750 pages for a mention of Husserl, in spite of the fact that, like W. R. Boyce Gibson, the translator of Husserl's *Ideas,* and Emmanuel Levinas, the translator of part of Husserl's *Cartesian Meditations,* William Kneale attended some of the lectures Husserl gave at Freiburg in the Summer Semester of 1928. That was a year before Husserl's *Formal and Transcendental Logic* was published and a year before Husserl travelled to Paris to give the *Paris Lectures* on which the *Cartesian Meditations* were to be based. In April of 1928 Husserl gave a lecture in Amsterdam where he met the intuitionist mathematician L. E. J. Brouwer. In the preceding month Brouwer had travelled from Amsterdam to Vienna to give the lecture on "Mathematics, Science, and Language." This lecture was heard by Wittgenstein and was the occasion of a switching of his attention from questions architectural back to questions philosophical and logico-mathematical, now in a style in some respects sympathetic with Brouwer's but antipathetic to that of Bertrand Russell and Frank Ramsey, who referred to Brouwer as "the Bolshevik menace."[1] Under that description Ramsey included too Hermann Weyl. Husserl had been chairman of the board of examiners for Weyl's doctoral dissertation at Göttingen in February 1908. I do not know whether after his visit to Vienna in February 1928 Brouwer was back in Amsterdam to hear Husserl deliver two lectures there the following month. Nor have I come across any explicit reference by Husserl to Wittgenstein. However, Wittgenstein refers to Husserl, and Husserl had read some Russell at least by 1936.

How, from the context of this chronicle of encounters, near-misses, and philosophical peripatetics in the early part of the twentieth century, does Husserl see the relation between his own ideas about logic and about grammar and philosophical movements in earlier centuries?

Plato, he says, set the ideal of a radical scientific responsibility in which his dialectical logic would be the science of all sciences and self-responsibly justify itself.[2] So, we may say parenthetically, Plato at the beginning of the history of philosophy is a paradigm of the moral responsibility—"the duty of genius," we might say, borrowing the subtitle of a book on Wittgenstein— which Husserl himself brings to his own philosophizing from the beginning, a responsibility which he seems to deem non-independent of logic when he writes "As one who judges, I remain true to myself (*Ich bleibe als Urteilender mir treu*), I remain self-consistent (*mir 'konsequent'*), just as long as I stick to my judgments. . . ."[3] It is as though Husserl is no more concerned with the logic of the consistency and truth of judgments than he is with the veracity of the judger and that he considers these to be ultimately inseparable.

The Platonic ideal of a science that gives unity to all science is embraced by Husserl in a course given in 1924 and 1925, when one of the members of his class was Rudolf Carnap. And if Plato responds to skepticism and sophistry by pointing a way to the ideal of an authentic science of science which will "found, assure and justify definitively every kind of activity of human reason . . . ," Husserl adds that it will achieve this "by means of theoretical reason and its predicative judgements."[4] To this extent at least Husserl is a Platonist even as late as the mid-1920s. But long before then, by 1910 and probably 1908, he is no longer a Platonist if Platonism is taken to posit Ideas as abstract objects existing separately in themselves. On the other hand, Husserl does not accept the Aristotelian way of denying such separation.

His first complaint about Aristotle is that his *organon* and other writings realize only imperfectly the Platonic Ideal of unity and self-justification. His second complaint regarding Aristotle is that if Plato was too ready to posit metaphysical givens, Aristotle marks the beginning of a too-precipitate willingness to assume physical and psychological givens. This is the attitude which for Husserl defines modernity and is an aspect of what he calls the crisis of European sciences. The plural form of the word "sciences" here signals that although the sciences have emancipated themselves from pre-Platonic naïvety, they are still naïve in adopting an uncritical attitude to their subject matters and pursue their topics in isolation from each other. It is sometimes suggested, we have noted, that Husserl's *Crisis of European Sciences,* begun in 1934, is his response to *Being and Time,* published by his erstwhile pupil Martin Heidegger in 1927. But already in *Formal and Transcendental Logic,* published two years after *Being and Time,* Husserl writes:

> The emancipated special sciences fail to understand the essential one-sidedness of their productions; they fail to understand that they will not encompass in their theories the full being-sense (*Seinssinn*) of their respective provinces until they lay aside the blunders imposed by their method, as an inevitable consequence of the exclusive focusing of each on its own particular province: in other words, until they relate their combined researches to the universality of being and its essential unity.[5]

It is not possible to miss the correspondence between this statement and Heidegger's call for an investigation of being as such by a philosophizing that precedes the division of labor into metaphysics, epistemology, ethics, aesthetics, philosophy of the sciences, and so on. But this citation from Husserl's book of 1929 can be matched by ones he made before 1927, for instance that in which in *First Philosophy* he lists logic, general metaphysics, mathematics, the sciences of nature and of mind and their diverse disciplines of physics, biology, psychology, ethics, and politics as fields which philosophy alas no longer seeks to unify within a philosophy that justifies itself.[6] The modern practice is to assume the data of this motley of disciplines and to allow the subject matter of logic to be dictated by them. The natural sciences assume an already given objective world. They assume factuality. But "The possibility of science cannot be *shown by the fact* of sciences, since the fact itself is shown only by [their] subsumption under that possibility as an idea. Thus we are led back to logic, to its apriori principles and theories. But now logic itself is in question with regard to its possibility."[7]

This is why, although Descartes, with his quest for a *sapientia universalis,* is an exception to the modern tendency and is rated by Husserl as the second of the great philosophical pioneers after Plato, even Descartes's method of radical suspension of belief is not radical enough. That method treats the ego as an ontological dangler. The ego is uncritically granted the status of a psychological *Endchen*, a fag end of the real world.[8] This is a convenient point at which to venture the remark that Husserl could be said to maintain that, in the Cartesian and Scholastic senses of the terms, "ob-jective reality" is the foundation of "formal reality." Hence *if* the ego is an ontological dangler because it is a psychological residue to which formal reality is uncritically ascribed, then it is not legitimate to rely upon it as a foundation from which to infer statements about transcendent reality in general. Its own existence must first be argued for or otherwise apodicticly demonstrated. And that means that the very principles of logic must be justified, however circular such an endeavor may seem to be. In the light of Husserl's teleological Ideal of unified science it is no surprise to learn that the legitimation of subjectivity and the legitimation of logic are for him inseparable. The subjectivity here mentioned is not, however, that of Cartesian (and Lockean) realism. Nor is it of course that of Descartes's more empiricist opponents Berkeley and Hume and their successors, for whom logic is a subsection of psychology, pragmatic technology, or anthropology. Here we anticipate the question whether along with these authors and with Avenarius, Mach, Mill, Spencer, Sigwart, Erd-mann, etc., criticized for their psychologism, technologism, pragmatism, or anthropologism in Volume I of the *Logical Investigations* under the subtitle *Prolegomena to Pure Logic,* Husserl would have included the author of the *Remarks on the Foundations of Mathematics* and the *Philosophical Investigations*. What would Husserl have made, for example, of the statement in paragraph 81 of the *Philosophical Investigations* in which Wittgenstein muses on what Frank Ramsey might have meant when he said that logic is a normative science? How does that remark (to my knowledge nowhere explained in the Ramsey archive) relate to what Husserl says, for example, under the section heading "Logic or theory of science as normative discipline. . . ."? It soon becomes plain that for Husserl any practical art of communication and any normative method of science must be based on the ultimate theoretical science of logic.

Implied in paragraph 81 and threaded throughout the length of the *Philosophical Investigations* is a quasi-Humean idea of logical necessity as based upon anthropological custom, and that idea is not at all friendly to the quasi-Platonic idea of ideality of crystalline essence "as if our logic were, so to speak, a logic for a vacuum."[9] Husserl's aim is to effect a synthesis of Plato and Hume to the extent that the objectivity of essences, which he claims to be valid not only for all humankind but "for any understanding whatever,"[10] is grounded in the subjectivity of human experience in which the psychological flux of impressions and ideas that are foundational for Hume is informed by a formal logic of judgment supplemented by a transcendental phenomenological logic of judging. We have just learned that Husserl holds that this logic is theoretical. Yet we have also learned that Husserl's transcendental logic is a logic which transcends itself under the norm of a Platonico-Kantian regulative "ideal of perfection."[11] How does one resolve this apparent tension? Perhaps, I suggest, by distinguishing the regulative normativity of an external ideal from the normativity internal to a system and inscribed in any constitutive rules which define the system. This is consistent with that system's being theoretical, with its not having any practical application, while being available as a standard for a practical methodology. So that the distinction between the theoretical and the practical or normative will be a distinction of attitude. This is borne out by Husserl's statement: "Logic *becomes* normative, it becomes practical; with a suitable change of attitude one can convert it into a normative-technological discipline. But intrinsically it is itself not a normative discipline but precisely a science in the pregnant sense, a work of purely theoretical reason—like all other sciences."[12] Hence the reference in the earlier cited heading in the *Prolegomena* to logic *as* a normative science.

I shall return to the normativity of what I have called the internal kind to show that it has a certain externality of its own from which it will be seen that from the non-absoluteness of the distinction between the normative or practical and the theoretical, a non-absoluteness of the distinction between the constitutive and the regulative ensues. Note first that this distinction between the constitutive and the regulative corresponds to two senses or contexts in which Kant speaks of the regulative, namely the regulative as applied to Ideas of Reason and the regulative as applied to the dynamic principles of the understanding deduced in the Analogies of Experience and the Postulates of Empirical Thought where, because the existence of appearances is at stake, there is a limit to constructibility which does not obtain in the case of the principles of transcendental mathematics.[13] We shall see that Husserl's pure transcendental logic does not extend beyond constructible existence, existence as understood by mathematicians. But other similarities and differences between Kantian and Husserlian transcendentalism call to be noted here.

Rightly or wrongly, Husserl includes Kant among those modern philosophers who simply take for granted the givenness of a natural world and of the sciences of it. This is the assumption of fact from which the transcendental arguments of the *Critique of Pure Reason* set out to deduce the presuppositions. Moreover, although Kant provides deductions or "exhibitions" of these presupposed principles, as a guide to them and as evidence of the exhaustiveness of his catalogue he uses the unsystematically collected forms of judgment listed by Aristotle. Although Kant finds Aristotle's ontological categories, predicaments, and postpredicaments to be something of a mixed bag, he says of Aristotle's formal logic and its theory of judgments that it has "not [been] required to retrace a single step" and that it is "to all appearance a closed and completed body of doctrine."[14] Husserl, on the other hand, is as scathing as Descartes about Scholastic logic and goes as far as to assert more generally that "Historically existing logic, with its naïve positivity, its way of obtaining truths as objects of naïve straightforward evidence, proves to be a sort of philosophic puerility (*eine Art philosophischer Kinderei*)."[15] If, as Husserl writes, "logic has not made much progress" since Aristotle or the Stoics it is certainly not because they had said more or less everything that was to be said about it.[16] For instance, far too little has been done to develop the project for a *grammaire générale et raisonnée*.[17]

From *The Port-Royal Grammar* to Kant's *Elements for a Grammar*

Husserl's French phrase here alludes to *The Port-Royal Grammar* (1660) of Arnauld and Lancelot, which describes itself in these very terms. In 1913, the year of the publication of Husserl's *Ideen*, Ferdinand Brunot wrote in his *History of the French Language* that *The Port-Royal Grammar* "for the first time applied to French the philosophical method of Aristotle. . . ."[18] This statement of what that book did would not have been much to Husserl's liking, unless he could have brought himself to read it as a statement to the effect that to return to Aristotle is to *reculer pour mieux sauter*. Nor could he have been enamored of the book's prefatory reminder that the word "grammar" comes from "*grammata*," the Greek word for the characters of writing. The entire first half of *The Port-Royal Grammar is* devoted to the written and spoken signs of natural languages, so that the English translation of the work contains many illustrative expressions that have inevitably to be kept in the original language, usually French, but also Hebrew, Latin, etc. More to Husserl's taste therefore would be the second half of the Grammar, where the topic is meaning, and the *Logic or Art of Thinking* by Arnauld and Pierre Nicole, which may be regarded as a continuation of the discussion begun in the *Grammar*. With its chapters dealing in turn with the idea and conception, the judgment and judging, reasoning and the syllogism, and scientific method or order, the Port-Royal *Logic or Art of Thinking* supports better Brunot's invocation of

Aristotle. Arnauld and Nicole have no compunction over drawing attention to errors made by Aristotle, but they are happy to adopt his logic as a list of rules, provided these rules are not regarded as norms to be consulted in order that we may think straight. Their normative function is retrospective. Only in this sense is logic the art of correct thinking. This is something Husserl would endorse, as any hints toward a universal Cartesian grammar that one might believe present in the Port-Royal logic of grammar are endorsed by Husserl when he writes that "operational laws of compounding and modification out of . . . primitive forms . . . hold pride of place over their empirical-grammatical expressions," so that one must ask, "How do German, Latin, Chinese, etc. express 'the' antecedent of a hypothetical, 'the' plural, 'the' modalities of possibility and probability, 'the' negative etc.?"[19] Further, "The notion of universal grammar can of course be carried beyond the *a priori* sphere, if the somewhat vague sphere of the universally human (in the empirical sense) is brought in. There can, and must, be a universal grammar in this widest of senses."[20] *Is* this the widest sense of universal grammar that Husserl allows? Have we not already observed that it is his ambition to seek the foundation of a grammar "for any understanding whatsoever"? So Husserl's *Prolegomena to Pure Logic* heralds a wider universality than that which Kant claims for grammar in his *Prolegomena to Any Future Metaphysics that will be able to Present Itself as a Science* (§39) when he writes there, in a passage already cited in part in our second chapter:

> To seek out from ordinary knowledge the concepts which are not grounded on any particular experience and none the less occur in all knowledge by experience, of which they constitute as it were the mere form of connection, presupposes no greater reflection or more insight than to seek out from a language rules of the real use of words in general and thus to collect the elements for a grammar (in fact both enquiries are very closely related to each other), without being able to state the ground, why any language has exactly this and no other formal nature, and still less that exactly so many, not more nor less, of such formal determinations of language can ever be encountered.[21]

The search for formal concepts envisaged here by Kant sets out from ordinary knowledge. That is to say, the concepts the search uncovers are restricted in their scope to human knowledge or experience. We have twice mentioned already §64 of the sixth Investigation in which Husserl argues that "The pure logico-grammatical laws are laws for any understanding whatever, and not merely for any human understanding." We shall come back a fourth time to this claim. Note here only that Husserl's reference, in the sentence reproduced from the fourth Investigation, to an extension of the notion of universal grammar beyond the *a priori* sphere to a specifically human grammar obviously does not itself imply the possibility of a grammar of nonhuman experience, a grammar that is wider than a grammar for human beings. The widening here mentioned is a widening not *of a priori* grammatical categories, but a widening *beyond* the *a priori* to the empirical, and Husserl makes it clear that the notion of the human which he has in mind here is an empirical one.

Intersubjectivity

In the second part of *Formal and Transcendental Logic,* where he has moved from formal logic to transcendental logic, in the sections treating of what he describes as the enigma (*Rätsel*) of intersubjective communication, which is the topic examined more thoroughly in the fifth of the roughly contemporary *Cartesian Meditations,* he distinguishes the other's and my own body as empirically physical, as the *Körper* which a physiologist studies, from the other's and my own body as lived psychophysical *Leib* with its involvement in what he calls a first nature in contrast to the second nature of the physiologist and the physicist. The second nature, he says, is an abstraction from the first. It suspends the empirical naturality of what in the citation from the fourth Investigation he calls the human. This distinction corresponds up to a point with Locke's distinction between the man and the person, the latter being for Locke not an empirical notion, but a forensic one, comparable with the French *"autrui"* whose quasi-legal status lends itself to the doctrine of the other person implied by Levinas's doctrine of veracity and face-to-face *droiture* which Locke would probably include along with such notions as perjury, sacrilege, and murder among what he names mixed modes.[22] We shall return to this doctrine. In so doing we shall be returning to the words in which Husserl emphasizes the responsibility and veracity which he places at the center of his theory of judgment and by implication of justice in the context of practice and evaluation and normativity which may be not as excludable as he thinks from the rules constitutive of theoretical systems. So the broadly ethical aspect of what both Husserl and Levinas refer to as the enigma of intersubjectivity is not as irrelevant to our interest in Husserl's theory of pure grammar as it may at first seem. Toward the end of the '20s that theory of grammatical objects and categories is harnessed to a theory of intersubjectivity that is itself an expansion of what Husserl had said in lectures at Göttingen in 1910–1911. This Husserlian theory of intersubjectivity, Levinas claims, requires a revolution of the notion of category whereby instead of being a form imposed on an object it becomes the subject's being categorized or questioned, the judger's being judged. Levinas finds hints toward this pre-reflective reversal of intentionality in Husserl's own underdeveloped doctrine of passive synthesis. Recall also Husserl's statement, cited in the section of our fourth chapter headed "Not in me, but among us": "Sensible data (and thus data in general) send, as it were, affective rays of force towards the ego pole. . . ." So, Levinas writes, "The room made in Husserlian phenomenology for non-representative phenomenology promised a signifiance (*signifiance*) not proceeding from knowledge, but the promise was not kept."[23] The promise not kept was the promise of a doctrine of proto-promise. The intentionality *à rebours* promised in this doctrine would be a twisting of the earlier-mentioned Cartesian and Scholastic notion of ob-jective reality into one of sub-jectility, of my being thrown, pro-jected before the other to whom I respond. It is a dimension beyond not only the straightforward (*gerade*) intentionality which Husserlian phenomenology ascribes to all consciousness. It accompanies the prereflective self-consciousness which accompanies that straightforward consciousness. So if grammatics or syntactics, semantics and pragmatics are the parts of semiotics treating respectively of relationships of signifiers to one another, to the meaning and truth of what they signify and to the users of signs, what I call semioethics is a further aspect of semiotics which concerns the users of signs as themselves signifiers.[24] Here pure formal logic or grammar as the *logos* of the said becomes pure nonformal logic as the *logos* of saying. Here we reach a formal/nonformal amphibology which is the quasi-transcendental condition of both the Austinian logic or rhetoric of speech-acts and of Husserlian pure formal and pure transcendental logic and grammar.

Bringing together the earlier references to Kant and these latest references to the social context, lifeworld, or form of life in which pure logic and grammar have their home, we now touch on the question whether Kant's discussion of the transcendental-empirical ego's self-affection is illuminated or darkened by Husserl's discussion of the enigma or riddle of intersubjectivity. I restrict myself to the obvious observation that this problem or puzzle of the double naturality of the ego, of the alter ego, and of the world is unavoidably a problem or puzzle for Husserl's phenomenology of pure logical grammar. The purity of that grammar is its suspension of allegedly second naturality. It is vital to remember that that is not a suspension of naturality *tout court*. It is simply a suspension that puts in parentheses questions relating to the real (*real*) world as studied by the empirical sciences, including the historically empirical sciences of language. This does not mean that the phenomenological science of grammar has no objects. It means that its objects are objects not regarded as just objects of the real world we happen actually to inhabit, but as objects of any possible world.

In the second edition of the *Logical Investigations* Husserl notes that what in the first edition he called pure grammar he prefers now to call more specifically pure logical grammar or grammar of pure logic defined as the theory of the pure forms of signification.[25] This marks a further respect in which his program differs from that outlined in the passage we reproduced from Kant's *Prolegomena*. The pure concepts which Kant holds to be conditions of all experience of a spatio-temporal world extend beyond the concepts of formal logic which he takes as a clue to them. He says that grammars of these two fields of forms are "very closely related" (*sehr nahe verwandt*). This is because, as he says in the *Critique of Pure Reason*, "The same function which gives unity to the various representations in a judgment also gives unity to the mere synthesis of various representations in an intuition; and this unity, in its most general expression, we entitle the pure concept of the understanding."[26] Therefore, "The functions of the understanding can ... be all [*insgesamt*; omitted by Kemp Smith] discovered if we can give an exhaustive (*vollständig*) statement of the functions of unity in judgments."[27] The claim to exhaustiveness in both the case of functions of judgments and the case of functions of the understanding mirrors the claim apparently implied in the *Prolegomena* respecting at least the elements of grammar that what "for any language" the forms are and how many of them there are can be established even though we cannot establish why there are no others.

The words "for any language" translate Kant's "für eine jede Sprache." These must be taken to mean that every language will have the same forms and the same number of forms. That seems also to be Husserl's contention, though restricted to the forms of elementary and complex judgment. Now, Kant says that we cannot give any ground for holding that these and these alone are the forms of any language whatsoever. Does Husserl say that we can? If he does not, is he not making a factual assumption, albeit perhaps the assumption of an absolute fact, like the assumption of the existence of the real world for which he criticizes Kant, Descartes, and Aristotle and could have criticized any philosopher who takes as more than a guiding thread the question, Why is there something and not rather nothing? Are not the even more specific assumption of the existence of a world of a certain sort and the assumption of a grammar of a certain sort "very closely related to each other," if not grounded in "the same function"? Might this same function be the "to us unknown common root" of sensibility and understanding?[28] I shall be saying something later about this idea of "same function" and this "common root," which I take to be the transcendental imagination. What must be stated first here is: to say that Husserlian phenomenology assumes the existence of the real world or of a certain universal grammar, and that it can therefore make an empirically verifiable postulation of an innate grammar in the manner of Chomsky,[29] is either to forget that phenomenology demands a methodological abstention from questions of empirical or metaphysical existence, or to question (as perhaps Derrida does) whether that phenomenology is coherent.

Husserlian phenomenology is the science of possibility. So it is the science of the possibility of the grammar of natural languages. Anything that it says about the possibility of anything whatsoever, including the spatio-temporally real, will hold for grammar as manifest in spatio-temporal expression. As Husserl writes, "*verbal expression,* which we excluded from our consideration of logic, is an essential presupposition for intersubjective thinking and for an intersubjectivity of the theory accepted as ideally existing; and that accordingly an ideal identifiability of the expression, as expression, must likewise raise a problem of constitution."[30] The existence here referred to is ideal existence in the sense which Husserl compares to existence in mathematics, where it is tantamount to the condition of being noncontradictory in the fields which are the topics of Husserl's *Philosophy of Arithmetic,* of his *Origin of Geometry,* and of algebra. It is thanks to this last that modern analysis prescinds from the materiality of geometry, mechanics, etc., that the formality of the Aristotelian logical analytics is possible, and that Husserl himself, following Leibniz, is able to project a science of the form of multiplicities the units of which have the maximal generality of "anything whatsoever." Such a formal *mathesis universalis* is the top deck of pure logic as Husserl conceives it. Before it is reached three other formally logical decks are to be distinguished. The lowest of these is that of grammar understood as the rules of the morphology of judgments, such rules as distinguish between the nonsense of strings like "Or if because king although" and the senselessness of "Here is a round square." This second string makes grammatical sense despite its being logically countersensical by the norms of the logic of contradiction or consistency which comprise the second level. Only at the third level do we reach the logic of truth and falsity. It follows that for Husserl the "objectivities" to which sentences refer are states of affairs (*Sachverhalten*), not, as they are for Frege, truth-values. It may seem to follow also that for Husserl analytic judgments are not strictly speaking analytically true and that self-contradictory judgments are not universally false, so there would be no room in his theory for a truth-table representation of tautology and self-contradiction. That, however, is not Husserl's view. His view, endorsed by Oscar Becker's Appendix to *Formal and Transcendental Logic,* is that there is a truth-principial version of a tautology, e.g. *modus ponens* or *modus tollens,* and a version of tautology expressed solely in terms of consequence, viz., for *modus ponens,* "'*N*" follows analytically from two judgments of the forms, 'If *M,* then *N*" and '*M.*'"[31] This, he says, is a "genuine purely analytic logical principle" which "belongs purely to the essence of judgments proper and to the relationships of analytic consequence peculiar to these." That seems to make consequence logic more fundamental than truth logic. Yet he writes that "The principles that originally connect truth and consequence must also be reckoned among the highest truth-principles of apophantic logic." I take the second part of this sentence to refer to the truth-principial versions of tautologies, which for *modus ponens* is "If an immediate relationship of total analytic antecedent and total analytic consequent obtains between any two judgments, *M* and *N,* then the truth of the antecedent entails the truth of the consequent." However, his phrase "principles that originally connect truth and consequence" alerts us to the need for a meta-logic treating the meta-principles that connect the principles of consequence logic and the principles of truth logic, the meta-logic that deals with what in Investigation IV he describes as the relations of equivalence that link the two sets of laws.[32] One of the lessons to be learned from this is that the levels (*Stufen*) are not independent pieces but non-independent moments of the whole compounded of formal and transcendental logic. In the present case the non-independence is that of the movement "up" from the logic of contradiction to the logic of truth. What about the movement "down" from the logic of contradiction to the level of grammatical morphology?

Varieties of Imagination

The question just posed takes us back to the questions with which we began as to the grammar of Husserl's logic and the logic of his grammar. A flood of dazzling light is cast on these questions by the following words:

> The whole support of form-construction [*Formenbildung*] is speech [*Rede*], with its well-differentiated indications, its references to sense, which attach to the sensuously differentiated signs and their sensuous configurations. And it is therefore not without reason that the theory of the forms of significations was characterized in my *Logical Investigations* as the "grammar of pure logic." In a certain manner, furthermore, it is also not without reason that people often say that formal logic has let itself be guided by grammar. In the case of theory of forms, however, this is not a reproach but a necessity—provided that, for guided by grammar (a word intended to bring to mind de facto historical languages and their grammatical description), guidance by the grammatical itself is substituted. Distinctly

understanding a statement and framing it as a possible judgment—this can and often does signify distinct grasping of the word-sequences (accompanied by an internal explicit following, in a quasi-speaking [*Quasi-nachsprechen*]) and also of their reference-articulation [*Verweisungsartikulation*], with which there accrues the unity of a judgment, confused and yet articulated in a definite form.[33]

Husserl goes on to repeat that the forms constructible at this level include self-contradictory ones like "No quadrangle has four angles." Then he says this: "Without the definite articulation of vague judgments by means of the sensuous articulation of verbal signs, no theory of forms, no logic whatever, would be possible—and, of course, no science either." But, we must ask, as Merleau-Ponty, Derrida, and others have asked, what kind of purity can there be if the grammar of a natural language like German or Greek or Hebrew or Hopi is taken as an example? What is it to take a natural fact *as* an example? What is an example *as such*? What is the grammatical as such, the grammatical itself, *das Grammatische selbst*? Answers to these questions in large part acceptable to Husserl can be reached only if the transcendental imagination is given its due in a manner indicated by Husserl himself going back through Kant to the things themselves and only if we remember that for Husserl—as, we shall later have occasion to remind ourselves, for Wittgenstein—it does not matter for the purposes of a phenomenology of grammar whether the example is fictitious or real, though it matters enormously that the transcendental phenomenological imagination be distinguished from fiction.

Speaking roughly, the imagination taken in its widest sense is that aspect of thinking expressed by the words *as, if,* and *as if.* The transcendental imagination is distinguished from purely fictive imagination as this latter is opposed to perception and to factual belief. The transcendental imagination transcends this opposition. So if we use the word "*Vorstellung*" for it, we must not limit the application of the word to epistemic representation. If we use the word "*Phantasie*" for it, we must not limit the application of the word to fantasy or fancy in senses that are incompatible with positing. One of Kant's words for imagination, "*Einbildungskraft*," may convey the idea of idea as image or picture, *Bild*, but, as the words "idea" and "*Idee*" (as in Husserl's title *Ideen*) mark more plainly, and as Kant's treatment of "*Idee*" as Platonic *eidos* and as a species of the genus *Vorstellung* suggest,[34] "*Bild*" and "image" lend themselves to quite formal senses. Indeed they lend themselves to the concept of form and, in the Kantian and Husserlian contexts, to formation or construction, as indicated in the nearly pleonastic word "*Formenbilding*," translated as "form-construction" in the passage just cited from *Formal and Transcendental Logic*. The neutrality with respect to content which the transcendental imagination implies means that this can be operative in the most formal realm not only of mathematics—which in Platonic, Aristotelian, and Kantian topologies mediates between or divides into the purely sensible and the purely rational. The transcendental imagination is also operative in the time-space of pure logical grammar where the "as" that characterizes imagination marks the "this as that" function of the copula and where the "if" marks the empty "if . . . then." These connective functions are themselves connected with each other, since "S is p" implies "If S then p" and the latter is short for "p is a property of S" or "S is the bearer of p" or the conjunction of these two, as we may want to say if we wish to accommodate Husserl's idea that although in using sentences of these forms we refer to the same state of affairs, their meanings are not the same. (Note however that although in the first Investigation he says that "$a > b$" and "$b < a$" have different meanings but refer to the same state of affairs, to the same *Sachverhalt*, in 1908 he prefers to say that the *Sachverhalten* differ but the sentences refer to the same situation, *Sachlage*).[35]

The imagination is operative typically in the thought of counterfactuality, but the transcendental imagination is neither factual nor counterfactual. "We . . . enact, instead of a judgement affirming a state of affairs, the qualitative modification, the neutral putting in suspense of the same state of affairs, which cannot be identified with any picturing of it."[36] This sentence encapsulates the double neutrality of the transcendental imagination. Indeed, although in the section from which this sentence is cited Husserl refers to the imagination as "*Einbildungskraft*" he notes the inconvenience of that word in so far as it suggests something "pictorial in the stricter sense." ("A whole cloud of philosophy condensed into a drop of grammar"?)[37] The philosophy of meaning against which Husserl is on guard is that against which Wittgenstein too puts us on guard both in the later writings and already in the *Tractatus*. For the abstention in the *Tractatus Logico-Philosophicus* from any naming of the nature of nameable objects is not merely a symptom of lack of interest but a consequence of the fact that the topic of the work is logic, as its title says it is.

Clarification of the status of the transcendental imagination is part and parcel of the story to be told about the relationship of the logic of contradiction to the logic of truth. For the distinction between these two logics straddles the dash of the noetic–noematic relation which in Husserl's *Ideas* puts into Greek the Cartesian relation *cogito–cogitatum* and the Scholastic notion of ob-jective reality and which is not yet articulated in the doctrine of the *Logical Investigations* that meanings or senses are abstract species. Translated into the context of logical grammar, the dash which separates and connects *noēsis* and *noēma* marks the division of analytics into the formal-apophantic and the correlative formal-ontological. If these two formalities are inseparable, to describe the subject matter of their jointure we shall need a notion other than truth, which is on the side of formal ontology. That notion is the notion of a possible object or of existence in the mathematical sense. This is the sense which gets transposed from the first love to which Husserl dedicated his *Philosophy of Arithmetic* to the even more fundamental sphere of logic. In that sphere he remains faithful to the first love not only in retaining its idea of existence, but in outlining a program of the countable as such. This is one reason why I thought it relevant to mention Brouwer in my opening almanac of the *anni mirabiles* 1928–1929. Another reason is that both Brouwer and Husserl are keen to give the imagination its due, as too am I. A third reason is that comparing the points of agreement and disagreement between them helps to identify the points of agreement and disagreement between the thinking of Husserl and the thinking of Wittgenstein at that moment of the art deco decade which is a turning point for both of them. I shall first make a few comments about the mathematical imagination which may seem to have little to do with the topic of pure logical grammar. I shall then say how I construe the connection between these topics. I shall then recite from the *Philosophical Investigations* a remark about imagination and grammar that will enable me to take further what I have already said on the question of the impurity to which the idea of pure logical grammar advanced by the author of the *Logical Investigations* has been said to be exposed.

Husserl's layered logic, with the theory of number at the top and the theory of grammatical form at the bottom, is generated from the consciousness of temporality where the "of" is a double genitive. The theory of temporal protention and retention which Husserl was working out in that other *annus mirabilis* of 1905 lends itself readily to the cell-division theory of number advocated by Brouwer, provided the latter's language of causality is replaced by the former's language of motivation and intentionality. According to Brouwer

> the first act of intuitionism completely separates mathematics from mathematical language, in particular from the phenomena of language which are described by theoretical logic, and recognizes that intuitionist mathematics is an essentially languageless activity of the mind having its origin in the perception of a *move of time*, i.e. of the falling apart of a life-moment into two distinct things, one of which gives way to the other, but is retained by memory. If the two-ity thus born is divested of all quality, there remains the *empty form of the common substratum of all two-ities*. It is this common substratum, this empty form, which is the *basic intuition of mathematics*.[38]

Both Brouwer and Husserl are going back to and through Kant's doctrine of imaginative schematism, and Husserl at least is going back to Hume, but intentionalizing Hume's accounts of association and of the flux of impressions and ideas. Both Brouwer and Husserl postulate a languageless continuum corresponding to the field of Kantian imagination. However, whereas Brouwer and the Wittgenstein of around 1930 agree that the mathematical part of that continuum is not based on logic, for Husserl the field of mathematics is a part of the field of logic, but that part which he calls formal ontology. Because formal ontology is distinguished from formal apophantics, Husserl's theory of mathematical multiplicities has to be distinguished from the logistic theory that mathematics is reducible to logic, as argued by Russell. Unlike Russell, and here like Brouwer, Husserl grounds mathematics on one or another kind of intuition of evidence. But that is because for Husserl intuition of evidence grounds the science of logic as a whole made up of formal apophantics and formal ontology and that is to say that for him it grounds mathematics. This difference leads to another one. Notwithstanding the consensus between Brouwer and Husserl on the point that empirical language is an extra to mathematics and logic because it is an aid to memory and communication with others, Brouwer denies that the principle of excluded middle holds for the logico-linguistic formulation of mathematical constructions, whereas Husserl holds that so long as a judgment is not either grammatically senseless or categorially absurd it is definitely either true or false.

One might think that Husserl's greater friendliness to classical logic and pure logical grammar would inhibit his friendship toward the imagination. This is not borne out either by Husserl's practice or by his preaching. What he calls eidetic variation in imagination (*Phantasie*), meaning by this transcendental phenomenological imagination, not imagination as fiction in opposition to perception or factual belief, is not restricted to sensibility (Hume) or to the zone between sensibility and understanding or reason (Kant). It ranges over these fields, but also over the field of pure logical and grammatical formality. However, despite his emphasis upon the freedom to imagine variations, and perhaps because of his faith in the principle of excluded middle and the definiteness of judgments, a faith shared with the Wittgenstein of the *Tractatus,* he is confident that it is in principle possible always to arrive at an invariant on this or the other side of the horizon. Compare this with the Wittgenstein of the *Philosophical Investigations* and the *Remarks on the Foundations of Mathematics.* This is the Wittgenstein who says about the principles of logic what is said about the principle of excluded middle by Brouwer. Brouwer writes that this principle was accepted historically only because for any single assertion it is noncontradictory and because classical logic worked well for so much of everyday experience that it is no more than "a phenomenon of the history of civilization of the same kind as the old-time belief in the rationality of π or in the rotation of the firmament on an axis passing through the earth."[39] How close to the spirit of this and how distant from the spirit of Husserl is the following remark from Wittgenstein's *Investigations*?

> If the formation of concepts can be explained by facts of nature, should we not be interested, not in the grammar, but rather in that in nature which is the basis of grammar?—Our interest certainly includes the correspondence between concepts and very general facts of nature. (Such facts as mostly do not strike us because of their generality.) But our interest does not fall back upon these possible causes of the formation of concepts; we are not doing natural science; nor yet natural history—since we can also invent fictitious natural history for our purposes.
>
> I am not saying: if such-and-such facts of nature were different people would have different concepts (in the sense of a hypothesis). But: if anyone believes that certain concepts are absolutely the correct ones, and that having different ones would mean not realizing something that we realize—then let him imagine certain very general facts of nature to be different from what we are used to, and the formation of concepts different from the usual ones will become intelligible to him.[40]

Wittgenstein indicates here how grammatical phenomenology puts invention and variation in the imagination at the service of the description of essence expressed by grammar,[41] at the service of the description of the essence of, for example, "imagination" itself understood as "*Vorstellung*."[42] That is done by explaining the forms of life in which the word "imagination" is employed. This stress upon the offering of reminders of how expressions are used in ordinary discourse is analogous to Husserl's increasing insistence from the late '20s onward upon the philosophical obligation to retrace the exact concepts of mathematical science to sources in the daily world of practice and evaluations. But this recourse to sources is a recourse from putatively formal logic to a transcendental logic that generates structures from examples, not from empirical data as such but from the empirical seen *as examples,* where the very notion of example brings with it the notion of the *as.* The purity of transcendental logic and grammar turned generative is not the purity of formal logic, as that is opposed to the empirically posited. It is as uncontaminated by this last as is formal logic because both are concerned with possibilities and with the imaginable in the sense in which the imaginable is the conceivable conceived as neutral with regard to fact and fiction. If, in the manner I have sketched, the science of transcendental possibility can escape the charge of being contaminated by natural factuality, it still has to face the difficulty that it pretends to be a theoretical science, so a science of objects. It therefore owes us a clarification of how the evidence of these can be traced back to a world lived practically and axiologically. One of Husserl's pupils provides such a clarification. I doubt whether Husserl himself does, since although he makes the Cartesian concession that there are many ways of being noetic (many varieties of what Descartes calls *pensées* or *cogitationes*), he does not relinquish the doctrine that nonpositing modes of *noēsis* like desire correspond with *noēmata* that are no different from those of positing modes. This seems to suppose that phenomenologists can strip themselves of the habitualities with which they are garbed. That may be no less difficult to do than to jump over one's own shadow. However, I leave this question hanging in the air in order to turn finally to a qualification of the defense I have just proposed on Husserl's behalf against the contention that the pretensions of purity made by his theory of logical grammar are incoherent. The qualification is compelled by the paragraphs reproduced from the *Philosophical Investigations*.

If those paragraphs may be read as a sign of semantic freedom, they must be read too as the elucidation of semantic necessity, a human and Humean necessity entrenched in history and custom. As applied to Husserl's science of "the grammatical" this means that the objectivity of that concept is constituted in part by historicality. John Austin wrote half a century ago:

> There are constant reminders in contemporary philosophy, which notoriously is much concerned with language, to a "logical grammar" and a "logical syntax" as though these were things distinct from ordinary grammarian's grammar and syntax: and certainly they do seem, whatever exactly they may be, different from traditional grammar. But grammar today is in a state of flux; for fifty years or more it has been questioned on all hands and counts whether what Dionysius Thrax once thought was the truth about Greek is the truth and the whole truth about all language and all languages.[43]

The abnormative imagination

It is evidence of a failure of imagination to say, as Husserl does,[44] that we cannot imagine other forms of consciousness than that "governed" by the pure laws of thought for which he claims intuited evidence. It is a failure of imagination in more than one sense. It is a failure that attention to Brouwer and Wittgenstein might have done something to repair, a failure to imagine that even the human imagination may stretch beyond the horizon Husserl sets for the regulative Idea in a Kantian sense. It may stretch to the abnormativity of what might be called the imadgination.[45] This is a conceptual point. That is to say, the "of" of the phrase "abnormativity of the imagination" stands for another double genitive. Husserl rightly makes much of the horizonal "and so on" of validation and of the liability of our expectations to be frustrated. But both the expectation of fulfillment and the preparedness for frustration on which he lays stress are of the kind to be experienced in practicing normal science, that is to say where we are following rules in the way that the point of having rules demands, that is to say in following them blindly.[46] Blindness is a blindness necessary to the vision of normal science and it remains a foothold for scientific or any other conceptual revolution. But it is also a blindness to the possibility of revolutionary science, the possibility of what is impossible by the norms of a historically given normality. That blindness, the blindness to alternatives to the entrenched ways of reading a rule, is not a blindness that a transcendental phenomenology of grammar can afford to have. It is to be blind to something that is perhaps readable between the lines of the ordinary normal grammar of the word "imagine." Imagine someone saying "Let him imagine such and such" or "Imagine such and such." He and you can obey that command, but it is a command to expect more than one can at that moment imagine. To put this in Husserl's terms, if all consciousness is noetic–noematic, the imagination is that pro-protentional aspect of consciousness ranging beyond that of which I am conscious at any given moment. Its "You can" announces something which you can *not*. It does not announce this because you cannot command sufficient strength or because your imagination is too weak. It announces something that exceeds psychological weakness and strength. "Imagine such and such" is essentially, logically, grammatically promissory. Half a century after Austin wrote about "ifs" and "cans" and grammar, a century since Husserl wrote about them, and I don't know how many centuries since Dionysius Thrax wrote about Greek language, truth, and logic, it calls to be written that "*the* imagination," "*the* grammar" of imagination in one of the manifold uses of those words is inherently prefatory of what is exterior to the imaginable understood as that of which we are able to present ourselves with an image or concept or idea. On this understanding imagination is analogous to knowledge by acquaintance, *connaissance*. But imagination can be more analogous to knowing that something is the case, *savoir*, provided the factuality of the case is not restricted to the present, and provided it is qualified by a conditional or subjunctive *if*. These distinctions cannot be overlooked if we are to avoid subjective idealism. The distinction between imagining *x* and imagining that *x* is one that cannot be overlooked either if there is to be a transcendental grammar with pretentions toward unified science. But imagining that *x* is still not sufficient for this. More is demanded of the grammar of science and the science of grammar if the idea or Ideal of pure logical grammar is to do justice not only to the subjects, predicates, and judgments that are the subject matter of Husserl's science, but also to the intersubjectivity which he himself says science presupposes. Imagine a turn from the logical grammar of countability to a logical grammar of accountability such as that begun by Austin's interpretation of Wittgenstein's remark that words are also deeds,[47] taken a few more degrees by Levinas. Such a turn would be one from both possibility and impossibility to the unpossibility latent in Husserl's binding of the logic of consistency and truth to the self-responsibility of truthfulness declared in his statement "Ich bleibe als Urteilender mir treu," "As originally Critical judger I remain true to myself." Here "Critical" is a word Husserl borrows from Kant and explicates in considerable detail in later chapters of *Transcendental and Formal Logic,* whence it is relayed further to Levinas. The phrase "originally Critical" expresses on the side of formal apophantics the idea of the partition of a whole judgment into subject and predicate and on the correlative side of formal ontology the idea of the partition of a state of affairs into object named and property. It is no dangling ontological fag end that gets appended to Husserl's declaration "As originally Critical judger I remain true to myself" if we say also "Ich bleibe als Geurteilter *dir* treu," "As aboriginally hypo-Critically judged I remain true to you." Beyond the non-empirical, pure logical grammar of *what* is judged or described or named or called, this second declaration announces a non-empirical, pure grammatological ethics of *who* is called to responsibility to another, an ethics of the *grammē,* of the mark made as signature. Making a mark *as* signature makes that mark a mark of imagination or imadgination and of the impossibility as un-possibility just mentioned (to which a return will be made in the first and last chapters of the second part of this book).

SIX

Meanings and Translations

Language

In *Speech and Phenomena* one reads that "*Bedeutung* is *reserved* [by Husserl] for the content in the ideal sense of *verbal* expression, spoken language. . . ."[1] This may not mean, as it is taken to mean by J. Claude Evans in *Strategies*, that "*Bedeutung* is used to characterize speech" by Husserl as opposed to characterizing something else.[2] What it says is that "*Bedeutung*" is used to characterize *the content in the ideal sense* of verbal expression, whereas "*Sinn*" is not limited to that.

Further, the statement in *Speech and Phenomena* that "for Husserl, the expressiveness of expression—which always supposes the ideality of a *Bedeutung*—has an irreducible tie to the possibility of spoken language (*Rede*)"[3] is compatible with the statement in *Strategies* that Husserl does not "reserve the power of expression . . . for *spoken* language." Assuming that the phrase "for Husserl" in the sentence from *Speech and Phenomena* signals that Derrida is here stating Husserl's express intentions and not what Husserl is committed to perhaps against his will, the expressiveness of expression could have an irreducible tie to the *possibility* of spoken language without the power of expression being reserved for spoken language. The expressiveness of *writ-*

ten expression could have for Husserl an irreducible tie to the possibility of spoken language.

By "spoken" here I do not mean, and do not take Evans or Derrida to mean, spoken in the certain sense in which Husserl allows in §8 of Investigation I that language is spoken even in soliloquy (*in der einsamen Rede*). In soliloquy one may view oneself (*sich auffassen*) as speaking to someone else or oneself, but there is no communication or indication. So if "spoken language" is taken in the wide sense that includes soliloquy, one may, "in the first analysis," to employ Derrida's phrase, share with *Strategies* the reservations it expresses over his statement about "spoken language . . . always containing *in fact* an indicative stratum"[4]—particularly given that when he first says this no mention has yet been made of Husserl's restriction that in communicative speech meaning (*Bedeutung*) is always interwoven with an indicative relation. This statement of Husserl's is cited two pages later in *Speech and Phenomena;* immediately after it is cited we are told "We know already *in fact* that the discursive sign (*le signe discursif*), and consequently the meaning, is *always* involved, always caught up in an indicative system."[5] In *Strategies* this sentence is read as an insinuation that all speech is indicative, even though, as *Strategies* allows, *Speech and Phenomena* goes on to admit Husserl's restriction, the restriction already announced in the citation from Husserl that *Speech and Phenomena* reproduces immediately before the sentence that *Strategies* regards as an insinuative plant or graft upon the text of the *Logical Investigations.* However, that sentence is so regarded because *Strategies* regards the words "the discursive sign" contained in it as a "supposedly explicative transformation Derrida immediately introduces" of, if I understand aright, Husserl's "*mitteilende Rede*" and of the Elie-Kelkel-Schérer translation of that as "*le discours communicatif.*" But these last phrases go back in their turn to phrases that they explicate or that are explicated by them in the German and French, namely "*im lebendigen Wechselgespräch*" and "*dans la conversation vivante.*" Therefore I take the adjective in the phrase "*le signe discursif*" as employed by Derrida to mean communicative in the sense of "*discursus*" as a running to and fro, an exchange, so that what in the French text of *La voix* is referred to at this point as "*discours*" is not to be equated with "speech." *Strategies* does so equate it in its construal of the sentence it deems to be strategically insinuative.

Incidentally, this construal is more implausible for the French original than for the published English translation. The latter begins "We know already . . . ," as though we have independent grounds for that knowledge. This translation fails to translate a word in the French text. According to that "Nous

savons donc déjà . . . ," which could be rendered "So we already know . . ."
or "We already know then . . ." where the "So" and the "then" signal a consequence of what we have just been told in the citation about communicative
discourse.

One soon learns not to underestimate the difficulties of translating Husserl's and Derrida's intentions. So I applaud the attention Evans gives to the
difficulties of translating, for example, *Rede.* If one were looking for a single
word to sum up or disseminate the topic of *Speech and Phenomena,* that
word would be "*Rede.*" This granted, and granted the reading I have just
given of the words "*le signe discursif*" on p. 20 of that book, we should recall
a phrase already cited from p. 18, the phrase "*discours parlé (Rede).*" Does
this imply that there could be *discours* that is not *parlé?* If so, the implication
relevant here is not just that there could be written discourse or semaphored
discourse. Since the word "*Rede*" and the words "*discours parlé*" are in apposition in this phrase and since Husserl says that strictly monological *Rede*
is noncommunicative, one would expect Husserl to say that strictly monological *Rede* would also not be, strictly speaking, speaking. And he does say
that. That still leaves room in Husserl's scheme for the possibility of unspoken
discourse that seems to be implied by the fact that Derrida uses the phrase
"spoken discourse." This is the possibility of imagining oneself speaking with
someone, another or oneself, in soliloquy.

However, to move to another difficulty, we have seen that it is the possibility of spoken discourse that Husserl is said to affirm in the sentence in
question. Now a point that I have already made regarding this in connection
with expression can also be made in connection with indication. Derrida
writes that for Husserl the expressiveness of expression, hence the ideality
of *Bedeutung,* has an irreducible tie to the possibility of language. In other
words, if it is not possible to utter unuttered, allegedly conceptual meaning, then there is no conceptual meaning to be uttered. Should one not say
too that it must be *possible* for unuttered conceptual meaning to be uttered
indicatively, communicatively? If so, although he has not yet cited Husserl's
remark restricting indication to communication, Derrida already has a reason for saying on p. 18 of *Speech and Phenomena* that spoken language always
contains in fact an indicative stratum which is difficult to confine within
limits, i.e., within the limits Husserl sets. The fact and the indicative stratum
will be that of the possible communicative utterance, an utterance that must
be possible even for strictly monological *Rede.*

What about the question whether in *Ideas* Husserl reserves logicality for
language, a question to which Evans says Derrida answers mistakenly that
Husserl does? Derrida cites from *Ideas* §124 Husserl's remark "logical *Bedeu-*

tung is an expression."[6] But he has cited from that section earlier in the same paragraph Husserl's statement that originally *"Bedeutung"* and *"bedeuten"* relate only to the linguistic sphere (*sprachliche Sphäre*), to that of "expression" (*des Ausdrückens*), but that "it is almost inevitable, and at the same time an important step for knowledge, to widen the *Bedeutung* of these words and to modify them suitably so that they can be applied in a certain way to the entire noetico–noematic field." Having said this, Husserl announces that for the sake of precision he will use *"Sinn"* more widely than *"Bedeutung."* He will use *"Sinn"* for all intentional experiences (*Erlebnissen*). And he will prefer (*bevorzugen*) *"Bedeutung"* for the original narrower use relating to the linguistic sphere. So he will speak of logical *Bedeutung* and expressive *Bedeutung*. Husserl's *"bevorzugen,"* which I have translated by "prefer," does not restrict his use of the word *"Bedeutung"* to the linguistic sphere and might suit better than "reserve," Evans's translation, the latter's argument that Husserl does not restrict his use of *"Bedeutung"* to the linguistic sphere. Husserl's words *"especially* in phrases like 'logical *Bedeutung*' and 'expressive *Bedeutung*'" could be taken to support the interpretation that Husserl is not purporting to restrict his use of *"Bedeutung"* to the linguistic sphere. All Husserl may be intending to say is that he is going to use *"Bedeutung"* of meaning where meaning implies a connection between the linguistic and the logical. Evans says that it is important to note that in *Ideas* Husserl does not reserve logicality for language at all. Husserl, he says, "was primarily interested in language as the instrument of cognition, but he did not for that reason deny that language has many functions."[7]

Does Derrida dispute this? How does the fact that Husserl does not deny that language has many functions undermine, as Evans says it does, Derrida's "claim that for Husserl the logical is the *a priori telos* of language, its proper destination"? Whether "for Husserl" refers here to an avowed or unavowed intention or to what Husserl is committed to whether he intends it or not, the logical could be the *a priori telos* of language in its many and varied functions. It could be said, for instance, as philosophers have said, that the manifold functions or deeds performed with words other than those reflected in classical propositional logic are analyzable as forms of propositional logic plus an imperative or optative or interrogative sign in place of the assertion sign of standard "cognitive" logics of falsity and truth. Is it not something like this that Husserl is suggesting when he writes in passages from §117 and §138 respectively of *Ideas I* (cited by Derrida in a footnote of "La forme et le vouloir-dire") that "Every act [including acts of feeling, will, axiology], as also every act-correlate, harbours explicitly or implicitly a 'logical' factor," and that axiological and practical truth or self-evidence "come to be expressed and known in the form of doxological truths, namely, in the specifically logical or apophantic"?[8]

This begins to say something about Husserl's conception of the *science* of logic. More about this will be said in, for instance, *Formal and Transcendental Logic*. It is to the transcendental conception of the logical expounded there that Derrida has just referred when he writes that "Husserl had, in a most traditional manner, determined the essence of language by taking logic as its *telos* or norm."[9] *Qua* phenomenological logician Husserl is interested in the ideality of language, not in its reifications.[10] It is only of language in its ideality that Husserl says that its *telos* is presence, following the metaphysical tradition that determines language (*logos*) from logic. It is only of language in its ideality that Husserl, subscribing to that tradition of rationality ("*ratio*" being the Latinization of "*logos*"), determines the essence and origin of language. So when it is asked in *Strategies* whether Husserl does really attempt to "determine the essence and origin of language," implying presumably that Derrida says Husserl does, at least two remarks are called for.

First, it is not said in *Speech and Phenomena* simply that Husserl attempts the determination of the essence and origin of language. It is said there rather that Husserl determines the essence of language by a theory of knowledge. Husserl does not attempt. He assumes in fact, a fact in the sense, by the way, of the factuality on which turns the argument we shall be analyzing in the chapter titled "Where to Cut."

Second, if by language is meant not language taken in its ideality but language in its real reifications, Derrida will be the last to say that Husserl attempts to determine the essence and origin of that. "From one end of his itinerary to the other Husserl had to postpone every meditation on the essence of language *in general*."[11] Otherwise put, as Husserl puts it in words Derrida goes on to cite, it can in no wise be said that the pure morphology of "*Bedeutungen*" embraces the entire grammatical *a priori* in its universality, since it does not embrace, for example, the psychological *a priori* of communicative relations. Husserl explains in the second edition of the *Logical Investigations* that this is why he there describes his topic in Investigation IV as pure *logical* grammar.

The logical and the teleological

What *Strategies* disputes is Derrida's construal of Husserl's conception of the relation between the logical and the linguistic, hence of the implication I have drawn from Husserl's words in *Ideas* that he is going to use "*Bedeutung*" of meaning where meaning implies a connection between the linguistic and the logical, though perhaps not exclusively. *Strategies* denies that Husserl conceives the essence and *telos* of language to be the logical. In view of the history of the words "logic" and "*logos*," whether we agree with this denial will depend on the specific senses ascribed to the words "linguistic" and "logical," a matter touched on in our introduction. The sense or one of the senses Evans attributes to "linguistic" is brought out by the use he makes of a passage from the introduction of the second volume of the *Investigations*, which he says Derrida neglects and which he himself finds "curiously indefinite and uncertain" on the question of the relation between language and thought. This indefiniteness arises in part, it seems to me, from the fluidity of the notions of language and logic and now thought, all of which, not to mention the word "word," are possible translations of the word "*logos*."

How might language be the instrument of thought without being the instrument of logicality? Perhaps if it is not logical thought? If thinking proceeds according to what are sometimes called the laws of thought and if language is the medium in which thinking is done, then would not that language also be the medium of logicality? And would this not be so *a fortiori* if by logic is meant the science of those laws of thought or rules of inference and sense? Even if by some standard or other the thoughts do not make sense, if the putative thinker is thinking at all she or he probably thinks that what is running through her or his head is consecutive by some standard or other. And if in talking about thoughts it is possible to abstract from the thinker, it would seem to be possible also to abstract from the thinker in the case of the thoughts talked about.

However, perhaps Evans would accept all this. His point may not be one that turns on any difference between logicality and thought, even if it might look as though it must be if it is to be read as an objection to what he considers to be Derrida's mistaken attribution to Husserl of the view that "logicality is . . . reserved for language." Perhaps when Evans concludes from Husserl's endorsement of Mill that for Husserl "far from being the medium of logicality, language is the instrument of thought, a help to thought," the contrast on which what is being said here turns is that between medium and instrument. That this is so is not obvious, not, at least, if one takes the "*mittel*" of Husserl's word "*Hilfsmittel*" to mean what is meant by the noun "means." And that the word "medium" is not being contrasted with the words "instrument or help" seems to be implied by the recourse made to the qualification "essentially" when we read further on: "To be sure, some judgments may be dependent on linguistic expression for pragmatic reasons, but this by no means indicates that thought *essentially* moves in the medium of language."[12] I take it therefore that the paragraph in question is concerned primarily with the curious indefiniteness and uncertainty in Husserl's statements, and that the objection against Derrida is yet to be made.

The objection is that this text, in which Husserl, agreeing with Mill, deems verbal expression to be only pragmatically necessary and linguistic discussions only "'philosophically' indispensable preparations" for the construction of pure logic, undermines Derrida's claim that for Husserl the logical is the *a priori telos* of language, its proper destination.

The *telos* in question in this objection is described by Derrida as an *a priori* one. Therefore it would not be sufficient for Derrida to reply to this objection by saying that if indeed according to Husserl language is an instrument or means for something it would not be unreasonable to infer that that something, the logical, is the correlative end it serves, the *telos*, the destination to which it prepares the way. For that reply does not demonstrate the priority ascribed to the *telos*. But the relevance of the objection is put in doubt if the already noted ambiguity of the words "for Husserl" leaves it open for Derrida to reply that he is not questioning what Husserl *says* in one place, but is questioning his right to say it in the light of what that which he says in another place *means* or *commits him to* in fact, *en fait* or *en effet*. In another place or in that same place. For what is meant by the adverb and by the single quote marks that protect it in Husserl's phrase "'philosophically' indispensable preparations"? And what is meant by "meant" and what is meant by "say"? This question has a direct bearing on the insistence in *Strategies* that Husserl's prime concern is not with language in general but with meaning. Since, as already observed, this is also stressed in *Speech and Phenomena*, is it not disingenuous and question-begging for the author of the latter book to propose as a definition or translation of Husserl's word "*Bedeutung*" the phrase "vouloir-*dire*"? A curious indefiniteness and uncertainty might seem to surround what is said and meant in *Speech and Phenomena* about saying and meaning. In order to explain this apparent indefiniteness and to remove it, or at least explain why it cannot be removed, something needs to be said about Derrida's response to the practice of using in discussions of Husserl the French "*signification*" or the English "signification." I shall later make some remarks on what needs to be said about this issue.

Meanwhile, I suggest that the theses and counter-theses at issue in the disagreement between Evans and Derrida that I have been commenting on here can be saved from tautology and contradiction by taking the word "logic" in Husserl's sense of pure logical grammar and in the sense of the science of formal logic intended in the title of Mill's *System of Logic*. From Husserl's endorsement of Mill's statement that "language is evidently one of the principal instruments or helps of thought" Evans concludes that (for Husserl) "far from being the medium of logicality, language is the instrument of thought." Language is, as we might put it, combining metaphors from Husserl and Mill, no more than a garment that can be hung on the hallstand as we pass across the threshold into logic. Separating the metaphors, Derrida's suggestion could provisionally be said to be that at the center of logic we find the threshold once again and that the garment is more like our own skin, but a skin that is being continually torn and in constant need of new grafts. New graphemes, Derrida might say, where one would have to remember that the material of the grapheme, whether graphite, ink, silicon chip, or whatever, matters no more, as Husserl, Wittgenstein, and Saussure all remind us, than it matters whether chess pieces are made of ivory, plastic, wood, or whatever, provided they are not made of ice cream or custard for contests to be played at a high ambient temperature. My metaphorical formulation of what Derrida says is provisional like any other metaphor, but it is also provisional in that it is a guiding thread that could easily misguide as to his construal of the itinerary from the outside to the inside. To state his "position" in the form of a provocative slogan: rather than affirming a materialism against the idealism of Husserl's *Ideas,* he is insinuating that materialism insinuates itself into idealism. And his insinuation is itself an insinuation into the materialistic idealism of ideas from Husserl's *Ideas;* in particular of the difficult idea that Husserl expounds as follows in a paragraph of §124 of the first volume of that book:

> The attempt to clarify here the relevant structures meets with considerable difficulties. Already the recognition that after abstracting from the stratum of sensory verbal sound, there lies before us in reality still another layer which we here presuppose, thus in every case—even in that of a thinking that is ever so vague, empty and merely verbal—a stratum of meaning (*Bedeutung*) that expresses, and a substratum of expressed meaning—is not easy, nor again is the understanding of the essential connections of these stratifications easy. For we should not hold too hard by the metaphor of stratification; expression is not of the nature of an overlaid varnish or covering garment; it is a mental formation (*eine geistige Formung*) which exercises new intentional functions on the intentional substratum and experiences from the latter correlative intentional influences. What this new image in its turn amounts to must be studied in relation to the phenomena themselves and all their essential modifications.[13]

Derrida would welcome Husserl's plea for an image or diagram different from parallelism. My name for this different diagram would be chiasmus. What this new diagram or image or picture in its turn amounts to is precisely what Derrida articulates in, for example, his essay "La forme et le vouloir-dire." Expression is indeed a remarkable form, *eine merkwürdige Form,* as Husserl remarks in a sentence to which we shall have to return. The new image he refers to is that of a mirror-image and therefore an image that may fail to lead us either into the center of the maze or fail to lead us right out of it. For the mirror in question would be a peculiar intentional medium or means, *ein eigentümliches intentionales Medium,* of which the distinguishing mark, *Auszeichnung,* is that it performs a drawing-out and "ex-graving," *Auszeichnung,* which *wider-spiegelt* (there happens to be a hyphen in the German text) what it *widerspiegelt,* and de-picts, *dé-peint,* what it pictures, as though a picture theory of meaning would at the same time be a de-picture theory of meaning. This, at least, is the interpretation some of Husserl's remarks seem to demand. It differs from Derrida's interpretation in one respect, though not, I think, in such a way as to make any difference to the inference to be drawn. Derrida's interpretation of what Husserl calls the new intentional functions takes its cue from Husserl's assertion that the stratum of conceptuality constituted by expression is not productive. So, Derrida writes, the newness is constituted by its adding nothing new. Its productivity is its improductivity. What's more, the deformation in the reflected copy (the *Abbild*) is not due to its unilateral imaginative projection (*einzubildung*). The intentionality mirrored in this metaphor by the mirroring is itself formed/deformed by the intentionalities mirrored. It is itself, in the mathematical sense of the word, a function of them. As Husserl puts it, it undergoes correlative intentional influences (*Funktionen*). As though its headlong intentionality encounters an intentionality already heading toward it before it ever gets under way. Impression and expression are embrangled with each other aboriginally, from both the thither and the hither side of origin. What this tells Derrida is not simply that the spatio-materiality that marks the written word off from the spoken word cannot after all be left on the hallstand as we pass from the impure grammar of natural language to the pure grammar of logic. Nor does it mean simply that the pure logic of sense and senselessness is as soundless as the grave. It means that the materiality of writing and the materiality of speech in the ordinary senses in which speech and writing are opposed to each other are both expressions of what, since names are lacking, may be called proto-archaic writing or trace or, as above in chapter 3, telescripture. Proto-archaism has a transcendental idealistic ring. This is what some would call Derrida's linguistic idealism. But let us not forget that, listening to Husserl's voice, Derrida hears that the *sinnvoll* noetic–noematic intentionalities that are expressed as *Bedeutungen* are already impressed, marked, by the metaphor of writing in the ordinary sense. What has a transcendental materialist ring and what has a transcendental idealist ring are echoes and pre-echoes of each other, to the point that perhaps one could say of them what Wittgenstein says about realism and solipsism in the *Tractatus* (5.64), that they coincide. Or that they form a circle, one that is both prior and posterior to the hermeneutic one Heidegger tells us we must take care to enter in the right way, and to the dialectical ones of the phenomenology of spirit, however determinate the negation that generates those dialectical circles may be. The circle Derrida finds inscribed in the phenomenology of Husserl is "dialectical" only in the sense of the word Derrida comes around to regretting he had so much recourse to in *The Problem of Genesis in the Philosophy of Husserl*.[14] Maybe we should do better to speak of a chiasmus. Or of an ellipse. For there are two foci or a double focus in the figures Husserl and we have to invoke in order to attempt to describe the difficult structures to which he refers. And these descriptions are elliptical in the sense that there is something that is left out or left behind. Something and nothing, no thing: the very "is" of the "there is," of the existence—the *es gibt*—of the existent that gives and is given away?

Indication

Without this allusion to omission or falling short (*elleipō*) the metaphor of the ellipse would suggest self-enclosure. It might suggest that the strategy of deconstruction is to show that instead of expression being the commander (*stratēgos*) of indication, indication commands expression, and that expression is only a species of the genus indication. *Strategies* sometimes suggests that this is a strategy of deconstruction, for example when it refers to "the suggestion that expression might be a species of indication."[15] *Speech and Phenomena* does indeed, as *Strategies* puts it, "entertain the possibility . . . that expression is a species of the genus 'indication.'"[16] This possibility might seem plausible, it goes on to say.

> Since, as Derrida has already noted, a sign can exercize an indicative function without being an expression, whereas, as he keeps insinuating against Husserl's express intent, expression is inevitably indicative, there might be two kinds of indications: those that do and those that do not express a meaning. In this case, Derrida claims, speech would be "but a form of gesture," as to mean or "want to say" would be a form of indication.

Now, just before saying this *Strategies* observes quite rightly that Derrida has just returned to Husserl's text. "Let us continue our reading," the relevant paragraph begins. Derrida is purporting to report Husserl's text. However,

Evans considers that report to misreport at least in respect of what he says it insinuates, namely that "expression is inevitably indicative" or—not to omit a phrase Derrida's report employs—expression is caught up in an indicative process "as though in spite of itself (*comme malgré elle*)." But the attribution made by "as Derrida has already noted" should not lead us to overlook that Derrida is also attributing to Husserl the claim that Evans does not consider to be misplaced, namely that not every indication is caught up in expression. It is on the basis of these two claims attributed to Husserl by Derrida that the latter says "So (*donc*) one could be tempted to make of the expressive sign a species of the genus 'indication,'" and that "Therefore (*Dans ce cas*) one should end up by saying that speaking, whatever dignity or originality one still allows it, is only a form of gesture." The temptation referred to is not one to which Derrida believes we ought to succumb. To conclude that all expression is a species of the genus of indication would be to suppose that we are clear about what differentiates the one from the other. Since Derrida is questioning the clarity of this distinction he can no more be clear that expression is a species of the genus indication than in his view Husserl can be clear that expression is not in principle interwoven with indication. That is why he says that although for Husserl no discourse is possible which has no expressive core, "one could *almost* say that the totality of discourse is caught up in a web of indication."[17] Moreover, if we cannot (in principle?) be clear about the essential difference between expression and indication, it is not clear how Husserl can state restrictedly that only expression in communication is interwoven with indication in, as Derrida puts it, an "essential intimacy."[18] If there is any force at all in Derrida's questioning of Husserl it will not be reduced by his making quite explicit the restriction to communicative discourse in those reports of Husserl which in Evans's view are misreports. For that questioning is ultimately a questioning of Husserl's assumption that he and we understand the difference (*écart*) between the *de jure* and the *de facto,* between truths of reason and truths of fact. What Derrida is ultimately questioning is what Husserl begins with without questioning: this, as Quine might say, dogma of empiricism which is also a dogma of rationalism, and a dogma of those who simply oppose rationalism and empiricism to each other. This does not mean that we can dispense with such oppositions in the course of showing them to be less reliable than they may appear. The same holds for the distinction between logical and pragmatic necessity. Because the pragmatic—and indeed pragmatism like Quine's or Rorty's—is also caught up in this quasi-dialectic of indeterminate chiasmic opposition, it is not enough for Husserl or anyone speaking for him to say that the interweaving of expression with indication is only pragmatic. More will be said about this "only pragmatic," about the *de facto* and about the *de jure* toward the end of part 2 of this book, in chapter 12, which applies to the distinction between the human and the inhuman some of the unsimplifications encountered in this last chapter of part 1.

Vouloir-dire

In his discussions of Hegel Derrida frequently uses the word "*signification*" where Hegel uses the word "*Bedeutung.*" In his discussions of Husserl he is reluctant to define or translate "*Bedeutung*" in this way. Dorian Cairns and the standard French translation of Husserl's *Logische Untersuchungen* use "signification" and "*signification*" where Husserl uses the word "*Bedeutung.*" Derrida (like Findlay) does not use "signification" or "*signification*" for "*Bedeutung*" as employed by Husserl.[19] Derrida wants to avoid begging the question whether there can be a *signe* without *Bedeutung* and vice versa. Husserl wants to allow for *Bedeutungen* that can stand independently of verbal or other sensory signs or signifiers, and this would appear to be disallowed the moment "*Bedeutung*" is translated by "*signification.*"[20] In signification as classically understood a signifier stands for a signified, and the signifier is a physical or psychological entity, or, in Saussurian semiotics, a relation between such entities. Real indicative signs (*Anzeichen*) belonging to a historical culture are necessary only for communication, Husserl maintains, but are in principle dispensable in his envisaged science of purely expressive meanings. Hence Derrida's decision to suspend employment of the term "*signification*" and to employ instead the locution "*vouloir dire.*"

In a note in *Autrement qu'être ou au-delà de l'essence* occurs a sentence that may be partially translated as follows:

> A word has a "Meinung" which is not simply a *visée*. M. Derrida has felicitously and boldly translated this word by *vouloir dire*, uniting in its reference to [the] *vouloir* (which every intention remains) and to the exteriority of language (*langue*), the allegedly interior aspect of meaning (*sens*). See Derrida, *La voix et le phénomène.*[21]

In his translation of this note Alphonso Lingis renders "*vouloir*" by "will" and "*vouloir dire*" by "meaning to say." A difficulty presented by using "will" for "*vouloir*" is that it appears to license the translation of "*vouloir dire*" by "will to say." Alan Bass, who also has "meaning to say" for Derrida's (hyphenated) "*vouloir-dire*,"[22] comments that the French "*vouloir*" is etymologically connected with the Latin "*voluntas*" and that "*vouloir-dire*" carries the connotation that meaning is the "will to say."[23] Whether this phrase is good, bad, or dubious English, it sounds more emphatically voluntaristic than the French. Yet, judging by Littré, the French word too has had a checkered career in its journey from Latin. Having cited Vaugel's remark that *"vouloir"* is no longer used, at least in prose, with the sense of *"volonté"* (will) and Voltaire's doubtless mischievous observation that the use of *"vouloir"* as in *"le vouloir de Dieu"* ("the will of God") is archaic, Littré goes on to say that usage has since proved them wrong. Nevertheless, Levinas implies that there is a diminishing of this voluntaristic force of *"vouloir"* in the Husserlian phenomenological usage for which he says in his note that Derrida's *"vouloir-dire"* is so appropriate. This is implied in what Levinas writes about *"volonté"* in his next note, where he says:

> The Mediaeval term intentionality, taken up by Brentano and Husserl, does indeed have in scholasticism and in phenomenology a neutralized meaning with respect to the will (*volonté*). It is the teleological movement animating thematization that justifies the recourse, however neutralized it may be, to voluntaristic language.[24]

It is the voluntarist teleology of Husserl's theory of meaning or intending to say that provokes the attention of Derrida and Levinas, as the voluntarist teleology of German idealism provokes also the attention of Heidegger.

When Levinas says that *"vouloir dire"* refers *"au vouloir"* he means to say, like Bass, that meaning and meaning to say allude to the will. This is what he wants to say about what in English we call wanting or wishing or desiring to say—although, presumably, wanting, wishing, and desiring do not have here the operative force of the testamentary "I will" or of "We desire you to approach" pronounced by a monarch whose wish is our command, like the *vouloir* of God.

However, if we translate *"vouloir dire"* by "wanting to say" we restrict it to what a speaker wants to say, whereas *"vouloir dire"* is the phrase one might use to ask what a word, sign, or expression means, or what is meant by a signifier, except that this is a word we are studiously avoiding here for Derrida's reason reported above and for another reason he gives that we shall come to below. Because in English we do not ordinarily ask what a *word* wants to say but ask rather what it means, *"vouloir dire"* invites translation by either "want to say" or "mean to say" in order to cope with the difference between what a word means and what a speaker means.

But if we ask of a word simply what it means, we still have to ask what "means" here means. We could begin to answer this question by asking how the word "means" would be translated into German, whether by *"meinen"* or by *"bedeuten,"* either of which would be possible in appropriate contexts (as too in some contexts "*heissen*" would be). We are already put under an obligation to ask this question anyway by what one is tempted to call Levinas's bold statement about Derrida's bold and felicitous translation, leaving open for the moment whether Levinas's statement also will turn out to be felicitous. Is Levinas's statement too bold, too bold because based on a mistake?

He says that Derrida proposes "*vouloir dire*" as a translation of "*Meinung.*" For confirmation he refers to *La voix et le phénomène*. However, when we turn to the page in that book where Derrida first proposes his translation or, rather, what he calls a definition, we find that he is talking about Husserl's use of "*bedeuten*" and "*Bedeutung.*" He writes: "Without forcing Husserl's intention we could perhaps define, if not translate, *bedeuten* by 'vouloir dire.'"[25] Derrida's first illustration of the use of this phrase is one in which something is meant by a person rather than a word. This would not prevent his equating "*vouloir dire*" and "*meinen.*" But that he intends to make this equation is rendered *prima facie* unlikely by the fact that his second illustration is of something meant by an expression. Although "*meinen*" is very much at home in the first case, it is less so in the second if, as Derrida says Husserl says, "An expression is a purely linguistic sign." If an expression is a purely linguistic sign we should be able to ask what the meaning of the expression is where Husserl says "Logical meaning (*Bedeutung*) is an expression." Although philosophers and others inquire into the meaning of meaning, and we all frequently ask after the meaning of an expression, it is unclear what it could mean to ask after the meaning of *a* meaning—or to affirm its meaninglessness: "When a sentence is called senseless, it is not as it were its sense that is senseless" (Wittgenstein, *PI* 500).

The solution of this difficulty lies in reminding ourselves of Husserl's observation mentioned earlier that the expression "expression" is a remarkable form. If by "expression" is meant the verbal sound (*Wortlaut*) or the sign understood as signifier, we must not forget that it owes its expressiveness to the fact that the meaning it expresses (the *Wortbedeutung*) is already an expression, an expression of a *Sinn*. Hence "One may *not* say that an expressing act *expresses* a doxic act, if by expressing act one understands, as we do here at every point, the act of meaning (*Bedeuten*) itself." The expressing act *is* the doxic act. "If, however, the phrase 'expressing act' relates to the verbal sound, one could very well speak after the manner in question, but the sense (*Sinn*) would then be altered."[26]

Hence Levinas's phrase "exteriority of language" would present a difficulty if the exteriority intended were that of a factual historical language. Derrida's endeavor to avoid begging the question against Husserl in the manner described at the beginning of this section would have been undermined

immediately by his recourse to "*dire*." The saying must be the phenomenologically reduced expression which we shall soon find Husserl distinguishing
from empirically audible speech, and the exteriority Levinas refers to must
therefore be understood as the nonreal exteriority of a systematic field of
meanings relative to the *vouloir* of the subject intending meanings in that
field. Only when understood in this way can saying be an exteriority within
what Levinas refers to as the alleged interior aspect of meaning.

"*Meinung*" and "*visée*"

No less worthy of comment is the fact that in successive paragraphs Husserl
calls the meaning that the act of *Bedeuten* expresses a "*Meinung*" or "*Gemeint*" and a "*Sinn*." In the essay "La forme et le vouloir-dire," first published
in the same year as *La voix et le phénomène*, Derrida cites the following sentence in which Husserl distinguishes *Meinung* from *Bedeutung*: "Whatever
is 'meant (*visé, gemeint*) as such,' every meaning (*Meinung*) in the noematic
sense (*im noematischen Sinn*) (understanding by that the noematic nucleus),
whatever the act may be, is *susceptible of receiving expression through 'meanings' ('Bedeutungen,' 'vouloir-dire')*."[27] Because Husserl favors the term "*Bedeutung*" for noetic–noematic acts which are interwoven with linguistically
expressive acts, allowing "*Sinn*" to range over those and all other noetic–noematic acts, it follows that his "*Meinung*" cannot be defined quite generally as
"*Bedeutung*," though, precisely because "*Sinn*" covers linguistically expressed
meaning as well as all other noetic–noematic meanings, "*Meinungen*" can
include "*Bedeutungen*": that is to say, some cases of the former will be cases of
the latter. Hence, if "*vouloir-dire*" is what is meant by Husserl's "*Bedeutung*,"
it cannot define his "*Meinung*," and unless Husserl is using the former as we
saw in the first section of this chapter he prefers not to use it; it can translate it only where the sense that is meant is expressed linguistically. This is
why in his translation of the passage just cited Derrida gives "*vouloir-dire*"
for "*Bedeutung*." So it seems that in this particular context Derrida would
have had no objection to allowing "*vouloir-dire*" to stand as a translation of
"*Meinung*" if Husserl had written this instead of "*Bedeutung*" in that or another context where what is meant is the expression of a concept or proposition. Restricted to translation in such contexts, therefore, what Levinas says
about *translation* would to that extent be consistent with what Derrida writes
about *definition*. The apparent divergence between them can be decreased
by taking Levinas at his word when he writes "translate" and Derrida at his
when he writes "define, if not translate."

But what if we take each at his word when we read that for *"Meinung,"* noetic meaning or intending, and for *"gemeint,"* what is meant or intended, Derrida has, respectively, *"visée"* and *"visé"* (which latter Elie, Kelkel, and Schérer have also for *"vermeint,"* "supposed" or "presumed"), and read that Levinas, also commenting on Husserl, decries the translation of *"Meinung"* by *"visée"*? To think that *Meinung* is simply *visée,* Levinas goes on to say at the end of the second of the two consecutive notes I have cited from him, is to misconstrue the manner in which *Meinung* operates in identificatory statements. If this attribution of *Meinung* to a statement attributes *Meinung* to the statement as a whole, an escape is offered from the threat presented by the attribution of *Meinung* in the first of the two notes to a word: the threat of inconsistency with the common German usage according to which what a dictionary gives a word is its *Bedeutung* or *Sinn* but not a *Meinung.* The complexity of a thought, proposition, or proponible is greater than that of a word. A thought or *Annahme* in this Fregean sense can be someone's *Meinung* in the sense of what someone thinks, means, or intends in saying what he or she says. However, this escape route is of little avail, for when Levinas speaks of the *Meinung* of identificatory statements it is of the *Meinung* of identificatory expressions in them that he is speaking, words identifying that *of which* something is said. The word, *le mot,* about which he writes in his note is not a lexicographical item of *langue,* so we can at least set aside as irrelevant the fact, if it is one, that although a dictionary definition gives a word's *Bedeutung,* it does not give its *Meinung.*[28] The word in question in Levinas's note is the word being used in discourse, what French refers to as *langage.*

Even so, we still need to know why Derrida is apparently happy to translate or define *"Meinung"* in the noetic sense by *"visée"* while Levinas is not. I propose that we adopt the simplest and laziest explanation, namely that Derrida sees no special need to depart here from Ricœur's translation of *"Ideen"* because his chief concern in *La voix et le phénomène* is with what he has suggested we call *"vouloir-dire."* He is not here speaking on this topic *in propria persona*—or not very univocally, perhaps one should say in view of the general difficulty of deciding when he is ventriloquizing, when he is being ventriloquized, and when he, or for that matter anyone else, is talking absolutely straight. This explanation brings with it the bonus that it also explains why Mohanty finds in *La voix et le phénomène* little if any explicit reference to reference, assuming that in his commentary on Husserl Derrida would allow that *"viser"* and *"meinen"* have or can have the meaning of "refer."[29] Husserl's account of conceptual or propositional ("doxic") meaning provides Derrida with a sufficient basis for what he wants to say in that book.

This could also explain, thirdly, why Levinas does not take Derrida to task over the translation of *"Meinung"* by *"visée."* When Levinas comes across this in Derrida's text perhaps he reads it as only a citation. So that if anyone is being criticized by Levinas here it is Ricœur. How *"Meinung"* and *"meinen"* are translated into French matters more to Levinas because, although reference is peripheral to Derrida's analyses in *Speech and Phenomena*, it is the topic of many pages in *Otherwise than Being* and in some of Levinas's essays.[30] Levinas would probably be happy with Suzanne Bachelard's word "opinion" in those places where Husserl uses *"Meinung"* in the noematic sense of view, belief, *avis*, or, as English has it, opinion. For Husserl's *"meinen"* or *"Meinung"* with the noetic sense of "to intend," instead of the *"visée"* of the Ricœur translation followed by Derrida, she, anticipating by twenty years the two brief notes from *Otherwise than Being* with which the two somewhat less brief notes on them in this part of this chapter have been concerned, has *"vouloir dire"*!

Meaning reduced

If the confidence with which I question the statement that in a discussion of Husserl *"Meinung"* should be translated by *"vouloir-dire"* is bruised by the discovery that Suzanne Bachelard translates it in this way, and by the further discovery that Paul de Man gives this translation, albeit in a discussion of Hegel,[31] my unsureness as to whether my questioning of this definition or translation is justified is almost converted into sureness that it is not when I discover that in discussing Derrida's interpretation of Husserl, Jean-Luc Marion in at least one place translates *"vouloir dire"* by *"meinen."*[32] However, he elsewhere gives *"intention"* for *"Meinung"* and, as Derrida does, *"viser"* for *"meinen."* This leaves room for one to say, as I have said, that although it is problematic whether *"vouloir dire"* is synonymous with *"meinen"* and whether Derrida says this, *vouloir dire* and *bedeuten* involve *meinen*, that is, *viser* or intending. Although the noun *"vouloir-dire"* does not mean the same as the noun *"Meinung,"* verbal *vouloir dire* means *meinen*: to mean is to intend. It will be with Derrida's phrase *"vouloir-dire as visée"* that the remainder of this chapter will be concerned, particularly with putting it in the context of some of Marion's remarks about Derrida's reading of Husserl that treat not only of the relations of intention and meaning, *Bedeutung* and signification, but of these and their relations to, first, intuition, and, second, donation. It should be borne in mind throughout my comments on Marion's remarks that the latter are made within the frame of what he describes as a paradox: while Derrida develops Heidegger's conception of metaphysical thinking as thinking oriented toward and limited by the presence of the present and oblivious of the *Sinn* or, as Heidegger later says, truth of presencing as such, Derrida disagrees with Heidegger's view that Husserl's doctrine of categorial intuition outlines a "new beginning," seeing it rather as a continuation of the metaphysics of presence.

More precisely, according to Marion, Derrida does not deny that although Husserl regresses to the metaphysics of presence at least in the *Logical Investigations,* he nevertheless makes a step away from this toward what could be called a new beginning; Derrida disagrees with Heidegger as to the direction of this step. According to Marion, Heidegger identifies Husserl's new beginning in what the latter says or implies about giving, whereas Derrida locates Husserl's break with metaphysics in those places where he states or implies the autonomy of meaning with respect to intuition and hence with respect to knowledge. Thus, on this account of Derrida's reading of Husserl in *Speech and Phenomena* Husserl's regressive step is precisely the reverse of his step forward. It is a step back to making meaning depend on knowledge. On Marion's reading Derrida's argument for attributing this dependency thesis to Husserl rests partly on a misreading of the following passage in §11 of Investigation I:

> If "possibility" or "truth" is lacking, an assertion's intention can only be carried out symbolically: it cannot derive any "fulness" from intuition or from the categorial functions performed on the latter, in which "fulness" its value for knowledge consists. It then lacks, as one says, a "true," a "genuine" meaning.[33]

Marion maintains that Derrida is mistaken in supposing that this passage states Husserl's own position. It states rather, he says, the position adopted in natural consciousness which Husserl is concerned to refute. That this is so is indicated, Marion holds, by Husserl's quotation marks and by his use of the phrase "as one says" (*wie man zu sagen pflegt*). This position, Marion suggests, is the one adopted by Sigwart and Erdmann which Husserl criticizes for confusing signification and meaning with intuition. So, Marion asks rhetorically, does this criticism not forestall Derrida's statement of Husserl's position according to which "The originality of *vouloir-dire* as *visée* is limited by the *telos* of vision"?[34] It is relevant to note, in view of comments made earlier in this chapter, that Marion omits "*comme visée*" from Derrida's statement.[35] In any case, I am not convinced by Marion's reasons for saying that this statement is forestalled by Husserl's criticism of the position taken up by Sigwart, Erdmann, and natural consciousness.

Nor am I as sure as Marion is that already in Investigation I the autonomy of signification is assured by the ideality and intentionality of its evidence. How do ideality and intentionality guarantee the freedom of signification from intuition? Husserl's argument for ideality in §11 is an argument against the idea that the meaning of a judgment, for example the judgment "The three perpendiculars of a triangle intersect at a point," is tied to any particular person's judging it or to the sounds or marks through which that judgment may be expressed. Showing that the meaning of this expression is not tied to a subjective experience of these kinds is not showing that it is not tied to the intuition of a non-subjective ideal intentionality. All it shows is that what an expression says is not to be confused with the empirical phenomena it evinces (*kundgibt*).

A further stage of Husserl's argument in §11 against this kind of subjectivist semantics is reached in the passage Marion, Derrida, and I cite. This passage is part of an argument to show that the subjectivist account of meaning fails too in the case of absurd and false assertions. It seems to me that when Husserl puts the words "possibility," "truth," "fullness," and "genuine" in single quote marks and uses the phrase "as one says," he does not do so because he wishes to dissociate himself from these words lest he become contaminated with the subjectivist view he is criticizing. Nothing he says in this section of Investigation I or in the pages of Investigation VI where he keeps his promise to say more about the distinction between intending and fulfilling meanings gives grounds for supposing that he himself cannot subscribe to the idea that the difference between possible and impossible concepts and the difference between false or absurd assertions and true or genuine ones is a difference between non-fulfillment and at least eventual fulfillment. It might seem, and it would seem to Marion, that if this is accepted then we must reject Derrida's reading of Husserl according to which "The originality of *vouloir-dire* as *visée* is limited by the *telos* of vision." This only seems to follow if, like Marion, we pay too little heed to Derrida's phrase "the *telos* of vision." In the passage cited from Investigation I Husserl is specifically concerned with the distinction between, for example, false assertions and those that, as we all innocuously say, are true, convey knowledge, or have "value for (or as) knowledge." This *Erkenntniswert* depends upon a fulfillment that we might provisionally describe as non-telic or visional, in order to distinguish it from the telic, pro-visional fulfillment upon which, on Derrida's reading, Husserl makes false and absurd assertions depend. Marion seems to give too little attention to Derrida's statement that in the case of these assertions the intuitionistic imperative operates at a distance, *à distance*.[36] Only thus can he believe that Husserl's charge that Sigwart and Erdmann confuse meaning or signification and intuition forestalls Derrida's claim that for Husserl the originality of meaning as intending, *vouloir-dire* as implying *visée,* is limited by the *telos* of vision.

Derrida cannot be charging Husserl with identifying meaning with truth or knowledge, for he gives an account of Husserl's idea of the meaning of false and absurd assertions like "The circle is square." He is claiming that Husserl subscribes to something like the verificationist principle of meaning to the effect that the meaning of a proposition is the method by which it is strongly or weakly verified or falsified, except that meaning—or perhaps one should say meaningfulness—in the case of assertions like "The circle is square," to which no intuition of a fulfilling object is directly correlated, is borrowed from the meaning of assertions of the same grammatical form, e.g., "The square is rectangular," to which intuition of a fulfilling object can be directly correlated.

This "directly" and the terms "non-telic" and "visional" which I used provisionally, as I warned a paragraph ago, must now be qualified. Derrida's statement that for Husserl the origin of meaning as intention is telic, that is to say, an unoriginal origin because always already ahead of itself, is a statement about Husserl's view of the meaning of all statements and concepts, including those that are what we call true or genuine ones. So that if the meaning and meaningfulness of the latter is, as was provisionally said, visionally, non-telicly, or directly correlated with an objective vis-à-vis it, this correlation must still have a certain pro-visionality of its own. One needs to distinguish two kinds of pro-visionality. There is the pro-visionality due to the incompleteness of verification and of falsification, about which the question arises as to whether it obtains only for statements that are not necessarily true or necessarily false. And there is the pro-visionality exemplified earlier by "The circle is square," which (unlike "Green is or," where only the parts have meaning, and so more unlike "abracadabra" in the context of which not even the parts make sense) has meaning as a whole "symbolically" thanks to the grammatical form it shares with "The square is rectangular," "The perpendiculars of a triangle intersect at a point," and so on. The meaning of these latter, too, will have this second kind of provisionality in so far as their grammaticality is defined structuralistically by comparison with classes of statements to which they belong and by contrast with classes of statements to which they do not belong.[37]

Intuition

Marion produces a second argument, one co-opted from Heidegger's *History of the Concept of Time: Prolegomena,* to cast doubt on two claims made by

Derrida: that Husserl's formal syntax backslides into an intuitionist semantics; and that, despite his acknowledgment that meaning intentions may not be correlated directly with intuitional intentions, in defining source and *telos* in terms of each other Husserl *at one stroke* both describes and effaces the liberation of meaning from truth and of language from knowledge, effecting a "subtle displacement" (reflected in the displacement of a hyphen, one might add) such that true and authentic *vouloir-dire* is *vouloir* (or *désirer*) *dire-vrai*. Against these claims Marion now argues that because Derrida's reading of Husserl does not recognize that donation is a mode of presence and that for Husserl donation is a mode of meaning, it is *insufficiently radical*.[38] This argument turns on the implications of the "extension" (*Erweiterung*) of the concept of intuition from sensible to categorial referred to in Investigation VI. Focusing on the notion of being, Marion purports to show that already in the *Logical Investigations* being manifests itself in a modality of meaning that is absent from intuition itself, even from categorial intuition, namely the manner of givenness or giving, donation. If donation is a modality of presence, Marion adds, it is a *sui generis* modality of meaning.[39]

Consider his assertion, implicating as much Beaufret and Adorno as Derrida, that neither in the *Prolegomena* of 1925 nor in the Zähringen seminar of 1973 do Heidegger's accounts of Husserl's doctrine of categorial intuition say that categorial being is intuited or intuitable. They say only, and in Marion's estimation more radically, that categorial being is *given according to* categorial intuition.[40]

Many of the paragraphs of Heidegger's repetition of Husserl in the *Prolegomena* are occupied with the Kantian point repeated by Husserl that being is not a real, that is, sensible, predicate. But there and when Heidegger cites in the Zähringen seminar Simplicius's expostulation "O Plato, I see the horse all right, but what I do not see is the horseness," the point is not that one does not see being or universals like horseness, the redness of a house, and the whiteness of a piece of paper, but that one does not see them *as* (*wie*) one sees the horse, the house, and the piece of paper. "I do not see substance in the same way as I see the white paper." This at least leaves open that one sees substance in some other way, and that, if "substance" (*die Substanz*) is what Marion calls categorial being, then what Heidegger is reporting here is tantamount to an admission that categorial being is intuited, whether or not one so regards his statement in the *Prolegomena* that "being-alike (*Gleichsein*) can be seen at a glance."[41] That much can be said too about his statements in the seminar that substantiality appears more shiningly than the very thing that has appeared (*erscheinender als das Ershienene selbst ist*) and that "the 'is' . . . is 'seen.'" As for his further statement that in order to be "seen" the "is" must be given, the point, and Husserl's point as Heidegger interprets him, is that the substantiality or being of the sensible thing is not *deduced*, as it is by Kant, following the guiding thread of the forms of judgment. Substantiality is what in §40 of Investigation VI Husserl calls a surplus that is *intuited* along with the sensible qualities. Husserl's phrase is *"Überschuss in der Bedeutung,"* Heidegger's is *"Überschuss an Intentionen."* But this surplus or excess over and above the sensibly real qualities, that is to say Husserl's doctrine of categorial intuition, cannot derive its importance as the focal point (*Brennpunkt*) of Husserl's thinking from the fact that by categorial intuition givenness is brought on to the scene. For givenness is already given with sensible intuition. And is not giving, indeed self-giving, although not *as* giving, given there too—*in* the very *sensibility* of sensible intuition and not only *with* it on account of its being supplemented by categorial intuition? For like all other "acts," all intuition is an intention that, according to §10 of Investigation VI, calls for fulfillment, which, according to §13 of Investigation V, is itself an act and therefore an intention. Although the word "intention" is wittingly employed by Husserl with an ambiguity that covers both aiming (*Abzielen*) and achieving the target, in both senses there is an act (*Akt*). And although this act is not to be confused with an activity (*Betätigung*), is not the intentional act of sensible intuition an act that gives giving to the essence of sensibility? Or, although in terms of Husserl's response to Kant it is not attributable to any spontaneity of the understanding or reason, would any giving apparently attributable to sensible intuition alone be properly attributable rather to its categorial excess? Or does this very notion of excess preclude this either/or? Perhaps Husserl's breakthrough is the warning that we should not take too literally the metaphor of stratification adverted to earlier in this chapter.

Donation

Following Heidegger, Marion maintains that the breakthrough made by Husserl's phenomenology consists neither in the widening of the notion of intuition from the sensible to the categorial nor in the thesis of the autonomy of meaning, but in the unconditional primacy accorded to the *donation* of the phenomenon.[42] In support of this he cites the statement made by Husserl in 1907 that "Absolute donation (*Gegebenheit*) is ultimate"[43] and points out that when in 1913 Husserl affirms the intuitionistic principle of all principles he affirms also that the perception of essence is a primordially donative act, an *originär gebender Akt*.[44] Already in 1900–1901, in §11 of Investigation V, Husserl writes "What is given to consciousness is essentially the same whether the presented object exists or is a fiction or even perhaps an absurdity." Marion refers in a footnote also to p. 5 of §2 of the introduction to Volume II of the *Investigations*. He does not cite the words he has in mind, but one may guess that they are those in which Husserl says that phenomenological analysis must not content itself with the data of linguistic usage. If this is the statement to which Marion is alluding and this statement is taken to imply reference to the givenness of pure logical concepts which the clothing of linguistic usage may conceal, it should be noted that Husserl expresses this implication by saying that "Logical concepts, as valid thought-entities, must have their origin in intuition." But is not an origin ultimate? Granted that it is, it does not follow that absolute donation is not ultimate too. However, it does appear to follow that if the origin that is ultimate is intuition, then the donation that is ultimate is the donation of intuition: not the donation of meaning as opposed to the donation of intuition, but maybe the donation of meaning through the donation of intuition—of, particularly, non-sensible intuition, including categorial intuition.

Would this still be the reduction of donation to intuition which Marion and Heidegger resist on Husserl's behalf? It depends on how we interpret the "of" in the phrase "donation of intuition," whether as a subjective genitive or as an objective genitive. Heidegger takes Husserl's "extension" to be guided by an analogy between sensible and categorial intuition. He is unwilling to limit the point of the analogy to their both being intuition. The point of the analogy is donation on his reading of Husserl's widening. But is this not a distinction without a difference if we take seriously such statements by Husserl as the statement in §65 of *Ideas I*, shortly after referring to a widening of this concept, that "under the title 'givennness,' where no contrary indication is added or obviously implied by the context, we understand at the same time [*mitverstehen*] being apprehended [*Erfasstheit*], and, where the givenness of the essence is concerned, the being apprehended primordially?"[45] Heidegger concedes that Husserl reaches only the brink of acknowledging the importance of givenness, and that, having glimpsed it, whether because he is too bedazzled by what he sees or because his vision is too narrowed by the blinkers of metaphysical tradition, he averts his eyes. But, one may ask finally, what is the difference between saying this, as Marion too seems willing to say with Heidegger, and saying, with Derrida, that Husserl both faces and effaces the emancipation of meaning and language from truth and knowledge? Perhaps a beginning of an answer to this question would be to remember the difference between, on the one hand, a present as that of which one may claim knowledge and which one may identify by giving it a name, and, on the other hand, a present as that which one may acknowledge and for which one may give thanks. It is perhaps this difference that, with the assistance of hindsight from Heidegger's, Marion's, and Derrida's own analyses elsewhere of the gift,[46] can be discovered in Husserl's analyses of dated time and the unnamed source-point of time's giving. It is the difference between two representations of representation, the one with which the first part of the book has been chiefly occupied and the one toward which its second part will gravitate.

Re-introduction

So far we have been considering chiefly the case where representation is se-mantic. But consider now more closely the case where representation is, for instance, ethical. Consider first such a case on analogy with legal representa-tion. Advocates represent their clients at the bar by making representations on their behalf. To make a representation in this context is to make or defend a claim. Further, it can be to make (or defend) a claim that a client has a claim. And the latter claim can be one that is founded in the claimant on behalf of whom the advocate pleads. Or on behalf of *which* the advocate pleads. For claims can be judged to be possessed by claimants not capable of the kind of intentional behavior manifested by their putting a claim on their own behalf into words. Their claim may need to be voiced by proxy advocates. These will usually conduct their case by appealing to matters of fact and of law. Usually too, so will lay persons making ethical judgments, though our appeals to moral principles will be motivated ethically only when such appeals to the general or universal are inspired by respect for the individuals concerned in their singularity.

"Concerned." This is another word of which the uses straddle the realms of the semantic and the legal and moral, the realm of, on the one hand, the true-or-false, a choice that may turn on what name one is called by, and, on the other hand, what one is called to do. These hands cross in so far as the name I am called by, the name to which I answer, is a quasi-legal aspect of how I am called to behave and how others are called to behave toward me, which are matters of morals. Reflected in this crossing, which is a crossing of the constative (for example, "My name is John") and the performative (for example, "I (hereby) admit that my name is John"), is the connection between the name I carry and my having been thus named. This connectedness is marked in Austin's recognition that the constative and the performative are not mutually exclusive opposites, for I can say "I hereby constate." To cite another illustration of the complicity that interests us here, the connectedness just referred to is incorporated in the duality of the notion of recognition itself (for instance Austin's recognition just mentioned) as standing for an acquisition of knowledge and, secondly, for more or less formally ritualized acknowledgment. Remember too that the notion of concern is invoked when one tries to describe the grammar of the middle voice. Grammarians commonly inform us that a verb used in the Greek, Sanskrit, etc. middle voice is one in which the "action" it describes somehow *concerns* the bearer of the verb's grammatical subject. One of the items on the agenda of the present book is the question as to the way in which that concern is enacted or suffered where the verb connotes a representation that is both a standing for and a standing up for.

Representation may be either semantic, a relation between a sign and something signified, or pragmatic, a relation or a more far-reaching proto-relation that is the condition of relationality between a sign and sign-users. Pragmatic representation will cover my standing for someone or something in the sense of exercising advocacy. And representation in this pragmatic and practical sense is operative when, announcing their names, I present someone to somone else. I am called, other things being equal, to give them the right name, to apply to them the *mot juste,* to do them at least nominal justice, to not misrepresent them. So that when we try to describe a phenomenon, as when someone practices phenomenology of language, his or her phenomenological representation of "the things themselves" (Husserl's *Sachen selbst*) is not a representation of the natural as opposed to the conventional or cultural or legal or aesthethico-politico-religious. The descriptive representations proposed by the phenomenologist are, as is any other account of meanings, articulated chiasmically with the prescriptions and norms that are institutive and constitutive of a culture, a legal system, an ethical practice, etc. Wherever the subject matter is meaning it is a matter of what is right and what is wrong, correct or incorrect. This is part of the reason why in the *Tractatus Logico-Philosophicus* Wittgenstein infers that the form of representation cannot be represented in a soft or hard and rigorous science of meaning, for to make a statement about a norm or a law is to turn its imperativity into an indicative, to neutralize its prescriptivity, to acquire the fateful *knowledge* of good and evil, which is not the same as being able to distinguish the one from the other. That the very conceiving of a meaning evacuates it of the normativity intrinsic to meaning is also part of the reason why, although Husserl claims to be founding a rigorous science of logical grammar, he lays so much emphasis on his responsibility and on the responsibility of those he hopes will take that science further. This again is part of the reason why, of those who attempt to take that science forward, one who acknowledges that responsibility, namely Derrida, encounters difficulties in some of the things Husserl says or implies regarding presence. One of the difficulties Derrida encounters arises from his wish to do justice to the need he is persuaded of by Levinas to recognize not only, on the one hand, the conceptual connection between semantic representation and cultural normativity, but also, on the other hand, the tie between that doublet (both facets of which have to do with cases, that is to say with particulars of a certain kind, instances of a concept) and what Levinas calls the ethicality of the face, that is to say of the singular. When I say that Derrida wishes to do justice to this, I mean that he wants to do justice to a certain justice that is not a matter of applying a law, not merely legal justice or right. He wants to do justice to the justice that is not only legal, not only *mishpat,* but is justice inspired by concern for the other's well-being, the *zedekah umishpat* of Genesis 18:19, justice animated by the kiss of life we call love, despite the etiolation this last word has undergone. Unadulterated love is the love that passes Simone Weil's test of the lover's imagining, in the beloved's absence, that the beloved may be dead. But it is not only Romantic love of which it may hold that "Un seul être vous manque, et tout est dépeuplé," "When she is gone, gone too is everyone else" (Lamartine). And what are the implications of "You mean the whole world to me"? One of the difficulties Levinas and Derrida probe arises from their hearing of the call for justice vis-à-vis the human law and for justice vis-à-vis the human face to be simultaneously maintained, and from a fear of being too precipitate in affirming that these different senses of justice are reconciled in justice before the law and face of God. In default of that exit from aporia and in default of a very subtle revision of notions of God, how are we to imagine, to represent, the logical grammar of the relation between a Responsibility of address that Levinas calls Saying and the responsibilities of what he calls the Said, responsibilities of one's historical circumstances, of, in F. H. Bradley's phrase, "my station and its duties"? Is this a difficulty that has to be endured? Is it an ingredient in at least the human being's temporality and freedom, the difficult freedom announced in the title of one of Levinas's collections of essays?

I beg leave to remind readers that in the preceding paragraphs I have used several times the word "imagination." I beg leave to remind readers too that this is a possible translation of the German *Vorstellung*, and that another possible translation of that German word is "representation." I shall remind the reader below that what we call imagination in English is often called *Phantasie* by Husserl, and that Kant's preferred word is *Einbildungskraft*. I note some of the consequences of these differences of translation in my *The HypoCritical Imagination*.[1] Notwithstanding these differences, I believe that many of the things Kant says in his Critiques about imagination as "constructing" remain valid for an analysis of *Vorstellung* and *Phantasie*, especially the idea that the "con-" in "construction" connotes a building-together of, on the one hand ("starting from above"), the universality of the law as sought in what he labels reflective judgments, and, on the other hand ("starting from below"), the particularity sought by what he labels determinant judgments. Once we raise the question of how singulars, as distinguished from particulars, relate to this con-strual of imagination we find ourselves obliged to reconstruct (or/and de-con-struct) imagination as imadgination in order to mark how the imagination as treated in the first and the third Critiques is penetrated by the moral and religious issues treated in the second of the Critiques and in *Religion within the Limits of Reason Alone* when these are exported beyond the universality of principles and archic law to the Sovereignty of God or to the an-archy of the otherwise singular. This exportation beyond Kant (and Hegel), which is also an exportation beyond what in *A Theory of Justice,* thinking of Kant, John Rawls calls "reflective equilibrium,"[2] is what gives rise to the difficulties experienced by Derrida and Levinas (and Kierkegaard) touched on above and to be returned to in the following chapters, in which an attempt is made to move toward a phenomenological and logico-geographical representation of representation that will respond not only to the human but also to the inhuman—for example the animal, whether canine, feline, etc.—and the divine. These chapters are gathered there under the heading "Table Talk" because they have to do directly or indirectly with the preparation, eating and not eating or sacrificing of meals, not to mention (most of us don't) the sacrifice of the animals that precedes or, with certain foods, is accomplished by their being consumed, either at a dining-room table or at that kind of table we call an altar. It is as though, in the spirit of some verses of Genesis, being consumed is being consummated, transsubstantiative *Aufhebung,* this German term being the one Hegel defines as a process of digestion that is both raising up and elimination.

The chapters that follow provide food for thought on food and on questions to my mind every bit as serious as those discussed in the *Banquet* of

Plato and, I would say, no whit less seriously religious—in a sense of the word "religious" that marks out a space between the religions and secularity—than those aired in the *Table Talk* of Martin Luther, who expresses his opinion of transubstantiation when he says there "I think that the bread and wine remain, just as the water remains in baptism and just as the human voice remains when I preach," adding, with Romans 1:16 in mind, "Yet it is in truth the power of God, as Paul calls it."[3] The opinion I express in *Margins of Religion* is that, whether or not they owe their existence to a divine creator, the elements and the human voice are already sacred. So it could be that the sacred and the religious in my widened sense of the word will haunt all of the chapters to come. However, only the first of them treats of theology, of an apparent turn of phenomenology toward that, and it is toward that alleged turn that we now turn our attention.

PART TWO

TABLE TALK

SEVEN

Approaches to Quasi-theology via Appresentation

Methodological phenomenology

The strictness of a conception may be measured in two ways. A conception will be more strict than another if it requires the fulfilment of a larger number of possible criteria than the other. Alternatively, it may be more strict than another if it insists on the fulfilment of a particular criterion that for the other conception is one of an optional set. That is to say, one may measure strictness either according to the standard of the number of conditions deemed necessary or according to the degree of necessity that is deemed to attach to a particular condition. So a conception that is more strict and more demanding than another according to one of these ways of measuring strictness may not be more strict according to the other way of measuring it.

Emphasized in the methodology of "the phenomenological turn" made by Husserl are (1) intuition or evidence as invoked in "the principle of all principles," (2) intentionality, (3) description of the as such, (4) bracketing off by reduction of matters of empirical or metaphysical fact and existence, (5) the horizonality of consciousness. That at least some of these factors overlap others among them becomes plain once we consider Husserl's assertion in the

Crisis that "in all cases the world is pregiven and, within this horizon, objects are given. . . . The pregiven world is the horizon which includes all our goals, all our ends, whether fleeting or lasting, in a flowing but constant manner, just as an intentional horizon-consciousness implicitly 'encompasses' ('*umfasst*') [everything] in advance."[1] Here Husserl is purporting to describe the world experienced in our natural straightforward attitude to it. The "flowing but constant manner" in which the world is lived under that aspect is something that becomes explicit when we make the phenomenological turn in order to describe the horizon of the pregiven in its howness. In this changed perspective "nothing shall interest us but precisely that subjective alteration of manners of *givenness*, of manners of appearing and of the modes of validity in them, which in its constant process, synthetically connected as it necessarily flows on, brings about the coherent consciousness of the straightforward 'being' of the world."[2] Pregiven in this synthetic connectedness is not only the pregivenness of the retained past, but the simultaneous protentiveness of the future. It is a law of essential being, Husserl tells readers of §82 of *Ideas*, "that every *present moment* of experience has about it a fringe of experiences, which also share the primordial now-form, and as such constitute the one *primordial horizon* [*Originaritätshorizont*] *of the pure Ego*, its total primordial *now*-consciousness."[3]

Hence it is not surprising to learn that, as reported by Jean-Luc Marion, Levinas once said to him, "Without horizon there is no phenomenology." Nor is it any wonder that Derrida agrees with Levinas on this. However, all three of these—as well as, we shall see, Michel Henry—discern a point at which there occurs a suspension of the horizon and therewith an at least partial suspension of Husserlian phenomenology. Horizonality, the last of the characteristics listed above, is for all four of these dissidents a component of Husserlian phenomenology. Yet Levinas would repeat on his own behalf Derrida's avowal, "I would like to remain phenomenological in what I say against phenomenology."[4] Indeed, in saying this Derrida takes himself to be echoing Levinas. "There are many places where he [Levinas] says that we have to go phenomenologically beyond phenomenology. That is what I am trying to do, also. I remain and want to remain a rationalist, a phenomenologist."[5]

In support of this apposition of rationalism and phenomenology Derrida could have referred to pages in Husserl where reason and rationality are topics, for instance the fourth section of *Ideas I* titled "Reason and Reality" or the second and third chapters of that section titled "Phenomenology of Reason" and "Grades of Generality in the Ordering of the Problems of Theoretic Reason." The pages of Husserl that Derrida in fact refers to here are those of the fifth of the *Cartesian Meditations*. These are the very pages that are crucial also in Levinas's departure from phenomenology. In neither case is this only a departure in the sense that, as a matter of empirical history and biography, Husserl's phenomenology was what Levinas and Derrida were reading and studying early in their philosophical careers. To go beyond phenomenology historically in this way would not necessarily be to go beyond phenomenology *phenomenologically*. It would not necessarily be simultaneously to go against phenomenology while managing to remain phenomenological. What then is it to do this?

A way of having one's phenomenological cake and eating it too is indicated by Derrida when he writes:

> what leads me in this matter about the non-phenomenality of the gift is also the non-phenomenality of the "other" as such, which is something I learned from Husserl's *Cartesian Meditations*. Husserl says that in the case of the alter ego we cannot have pure intuition, an originary perception of the other; we have to go through appresentation. That is the limit of phenomenology that appears within phenomenology. That is the place where I work also.[6]

That is the place of the possibility of taking place which is yet an impossibility, but an impossibility that is other than straight negation of possibility as defined in the classical logic of noncontradiction, and other than the negation of negation operative in dialectical logic that can lead to a conceptual synthesis as smooth as the perceptual synthesis of the givenness and pregivenness envisaged in Husserl's sentences about these cited above. This impossibility of possibility that is not simply opposed to possibility, but is a destabilization of power and faculty, is the condition that makes it possible for one to pass beyond phenomenology phenomenologically.

"Impossibility of possibility" is the phrase Levinas uses for what he maintains has priority over the being toward one's own death that is according to Heidegger the possibility of impossibility. The impossibility of possibility according to Levinas is the other's death, the ethical impossibility encapsulated in the other's commanding me "You shall not kill," defying my "I can" and limiting while giving power to the freedom of my will. Observe that in the sentences just cited from Derrida a reference is made to "the 'other' as such," the "as such" being the third of the conditions mentioned in our list of the conditions that might be judged constitutive of phenomenology. That is how it is regarded by Derrida. "Phenomenology without as such!" he exclaims, leaving us in no doubt that he believes that if Marion is abandoning the as such he is abandoning phenomenology.[7] And Marion signals his own awareness that in not remaining faithful to the as such he is exposing himself to being charged with a second heretical break with phenomenological orthodoxy beyond his already avowed readiness to relax the condition of horizonality, that is to say, as the Greek root of this word says, determination and being determined.

What is the as such? What is the as such as such or not as such? What is the *kath auto*, the *per se*, the *comme tel*, the *en tant que tel*, or the *als solche*? These phrases sometimes translate what is said by Husserl in phrases of the form "*x* as *x*," as in, for example, "*Erfahrung als Erfahrung*," "experience *qua* experience," near the beginning of §7 of *Ideas*. In the passage cited above from the discussion between Derrida and Marion presided over by Richard Kearney "as such" qualifies "the 'other'," and the other understood as the alter ego is described as that of which, according both to Husserl and Derrida, no pure, originary intuition or perceptual evidence can be had. That is to say, the possibility of such perception is not entailed by something's being described as such-and-such "as such." At least no such entailment holds according to Derrida.

Where does Marion stand on this matter? The matter at stake between him and Derrida is the question of the givenness or otherwise of the gift, "the matter about the non-phenomenality of the gift," of whether or not the givenness (*Gegebenheit*) or being given (*Gegebensein*) of the gift can appear. The inclination to deny that it can arises from the so-called paradoxes of the gift treated by Marcel Mauss in the *Essay on the Gift*[8] and analyzed by Derrida in *Given Time: 1. Counterfeit Money*.[9] Giving seems to be impossible because it seems to turn into exchange once a gift presents itself as a gift, as a present that provokes a return from the donee, if only in the form of gratitude and whether the gratitude be expressed or not.

Derrida qualifies not only the "other" with the phrase "as such." He writes also of "the gift as such." This means for him that the gift does not entail givenness (*Gegebenheit*) if this is understood as phenomenality. The gift, Derrida maintains, does not appear. This does not mean that there can be no gift. The gift as such is not an object or objective of theoretical knowledge. Therefore it is not an object or objective of phenomenology as this is understood by Derrida. Phenomenology, he writes, purports to be constative. As is said in our list of characteristics, it is descriptive. In order for phenomenology to be descriptive it must meet also the first of the requirements or axioms in our list, Husserl's principle of all principles, according to which "*every primordial dator Intuition* [Anschauung] *is a source of authority* [Rechtsquelle] *for knowledge, that whatever presents itself in 'intuition'* ['Intuition'] *in primordial form* (as it were in its bodily reality), *is simply to be accepted* [hinzunehmen] *as it gives itself out to be* [als was es sich gibt], *though only within the limits in which it then gives itself* [da gibt]."[10]

The quotation marks around the learnèd word *"Intuition"* may be intended by Husserl to indicate its Latin formality. It also marks the generality pointed out a few pages earlier when, having glossed "primordial dator intuition" as "immediate 'seeing,'" with quotation marks again, he warns that this is to be understood as "not merely the sensory seeing of experience, but seeing in general as primordial dator consciousness of any kind whatsoever" including "the meaning of judgements, or the proper essential nature of the objects and contents of judgements."[11] Intuition as Husserl would have it understood includes categorial intuition. It includes, as Marion insists, significations. And Derrida agrees with this interpretation of Husserl. That is to say, he and Marion agree that at least the first and the last items on our list are axioms of the methodology of strictly Husserlian phenomenology at at least one stage of Husserl's thinking.

Why is it then that while in *Phenomenology and the "Theological Turn"* Janicaud includes Marion among those whose turning of phenomenology toward theology he criticizes on the grounds that it falls short of phenomenological method in doing so, Derrida seems not to be included in that company?[12] The explanation for this could be that Derrida insists on more of the requirements in our list being met than Marion does and that those to which Marion adheres are fewer than Janicaud considers essential to Husserlian phenomenology. Another explanation could be that Janicaud considers that Marion interprets one or more of the requirements or axioms in a way the former takes to be untypical either of one variety of Husserlian phenomenology or of phenomenology more generally. Perhaps he agrees with Derrida's hypothesis "that Jean-Luc Marion, of course, has his own concept of phenomenology."[13] Might what leads Derrida to say that Marion has his own concept of phenomenology be what leads Janicaud to say that Marion is not loyal to the laws of Husserlian phenomenology? Suppose that Marion abides by a principle of all principles in a way that allows for Revelation, not just revelation, to be an object or objective of intuition, including intuition that floods every concept and therefore every phenomenon, that is to say, overbrims every product of a marriage between intuition and concept. One might well wonder whether that would be in the spirit of Husserlian phenomenology. However, if this would amount to a difference between Marionian and Husserlian phenomenology, the difference would not be a good reason for Derrida or anyone else to distinguish Marion's phenomenology from any other phenomenology whatsoever. It would not be this because Marion himself says that at the point at which revelation and its saturated phenomena are superseded by Revelation, the phenomena and phenomenology are in a certain manner superseded by theology. But the manner of this supersession would still allow for phenomenology to serve as an ancillary to theology in that phenomenological descriptions of how concepts may be overbrimmed, "saturated," or flooded by intuition in the revelation of phenomena involving historical events, idols, flesh, or icons could serve as a guide to descriptions of the conditions of possibility of Revelation, notwithstanding that only theology can pronounce on the actuality or non-actuality of Revelation.[14] In Marion's earlier treatment of saturated phenomena Revelation overlaps with the fourth of the kinds of phenomenality just listed. Revelation with an uppercase initial overlaps with revelation and so with what Marion includes among topics of phenomenology. In his later treatment the four "banal" kinds of saturated phenomenality are kept separate from revelation and the possibility of Revelation. From this follows a separation between phenomenology and theology,[15] notwithstanding that the transition from the former to the latter is facilitated once the distinction between *Offenbarkeit* and *Offenbarung* is blurred when "revelation" is spelled with a lower case initial. This typographical turn yields an ambivalent middle term that might be suspected of smoothing too conveniently the path to the turn from phenomenology to theology in France. In order to get a fuller story of how this turn is taken in France, a little attention must be given at this point to how it is prepared for in post-Husserlian Germany, for instance by Heidegger's interpretation of Luther's statement "Faith is permitting ourselves to be seized by the things we do not see."[16]

Presents and presence

Religious faith as thus defined by Luther is presupposed by theology as conceived by Heidegger. But phenomenology as conceived by Heidegger would be independent of such religious faith. The disclosure or opening (*Offenbarkeit*) proper to phenomenology differs from religious Revelation (*Offenbarung*) in being independent of religious credal commitment. This means for Heidegger that phenomenology is independent also of theology. This inference would be questioned by philosophers who hold that there is sense in the idea of a science of God that abstracts from religious commitment. It would be questioned too by philosophers (myself among them) who argue that the religious understood as dependent for its sense on historical religions must not be confused with the religious understood as not thus dependent.[17] Janicaud, like Heidegger, is thinking of the religious as thus dependent. Although he would probably not want to say that religion in either of these senses plays an essential role in the phenomenologies of the French philosophers of whom he treats, we shall find that at least one of these philosophers, Michel Henry, presents *prima facie* a serious challenge to the possibility of such a neutral reading of his phenomenology.

What would it be for the religious in either of the senses just distinguished to play a nonessential role in phenomenological thinking? The answer to this question would turn on our interpretation of the fourth in the above list of requirements that might be taken to be axiomatic for phenomenology. It would depend on how we conceive the relation of empirical or metaphysical existence to the eidetic and transcendental. It is arguable that human nature happens to be so constituted that presence to an *eidos* presupposes presence at some time or other to an empirical instance of an *eidos*, whether an *eidos* of the given empirical example or an *eidos* at least of some other given empirically experienced particular. The essentiality could be described as the essentiality of an occasion, not the essentiality of a ground. Like Husserl, one could be tempted to flirt with the notion that the availability of an example or instance would be only a contingent necessity, and that "in principle" there could be eidetic givens without non-eidetic data. The situation has the same structure as that which motivates Husserl's *Crisis*. On the one hand, the archive of a science, whether a formal or an experimental science, is what makes objectivity possible in that science. On the other hand, the documents and other records thanks to which scientific data are passed on distance the scientist from the observations on which the theories of the science or their refutations are based. The difficulty here is a difficulty of memory. It arises from the paradox of remembering. A mnemonic helps one remember, but its remembering is predominantly rote: rote because, more often than not, written. So it can also help one to forget. It can divert one from engagement with what one is wanting to remember, as engagement with the religious would be shelved in theology or meta-theology as distinguished by Heidegger from faith.

Remembering and forgetting as just described are a remembering and forgetting of the given and pregiven in the senses that arose when near the beginning of this chapter Husserl's conception of horizon was explained. These pregivens are cases of *Gegebenheit*, this latter being the concept over the scope of which Derrida and Marion take different views. Givenness, including the givenness of the gift, ranges according to Marion more widely than Derrida is ready to grant. According to Derrida, its range is restricted, as is the range of horizonal remembering, by an absolutely unrememberable past corresponding with and inseparable from an absolute future irreducible to a fullness of presence. Being irreducible to presence, this absolute past and this absolute future are not subject to constative description. Beyond theoretical knowledge, they belong rather to the field of something like what Kant calls thinking, in contrast to knowing, and they belong to what we have been calling faith. They belong to the field of practical faith, as confirmed by Derrida's assigning them to the field of performativity, except that their belonging is also an unbelonging, and their field is the displaced place marked by what, in the wake of the *Timaeus*, Derrida calls "*chōra*," which brings with it the unpresence that is alluded to when Jesus says to Thomas "blessed are they that have not seen, and yet have believed" (John 20:29). But whereas this unpresence is an unpresence that is presupposed by a faith arising in a special religion, Derrida is investigating the unpresence of a faith that arises in "religion in general," religion without [special] religion. This faith is, on the one hand, distinguished from the faith of positive religions and theologies. Because, on the other hand, it is distinguished also from knowledge, it is distinguished from the knowledge that is the topic of the would-be rigorous science of phenomenology. The conceits Derrida is endeavoring to discover or invent or forge are quasi-transcendental conditions of the opposition between the phenomenological and the specifically religious or theological. These quasi-conditions are the denizens, that is to say legitimated asylum-seekers, of the displaced place that Derrida calls *chōra*, religion without religion, and religion in general. They are not plain transcendental conditions but quasi-conditions because they are the conditions not of plain possibility, but also of un-possibility, of what is more than what is constituted by law, more than what is legitimated universally, more even than a particular case. This more is the more of the singularity that happens when one human being says to another "I promise" or when human beings hear those words addressed to them by God.[18]

In a manner that mirrors Janicaud's precaution, Derrida writes of Marion that "he cannot practice any phenomenology without at least keeping some axioms of what is called phenomenology—the phenomenon, the phenomenality of the appearance, meaning, intuition, if not intuition, at least the promise of intuition, and so on."[19] Then he says, "I do not say this against phenomenology. I do not say this even against religion or even against *donum Dei*." Derrida is no more "against religion" than is Janicaud against whatever religions, if any, are embraced by the French phenomenologists whose application of phenomenological method he judges deficient.

So far Derrida and Janicaud are in step with each other. Whether the next step taken by Derrida is one that Janicaud would take, it is one that discerns a structure sufficiently flexible to deter Janicaud from including

Derrida among the phenomenologists he criticizes for not attending to the demands of phenomenological method. This is how Derrida describes this further step: "I try to think the possibility of this impossibility [the possibility of the impossibility of a phenomenology of the gift] and also to think the possibility of *donum Dei,* or the possibility of phenomenology, but from a place which is not inside what I try to account for." Does this not go against what we cited him as saying earlier when we reproduced his statement "I would like to remain phenomenological in what I say against phenomenology"? Recall, however, that he considers doing this to be doing what Levinas is doing when the latter says that we have to go phenomenologically beyond phenomenology. Derrida's and Levinas's way out of phenomenology, their "*Weg* aus *der Phänomenologie,*"[20] is a way that shows phenomenologically that phenomenology is outside itself. So that when Derrida writes that he seeks to think the theological gift and the phenomenological gift "from a place which is not inside what I try to account for," the place is not simply outside what he tries to account for. The place is *chōra,* the place that resists the over-simple placement in which interiority and exteriority pretend to be polar opposites of each other.

Exteriority

Exteriority is the topic of Levinas's *Totality and Infinity.* That book and other works by its author are a topic of one of Janicaud's chapters. The gist of Janicaud's main criticism of Levinas is conveyed in Derrida's remark that there appears to be a certain empiricism in Levinas's work. Both Janicaud and Derrida are raising the question of Levinas's right as a self-styled phenomenologist to rest his case, as they say he sometimes seems to do, upon the input from outside of what Levinas calls the affect or experience or "experience" of alterity. Stressing absolute passivity, does not Levinas pay too little respect to the part played by active constitution in this transaction? Should he not acknowledge that if ethical exteriority invades the self's phenomenologico-ontological interiority, the latter to some degree conditions this transaction or transpassion?

Levinas could begin his reply to this criticism by maintaining that it neglects his insistence that what he calls absolute passivity is not to be confused with passivity as this is opposed to activity in debates between classical empiricism and rationalism. He could go on to remind his critics that *Totality and Infinity* devotes many pages to the topic of the enjoyment of one's embodiment, and that the exposure of the body to being wounded is intrinsic to ethical traumatism. On the other hand, Janicaud could still maintain that Levinas does not bring out in sufficient detail how these responses enable him to "go phenomenologically beyond phenomenology." One way to do this would be to imagine a phenomenology where something like the middle voice is what is audible in the "permitting ourselves to be seized" of Luther's sentence cited by Heidegger, as noted above, "Faith is permitting ourselves to be seized by the things we do not see."[21] This permitting or suffering is *Sichge-fangengegeben*. That is to say, it is a self-giving, a giving of the self by the self. It raises again the questions debated between Marion and Derrida, first the question whether the things (*Sachen*) we do not see are gifts, a question both Marion and Derrida answer in the affirmative, and, secondly, the question whether these invisible things are *Gegebenheiten*, a question to which Marion answers Yes and Derrida answers No or Perhaps Not.

Derrida's non-affirmative response to this second question draws on something like negative theology. But he prefers not to call by that name what passes for negative theology. The "logic" of the gift is more complex than the logic of negation, which leads either to clear-cut exclusion or dialectical inclusion. Marion's affirmative answer to the same question also draws on the tradition of so-called negative theology. He prefers to call this mystical theology, however, precisely in order to protect the idea that in the gift, which is neither simply an object nor simply a being, there is *Gegebenheit*, givenness or givenhood, the nesshood and hoodness of which tell us that it is apt for phenomenological *Offenbarkeit*, transcendental openness to the seeing of eidetic essences as distinguished from theological Revelation, *Offenbarung*. Something is received that would, Marion says, borrowing Derrida's language, "deconstruct the transcendental condition of the ego."[22] This "original passivity of subjectivity" would leave room for the absolute passivity of ethical alterity described by Levinas. But both in its Levinasian and in its Marionian versions it invites Derrida's increasingly frequent warnings against the assumption that every trace of every kind of narcissism can be eliminated. That warning is at least implicit in Janicaud's appraisals of Marion and Levinas. It is explicit in Ricœur's difficulties with Levinas and in his thoroughgoing attempts to demonstrate that the absolute passivity described by Levinas in terms of one's being persecuted and taken hostage by the other calls to be qualified by an admission of the necessity to make room for self-attestation.[23] This necessity may be presaged in something Levinas himself says: "The term welcome of the Other expresses a simultaneity of activity and passivity which places the relation with the other outside of the dichotomies valid for things: the a priori and the a posteriori, activity and passivity."[24] Janicaud does not hear what I sometimes fancy I hear in this sentence, namely, something like the middle voice. He suspects that this medially diathetic reading underestimates the purity Levinas claims for the alterity, otherwiseness, and otherwisdom—wisdom of love as distinguished from love of wisdom—of the ethical exteriority announced in the subtitle of *Totality and Infinity*.

Interiority

If Levinas and Marion run the risk of overemphasizing the priority of Exteriority, it is the priority of Interiority that is in danger of being overemphasized by Michel Henry. This is the fear evinced in Janicaud's chapter about him. In that chapter theology figures more centrally than it does in the chapter on Levinas, where the focus is on the ethical and where the theological is approached only through the ethical. But the ethical is already the religious in Levinas's use of the word, a use in which the religious purports not to demand interpretation in terms of any "Oriental wisdom," be it Judaic, Christian, or Islamic.[25] Even Marion, in his studies of saturated phenomena, aims to describe a phenomenological landscape that postpones inhabitation by specifically Christian figures. Further, if Derrida is aware that he is borrowing not only from Plato but also from the history of Christianity when he attempts to give an at least provisional description of the non-historical, quasi-transcendental place he calls *chōra* that may be occupied by historical religions, it is the non-historical status of this religiousness in general that he emphasizes, notwithstanding that the "non" of its non-historicality is not to be confused with the "not" of classical logic, of dialectical logic, or of a too naïvely read negative theology. Instead of opposition and parallelism or synthesis there is chiasmus. Derrida is willing to say that this chiasmus is religious, but it is religious in a sense that is not derivative from particular historical religions and is not open to their positive or negative kind of revelation, *Offenbarung*. Nor is it open to the disclosure, *Offenbarkeit*, of phenomenology. Prior to both revelation and disclosure, the religious in Derrida's sense of the religious without religion is prior to the question as to which of these is prior to the other. It is in the difference between them.

Where Levinas explicitly denies that his quasi-phenomenology depends on any empirically historical religion, where, after *God Without Being*, Marion strives to keep to a phenomenology that assumes no commitment to an empirically historical religion, and where Derrida, while defending the claims of a non-historical religiousness, complicates the relation between the historical and the non-historical, Henry maintains that any allegedly non-historical principles that phenomenology may disclose are rooted in the empirically historical religion of Christianity. Henry's so-called radical phenomenology is less radical in the sense of less basic than the *archē* or *archi* unearthed by Derridean deconstruction, except that in Derrida's adaptation of these Greek expressions the senses of firstness and controlling sovereignty they normally express are subordinated—etiolated, one might dare say, borrowing an expression Derrida once cited from John Austin.[26] In Derrida's employment of them these Greek archaisms do not stand for a first principle or a root. Hence they subvert any simple opposition between the fundamental and the derived. Henry, however, has no qualms about positing a foundation, namely the *Fond* (his upper case) that is the subject of the positive revelation and Revelation of Christianity. And because this foundation is, he says with Kierkegaardian undertones, Interiority, its "Christian" phenomenology is *prima facie* a polar opposite to the "Judaistic" ethicality of Exteriority proposed by Levinas. Even so, Levinas's ethical exteriority of transcendence is analogous or quasi-analogous to Henry's interiority of immanence in that both the exteriority according to Levinas and the interiority according to Henry purport to be a presupposition of any intentional practical or theoretical dealings with the world and its horizonality. Therefore both reach beyond the phenomenology of which the methodology assumes intentionality and horizonality. Anyone questioning the fundamentality of this latter historical, classical, Husserlian phenomenology is faced with the question whether what is held to challenge its claim to fundamentality should still be called phenomenology. Because Levinas, as noted above, sometimes sees himself to be making a transition to the non-phenomenological from the phenomenological, I have called the methodology or way he follows in doing this quasi-phenomenological. The *archē* and the *archi* of Levinasian quasi-phenomenology, as of Derridean deconstruction, which is another version of quasi-phenomenology, are an-archic. The universality of its principles and laws collides chiasmically with singularity.

Where what is at issue is what in classical Husserlian phenomenology would be described as the imaginable variations that the essence of phenomenology can tolerate, questions of nomenclature can be decided rationally only in light of the things themselves. Thus, although Marion is keen to continue calling what he is doing phenomenology, at one point in his debate with Derrida he writes: "As to the question of whether what I am doing, or what Derrida is doing, is within phenomenology or beyond, it does not seem to me very important. . . . Whether *Being Given* is still phenomenology we shall see ten years from now"—ten years that have since expired.[27] He cites Heidegger's remark "We are not interested in phenomenology, but in the things phenomenology is interested in." He could have cited Wittgenstein's remark to the effect that whether or not we persist in using a particular word will depend not only on the meaning of that word but on the point (*Witz*) of using it.[28] In the context of an interest in deciding what is to count as phenomenology the point is not only the point we may have in mind. It is also the point that our successors may see in retaining this description in their contexts, contexts that will be contexts of our contexts. But the point of using the word can make a difference to the word's meaning. So what is pregiven in that meaning will be known only in the distant future, a future that comes from a future. Not only psychoanalytic meaning is *nachträglich*, behind-itself-ahead-of-itself. Meaning as such is, including meaning in the "rigorous science of meaning" known as phenomenology.

The complaints made by Janicaud in *Phenomenology and the "theological turn"* against certain French *soi-disant* phenomenologists arise in large part from the author's conception of phenomenology as a rigorous science defined by the five or so methodological requirements listed at the beginning of this chapter. The conservative nature of this conception is manifest in his comment on Marion's procedure in *Reduction and Donation* that "It displays no respect for phenomenological order, which is manipulated as though it were an elastic mechanism yet at the same time purports to be strict."[29] He goes as far as to suspect that this mechanism is a *deus ex machina*. For although he recognizes that Marion does not rush his reader toward theological conclusions, this, he holds, is only because in *Reduction and Donation* Marion bends phenomenology in the direction of a negative phenomenology that will make ready a philosophical place for the negative or mystical theology defended in *God without Being*.[30] Janicaud's reservations regarding Marion turn on the thought that if, in the wake of Heidegger's turning of Husserlian phenomenology and his own phenomenological ontology in the direction of *tao*, methodological phenomenology is to become a phenomenology of way, the latter should not masquerade as the former.

No such pretence is made in Michel Henry's break with what he calls "historical" Husserlian phenomenology in favor of a "radical" phenomenology of the way. Which way? None other than the way to which Christ points when he declares: "I am the way, the truth, and the life: no man cometh unto the Father but by me" (John 14:6). No man or woman cometh unto a recognition of the barbarism of a purely Galilean philosophy of reality but by a Galilean (Galilee-an) reinterpretation of sensibility. With reference to the Galilean science against whose philosophical pretentions he rails in *La barbarie*,[31] Henry writes, "What escapes science is that sensible qualities never exist as the simple properties of an object. Before being projected onto that object, they are pure subjective impressions that in fact presuppose sensibility, that invisible essence of Life that is Christian Truth."[32] And Christian truth is God himself.[33]

So where Levinas says that no human being cometh to God but by another human being, Henry stresses that the human being begins in the life of God as told in the words in which the life of the God-man Christ is told. One of the crucial intuitions of Christianity, Henry writes, is that the relation to the other, to my neighbor, is possible only through God.[34] Because God is Life, life is more than the human being or *Dasein*. On Henry's reorientation of Heidegger's analysis of *Dasein*, *Dasein* is being toward birth and rebirth rather than being toward its death, and the ontology of life is not to be understood, as maintained in *Being and Time*, through a privative interpretation of *Dasein* or of the human being defined as animality supplemented by *logos* or language.[35] Further, human language, language that deals with others and things as inhabitants of the exterior world, is supported by the word of Christ that is one with the word of God. Our human language, the language of what Henry calls the sons of Christ, is not self-supporting. It derives its life from the language of Christ and the language of God. According to the Prologue to John, Christ *is* the word of God.[36] That Prologue situates itself at the threshold between the Old and the New Testaments, inviting us to reread Genesis not as a factual description of the origin and development of humankind, but as "the first veritable and rigorous analysis of the human condition."[37] Moreover, that Prologue invites us to read the New Testament not only as the *first* but as the *only* veritable analysis of the human condition. The book *I Am the Truth* is a reading of the words of Christ as recorded in the New Testament, and its subtitle is *Toward a Philosophy of Christianity*. In that book Henry writes that "the obsolete knowledge of Christianity, a knowledge that is two millennia old . . . furnishes us not with entirely limited and useless data about humans," but, on the contrary, "it alone can tell us . . . what man is."[38]

How does this telling take place? Knowledge of Christianity tells man what he is only because he already has this knowledge. The Scriptures that are a "rigorous analysis" of it elicit a knowledge we are already possessed of, somewhat as the Greek-speaking slave-boy in Plato's dialogue *Meno* is shown to have already known the propositions of geometry elicited from him without having been given any new information. This analogy is limited, however, by the disanalogy that the slave-boy's knowledge is a scientific knowledge of general and abstract facts, a *logos*, a *scientia*, and a *savoir*, whereas the knowledge the human being has as to what it is to be human is a *savoir* sans *savoir*, a *connaissance*, a co-*naissance*. It is nothing less than a self-affecting, self-affectionate, emotional, and emotive experience (*épreuve*) of the human being's co-generation with the Son of God and His Father. The human being's recognition of this is a reconnaissance and a renaissance that opens our eyes to the superficiality of the kind of knowledge prized in the historical period known as the Renaissance, in so far as that took as its ideal the methodology of the Galilean sciences of so-called primary qualities. Perhaps to the pun on *connaissance* on which Henry's story turns we may be allowed to add the already sounded pun on *galiléen,* which does duty in French both for that which appertains to Galileo and for that which appertains to Galilee. Only when the Galilean in the former sense is put into the context of the latter sense is the human condition properly understood.

Therefore, Henry writes, although "God said, Let us make man in our image, after our likeness" (Genesis 1:25), and although God is Life and man is a living being, human intelligence demands that our extrinsic relation to a transcendent world of ob-jective entities spread out before our eyes or under our hands be apprehended in the perspective of its dependence upon the living of a life of radical interiority. This dependence is the dependence of the human language of worldhood and external existents upon the language of immanence, which is the language of God, which is the language of generation and Life. The derivativeness of the language of worldly existence is its way of being accessory after the fact in the sense that the facts reported by such expressions as "that is" and "there are" are independent of their being put into language. By contrast the language of God, the language of Life, is essential to what it reveals. That language, that word, is the flesh of what it reveals:

> whoever is born of the Word of Life has no leisure to withdraw itself from the Parousia of its Revelation. . . . Life has but one word, that word which never harks back over what it has said, that word that nothing escapes. This Parousia without memory and without project of the Word of Life is our birth.[39]

The word that is with memory and with project is the word of intentionality and horizonality. In this respect it has the noetic–noematic structure of Husserlian phenomenology and/or the ecstatic structure described in the phenomenological ontology of Heidegger. It is "the word that enables us to see while being absent," even when the seeing is phenomenological in the classical Husserlian sense. But radical phenomenological signification is the signification this word of the visible world refers back to, "the word that generates in life."[40] Further, "all Christian 'morals,'" as expounded in the Scriptures and elsewhere, makes this a retro-reference—a retro-reference that, be it noted in passing, has dire implications for the New Critical teaching on the self-contained "isness" of the word of the Scriptures and the work of art discussed above in chapter 3.

> It is not the word of the Scriptures that gives us to hear [or understand, *entendre*] the Word of Life. It is the latter, in engendering us at every instant, in making us Sons, that reveals, in its proper truth, the truth that is recognized by and testified to by the word of the Scriptures. . . .
>
> What need have we of the Scriptures? Are they not there only to be recognized retrospectively in the light of a truth that we already bring with us and that in its prior accomplishment, in the accomplishment of life in us from always, would easily manage without them?[41]

On the one hand, Henry's radical phenomenology calls into question the pretensions to fundamentality claimed by Husserlian phenomenology. On the other hand, it shares with Husserl a scorn of the pretensions to fundamentality of "the word that enables us to see while being absent," typically the typographical or otherwise written word, scripture generally, for instance marks that are merely indicative, like token reflexives, as distinguished from words that have what Husserl calls expressive meaning. Token reflexives such as "here" and "I" and "now," as in "Here I am now, at your service," *Hineni,* have force only in so far as they mark a time, hence only if they function in the horizon of a temporal past and future. In this perspective even Holy Scripture is an incidental distraction. Even it is an infraction into the language of Life by the language of the historical world. It is an *écart,* precisely what for Levinas is the strength of the Torah because it is a safeguard against the human temptation to desire fusion with God. For Henry *Écart* spelled with a capital initial is a name for what is not a virtue precisely because it intrudes a fission into every fusion. It is a name for what he refers to as culture when, despite his contention that knowledge of Christianity "alone can tell us . . . what man is," and in line with his marginalization of scripture in general and biblical Scripture in particular, he writes in the final paragraph of "Speech and Religion: The Word of God" that culture limits the privilege he accords Christianity as a key to a radical phenomenology of human nature.

Worldly word, godly word, given word

Paradoxically, stretching further than *doxa,* Henry's turn to Christian theology is a turn from theology and dogmatic religion to phenomenology. The turn is a return, a return that accords recognition (*re-connaissance*), however grudgingly, to the possibility that the key to the phenomenological essence of what it is to be human, the key that Henry calls knowledge of Christianity, is not the Judeo-Christian Bible. For the Bible is a part of culture.

Of culture Henry speaks in two voices. In the first chapter of *La barbarie*, rethinking, as he so often does, thoughts expressed by Husserl in the *Crisis*, Henry writes of culture as an aspect of the world as lived, the *Lebenswelt*, and as what saves us from the death represented in the world of primary qualities to which Galilean science is confined. On the other hand, in the final paragraph of "Speech and Religion" Henry describes culture as an aspect of what disrupts the immanence of the psyche's self-affection. Thus viewed, culture is an aspect of transcendence, of the *Écart*, and as such only a complexification of the Galilean world. In a penultimate paragraph that invites comparison with paragraphs in the writings of Marion, Henry affirms that radical revelation experienced through the work of art is not primarily revelation to the intellect, but revelation to the feelings. He concludes:

> But the overturning [*bouleversement*] of life that opens it emotionally to its own essence dispenses as well with every condition in the sense of an encounter, circumstance or occasion, of every form of culture of whatever order it might be. It is born and can be born of life itself as that re-birth that gives to experience suddenly its eternal birth. The Spirit bloweth where it listeth [*où il veut*].[42]

If those dispensable forms of culture include the cults that rely on the word (of) God, the wind of the Spirit will turn the pages not only of the Christian Bible. The Jewish Bible and the Koran, not to mention the Hindu Vedas and the Buddhist scriptures that go under the names of the Greater and Lesser Vehicles, may be vehicles of God's word as well. Or as ill. For in so far as scripture is a human contrivance severed from the word of God, the only power Henry grants it is such power as it confers on the scribes and the Pharisees to deceive. But Henry grants to Christianity a special power to reveal the truth about what it is to be a human being. Does this mean that the Spirit bloweth where it listeth only if the "where" is limited to the confines of Christian knowledge? Or does it blow beyond those confines in the space of Judaism and Islam and elsewhere because these other religions anticipate or retain elements of Christian knowledge? Before we condemn either of these forms of imperialism we must note that the very first sentence of the introduction to *I am the Truth* warns the reader that this book does not aim to consider whether Christianity is "true" or "false." As already observed, the subtitle of the book is *Toward a Philosophy of Christianity*. So that if there is imperialism here, it is philosophical rather than religious imperialism, notwithstanding that the phenomenological philosophy it favors is called Christian. It is not the truth of a religion that Henry is seeking to establish. "Rather, what will be in question here is *what Christianity considers as truth*," whether or not it be true as a matter of fact. Radical phenomenology, like its Husserlian predecessor, suspends matters of fact and questions as to the existence of this, that, and the other, including the question of the existence of the Other we call God, "*Dieu, si vous voulez,*" as Derrida writes, "God," he might have written, "if the Spirit so listeth (*veut*)."

Otherwise than being, but not beyond essence, the essence of what it is to be human is passion, passion to the phenomenology of which our guide, according to Henry, is the Passion of Christ. Passion, but without Christ, is also at the heart of the thinking of Levinas. His phrase "reversed intentionality" stands for the passivity he, Marion, and Henry are all, in their different ways, attempting to find a place for which, even in the case of Marion's tentatively so-called negative theology without being, is not usurped by formal or dialectical negation. This agenda is also Derrida's, one that shares with Ricœur reservations regarding what they both take to be the danger that in trying to do justice to the ego's *bouleversement* by the other, Levinas underestimates the contribution of the self.

No one could charge Henry with being guilty of this last-mentioned injustice. Now although, without mentioning his name, he must deem Derrida to be among the leading detractors of presence and chief defenders of separatism alongside Levinas, for whom *kadosh* denotes the holy and the distance of respect, Derrida is also a defender of the variety of self-affective narcissisms courted by the self. Henry and Derrida appear to be at opposite extremes of a polarity of interiority and exteriority only if we do not make the distinction the former makes between the language of the world and the language of God. According to Henry, the language of the world, whether in the starkest and most skeletal form it takes in Galilean quantitative science or fleshed out in the garbs of culture, is as shot through by gappiness, as hyphenated, as according to Derrida the spoken word, *parole,* is by archi-scripture. The difference between them emerges when we turn to what Henry calls the language of God. This difference is not that Henry appeals to that language while Derrida does not. For Derrida too invokes the language of God or, as we have seen he sometimes prefers to say, the language of God-if-you-wish, or of God maybe, *Dieu avec le peut-être.* The language of God is *parole* in the sense of the given word, the promise performed by a "Thereby" that is presupposed by my and John Austin's "Hereby" and Levinas's and your "Here I am," *Hineni,* even if the given word is without givenness, *Gegebenheit,* because a promise is always called from out of the future to be repeatedly endorsed. The a-coming-ness of this future trails an absolute past that is as immemorial in the thrownness of *Dasein* toward its death described by Heidegger, in one's being faced with the death of the other treated by Levinas, and in the life-death of historicity construed and deconstrued by Derrida, as is our birth as told in the language of God of which Henry has told us that it is without memory and project, therefore absolutely unforgettable, *inoubliable*.

Henry maintains that *Dieu* "is" or happens as *Devenir* (*Dieuvenir!*), or as *Parvenir* or as *Advenir,* that "Life 'is' not," that it "occurs (*advient*) and does not cease occurring," that "This incessant coming of life is an eternal coming forth (*parvenir*) in itself."[43] He says of life that "it 'is' not," and that it could not be "all that it 'is.'"[44] In light of Henry's "reduction" of culture and cults, might his saying these things be tantamount to saying that God "is" other, and more than anything is, even more than a Messiah, perhaps as much or as little as a messianicity minus a Messiah—what Derrida too calls advenience, the advenience of democracy, despite the unique privilege Henry reserves for the religion of Christianity? Derrida acknowledges that in the languages of the West at least since the Enlightenment the language of Christianity has been privileged, and not only in the language of those who swear by that religion. It may be pointed out that Derrida acknowledges this as a matter of fact, but that Henry contends that in radical phenomenology matters of fact are at most secondary to the transcendentally essential. However, the simplicity of this opposition between the empirically or otherwise factual and the transcendental is judged by Derrida to be an oversimplification. The turn of French phenomenology toward theology is in its turn overturned, *bouleversé,* to use a word both Henry and Levinas use, by a turn from phenomenology and theology toward quasi-theological deconstruction. In this last or latest turn—with all due respect to the religions, and with a return of regard for the "things" that are excluded by some of those religions (for example Eckhart's) and, in their almost idolatrous respect for the *Sachen selbst,* by some of the phenomenologies of those religions (for example Henry's)—attention is given to a religiousness that is not necessarily the religiousness of a god-affirming or god-denying religion.

Appresentation

If at least some of the theological and quasi-theological twists and turns described in the preceding pages are, as Janicaud holds, departures from the standards of methodological rigor set by Husserl, it is arguable that all of them take as their point of departure notions left ambiguous by Husserl himself. One such ambiguity leads to an equivocity in the discussion between Marion and Derrida of the relation between the gift and givenness. At one point in that discussion Derrida says to Marion, "you interpret everything, every *Gegebenheit* as gift . . . ," whereupon Marion interjects, "Every gift as *Gegebenheit*," as though to correct Derrida.[45] The latter does not register or accept this as a correction of his opinion as to what Marion is arguing. That this is so is shown by his attributing to Marion a few moments later the claim that every phenomenon is a gift. He protests that Marion cannot make this claim, for a phenomenon is a presence whereas a gift, they agree, is not.

This misunderstanding arises because Marion, reading Husserl through the lens of what Heidegger writes about "*es gibt Sein*," interprets *Gegebenheit* more liberally than Derrida does. Despite Marion's protestations that he is steering clear of theological commitments, Derrida may well suspect that the generosity implied in Heidegger's analysis of the "giving of Being" is being used by Marion as a bridge to reach a phenomenology that will prepare a comfortable place for a Christian theology. On the other hand, Derrida himself offers a reading of the "as such" clause in the table of laws of Husserlian phenomenology that is liberal enough not to be restricted to the intuitional givenness referred to by the principle of all principles. In this way Derrida can hold open a space for the given as such that is less comfortable than the specifically theological space of which Marion seeks to describe the phenomenology. But in their engagement with the other as such Marion, Derrida, Levinas, and Henry are all taking as their clue what is implied regarding the as-suchness of the other and the Other or God by Husserl's never rigorously defined notion of analogical appresentation.

The notion of analogical appresentation is not rigorously defined by Husserl because it exceeds the limits of definition, essence, and presence. It straddles analogy as, on the one hand, repetition (*ana*) of *logos* as something stated and, on the other hand, analogy as repetition of a deed of address. It straddles the limit to which Derrida refers when, in the words cited in the first section of this chapter, he writes that "appresentation . . . is the limit of phenomenology that appears within phenomenology," adding, "That is the place where I work also." It is the place where Marion, Levinas, and Henry work also, working toward an engagement of phenomenology with theology. It is the place of the other as such and of the given as such, where the as such as such subverts the principle of all principles, where intentionality is turned through a hundred and eighty degrees, and where whatever may be said is turned into a saying. This turn is not simply a replacement of outward-going intentionality by inward-coming intentionality if intentionality is taken to be aimed at an actual, possible, or promised noematic presence. Such a simple reversive revolution would be a revolution within the sphere of the constatable, whereas the revolution from the givenness of data and dicta to the giving of one's word—my, yours, or God's—is a switch to the word as performative deed. It is the moment of faith at the brink between Marion's lowercase revelation and uppercase Revelation, and between the call and what he calls the responsal.[46] This is the moment when there happens what, in his second study of Levinas, Derrida calls the seriature (*sérirature*) of message and address.[47] In Henry's radical phenomenology it is the moment of the crossing of the language of the world and the word of God in the *Parole* of the Crucified Signifier. At once widening and narrowing the focus of the linguistic turn made in Anglo-Saxon self-styled phenomenology of language, the theological turn in French phenomenology is a linguistic turn of *langue* toward *parole* and toward an event which is as such more and less than any such and which makes this opposition both a possibility and an impossibility. The very experience of this impossibility is perhaps what motivates each of the authors treated by Janicaud toward, in Derrida's words, the deepest ambition of their thought,[48] in Janicaud's own words: the theological turn. In this turn presentation as the phenomenal presence denied in Husserlian analogical appresentation turns into presentation as the introduction at the heart of a chiasmus of one addressee to another or an Other.

EIGHT

Who Is My Neighbor?

Et quis est meus proximus?

Who is my neighbor? The discussion of this question throughout the ages has ranged from asking whether my neighbor is the Jew and the friend, through asking whether my neighbor is any and every other human being including the stranger and my enemy, to asking whether he or she is God. Is it conceivable that my neighbor might be a nonhuman animal? Would this be conceivable to Levinas? If it is claimed that Levinasian "metaphysical" ethics as ethics of human beings beyond their being (*phusis*) can meet a shortcoming in the ethics of utilitarianism at least as this is understood by John Stuart Mill, it must not do so at the cost of ignoring the fact that utilitarianism requires that in determining the morality of an action, rule, practice, or institution consideration must be given to the welfare of *any* and *every* sentient being. Of what classical utilitarians have said on this matter nothing is more eloquent than the words in which Jeremy Bentham declares his hope that:

> The day *may* come when the rest of the animal creation may acquire those rights which never could have been withholden from them but by the hand of tyranny. The French have already discovered that the blackness of the skin is no reason why a human being should be abandoned

without redress to the caprice of a tormentor. It may one day come to be recognized that the number of legs, the villosity of the skin, or the termination of the *os sacrum,* are reasons equally insufficient for abandoning a sensitive being to the same fate. What else is it that should trace the insuperable line? Is it the faculty of reason, or perhaps the faculty of discourse? But a full-grown horse or dog is beyond comparison a more rational, as well as a more conversable animal, than an infant of a day, or a week, or even a month, old. But suppose they were otherwise, what would it avail? The question is not, Can they reason? nor Can they *talk?* but, *Can they suffer?*[1]

Is Levinas of the opinion that the question is, Can they talk? It is not easy to determine his opinion because almost always when he touches upon the subject of animality he is thinking of the animality of man. There are however a few places where he writes explicitly about a nonhuman animal. In particular I am thinking of Bobby. Not Greyfriars Bobby of Edinburgh, the Franciscan terrier that is said to have mourned on his master's grave for fourteen years until he himself died, but the dog referred to in an essay titled "Nom d'un chien ou droit naturel" published in 1975 in a collection titled "Celui qui ne peut se servir des mots" and reprinted in *Difficile Liberté.* No less eloquent than those words of Bentham's are those of the opening paragraph of this essay where Levinas mentions that according to Genesis Adam was a vegetarian and where he all but proposes an analogy between the unspeakable human holocaust and the unspoken animal one. The reader of that paragraph may well feel his leather shoes beginning to pinch.[2] I am thinking of Bobby in order to understand whom or what Levinas means by *Autrui.* Is *Autrui* a strictly personal pronoun? Can it stand for God? Can it stand for a dog? The question is not as rum as it may seem. Not as rum as the idea that occurred to George Borrow when, learning that the Romany word for God is Duvel, he muses in *Lavengro* "Would it not be a rum thing if divine and devilish were originally one and the same word." We are not about to find Levinas arguing that the words "God" and "dog" have a common root. Although Bobby has his origins on the Egyptian side of the Red Sea, he is not a metaphorical Anubis. Throughout the entire essay about him Levinas tries to keep the metaphorical at bay, for the sake of the literal truth about the dog of the verse in Exodus 22 which his essay takes as its text: "neither shall ye eat any flesh that is torn of beasts in the field; ye shall cast it to the dogs." It is an uphill task, both for him and for the Talmudic interpreters of this text who explain what Levinas calls "the paradox" of a purely natural creature having a right, here the right of the dog to feed on this particular sort of meat, by referring to Exodus 11:7, which says that no dog shall move its tongue at the midnight when the first-born in the land of Egypt are threatened with slaughter and the Jews are about to be led into captivity. Threatened, be it noted, are the first-born not only of man, but of the chain of being "from the first-born of the Pharoah that sitteth upon his throne, even unto the first-born of the maidservant that sitteth behind the mill; and all the first-born of beasts." But one of these beasts, the silent dog sans ethic and sans *logos*, by holding its tongue bears witness to the dignity of man. Man's best friend signifies a transcendence *in* its animality, *dans l'animal!* For which service he has the everlasting right mentioned in Exodus 22.

It makes a nice story, Levinas seems to say, but have not the Talmudic exegetes lapsed into merely rhetorical figures of speech? He decides that they have, no less than Aesop and La Fontaine, but he goes on to tell of another dog, the dog that strayed into the German camp for Jewish prisoners where Levinas himself and his companions had become accustomed to being treated as less than human, sometimes subjected to looks that were enough, as he chillingly expresses it, to strip them of their human skin. Yet Bobby, during the few weeks the guards allowed him to remain, was there every morning to welcome them with wagging tail as they lined up before leaving for work and, unconstrained by the prohibition placed upon his Egyptian ancestors, was there waiting when they returned at night to welcome them one and all with an excited bark. The last Kantian in Nazi Germany, Levinas comments, and one wonders if he intends us to take that comment as nothing more or less than the literal truth. How can we? How, any more than Aesop, La Fontaine, and the Talmudic exegetes, can Levinas be speaking otherwise than figuratively? For in the very same breath he adds that Bobby lacks the brains to universalize his maxim. He is too stupid, *trop bête*. Bobby is without *logos* and that is why he is without ethics. Therefore he is without Kantian ethics; and so he is without Levinasian ethics, since the ethics of Emmanuel Levinas is analogous to the ethics of Immanuel Kant in that each is an ethics with a God within the limits of reason alone, but without a dog or any other beast, except indirectly, if we are to judge by reason alone.

> To judge by reason alone, man has no duties except to men (himself or others), for his duty to any subject at all is the moral constraint exerted by his will. Accordingly, a subject who constrains (obligates) must, first, be a person; and he must, secondly, be given as an object of experience, because he is to influence the purpose of a man's will; and such an influence can occur only in the relationship of two existing beings (for a mere creation of thought cannot become the cause of any purposive achievement). Since in all our experience we are acquainted with no being which might

be capable of obligation (active or passive) except one, man therefore can have no duty to any being other than man. And if he supposes that he has such another duty, then this happens through an amphiboly of the concepts of reflection; and so his supposed duty to other beings is merely his duty to himself. He is led to this misunderstanding because he confuses his duty *regarding* [*in Ansehung*] other beings with a duty *toward* [*gegen*] these beings.[3]

To judge by reason alone, Bobby cannot even say "Good day," no matter how gaily he may wag his tail and no matter how excitedly he may bark. If I think that I have duties to animals it is because I am failing to distinguish direct duties to or toward from indirect duties regarding. "Even gratitude for the long-performed service of an old horse or dog (just as if they were members of the household) belongs indirectly to man's duty, namely his duty *regarding* these animals; but directly considered, such a duty is always only his duty *to* himself."[4] If a man is not compassionate in his relations with animals he is likely to become insensitive in his relations with other human beings. According to Kant a man can have obligations only to a being that has obligations, which means, on his account of human experience, that human beings have obligations only to other human beings. The argument turns on the difference between doing something which falls under a single law and doing something which falls under two laws, the law of human animality and the law of human rationality, and it is this duality that gives rise to the experience of constraint and tension which is implied in the notion of being bound. So a being that is a purely animal nature will have no sense of obligation, of oughtness. Nor will a being that is purely rational. Hence, Kant maintains, we can have no moral obligations to God. We have, according to Kant, duties of religion, that is to say, duties "of recognizing all duties as [*instar*] divine commands." The duty of religion, however, is correlated with an Idea of Reason that, from a theoretical point of view, helps us to make sense of the apparent purposefulness of nature; and, from a practical point of view, Kant holds, this Idea is of the greatest moral fecundity in availing an incentive to virtuous conduct. Thus what we take to be a duty to God is a duty to man himself, namely a duty each man has to himself, the duty to make himself virtuous.

Does Kant think that a man cannot have a duty to a being he does not know exists? He writes: "we do not . . . have before us [*vor uns*] a given being *to* whom we are obligated; for the actuality of such a being would first have to be made known by experience." He also writes, in the paragraph already cited, that we can have no duties except duties to human beings because "we are acquainted with [*kennen wir*] no being which might be capable of obligation (active or passive) except man." We can be under an obligation only to a being with whom we can be, as we say, face to face. In the very human world of Immanuel Kant the other man is the only being with whom I come face to face. So too in the very human world of Emmanuel Levinas. The only face we behold is the human face and that is the only face to which we are directly beholden. Ethically, that is all that matters. In this, despite their fundamental disagreement over what it is for two human beings to be face to face, there is a considerable area of agreement between Levinas and Kant. Just as Kant maintains that I can have obligations only to a being that has, or (to cover the infantile and the senile) is of the kind that can have obligations, so Levinas seems to imply that I can have responsibilities only toward beings capable of having responsibilities.

We have seen why Kant thinks that God can have no obligations. He thinks this because he thinks that the notion of obligation carries with it the notion of constraint, of a tie. So although we may coherently think of God acting according to the moral law, that law is descriptive, not prescriptive, of his action, and it is not a law for which he can feel respect or by which he can feel obliged. He can command, but he cannot be commanded. And this is what Levinas says, speaking of *Autrui*. I do not judge the Other. The Other judges me. I do not categorize him. He categorizes me. He makes me stand out (*m'accuse*), identifies and accuses me. I do not simply appear, but am summoned to appear before him. And in this court of appeal it is he who does the calling, calling me to testify: to testify to my responsibilities even for his responsibilities. So that where Kant allows that I have responsibilities to myself, namely to make myself virtuous, my responsibility toward myself according to Levinas is mediated by my responsibility for the Other's responsibility toward me. Further, in contrast to Kant's view that I have a duty to promote the happiness but not the virtue of others, Levinas holds that I go bail for the Other's obedience to the Law. "His business is my business."[5] But, Levinas goes on to ask, "Is not my business his? Is he not responsible for me? Can I therefore be responsible for his responsibility for me?" To this last question Levinas answers Yes. For every responsibility that the Other has toward me and others I have a pre-ordained meta-responsibility.

Starting from below, as it were, from my responsibility toward the other human being, an infinite progress is generated, an infinite progress that is not to be confused with the agent's infinite progress toward moral perfection as postulated in the ethical theory of Kant, even though both Kant and Levinas call what gives direction to this progress an Ideal. In the Kantian Ideal happiness is commensurate with virtue. It is an Ideal toward which one strives by exerting a good will, and the realization of the Ideal would be a fulfillment.

The Levinasian Ideal, as viewed from my subjectivity, recedes unmeasurably further and further away the more I take up my responsibilities. The incessant realizing of it would be a derealizing of my self, an emptying of myself, a *kenōsis*, but an emptying that could never be complete. And this taking up of my responsibilities is not an exercise of power, not even of the power of a good will. It is a being taken up by the idea of Infinity and Goodness, the idea which is presupposed by the infinite progression–regression and which prevents it becoming the bad infinite that it would otherwise be.

This explains the structure of Levinas's important essay "God and Philosophy." The first part of this starts from above with the idea of God, *En Sof,* the topic of Descartes's Third Meditation. Then (on pp. 113–115 of *De Dieu qui vient à l'idée*)[6] it starts again, this time from below, with the topic of the First and Second of the *Meditations,* subjectivity, and therefore in Levinas's text, since subjectivity is ethical subjection, with *Autrui. Autrui* is the difficult pronoun that seems to do service for God in the meditations of Levinas rather as the name of God seems to do service for the scarcely mentioned "other minds" in the *Meditations* of Descartes.

Is God *Autrui*? Not if by God is meant the God of positive or negative theology. The Other is not some Plotinian avatar of God. "The Other is not the incarnation of God, but precisely by his face, in which he is disincarnate, is the manifestation of the height in which God is revealed,"[7] revealed in discourse. "It is our relations with men . . . that give to theological concepts the sole signification of which they admit." "Everything that cannot be reduced to an interhuman relation represents not the superior form but the forever primitive form of religion." As indeed Hegel might have said, except that the infinity of the interhuman relation in his conception is an infinity that totalizes a symmetrical intersubjectivity. Hegel's God is beyond any gulf between subject and object, but it is, Levinas would contend, not beyond the participation of what according to Hegel too are primitive forms of religion, the mythological religions of faceless gods. The superior form of religion is one in which God is not numinous, and in which he is "in-himself," *kath auto,* only on the assumption of ontological atheism or atheistic de-ontology, the atheism which results from the death of the pagan gods before which we are in danger of confusing God with the nocturnal shuffling of the *il y a*.[8] "The Other, in his signification prior to my initiative, resembles God."[9] "The Other is the very locus of metaphysical truth, and is indispensable for my relation with God."[10] But even when he is no longer conceived as the God of positive or negative theology, God is not the Other, *Autrui.* Far from it. He is closer to this farness. Not the impersonal *il* of the *il y a,* the "there is," not the third person of justice nascent in the dyadic face to face, God is the third personal *Il* over and up there, *illic,* and, as Descartes says, echoing the *Banquet* of Plato, majestic. God is the eminence of illeity of which the trace is inscribed in the face of the second-person You as well as in the third-person nascent there. Still speaking in Cartesian terms, Levinas says that the idea of God is the idea of Infinity thought by the first personal but never nominative me, the "in" of this idea of infinity connoting both the being of this idea in the finite me and the negation implied in the idea of my own finitude revealed to me *a posteriori* by my doubt and desire but *a priori* by the immeasurable degree to which the "objective reality" of my idea of infinity falls short of the "formal reality" of its metaphysical and ethical origin. Infinity, the Desirable, God is the transcendence and holiness or distance that makes my nearness to my neighbor more than a relation of love, as for Kant, *mutatis mutandis,* love is that which unites while respect is that which sets a distance between us. "God is not simply 'the first other [*autrui*],' or 'the other par excellence,' or 'the absolutely other,' but other [*autre*] than the other [*autrui*], otherwise other, other with an alterity prior to the alterity of the other [*autrui*]."[11]

Levinas's phenomenological analysis of love is a reflection on Plato's *Banquet* and Rosenzweig's *The Star of Redemption.*[12] Love is ambiguous. On the one hand it points to the exteriority of the beloved and to an exteriority beyond that exteriority, beyond the face. On the other hand it enjoys the interiority of sensation and return to oneself,[13] to the concupiscence that Pascal describes with the help of the proclamation of the First Epistle of Saint John, 2:16. "Everything in the world is lust of the flesh, or concupiscence of the eyes, or vaingloriousness of life," *libido sentiendi, libido sciendi, libido dominandi,* the very same *cupere* that throws us back from the Cartesian idea of God to the *cogito* that would like to have everything under its command. Levinas writes that there is a touch of the erotic in all love, but he goes on to write of an *Amour sans Eros.* It is as though the pagan god is left behind as Levinas's thoughts turn from Plato to Rosenzweig. Rosenzweig writes of the love of a non-pagan God, of God's love for man and of man's love for God. In a footnote Levinas makes the comment that "Franz Rosenzweig interprets the *response* made by Man to the love with which God loves him as the movement towards the neighbor." He probably has in mind the sentences:

> Since love cannot be commanded except by the lover himself, therefore the love for man, in being commanded by God, is directly derived from the love for God. The love for God is to express itself in love for one's neighbor. It is for this reason that love of neighbor can and must be commanded.[14]

We saw how in the spirit of these sentences the love without *eros* to which Levinas refers—and which Rosenzweig champions,[15] though in treating of God's love for man—gets spoken of henceforth as responsibility in order to mark its difference from ego-based desire and to mark that it is a response.

Am I obsessed by Bobby?

Why however must responsibility be limited to responding to a being that has the gift of speech? Is there no room for direct responsibility to dumb animals?

Responsibilities may be responsibilities *toward,* but not all such responsibilities are responses *to* in the strict sense of answers or other responses to a question or command. They may be responsibilities *for,* and it is of responsibilities *pour* or *de* that Levinas mostly writes, explicitly distinguishing them only once or twice from responsibilities to, responsibilities *à.*[16] We could of course take up the question whether animals talk and, if so, which, if any, can talk to us. There are grounds for believing that Levinas would consider it crucial for his account whether Bobby merely barks or whether in doing so he can say *Bonjour.* When asked about our responsibilities toward nonhuman sentient creatures he is inclined to reply that our thinking about them may have to be only analogical or that the answer turns on whether we can discern in the eyes of the animal a recognition, however obscure, of its own mortality, on whether, in Levinas's sense, the animal has a face.[17] If this question is crucial, we may have to be satisfied with falling back on the need to appeal to agents to speak on the animal's behalf, as we do in the case of infants. However, the agent who speaks for the child says what he says on the child's behalf on the basis of the certainty that the child does not enjoy being battered or starved. Is not the fact that this is also how it is with nonhuman animals enough to prove that I have responsibility for them, and that responsibility does not depend upon their having responsibilities, for example responsibilities to their offspring or to humans they guard or guide? Suppose we agree that talk of the animal's responsibilities is anthropomorphism or rhetoric, still, as Bentham and other utilitarians put it, the question is not Can they reason? or Can they talk? but Can they suffer?

The first and perhaps the second of these questions has been seen to be all-important for Kant. Yet the last is not for him, as some of his readers have inferred, morally irrelevant. It is argued that Kant's concession that we have indirect duties to animals can be reduced to absurdity on the grounds that rationality is the only morally relevant characteristic that he can admit by which to distinguish animals from other nonhuman beings and that therefore, if we are to refrain from treating animals only as means because that is likely to lead us to treat fellow human beings as means only, we should for the same reason refrain from treating only as means inanimate objects like hammers. (We shall return to this alleged absurdity.) This argument derives its plausibility from the failure to distinguish a necessary condition of moral agency, where the moral is opposed to the non-moral, from a condition of the circumstances in which an action is performed that might determine whether the action is moral as opposed to immoral. The former condition is one that holds for any rational beings that may exist. The latter condition holds only for the actions of those we know to exist, human beings. That Kant agrees that the animality of rational animals can be determinative of our duties toward them is implied by his claim that we have a direct duty to contribute to the well-being of other humans and to support them in distress, and an indirect duty to assure one's own happiness as far as one can consistently with one's other obligations.[18] The practical contradictoriness that makes some of my actions wrong depends on the fact that it is natural for men to seek their own happiness. The moral law is a test for practical, and that means teleological, consistency, and it applies to maxims prescriptive of how men can achieve that natural end. Since that natural end includes man's well-being as an animal, the maxim "Treat nonhuman animals as if they have no capacity for suffering" is not one that can be consistently conceived as a law of nature or willed to become one.[19] Such conception is inconsistent with what one knows about animals from one's own experience of being one. This removes one obstacle preventing Kant admitting that we have direct duties to brutes.

There remains the obstacle presented by Kant's doctrine that as far as we can tell on the basis of reason alone, in other words setting aside matters based on faith and on feelings other than the feeling of moral respect, man has no duties except to men because his duty to any subject is moral constraint by that subject's will. We should be well on the way to clearing Kant's path to admitting direct duties to animals if only this reference to the subject's will could be interpreted as what the subject desires. If that were allowed, and if similar translations of the accommodating word *Wille* were permitted elsewhere in Kant's text, we should also be well on the way to converting Kant's theory of ethics into the tacit utilitarianism that Mill holds it to be. Kant himself is less accommodating than the word, taking pains to distinguish two of its primary senses. He is adamant that we can have direct duties only to beings that have *Wille* understood as pure practical reason.

In the metaphysical ethics of Levinas I can have direct responsibilities only toward beings that can speak, and this means beings that have a rationality that is presupposed by the universalizing reason fundamental in the

metaphysics of ethics of Kant. However, the proto-rationality of primary justice between two unequals, one of whom is oneself, anticipates the rationality of secondary justice among many, but without this entailing that I cease
being more responsible than anyone else.

Both Kant and Levinas are so sensitive to the dangers of the *Schwärmerei*
threatened by what Kant calls pathological love that they require an obligat-
ing being to be able to make a claim in so many words. No claim goes without
saying, even if the saying is the silent saying of the discourse of the face—a
silence not to be confused with the nocturnal silence in which the insomniac
hears the menacing rustle of the anonymous "there is," the *il y a*.[20] The Other
has to look at me. Indeed, what is expressed in his face may be expressed by
his hand or the nape of the neck.[21] And for Kant at least the claim does not
have to be a claim to a perfect right. I can have duties to others without any
of those others having a right to require that that duty be exercised toward
him or her by me. Levinas however seems to be more demanding. The very
droiture of the face to face, its uprightness or rectitude (*Gerechtigkeit*, justice),
is the expression of the other's right over me, *droit*.[22] And in one place at
least Levinas says "I support the universe," *Je soutiens l'univers*.[23] This might
seem to augur well for Bobby. He is presumably part of the universe. So if
supporting means being responsible for, I am responsible for, that is to say,
obsessed by him. But Levinas distinguishes my support of the universe into
two aspects. My support of the universe performs a role analogous to, though
at the same time very different from (as different as "I should" is from "I
know"), the role that Kant assigns to the transcendental unity of apperception, the role of giving the universe its uni-ty. Prior to transcendental unify-
ing, Levinas maintains, is the unity of human society of which the oneness
is brought about by my responsibility. Society starts with the disunity of a
sociality in which your commanding me both gives me my identity and prevents it being an identity without difference. Identity as sameness is usurped
by a de-con-structed identity in which withness is disrupted by outwithness.
This is a society of the other human being. There is no place in it for direct
responsibility for Bobby.

What about the other respect in which I am responsible for the unity of
the universe, the ontological, epistemological, and phenomenological unity
of apperception? According to Levinas this aspect is dependent upon the
ethical aspect. So, because according to Levinas the latter begins with a human being commanding me, the unity of apperception conditioned by it
could not allow a place for direct responsibility for the nonhuman animal.

The one space of the universe is ultimately the space of justice in the
proximity of the third party under law. But this justice is saved from the

violence of totalitarianism only if it is exposed to the peace-bearing violence in which I am looked at and looked to by the singular face that *me regarde* in both senses of the word: the face of one who looks at me and concerns me, the face that *m'accuse* in both senses of that word: the face whose look makes me stand out and accuses me.[24] The face that calls me into question is not the face of the animal. It is thanks to human faces, Levinas writes, that "Being will have a meaning as a universe, and the unity of the universe will be in me as subject to being. That means that the space of the universe will manifest itself as the dwelling of the others." The door of that dwelling would seem to be slammed in Bobby's face, assuming it be allowed that he has one.

This impression is confirmed by Levinas's endorsement of much of what he finds said in Rabbi Hayyim of Volozhin's *Nefesh Hahayyim, The Soul of Life*. In the doctrine expounded in this book Levinas recognizes a basis for his own teaching that man is responsible for the universe. The soul of the universe, according to Rabbi Hayyim, is man and, significantly for our present question, man defined not Hellenistically as a rational animal, but man understood biblically as the being created in the image of God and, more precisely, Levinas hastens to add, of God as Elohim, God as the principle of justice, not God as the principle of mercy unpronounceably named in the Tetragramme. Elohim is also the soul of the world. *Nefesh Hahayyim* describes a cosmology, Kabbalistic and Hellenistic, in which is postulated a hierarchy of worlds with God at the top. But this cosmology has to be read ethically. The principle of justice at the head of this hierarchy of worlds is the source on which feeds the root of the soul of man. Thanks to this, man in turn nourishes the intermediate worlds. Man is dependent upon Elohim, yet Elohim is at the same time dependent upon man as mediator.[25] In Rabbi Hayyim's ethical cosmology man is *homo Israelis* understood non-racially, and on the Israelites' obedience to the commands of the Torah depend the life and death of all the intermediate worlds. This "power" of life and death is man's responsibility or, as Levinas would say, his passivity more passive than the receptivity to which activity is traditionally opposed.

Does this responsibility include responsibility for the lower animal? The answer to this question would appear to be Yes, if we are to go by the following statement cited by Levinas from *Nefesh Hahayyim*: "Just as the way in which the body moves depends on the soul that is interior to man, man in his entirety is the power and living soul of the innumerable worlds in his charge, above him and below."[26] And below. These two words get lost in Levinas's interpretation. On the very same page on which he cites them he writes, "It is at the lowest (*au plus bas*), in man, that the entire fate of the universe is decided," and on the next page he cites from the Talmudic treatise

Aboth "Know what confusion your action brings about in the worlds above you." That is to say:

> It is not by substantiality—by an in-itself or for-itself—that man and his interiority are defined, but by the "for-the-other": for what is above one-self, for the worlds—but also, interpreting "world" broadly, for collectivities, persons, spiritual structures. In spite of his creaturely humility, man is engaged in injuring them (or preserving them).

Is this broad definition of "world" not still too narrow to allow for direct responsibility for the lower animal? Where does he or she fit in? There is no sign that Levinas would place the lower animal "above oneself" among the collectivities, persons, and spiritual structures. It is as though the universe to which Levinas applies Rabbi Hayyim's cosmology is the universe of discourse between the Creator and the human creature in the traditional great chain of being. The creatureliness of any creature more humble than man is a purely (or should we say "impurely"?) cosmological creatureliness, recalcitrant to production into ethics, whereas creation is the intake of ethical breath which Levinas calls *psychisme:* the reveille of the inner life by a *Wachet auf* that rouses it from the twilight of its dogmatic slumber, apparently re-creation but in truth older than cosmological creation as ontologically understood—the very pneuma of the psyche.

Man is an unreasonable animal

In *Otherwise than Being or Beyond Essence* Levinas writes: "The soul is the other in me. The psyche (*psychisme*), the one-for-the-other, can be possession and psychosis; the soul is already the seed of folly."[27] Where the *conatus* of the synoptic ego is a desire to possess, ethical and metaphysical Desire is psychotic being possessed, possessed not by being or language however, but possessed by God: sobered (*dégrisé*) enthusiasm in which there is a response to the word of the Other. Levinas maintains that the first word addressed to me by the Other is "Thou shalt not murder/kill" where the oblique stroke we insert signals the question, How are we to translate the Hebrew word *ràsah*? The answer to this question will have repercussions for the question whether I am obsessed by Bobby, whether I have direct responsibility for him. We have failed to discover any evidence that Levinas allows that Bobby and I can be face to face such that I could read in his own eyes "Thou shalt not kill." We must therefore retreat to the question whether in the face to face the other man addresses me not only on behalf of himself and other men, but also on behalf of the nonhuman animal; and to the question whether, if what the human face tells me is "Thou shalt not murder," the legal and quasi-legal connotations of the word "murder" prevent our saying that the commandment includes within its scope the nonhuman animal.

Commenting on Exodus 20:13, J. P. Hyatt states that *ràsah* refers to the murder of a personal enemy and that it is used much less frequently than the two words meaning to kill, *hàrag* and *hèmît*. He adds:

> It originally had nothing to do with capital punishment (administered by the avenger of blood or by the community), killing in war which was certainly sanctioned by the OT, or the killing of animals. Careful studies have shown that it is not confined, however, to intentional murder, but is occasionally used of unintentional homicide.[28]

When we turn to Levinas's statements of the commandment we find that he sometimes formulates it as "Thou shalt not kill," but other times replaces *tuer* by *meurtrir* with no contextual indication that he would not be willing to use the latter in all his mentions of the commandment. Of course this must not be taken to imply that he is not fully aware of the strict injunctions of the Torah against causing animals unnecessary pain. He also knows very well that the later Priestly sections of Genesis which speak of man's dominion over animals have alongside them passages from the earlier Jahwist sections which speak of animals as man's companions and affirm that God's covenant is made between him and man and every living creature.[29] But what sort of relevance is to be ascribed to this sensitivity and knowledge on Levinas's part, or indeed to any of the citations he makes in the course of his more philosophical writings of texts from the Jewish Bible or the Talmud? The face to face faces us with a dilemma. If the first word addressed to me derives its authority from, say, Sinai, does that not prevent Levinas making his claim that metaphysical ethics makes no appeal to the content of any positive religion? Even if Levinas's ethics cannot be an ethics of the other animal, even if Bobby cannot be my neighbor according to that ethics, we must take Levinas seriously when he insists that the ethics of which he speaks is a humanism of the other human being. This means that we cannot avoid asking how in the face to face the other human being can say *anything at all* and how, without the constraints imposed by the importation of commandments from positive religions, he can be prevented from saying *anything whatsoever.*

The best solution of this dilemma that Levinas's writings seem to offer is to understand the encounter that Moses had on Sinai, where he was told by God "my face shall not be seen," as a face to face encounter with the other human being, and, second, to understand "Thou shalt not kill" not as a proposition said or commandment affirmed as a principle of ethics, not as something *dit*, but as the nearest one can come to an enunciation of the force of any saying, the *dire* that is left when what is said is unsaid, *dédit*. This remainder is not as big a challenge to our understanding as the smile left behind after the subtraction of the face of the Cheshire cat. For to every unsaying there immediately accrues another said calling to be unsaid again to infinity. Since Levinas replaces or translates the commandment "Thou shalt not kill" sometimes by such words as "Thou shalt give the other the bread from thy mouth" and "Thou shalt not let the stranger die alone," it would seem not improper to conclude that these various forms of words are different ways of expressing the vulnerability of the human being, symbolized by the fact that these words are read in the eyes of the other, the most vulnerable part of the face. This symbolism does not prevent his granting that any part of the body can be the face in his ethical or proto-ethical sense.

One problem raised by the suggestion we have just made is that the vulnerability in question is the vulnerability of the other, whereas saying, *Dire,* is not restricted to that side. This problem is a difficulty intrinsic to the saying of the face to face, not necessarily an objection to what Levinas says about this. What he says is intrinsically difficult to comprehend, and perhaps it is impossible to do so if comprehension is subsumption under concepts. But this particular difficulty can be at least articulated if we recall that there is an asymmetrical chiasmic exchange of places in the face to face which Levinas tries to describe in sentences we quoted above from which it appears that, despite the radical alterity of the other, this alterity is somehow already immemorially on my side because it is the anarchic condition of my identity. I am neither at one time nor at one place. Because I am diachronic and diaconal I am situated in the place of the other, substituted ethically in his stead to the point at which my so-called subjectivity is the other in my place, *au lieu de moi*, as Blanchot says, and therefore no more subjective than ob-jective, like the Cartesian idea of God, where the "of" is both a subjective and an objective genitive.[30] So my *dire* is a speaking for him, prophecy. My word is *a priori* and from before the beginning psychotically possessed by him. Its authority is independent of my authorship.

Our main problem in this chapter has been and still is to understand why Levinas gives so much ethical weight to the ability to speak; why calling or claiming is required in so literal a sense, though that sense is already extended some way by him from what one ordinarily thinks of as speech. If calling or claiming are to be understood in such a way that they do imply speech, why cannot the speech be that of persons who speak on behalf of those that cannot speak for themselves? Does not their being unable to speak for themselves magnify my responsibility? Does their not being able to speak make my responsibility for them any the less direct than my responsibility for the other human being? This may not be a responsibility *to* or *toward* if by that is meant a response to a being that can put his or her request into words—though in the case of at least some nonhuman animals it is only on an extremely exacting definition of language that it is plausible to hold that such a response is ruled out. But is it not a responsibility *for*, and a direct one in the sense of underivative?

Now, it is obligations that Kant distinguishes into direct ones *to* or *toward* (*gegen*) and indirect ones regarding (*in Ansehung*). And if we distinguish also obligations from responsibilities, the prospect Levinas offers Bobby begins to look less bleak. In an interview published in 1988, in reply to the question whether we have obligations to animals, he answers, as we have never doubted for one moment that he would, Yes we do.

> It is clear that, without considering animals as human beings, the ethical extends to all living beings. We do not want to make an animal suffer needlessly and so on. But the prototype of this is human ethics. Vegetarianism, for example, arises from the transference to animals of the idea of suffering. The animal suffers. It is because we, as human, know what suffering is that we can have this obligation.[31]

That is his answer to Bentham. But this answer leaves unclear whether "we, as human" *transfer* the idea of suffering from ourselves to other human beings (by analogy?), and if not, why we need to transfer the idea of suffering from human beings to animals. The answer also leaves unanswered the question whether the obligation to which it refers is direct or, as Kant maintains, only indirect and derived. And it leaves unanswered the question whether our obligation is also a responsibility. A negative answer to this last question seems to be implied by the notion of the face to face which is at the center of Levinas's rethinking of the ethical. Notwithstanding his statement "the ethical extends to all living beings," on Levinas's analysis ethical responsibility "originates" in the face to face. Hence it is not enough for the bearer of that responsibility to have a face. The being to or for whom I am responsible must also have a face in Levinas's ethical sense. Despite his granting that we have obligations with respect to animals, and that the ethical extends to all living beings—where, if the "all" includes vegetable as well as animal life, the position of the vegetarians he goes on to mention becomes still more complex—he appears to continue to think that in ethics proper, that is to say in the "prototype" of ethics as distinct from its extension (whether this be an extension of ethics or an extension of proto-ethics), the other, whether it be animal, vegetable, or mineral, can be an other in respect of whom or which I have responsibilities only on condition of having a face. On being asked whether having a face in the ethical sense means being able to speak, he replies:

> I cannot say at what moment you have the right to be called "face." The human face is completely different and only afterwards do we discover the face of an animal. I don't know if a snake has a face. I can't answer that question. A more specific analysis is needed.

This seems to confirm that the distinction between obligation and responsibility is important for Levinas. Since "It is clear that, without considering animals as human beings, the ethical extends to all living beings" and that we have an obligation to animals because they suffer, the implication appears to be that we can have an ethical obligation without having a proto-ethical responsibility to animals. Therefore when at the end of his great poem, after describing how he threw a log in the direction of the snake he encountered at his water-trough, D. H. Lawrence writes

> And so, I missed my chance with one of the lords
> Of life.
> And I have something to expiate:
> A pettiness.

the expiation will be either of a failure to meet an ethical obligation or of the shirking of a proto-ethical responsibility, depending on what is the right answer to the question asked earlier in the poem and on the reasons for its being right:

> Was it perversity, that I longed to talk to him?

What answer and what reasons Levinas would give depend on what answer he would give after further analysis of the question to which he says he does not yet know the answer, namely whether a snake has a face. And his answer to the latter question appears to depend on whether in some sense the snake can talk. Since he grants that the fact that animals suffer is enough to put us under an obligation in respect to them, has he not granted what matters most? Why do we need to pursue the question of responsibility in respect of nonhuman beings? We need to do this in order to understand what Levinas means by ethics and how the ethical is related to responsibility. Despite his granting that we are under ethical obligations to animals, these obligations appear on Levinas's account to have a lower status than obligations to other human beings because the latter, but not the former, are clearly expressions of proto-ethical responsibility. When Levinas says that the human face is completely different from the face of the animal and then adds "I don't know if a snake has a face," we have to ask whether if he discovered that the snake has a face it would be a face in the same sense as that in which a human being has a face.

For an animal to have a face in the same sense as that in which a human being has a face would mean, on one interpretation of some of Levinas's words, that the animal is capable of holiness or saintliness, understanding by this that the animal is capable of being "more attached to the being of the other than to his own." I do not know whether Levinas would accept as evidence of this reports of apparently altruistic and self-sacrificial behavior among nonhuman animals—it is said that elephants even mourn—or whether he would interpret these as manifestations of individual altruism in the interest of the preservation of the genus or the gene. The first alternative seems to be ruled out by the following remarks:

> You ask at what moment one becomes a face. I do not know at what mo-
> ment the face appears, but what I want to emphasize is that the human
> breaks with pure being, which is always a persistence in being. This is
> my principal thesis. A being is something that is attached to being, to
> its own being. That is Darwin's idea. The being of animals is a struggle
> for life. A struggle for life without ethics. It is a question of might. Hei-
> degger says at the beginning of *Being and Time* that *Dasein* is a being
> who in his being is concerned for this being itself. That's Darwin's idea:
> the living being struggles for life. The aim of being is being itself. How-
> ever, with the appearance of the human—and this is my entire philoso-
> phy—there is something more important than my life, and that is the life
> of the other. That is unreasonable. Man is an unreasonable animal.[32]

Like Heidegger, Levinas takes exception to the traditional definition of man as a rational animal. Levinas here has the adjective take the weight of his disagreement with this definition. As we have seen, it would be a mistake to suppose that he is arguing for an irrationalist or non-rationalist philoso-phy of man; he is arguing for a definition of rationality that brings out that the height of rationality is what by the standards of rationality as tradition-ally understood would be deemed the height of folly. However, Heidegger separates the human from nonhuman animality more sharply than Levinas does, so sharply that he would be very unhappy with the equation Levinas draws between *Dasein*'s being concerned for its being and the Darwinian idea that the living being struggles for life. First, the being of *Dasein* is not a struggle for life. However paradoxical it may be to say so, the being of *Dasein*, notwithstanding its beingness toward its own death, is not fundamentally (*pace* Dilthey) a living being. Concern for its existence is not concern for its life. Second, *Dasein* is indeed concerned for its being according to the analysis given in *Being and Time;* but it is concerned for—one might say also concerned or obsessed by—being, and this concern cannot be construed as a concern only for its own survival and/or the survival of other beings. Although the ethical as understood by Levinas is not based on the principle affirmed as Proposition VI of Part III of Spinoza's *Ethics,* "Every thing, in so far as it is in itself, endeavours to persist in its being," it is by no means evident that according to Heidegger the surplus of concern for being should be construed as a requirement for persistence in being, or at least persistence in authentic being. It will become evident before we have proceeded much further that adherence to Spinoza's Proposition VI is a requirement of "the rigor of a certain inhumanity" referred to in the title of this book and of its last chapter.

NINE

Who or What or Whot

A stumbling block

Kierkegaard's statement "The metaphysical, the ontological, is [er], but it does not exist [er ikke til]" draws the line that separates him from Hegel and both of them from Levinas.[1] His Danish does this distinctly. On the one hand, the preposition "til," "to," indicates a relation between subjectivity and otherness that, Kierkegaard maintains, cannot be subsumed within the sphere of being or essence. On the other hand, while agreeing with Kierkegaard's denial, Levinas argues against Kierkegaard (and Heidegger) that the ec-static, ex-sistent to-ness and toward-ness of the relation indicated by Kierkegaard's preposition presupposes an inward-ness without which there can be no relations. This in-wardness is not the inwardness of subjectivity as Kierkegaard describes it. It stems not from the singular individual's decision and free will, but from finding itself subjected to and responding to another's command. Before investigating this difference more closely, let us review briefly the Hegelian conception they agree in rejecting.

Hegel teaches that the other is the negative of the same, "the necessary other," as Kierkegaard calls it. In *The Concept of Anxiety* Kierkegaard applies to Hegel a criticism he has heard made of Schelling. Having affirmed that the negative is the evil, it is a short step to a position in which transitions in logic are declared illogical because they are evil and transitions are declared unethical in ethics because the evil is the negative. "In logic they are too much and in ethics too little. . . . If ethics has no other transcendence, it is essentially logic. If logic is to have as much transcendence as common propriety requires of ethics, it is no longer logic."[2] It is to this panontologicism that Levinas too is objecting when he writes that "the fundamental fact of the ontological scission into same and other is a non-allergic relation of the same with the other."[3] To say that this relation is non-allergic is to say that it is not a relation in which there is a conflict between forces, not an inter-action (*ergon*). Hence the quotation marks when he writes that "The 'resistance' of the other does not do violence to me, does not act negatively; it has a positive structure: ethical."[4] The other resists me in being undesirable, because he or she is my accuser. This resistance is also a resistance to system "without its resistance to system manifesting itself as the egoist cry of the subjectivity, still concerned for happiness or salvation, as in Kierkegaard."[5]

For both Kierkegaard and Levinas the other is the one I am commanded to love. For both Kierkegaard and Levinas the other is my neighbor. According to both Kierkegaard and Levinas I am commanded to love my neighbor by God. According at least to Levinas I am commanded to love my neighbor also by my neighbor. Furthermore, God commands me to love my neighbor as I love myself. "You shall love your neighbor as yourself" (Leviticus 19:18, Matthew 22:39). You *shall* love your neighbor. I *do* love myself. According to Kierkegaard self-love is part of all preferential love, whether the latter be friendship or erotic love. These are forms of temporal love. They fall short of commanded love as the temporal falls short of the eternal. But if they fall short through being forms of self-love, how can I be commanded to love my neighbor as myself? Only if self-love can be unselfish.

"The concept 'neighbor,'" Kierkegaard writes, "is actually the redoubling of your own self; the 'neighbor' is what philosophers call 'the other,' that by which the selfishness in self-love is to be tested."[6] The friend and the beloved are nearest to me by preference. Their being near to me is exclusive of others. My love ceases to be exclusive only when the other is as near to me as I am near to myself. As such the other is my neighbor. The selfishness and narcissism of preferential love is superseded by a love of oneself as neighbor to a neighbor. The former love differs from the latter in that while in the former love I make demands on the beloved, in the latter love demands are made on me. The latter love is a test of the former in that the beloved as neighbor makes demands on me *as myself* a neighbor, as one who loves the other *as myself.* There therefore appears to be no difference between the beloved as neighbor making demands on me as neighbor and my making them on myself as neighbor. This would follow from Kierkegaard's subsumption of these demands under the commandment "You shall love your neighbor as yourself."

Levinas observes that in Buber's and Rosenzweig's translation of the Hebrew version of this commandment its last word, "*kamocha*," "as yourself," is separated from the beginning of the verse, yielding "Love your neighbour; this work is (as) yourself."[7] The work will be the work of love, but *my* love, not, as in Kierkegaard's interpretation, the love of God or the love that God is. Kierkegaard writes: "In erotic love and friendship, preferential love is the middle term; in love for the neighbour, God is the middle term."[8] That is to say, the other is your neighbor on the ground of equality before God.[9] With this we seem to reach what for Levinas would be a stumbling-block, a double difficulty, partly a difficulty relating to the difference between Kierkegaard's Christian construal of God, partly relating to God independently of that construal.

Kierkegaard's concept of God is a stumbling-block for Levinas on account of what Kierkegaard himself calls the absurdity of the absolute paradox that God became man. In Kierkegaard's concept of God the way to Christ is the way to God and the way to God is the way to Christ. The way to Christianity is guarded by the incarnation. And the incarnation is an offensive absurdity. Its offensiveness is essential to Christianity. It is not, however, because the incarnation offends Levinas's Judaism that he cannot as a philosopher follow Kierkegaard. It is because no positive religion, including Judaism, can be the key to an understanding of ethicality. To repeat words cited in chapter 8, "The Other is not the incarnation of God, but precisely by his face, in which he is disincarnate, is the manifestation of the height in which God is revealed."[10] The key to the understanding of ethicality is the "Western," Greek idea of the Good beyond being. "If it has played no role in the Western philosophy issued from Aristotle, the Platonic idea of the Good ensures it the dignity of a philosophical thought—and it therefore cannot be traced back to any oriental wisdom."[11] If the offence that Kierkegaard holds to be essential to Christianity were not the incarnation but the crucifixion there might be a chance of building a bridge from him to Levinas by going back from the crucifixion to what Christian theologians call its prefiguration in the story of Abraham and Isaac told in the Hebrew Bible. This chance is weakened by the fact that Christ was crucified but Isaac was not killed. The chance is still further weakened by the fact that in his reading of Kierkegaard's account of the story of Abraham and Isaac Levinas says that primacy should have been given to the restitution of the purely ethical relationship after the angel of the Lord cried "Lay not thine hand upon the lad." That is to say, independent of the difficulty raised for Levinas as a Jew by Kierkegaard's Christian conception of God is the difficulty for Levinas that Kierkegaard not only ends with a positive religion but *begins* there too, with God, rather than with an ethics of the other human being.

Order of priority

This statement of how Kierkegaard and Levinas differ from each other in one respect raises the question whether, notwithstanding the latter's emphasis on the importance of the return to ethicality in the story of the events on Moriah, he himself retains a place for a religiousness that he does not oppose to ethicality. At the very least he would want to retain for ethicality the sense of binding that the second syllable of the word "religion" is commonly taken to signify, whether or not this signification is supported by etymology. The opposition between the ethical and the religious is starker in those places in Kierkegaard's writings, for instance the *Concluding Unscientific Postscript,* where so many of the references to the ethical are references to general objective ethics as conceived by the Hegelians. He is there writing about ethics particularly as *Sittlichkeit,* custom, practice, morals as *mores.* Levinas maintains that the generality and historicality of ethics or morals thus understood is conditioned or quasi-conditioned by what he calls the ethical. For Kierkegaard it is animated by the religiousness in which the finite collides not only dialectically but also paradoxically with the absolute otherness of the transcendent infinite. He calls this religiousness B. Levinas would call this Christianity. But it would not be making too crude an assessment of the difference at this point between the two thinkers if we said that both aim to find room for what, using a locution Kierkegaard employs, we could describe as the ethico-religious.

For both Kierkegaard and Levinas the second word of this hyphenated expression evokes the individual in his or her first-person singularity. But while for Kierkegaard in this context this first-person singularity is that of the I, for Levinas it is that of the me. For Levinas the first-person singularity is that of the I when I am the one that seeks to enjoy myself; it is the first-person singularity of the self of the world of happiness in time as distinguished by Kierkegaard from eternity. One of Levinas's criticisms of Kierkegaard is that the projective character he attributes to the enjoyment of worldly life carries over into what in Kierkegaard corresponds to what Saint Paul describes as the new life or at least into what Kierkegaard himself describes as the serious matter of choosing not between good and evil, but between choosing between good and evil and not so choosing: between decisiveness and indifference. Choosing or decision is an act of free will, and an act of will relates to what will or will not be. Such an act, Levinas maintains, depends upon a passivity which, if it has any intentionality at all, has an intentionality that is reversed, whether intentionality be understood as an intending to do something or in the broader phenomenological sense in which all so-called mental acts or states of consciousness are intentional in that they are directed at an objective or accusative. The primary accusative, Levinas holds, is the first-person singular in the accusative case: me, the one whose very selfhood is due to its being singled out, elected, by the other one who accuses me of not fulfilling my duty. My selfhood is not a matter of consciousness. If it is not misleading to speak in the Levinasian context of selfhood being constituted—for in this context constitution is also deconstitution of consciousness—the constitution of my selfhood is due to duty or, to use the term that Levinas prefers, to responsibility, meaning by this the absolute responsibility without which no specific relative duties are ethical.

Kierkegaard defines this responsibility or answerability (*Ansvar*) in terms of God and his laws. The religious and the responsibility that goes with it is the religiousness of a religion, albeit that this responsibility is spelled out in terms of responsibilities to my neighbor, the other human being. The responsible love that helps my neighbor is the love that helps my neighbor to love God. Similarly for my neighbor's love of me. Not least when my neighbor is my wife.

> This the world can never get into its head, that God not only . . . becomes the third party in every relationship of love but really becomes the sole object of love, so that it is not the husband who is the wife's beloved, but it is God, and it is the wife who is helped by the husband to love God, and conversely, and so on.[12]

The world can never get into its head that for the truly loving husband and wife God is between them when they are in bed. They make up a threesome. But the third, God, is love. And the third is first where the love between husband and wife is love of the other as neighbor. This is what distinguishes the Knight of Resignation from the Knight of Faith in the "Preliminary Expectoration" in *Fear and Trembling*. The Knight of Resignation, unlike the Knight of Faith, thinks erroneously that he can give up the girl and without giving up himself hope to graduate to faith.[13]

"Ultimately, love for God is the decisive factor; from this originates [*stammer*] love for the neighbor" Kierkegaard writes.[14] As though with this sentence in mind Levinas writes about the word "God": "What matters here is that it is from the relation with the other, in the depth of Dialogue, that this inordinate word has significance for thought, not vice-versa."[15] This difference in order of priority stands even when allowance is made for two facets of Kierkegaard's exposition that may seem to be passed over in Levinas's explicit and implicit criticism.

First, does not the place Kierkegaard leaves for grace mean that a moment of reversal must be admitted by what was called earlier the projective structure of Kierkegaard's interpretation of first-personal subjectivity? Does this not to some extent forestall Levinas's critique by admitting a so-to-speak "in-static" interference into the centrifugal ec-staticness that he finds in Kierkegaard's account of the self, as he finds it and finds it objectionable in Heidegger's analysis of *Dasein*? However, grace does not meet the requirement of perspicuity that Levinas believes ethicality imposes, and without which there would be no safeguard against fanaticism.

> When I maintain an ethical relation I refuse to recognize the role I would play in a drama of which I would not be the author or whose outcome another would know before me; I refuse to figure in a drama of salvation or of damnation that would be played in spite of me and would make play of me.[16]

Here Levinas is manifesting the distrust in which Kierkegaard and Kant hold the insobriety of enthusiasm and *Schwärmerei*. Grace would belong to the realm of "mysterious designs." Therefore it could not belong to the realm of the ethical or indeed of the ethico-religious.

Levinas's analysis of Kierkegaard's notion of the first-person singular as ecstatic or projective may appear to need qualifying also in order to do justice to Kierkegaard's exclamation: "*You* shall, *you* shall love the neighbour. O my listener, it is not *you* to whom *I* am speaking; it is *I* to whom eternity says: *You* shall."[17] In so far as the pattern here is that of being addressed it resembles that of the *you* addressing the *me* as described by Levinas. But what Kierkegaard here calls eternity is not what he refers to earlier in *Works of Love* as "the *first you*,"[18] meaning the neighbor as neighbor in contrast to the *alter ego* of erotic love or friendship who, despite his or her otherness, is still the self-loving I. By eternity here is meant God. Now late in *Totality and Infinity* Levinas writes about eternity as follows:

> The dream of a happy eternity, which subsists in man along with his happiness, is not a simple aberration. Truth requires both an infinite time and a time it will be able to seal, a completed time. The completion of time is not death, but messianic time, when the perpetual is converted into the eternal. Messianic triumph is the pure triumph; it is secured

against the revenge of evil whose return the infinite time does not pro-
hibit. Is this eternity a new structure of time, or an extreme vigilance of
the messianic consciousness? The problem exceeds the bounds of this
book.[19]

Although it is a special problem concerning eternity that Levinas here declares out of bounds in his book concerning the ethical, and although the
ethical itself breaks the bounds of being and knowledge, no problem or mystery concerning eternity can belong to the ethical Exteriority which the subtitle of *Totality and Infinity* announces is the topic of that book. The eternity
of what Kierkegaard calls inwardness is beyond the bounds of that book for
the same reason.

Nevertheless, Levinas grants, "The movement that leads to the other
human being leads to God."[20] The ethico-religious leads to religion. And
provided the priority of the movement that leads to the human is preserved,
the religion to which it leads is the superior form of religion. "Everything
that cannot be reduced to an interhuman relation represents not the superior
form but the primitive form of religion."[21] The word "reduced" reproduced
here from the published translation should be interpreted, with its Latin
original in mind, as "led back." The French text has "*se ramener*," which
itself leads back to the "leads" (*mène*) of the sentence cited at the beginning
of this paragraph. God and be-godded religion cannot be reduced to the
ethicality of interhuman relations in the sense that there is no more to religion than these relations. It cannot be in terms of such be-godded religion
that the religiousness of the ethico-religious in Levinas is to be understood.
To understand Levinas in this way would be to reduce his notion of the
ethico-religious to Kierkegaard's in the sense that it would be to say at least
that the other as God is the way to the other as human being. When the
risk is taken of transferring Kierkegaard's expression "ethico-religious" to
the Levinasian context the second component must be given a sense that
is not defined only through the idea of God. It includes the sense Levinas
gives to "metaphysics" when he writes "In metaphysics a being is in a relation with what it cannot absorb, with what it cannot, in the etymological
sense of the term, comprehend." Metaphysics is *meta-phusis*, beyond being.
The ethico-religious is the ethico-metaphysical and vice versa for Levinas
because "For the relation between [the] being here below [*l'être ici-bas*] and
[the] transcendent being [*l'être transcendant*] that results in no community
of concept or totality—a relation without relation—we reserve the term religion."[22] That is to say, (the) transcendent being is beyond being, and because
(the) transcendent being is related, albeit unrelationally, to (the) being here
below, the latter too is beyond being. But the beyond of being is the Good,

not God. More precisely, for Levinas the beyond of being is God only if God is the Good. Kierkegaard too sometimes refers to the Good and to God as though they were interchangeable, but only where the Good is defined in terms of God. Thus at the beginning of the third chapter of *Purity of Heart,* after citing the Epistle to James 4:8 ("Draw nigh to God, and he will draw nigh to you"), he adds this explanation: "For only the pure in heart can see God, and therefore draw nigh to Him; and only by God's drawing nigh to them can they maintain this purity. And he who in truth wills only one thing can will only the Good. . . ."[23] The Platonic Good is Levinas's guide to the ethical, and, as has been seen, the ethical is an exteriority where all is above-board. It is the realm of frankness and sincerity. What Levinas refers to as "the final secret of being"[24] is that there is no secret in the realm of the ethical. This realm is ethico-religious as against the realm of the unregenerated political, because the latter is the field in which the struggle for equality and reciprocal recognition takes place.[25] It aims at a happy totality. That totality is made possible and impossible or unpossible—otherwise possible—by the infinity of Desire which interrupts it. It is for the latter that Levinas reserves the word "religion," meaning by this "the surplus possible in a society of equals, that of glorious humility, responsibility, and sacrifice, which are the condition for equality itself." "Religion . . . is the ultimate structure" or, "if one may so put it, de-structure." This de-structure is testified to by texts from Holy Scripture, for example by Micah 1:3–4. "For behold, the Lord cometh forth out of his place, and will come down, and tread upon the high places of the earth. And the mountains shall be molten under him, and the valleys shall be cleft, as wax before the fire, and as the waters that are poured down a steep place." But the power of such texts to stand witness to the ultimacy of religion as de-structure or dis-structure or cata-strophic structure does not depend upon their scriptural authority.[26] In that regard it is, to borrow a phrase and a title from Kierkegaard, without authority (a phrase and a title through which resounds a note that in chapter 7 was heard in what Michel Henry says about Scripture).

That is, even in those studies devoted to the exegesis of the Torah, the Talmud, and other texts of Jewish religious tradition, it must be possible to express in Greek what is testified by them, meaning by "Greek" that discourse of philosophy transmitted from Athens, not least in what Levinas hears in Plato's doctrine of the Good beyond being. This beyond is the beyond of the title of those readings and discourses Levinas collects under the title *L'au-delà du verset.*[27] His title is not *Au-delà du verset, Beyond the verse.* It is *The Beyond of the Verse.* The beyond is *in* the verses of Scripture. In their words is their transcendence. But the transcendence of the word is the deed. It is, to borrow again the words of another of Kierkegaard's titles, works of love. And the love is love of the other in both senses and directions (*sens, Sinne*) of that genitive, and of the other in two senses too: the other human being, *Autrui* or *l'autre*, and the Other, *l'Autre*, meaning God.

World without end

A warning was given above against inferring that Levinas would have the other take over the work of the Other as just distinguished. Although because of his confessional commitment to Christianity Kierkegaard is unable to allow this, it cannot be only because of Levinas's confessional commitment to Judaism that he is unable to dispense with the word "God." There are philosophical reasons why he cannot do this, Greek reasons, and not ones derived simply from the fact that the Greeks needed the word. Levinas says that the word "God" is extraordinary. But without it we should be unable to understand ordinary words. Or, rather, we should be unable to understand that all ordinary words are extraordinary, not only those that carry their extraordinariness on the face, but words in daily use like "Goodbye" and "Adieu." The transcendence of words is their being for the other, *pour l'autre*. What is added, we may ask, if, having said "For the other human being" we go on to say, as Levinas does: "and thereby unto God," "Pour l'autre homme et par là à-Dieu"?[28] What is the force of this "thereby"? Does it link the for-the-other to the unto-God chronologically or ontologically? This is a question that is raised in Descartes's Third Meditation, so frequently referred to by Levinas, where the answer seems to be that the idea of the existence of the self that is conscious of itself, the *pour-soi*, is prior in the temporal order of discovery to the idea of the existing God, while God is prior to the self ontologically. But what Levinas's "thereby" signifies is neither in the *ordo cognoscendi* nor in the *ordo essendi*. It signifies in the space of *dés-inter-essement* in the etymological sense of this word. On page 9 of the 1982 edition of *L'au-delà du verset* where this is said there are two typographical curiosities that may not be unintended misprints.[29] Instead of "*dés-*" the published text has "*dès-*," which usually means "from" in a temporal sense. But a misprint so apt that one hopes it is intended is *éthymologique* [*sic*]. For it is ethics or the ethical, *l'éthique*, that disorders both the order of being and the order of knowing, the ethical not as exclusive of the religious, but as leading us and Descartes both to the idea of God and to the God that comes to the idea or to mind, *Dieu qui vient à l'idée*. The God that comes to the idea or to mind cannot be comprehended in any idea or finite mind, as Descartes confirms when he breaks off ratiocination and instead offers a prayer in praise of God's majesty. Levinas would say that prayer, *oraison*, is a reason, *raison*, that is prior to rationalist ratiocination.

The rationalist Descartes is of course interested in establishing the existence of God. The question how the existence of God is established is treated by Kierkegaard almost as an irrelevance. He is content to say that he knows God exists because his father told him so.[30] This question of how we know God exists is deliberately set aside by Levinas. He states at the beginning of the foreword to *De Dieu qui vient à l'idée* that this book makes no pretence to deal with the question of the existence or nonexistence of God or indeed with the question whether it makes sense to talk of deciding this one way or the other. His approach is phenomenological, and phenomenology suspends questions of existence. Levinas's non-dogmatic quasi-theological phenomenology has in common with the rationality of Descartes's theological ontology that it seeks "a reasonable way to speak of God."[31] It does this by binding back speaking about God into one human being's speaking to another. It shows that the abstractness of the Other as God is given meaning through being placed within the context of concrete relations with the human other.[32]

One illustration of this passage from the abstract to the concrete is a passage to a dimension of otherness that has not yet been mentioned. At the end of the essay titled "Meaning and Sense" a reference is made to Exodus 33. At the end of that chapter of Exodus we read God's words to Moses: "And it shall come to pass, while my glory passeth by, that I will put thee in a cleft of the rock, and will cover thee with my hand while I pass by: And I will take away mine hand, and thou shalt see my back parts; but my face shall not be seen." Levinas's gloss on God's not showing his face is that God shows himself only by his trace, where a trace is to be understood in terms of God's having passed and—in contrast with what is representable by an image or sign—of his never having been present and never being capable of becoming present to view, not even as an objective to the mind. Viewing and visibility are out of the question precisely because the "thereby" (*par là*) cited above does not usher in a being or the being of a being. It marks that the meaning of the word "God" is our addressing ourselves to the other human being. Address is not a relation to an object or objective. It is being face to face, which, we have learned, is not strictly a relation, but the precondition of relationality.[33] Levinas then gives an ethical exegesis of the words cited above from Exodus: "To go toward Him is not to follow this trace, which is not a sign; it is to go towards the Others (*les Autres*). . . ."[34] But there has already taken place in Levinas's text, if not quite a reversal of this humanizing move, a reaching back to what makes the move possible, to a kind of compromise (which is also a com-promise), a common origin of alterity which he calls illeity. The third-personality (*il*, he) of this neo-logism is apt because it is in the trace of illeity that we go toward the plural Others.

It would be more accurate to say that illeity is not a neologism, but a neo-graphism. For it alludes to a Scripture beyond the biblical Scripture that Levinas takes as his clue. Parallel to the philosophical and ethical issue at stake here is the doctrine invoked by Levinas that the Torah stands as a safeguard against a too familiar proximity to God.[35] Tangential to this doctrine is the Kabbalistic doctrine that God is the Torah.[36] He reminds us too of the place in the *Phaedrus* (p. 275) where we read that—like God in Exodus 33—the author of a piece of writing or of a drawing is typically unavailable and unanswerable to the reader or viewer. And it is in this Platonic dialogue that we find the theory of knowledge as recollection illustrated by the analogy of truths written on the wax of the mind. Kierkegaard too harks back to this theory in order, like Levinas, to substitute an ethical transcendentalism for the epistemological immanentism of Plato's theory of *anamnesis*. In Kierkegaard's case, this transcendentalist alternative is what he calls repetition (*Gjentagelse*). Repetition does not retrieve something remembered. It is directed not simply toward a temporal future and past. It is directed to eternity. And it is teleological, as confirmed by the thought in *Fear and Trembling* of a teleological suspension of the ethical. Although illeity is not recollected, neither is it teleological. Yet the absolute past of its immemoriality is matched by an absolute futurity. So if illeity is an origin, as Levinas says it is, while denying it any cosmogonic or cosmological status, it could be regarded as the common origin of doctrines found in the Hebrew and Greek traditions. This brings us to a critical question. Would the absolute otherness of this common origin offer a way of getting behind and subverting the Other called God?

Pertinent to this question are the following rhetorical questions from *Purity of Heart*:

> For, after all, what is eternity's accounting other than that the voice of conscience is for ever installed with its eternal right to be the exclusive voice? What is it other than that throughout eternity an infinite stillness reigns wherein the conscience may talk with the individual about what he has done of Good or evil?[37]

There is mention of conscience and of good and of evil here, but there is no mention here of God. So is Kierkegaard contemplating the possibility of an ethics of eternity that is ethico-religious but neither an ethics of generality in the style of Hegel nor an ethics of religion? No. For, in the paragraph preceding the one in which he may seem to be leaving an opening for this possibility he has written: "In eternity . . . each one shall render account to God as an individual." And here the name of God is being used essentially, not borrowed as a manner of speaking as it seems to be when Levinas employs the expression "judgment of God" for the judgment that calls me to a justice more exacting than that of the universal judgments of history.[38] As in the sentences cited from Kierkegaard, the Hegelians are again being targeted. But Levinas would acknowledge Nietzsche as well as Kierkegaard to be a marksman alongside himself, except that the eternity of Nietzsche's eternal return of the same is neither the eternity that gets mentioned in the sentences just cited from Kierkegaard nor the eternity that gets mentioned toward the end of *Totality and Infinity* only in order that its author may tell us that it raises a problem that exceeds the frame (*cadre*) of this book. Has not the book been treating throughout problems that exceed any frame? This is a question that exceeds the frame of this chapter. I therefore pass, as that book does, to some Conclusions, or, as Kierkegaard might say, to a concluding unscientific postscript, pausing only to observe in passing that a postscript is something that exceeds a frame, and that this can be said of the entirety of Kierkegaard's *Concluding Unscientific Postscript* as confidently as it can be said of his collection of nothing but prefaces titled *Prefaces*.

Neographisms

If with Kierkegaard we give priority, ethico-religiously speaking, to the Other as the God of Christianity over the other as the other human being, are we not in direct conflict both with secular ethics and with any religion which, like Levinas's, does not give a central place to the Incarnation? The conflict will not flare up into warfare if the Christian, the Jew, and the Muslim not only tolerate one another but listen to one another. Levinas purports to keep his Jewish faith separate from his thinking of ethicality. This thinking helps us to understand how not only tolerance but active listening to and welcoming of the other as stranger can happen. It opens a way, as Christianity also does, to loving the enemy, but it does so without requiring that that love be offered only on condition that the Christian or Jewish or Islamic doctrine be accepted as fundamental in ethico-religious intersubjectivity and sociality. To accept a doctrine as fundamental is to accept it not merely as a doctrine or theoretical tenet, but in one's actions and, Kierkegaard would say, as an "existence-communication."

Kierkegaard keeps his Christian faith separate from his thinking of un-regenerate Hegelian ethicality, but that faith is the heart of his thinking of ethicality as given back dialectically in the absurd paradoxicality of Religiousness B. In Religiousness B eternal happiness is at one and the same time, or, rather, at the intersection of time and eternity, worldly suffering. In Religiousness A happiness is the *telos* one hopes to achieve via suffering. It takes this end to be achievable through things of this world, the world understood as a totality to which these things belong together with the individual. That is to say, it is a religiousness of immanence, and its pathos is aesthetic. Hence it is available to the pagan. None of this means that Religiousness A does not share with Religiousness B a consciousness of culpability. Without that there would be little plausibility in the proposal I hereby make that Kierkegaard's Religiousness A be taken together with Levinas's description of the ethico-religious as pointers toward a Derridean notion of religiousness that is more comprehensive than those proposed by Kierkegaard and Levinas yet is no less demanding upon the singular individual than are their teachings regarding the ethico-religious. It is this demandingness that distinguishes the proposed revision both from paganism as conceived by Levinas when he distinguishes the sacred (*le sacré*) from the holy (*le saint*), and from paganism as conceived by Kierkegaard when he dismisses paganism with the remark that "The highest well-being of a happy immediacy, which jubilates joy over God and all existence, is very endearing but not upbuilding and essentially not any relationship with God."[39] It is not essentially a relationship with God according to Kierkegaard because in place of existentiality it puts "all existence," that which is comprehended. The paradox and the absurd "are employed aesthetically with regard to the marvelous among many other things, the marvelous that certainly is marvelous but that nevertheless can be comprehended."[40]

Derrida demonstrates that the greater comprehensiveness of a religiousness beyond religiousness as portrayed by either Kierkegaard or Levinas does not mean that it is a religiousness in which everything can be comprehended. He keeps open the path to a greater comprehensiveness by observing that the question "Who is my other?" begs a question. He asks us to ask instead "Who or what is my other?" To put this in Levinas's terms, he questions the opposition between the sacred and the holy. Levinas's word "*saint*" translates the Hebrew "*kadosh*," meaning separated. But the Hebrew word can also mean sacred. Derrida invites us to follow this hint of the Hebrew when he expands the scope of what Levinas first calls reversed or inverted intentionality but comes to think of rather as an interruption of intentionality and its noetic–

noematic structure. Intentionality implies consciousness and, on Levinas's interpretation of it, consciousness implies a synthetic unity of apperception over against an objective accusative. In responsibility this objective accusative of what is said or what appears (*apparaît*) becomes the subject's appearing (*comparaît*) as though in a court of law, except that I am found culpable not on account of anything I have done or left undone, not because of a contravention of a law, but simply through my excluding the singular other from my singular place in the sun. Derrida reopens the question whether this excluded other is divine, human, animal, vegetable, or mineral, whether we must extend what he calls, paradoxically, democracy to come "to the whole world of singularities, to the whole world of humans assumed to be like me, my compeers . . . even further, to all nonhuman living beings, or again, even beyond that, to all the nonliving, to their memory, spectral or otherwise, to their to-come. . . ."[41]

My other according to Levinas is someone, a he or a she, who can speak. Although the nonliving understood as the no longer living is not the nonliving understood as the inorganic or the artificial, Derrida invites us to consider whether no less other than the other who can speak is the other who cannot speak, the it on behalf of which it is therefore my responsibility to speak, however unimaginably other the other may be. So unconditional is the welcome this ultimate other invites me to make that its alterity cannot be marked by the paleonym or pronym "God" or by the neographism "Illeity" unless these markers are undecided as between who and what. Following the suggestion made by the relative pronoun in "Our Father *which* art in Heaven . . ." in the King James version of Luke 11:2, this undecidedness could be marked by the neographism "whot."

In the phenomenological description of the experience that manifests the speculative system that Hegel constructs occur moments when alterity is the alterity of a who, for example the alterity of my master. But as the dialectic of "the necessary other" who negates and elevates me progresses, the personal Who becomes an impersonal What, for example the alterity of the impersonal and universal "absolute master" called death. Kierkegaard and Levinas seek to save the Who in its singularity. So too does Derrida. But he seeks to save also the What. Not principally the What of essence nor the Hegelian What that is singular through being an ultimately single and all-comprehensive It, but a What that respects the plurality of unique Its. This fails to be marked by Levinasian Illeity, of which the third-personality is indeed that of the third person, whether another human being or God. To do justice to the singularity both of human and all nonhuman others, a justice that is done by neither Levinas nor Kierkegaard, Derrida is in effect inviting us to widen our notions of representation and suffrage by giving asylum in our thinking of what he calls the New International democracy to come a barbarism, neither Greek nor Hebrew nor Arabic nor yet English, neither simply spoken nor simply written, at the heart of the chiasmus of *logos* as saying and of *logos* as said, the archic yet anarchic pronoun "Whot."

TEN

Ecosophy, Sophophily, and Philotheria

Subwholes and singularity

Once upon a time I took part in a trek along a network of valleys to the base camp of the 1970 British expedition to the south summit of Annapurna in the Himalayas. Although our final destination was merely the edge of the Hiunchuli glacier, our sirdar Yong Tenzing acceded to my request that I might proceed on my own to a cairn a little higher up. On top of the cairn was a Norwegian 10-*øre* coin. Had this been placed there, I mused, by the philosopher and mountaineer Arne Naess with some of whose writings I was familiar? If not, had it been put there by his namesake and nephew, the Arne Naess who has sponsored Himalayan climbs, supporting them financially to the tune of rather more than 10 *øre*?

In his *Ecology, Community, and Lifestyle: Outline of an Ecosophy,* Arne Naess senior describes how each thing belongs to a whole and to a plurality of subwholes according to an indefinite range of possible *Gestalten* in which it may appear as a figure or ground.[1] That belonging is not the belonging only of an instance that falls under a concept. Belonging as the belonging of an instance that falls under a concept, the belonging in terms of which rights and justice are defined, itself falls within a notion of justice as concordance that is closer to the idea of justice as expounded in Plato's *Republic* and to Anaximander's notion of *dikē* as expounded in Heidegger's "The Anaximander Fragment"[2] than it is to the Enlightenment and Kantian idea of justice and injustice determined as cases or maxims falling under or falling foul of a natural or moral law by which they are taken to be covered. However, in the Critical system of Kant this hierarchical idea of justice falls under the regulative Idea of orderedness in an organic whole that has more in common with the Platonic conception of justice as synergic harmony. Instead of prescribing principles entailing conclusions unidimensionally, this conception of justice as balance within a multidimensional whole offers guidelines. Deductive rigor makes way for persuasion, as in the cosmogony outlined in the *Timaeus*. Instead of a blueprint we have a recipe, instead of a tracing a map. A recipe leaves room for practical judgment and imagination. It therefore leaves room for their misuse. The difference between use and misuse is a difference of *phronēsis*, practical understanding in our ways of conducting ourselves in the regional ecologies of the world.

From this willingness to invoke Aristotle's notion of *phronēsis* it must not be inferred that the conception of ecology referred to here is an endorsement of his doctrine that each of the elements composing an ecology has a natural directionality of movement. What the conception of ecology referred to here does endorse is more like what is described in the following paragraphs from Aloo Dastur's *Man and His Environment*. They capture something of what is important in the conception of ecology articulated by Arne Naess. And they take us back to the mountains at the head of a valley, where this chapter began.

> A river, in its journey from its source to its mouth exhibits, as it were, a section of our civilisation. At its source among mountains or hills are found stone and rocks and minerals; hence, man can live there and maintain himself by mining. Adjoining this part of the valley section are woodlands where man can fell trees, while his neighbour in the forest is essentially a hunter. On the expansive grasslands the shepherd and his sheep can thrive with advantage. As we enter the lower slopes of the valley we see the crofts of the crofter, while further down on fertile plains the farmer and the gardener. Of course, at the mouth of the river the fisherman plies his boat and/or casts his nets and baits. Thus does each part of the valley section represent a unit of environmental advantages for some specific human activities and difficulties for some others. Each has its own possibilities, its own specific fundamental occupation and along with it its subsidiary occupations. To these eight typical occupations can be traced the several occupations and professions of the present day world. In each part springs up a distinctive culture with its

characteristic arts, crafts, sciences, ideas and ideals, beliefs and religions, and even its super-social and anti-social representatives.

The valley section is a corrective on the hypothesis of geographical determinism because of its occupational bias and ecological approach. It classifies regions not merely in terms of climate or location or size, but with special reference to the possibilities which every region offers to its inhabitants for specific, fundamental pursuits. Each of its parts is the smallest regional unit from which all inquiry pertaining to regional surveys should proceed. The various divisions of the earth into zones, climatic or botanico-zoological, given by geographers are unsatisfactory by themselves and there is no regular, scientific basis of division adopted by them. Each of their final regional units can be further sub-divided into several regions. . . . Moreover, the typical problems of "transitional" or "pocket" regions are wholly ignored in these earlier divisions.

The various parts of the valley section are not conceived as isolated, water-tight compartments. Rather, they are so many necessary links in a chain having points of contact with and/or divergence from each other. Each part is related not merely to its immediate neighbours but also to every other; and these linkages are not casual but causal. This enables us to view a world of linked valley sections as one co-ordinate whole with life and activities, plant, animal and human, continually going through different processes of transformation and change. It thus offers the widest scope for the study of relationships between man and his environment not only analytically in each region but also synthetically along the entire valley, not only statically but also dynamically.[3]

Aristotle studied the interactions between organisms and their environment, but it was not until 1866 that the term "oecology" [sic] was introduced as a name for such a study in Ernst Haeckel's *General Morphology of Organisms*.[4] An *oikos* is a house, an inhabited place. But unless it is specifically to animal or human ecology that reference is being made, I shall understand by the term "ecology" either *any* inhabited place or the study of any inhabited place, with the unlimited universality that the word "ecumenical" implies, not the limited universality such as that which the Greeks imposed when they restricted the *oikoumenē* to that part of the world inhabited by them as contrasted with those they called barbarians, or which the Christian church laid down when ecumenism extended no further than Christendom. Although this uncircumscribed universality does not exclude any inhabited region from its scope, it allows for regional ecologies and ecologies of ecologies like those which, following the biologist and pioneer town planner Patrick Geddes, Dastur calls valley sections. The question as to what constitutes a regional ecology is a descendant of the Platonic question about separating at the joints, but we must follow Dastur and Geddes in allowing for pockets, limitrophes, interregna, and change.

Who or what are to count as inhabitants? Organisms at least, according to practitioners of the science of ecology going back to Haeckel and beyond to Aristotle. According to Aristotle an organ is something living that performs a work, an *ergon*, something with which we toil (*ergazomai*). If it is also Aristotle's view that an organ is a tool (*ergaleion*) and that an organic body (*soma organikon*) like the human body is a kit of tools, we have a problem on our hands, indeed a problem posed by our hands. For there is a vital difference between the way work is performed by the hand that holds a hammer and the way work is performed by the hammer itself. My hand can work like a hammer when it is taken in my other hand or in the hand of someone else and brought down heavily on a lump of clay in order to flatten it out. Only when it is used in such a manner does it function instrumentally. Only then is my hand handy or unhandy. So something seems to be going wrong right from the beginning of the history of the word *organism,* already in the work of the thinker who set out to provide an *organon,* an ordered classification of whatever there is, logical, biological, physiological, psychological, anthropological, cosmological, theological, ecological.

The last-mentioned of these domains is the concern of this chapter in respect of its ethological and ethnological dimension, but its concern is above all ecology considered from the, broadly speaking, ethical point of view. Common to the ethological, the ethnological, and the ethical is the idea of the habitual expressed in the Greek term *ethō.* So there is a connection here with our question as to who is to count as inhabitants. An *ethnos* was for the Greeks a people and a nation. For the authors of the Bible the nations were the Gentiles understood either as non-Jews, *goyim,* or as those who were neither Jews nor Christians. It is as though the biblical use of the words *ethnos* and *ēthea* inherited the force they had already in some contexts for the Greeks when they were used of herds and flocks and the places occupied by them. That force is ambiguous. It could be either exclusive or inclusive. It permitted these words to be used to connote either cohabitation and inclusion or alienation and exclusion. In our exemplary paragraphs from Dastur the inclusive force of *ethnos* has become absorbed into what she understands by ecology, just as ethology as understood by Konrad Lorenz and Desmond Morris is the study of what they claim nonhuman animals and human beings have in common. Their claim implies that nonhuman animals, like humans, inhabit, inherit, and transmit non-genetic social and cultural structures. Ethology as Lorenz and Morris understand it is part of ecology as understood by Geddes and Dastur. This is evident from the paragraphs cited from her. In each part of the valley there arises, she writes, "a distinctive culture with its characteristic arts, crafts, sciences, ideas and ideals, beliefs and religions, and even its super-social and anti-social representatives," and, she goes on to say, we are able "to view a world of linked valley sections as one co-ordinate whole with life and activities, plant, animal and human, continually going through different processes of transformation and change."

Transformation and change are undergone by the view of the world and the words through which that view is constituted and expressed. A *Gestalt* switch of worldview is often a *Gestalt* switch of wordview. That this is so needs saying because the linguistic *ethos* we inhabit at any one time is a habit, so it conspires to conceal from our view that a given word belongs to a history of the mutations it has undergone and will go on undergoing. This holds for the words *oikos* and "ecology" and *ethos* and "ethics." Ethics, hence ecological ethics, is unethical unless it is simultaneously undergoing and transmitting an education, hence an education about its own name.

Dastur's and my definition of ecology will embrace human and nonhuman animals, and plants. Such a definition is not altogether uncontroversial, since the ecological is sometimes equated with the natural and opposed to the human in line with the tendency to oppose the human to nature, even to prize the human because it is anti-natural. This tendency is manifest, for example, in the context of an interpretation of Genesis impressed by the idea that the human being is created in the image of God. This tendency is reinforced by the seemingly axiomatic status of the idea that the God at least of Judaism, Christianity, and Islam must be extra-ecological. How can it not be that if it is extra-territorial, extra-terrestrial, the ET by whom the earth is created? If God or the gods are excluded from the natural, is It, are they, to be included in the super-social that is yet included within the ecosystem as defined by Geddes and Dastur?

How could the Good God be intra-systematic, any more than the Good could be other than beyond being, *epekeina tēs ousias*? How can the one that is responsible for creating and organizing the cosmos be part of the cosmos itself? How can the transcendent be immanent? The answer toward which this chapter has so far been tending learns something from the way in which in the context of those ancient questions, as in the not-so-ancient context of secular Enlightenment, we find that our thinking turns on analogy and equivocation. But in the response toward which the present chapter would progress the notions of analogy and equivocation are invoked in a manner that seeks not to beg theological questions either way. It tries to remain neutral with regard to the tradition of positive theology, negative theology, and their secular competitors. It would aim to outline a conception of ecology that does justice both to the whole and the singular existents within it. As indicated above, it would attempt to do justice to a notion of justice that is, in the terms of the distinction made by Arne Naess, holistic but not totalistic.

This distinction between holism and totalism can be developed with the assistance of what Levinas writes about the difference between infinity and totality.[5] Readers of his works will perceive that I have learned something from what he writes about the face. Some will say that I have not learned enough from what he says about this. For, as was underlined in chapter 8, he is very resistant to the thought that a human being can be face to face with anything other than another human being, allowance made for the eventuality that in the face of the other human being we are being looked at by God. Leaving that eventuality on one side, and without ruling out or ruling in the eventuality that God is an existent, I ask my reader to consider each and every existent, as an existent, as *ipso facto* also a face. That is to say, each existent is *ipso facto* not just a fact or a constituent of a fact. Not to acknowledge a responsibility to an existent as a sheer existent is to be irresponsible. Not to consider it as putting me under a *prima facie* obligation is to be inconsiderate. Not to want, other things being equal, to support its existence—and to support it not only because it supports us—is to be wanton. I shall return to this question in the final part of the next chapter.[6]

The totalizing justice of cases falling under laws falls under the ecological justice of wholeness, but the latter justice as synergic harmony within a non-totalized ecological whole in turn *falls*. The whole is itself a singular existent. However, it loses any automatic autonomy its wholeness may appear to confer on it when a response is made to the appeal of every thing in the singularity of its incomparable existence as such. It may seem that an ecology cannot tolerate singularity except in so far as the contained singular existent is internally related to the containing singular existent, every thing being internally related to everything. Does not the very notion of an ecology imply a systematic relationship between the whole and the items within the whole? And what else could a systematic relationship be than one in which the terms are defined in terms of each other? This conception of internal relations is far stricter than the gestaltist notion of internal relations appealed to by Arne Naess. It is too strict because too conceptual. It is too procrustean to serve as a basis of our understanding of how the parts of an ecological system participate in the whole. This does not mean that one must adopt a notion of ecology in which all relations are loose and external. This is why Dastur says that the relations are causal, not casual. A relation that is external to a sub-ecology will usually be internal to a super-ecology. In which relation a thing stands will depend on the "valley section." That expression implies differences of location, higher up and lower down. But Dastur's description makes it clear that the series of sections also represents different historical stages. Practices that fit well in an earlier way of life in the uplands may be a misfit in the valley plain. And vice versa. For what is earlier in the life of society may not correspond to what is earlier in the course of a river. The region surrounding a port is likely to be settled before there is settlement in the less accessible hinterland near the source. But because when a people grows older in the same place or migrates its history stays with it, memory may exert upon it pressures conducing to a retention of ancient practices in a later age when very ingenious arguments indeed have to be invoked to justify the continuance. I want now to show how this holds for the ancient practice of hunting mentioned by Dastur as it is defended in José Ortega y Gasset's *Meditations on Hunting* and Roger Scruton's *On Hunting.*[7]

A shabby sophism

I choose the two texts just mentioned because what is written in them is contrary to my own feelings about hunting in self-styled civilized societies and because they demonstrate the extent to which what is fitting is a matter of that with which we feel comfortable. However, I shall preface my samplings of those texts by citing an author who began with a view close to that of Ortega and Scruton but became converted to the view I find it easier to share. The scene about to be described in my first citation may cause you some distress. Nevertheless, please do not look away.

> One day, stationed on the edge of the forest, while beaters were driving the game, with a gunshot I bring down a wolf, then I run up in order to dispatch him with a huge stick prepared for this purpose. I hit him at the base of the nose, the most sensitive part of the animal, and he looks at me right in the eyes and at each blow a stifled sigh escapes him. Soon his paws are convulsed, they draw themselves up, a slight shudder runs through them, they grow stiff. I return briskly to my place, quite stirred up, and hide myself behind my tree to lie in wait for a new victim. . . . But little by little a kind of trouble took possession of me; then, suddenly, I understood, by means of the heart and not by reason, that this murder was in itself a wicked action and that worse than the action even was the pleasure that it procured, and worse still was the dishonesty with which I sought to justify myself. Only then did reason show me the emptiness of my previous arguments in favour of hunting. I understood that the pretext with which I had provided myself was false, and that the wolf could with the same justification say that in eating the hares, he was saving the insects swallowed with the grass, the hare would be able to reason in the same way, and the insects in their turn.[8]

Thus Tolstoy in an essay titled "The Hunt," after reporting his "shabby soph-ism" that every animal, beast of prey or not, destroys other living beings, so why should not human beings follow suit, for in doing so they would be sav-ing the life of the being on which the hunted animal lives?

Judgments and adjustments

Promising to come back to the issue raised here by Tolstoy's distinction be-tween heart and head, we can turn away now from this bloody scene to the safety of the abstractness of the general topic of deep ecology. Deep eco-logical attitudes may be expressed both by those who are for hunting, the philotheriasts, and those who are against it. And the depth will be in part a depth of feeling. This does not mean that these feelings are not backed by beliefs concerning matters of empirical or metaphysical or theological fact. These beliefs may not be blind. But they may be biased, and biased either way; that is to say, the pressure exerted by habituation may be so great that, in contrast to Tolstoy's experience, one's belief continues unchanged under its own momentum in the face of evidence and arguments against it. This is why the most persuasive evidence is either that of firsthand experience or that of firsthand experience mediated by someone with filmic, literary, or other artistic skill. That Scruton has literary skill in no little measure is manifest in the descriptions of the more or less immediate pleasures of closeness to the natural world he discovered through being introduced to fox-hunting, "an involvement" he writes, "which changed my life."[9] Closeness, for instance, to Dumbo, his first horse, who was initially as unfitted to join the smart hunt-ing set as his rider makes it clear he felt himself to be. More at home in that society is another horse, Bob. Of him Scruton engagingly writes: "Each field he entered he scanned at once to find the points of exit and if, in the distance, he saw that a horse was jumping, he would smile all over his body and make for the place."[10] Then there is Barney, who inspires the final paragraph of the book's epilogue.

> But let me give the last word to Heidegger, for whom "care" is the relation to the world that distinguishes you and me. He defines care thus: "ahead-of-itself-Being-already-in as Being-alongside." And that, more or less, is what it feels like, jumping hedges on Barney. The being-alongside is mine; the ahead-of-itself-Being-already-in is Barney's. Hunting gives sense to everything—even to Heidegger.[11]

With rather more humor than Heidegger is able to muster, Scruton nonethe-less shares with him the respect for roots that can easily, but not necessarily, lead to a lack of respect for those whose roots grow elsewhere than our own, those who are torn from their roots or those who never had any roots at all. He believes that the fox is better served by hunting because hunting causes the fox less suffering than any other form of cull; yet he grants that only a very small number of foxes are killed by hunting with dogs; and anyway ("anyway" is often the sign of what Freud calls an argument from the kettle, that is to say, one argument too many) the maintenance of fox hunts leads to the maintenance of foxes. He considers that because other species nowadays depend upon us for their survival we have a duty to preserve these species, but that unless the animal is one we have undertaken to care for as a pet or on a farm, there is no room for grief at its death.

This view that there is room for grief over the death of an animal only when the animal is for instance a pet dog would seem to exclude the possibility of grief over the death of someone who has undertaken to care for us, for instance a human guardian or a god. Or, in order to keep open this possibility, are we to take Scruton to be saying that for there to be room for grief it is sufficient that the grief be for a being we have loved? He does say that grieving is the offshoot of love, so, "unless the rabbit is our loved companion, we must not grieve for him." (Is our guardian or our god a loved companion?) Yet he cites the following words from Sir William Bromley Davenport's confession "that when alone I have come across the hiding place of a 'beaten' fox, and he has, so to speak, confided his secret to me with big upturned and indescribably appealing eye, it has been sacred to me; I have retired softly, and rejoiced with huge joy when the huntsman at last calls away his baffled pack." According to Scruton, Sir William's pity should not be allowed to betray the relation between huntsman and hounds. If the hounds are called off too often they will be so baffled that they will lose all gusto for the chase and in due course the hunters will lose their hunting.

Scruton's most fundamental reason for thinking that this would be a great loss sometimes seems to be that the practice of hunting is the essence of Old England. He allows that fox-hunting has been the essence of Old England only since the seventeenth century, when it began as an aristocratic pursuit. The hunting for the continuing practice of which Ortega argues has a more ancient history, for it is not only of fox-hunting that his book treats. Scruton and he stress that hunting did not remain the diversion of only one class. It is, along with racing, dancing, and conversation, says Ortega, among the most enjoyable occupations of "the normal man." It belongs to "the repertory of the purest forms of human happiness." Why?

One of his answers to this is ingenious. Natural to the wolf is the feeling that it is a prey. Wolves "by nature, count on an 'ideal' hunter." Now "The only adequate response to a being that lives obsessed with avoiding capture is to try to catch it." We are doing it a favor in pursuing it to its death. So we can imagine the fox saying with Scruton that his, Reynard's, being introduced to fox-hunting was an involvement "which changed my life." And—English sentimentalists note well—pursuit that ends not in a kill but in a photograph is a cheat; it cheats both the hunted and the hunter. Or, rather, it is the destruction of hunting altogether. Although the hunter's goal may not be the kill, the goal of authentic hunting itself is the kill. Scruton writes: "The kill is the goal of hunting. . . ." Ortega writes: "the killing of the animal is the natural end of the hunt and the goal of hunting itself, *not* of the hunter." Yet for Scruton the kill is the goal of the hounds, their "single-minded motive." Scruton and Ortega are agreed on what the word "hunting" means. It means, among other things, that its end is the end of the wolf or the fox, even if that death is not what interests the hunter, what interests him being what he has to do in order that this death will ensue. As Ortega puts the matter aphoristically: "one does not hunt in order to kill; on the contrary, one kills in order to have hunted." He is giving us enlightenment about the meaning of a word.

Let us let Ortega have that meaning. But let us add that the most likely reason why the word has that meaning is that, in earlier valley sections or others contemporary with that in which hunting is a sport, hunting was necessary to the sustenance of human life, as necessary as it still sometimes is, we are told, for the maintenance of wild animal life. Ortega himself says, "the general lines of the hunt are identical today with those of five thousand years ago." They are identical in particular, he explains, in that whatever rules may have been introduced to assure that the hunted creature is fair game, and provided the inequality of the hunter and the hunted is not allowed to become too great, when it comes to the moment when the hunt gets under way, "reason does not intervene in any greater degree than it did in primitive times, when it was no more than an elemental substitute for the instincts." Too true. But in the valley section in which hunting is a way in which human beings disport themselves the hunt is not as locked into its ecology as it was five thousand years ago. It no longer fits so tightly into its regional ecosystem that it would be much missed if it were acknowledged to be a relic of the past. It is not so locked in that it cannot be reconceived in such a way that its goal is not a kill but a click of a camera or simply a delight to the naked eye.

No less ingenious is Ortega's second answer to the question why hunting is one of the purest sources of human happiness. It is one of the purest sources of human happiness because it lowers the human to the animal. It does something "more spiritual," he says, than raising the animal to the level of man. Without assuming an equality between humankind and animalkind, the ethics of hunting requires that restrictions be imposed on the hunters that give the hunted animal a chance to escape. This is tantamount to "a conscious and almost religious humbling of man which limits his superiority."

> I have said "religious," and the word does not seem excessive to me. . . .
> [A] fascinating mystery of Nature is manifested in the universal fact of hunting: the inexorable hierarchy among living beings. Every animal is in a relationship of superiority or inferiority with regard to every other. Strict equality is exceedingly improbable and anomalous. Life is a terrible conflict, a grandiose and formidable mystery and therefore contains something of religious rite and emotions in which homage is paid to what is divine, transcendent, in the laws of Nature.

The least that can be said about this is that it acknowledges the animal in man without implying that he is contaminated by his animality. This humbling of man through his dim recognition of his own animality and "the equivocal nature of man's relationship with animals" leads every hunter to experience a certain uneasiness "when faced with the death he is about to inflict on the enchanting animal." Why does it not lead him to stay his hand, thereby demonstrating that the humbling of man is consistent with recognition of the human component in the ambivalence of his relationship with animals and animality? There are other ways of paying homage to what is divine in the laws of nature than killing the enchanting animal, other ways of recognizing their charm when the animal is hunted for sport, not out of a need for food. The ambivalence in question is double. It is the ambivalence between feeling (pity, for instance) and reason, and an ambivalence between reason and the capacity for language. This second ambivalence is literally an equivocality, but it is one that relates back to the first ambivalence, since language is the vehicle not only of propositions and inferences but also of feelings. Whereas Scruton argues that we should not give the last word to pity but to reason in the circumstances described by Sir William Davenport—though Sir William too could have been acting out of both reason and pity—Ortega is perhaps a little too ready to luxuriate in the grandiosity of the conflict in which the human being finds himself. He appears to welcome the opportunity to plunge into and remain mesmerized by the "formidable mystery" of the dilemma with which the hunt is said to confront men—and, presumably, women, though he is quieter about them than Scruton is about "the hunting harpie."

Ortega is less sanguine (if that is the right word) about the scope of reason than is Scruton. At one of the few places where Ortega does refer to a woman explicitly it is to chide her for her presumption. The woman in question, "an Englishwoman, or a woman raised in England," had donated money for the wounded in the Spanish civil war. It turned out that by the wounded she meant injured dogs, for, she observed, "It is men who make war, and dogs are not to blame for the injuries they themselves suffer." Stopping short of saying that the dogs may be responsible for the injuries the soldiers suffer, Ortega scolds her for supposing she can be so sure that men are ultimately to blame for war.

> Why does this woman, who manipulates the apothegm like one of Plutarch's philosophers, have enough perceptiveness to discover the blamelessness of the dog and yet be completely blind to the ultimately doggish in man, lost in an existence that he does not dominate and cudgelled from the one side and another by the most impenetrable Destiny?

Ortega is for letting be what is "absolutely or for the present, indiscernible." So although he is careful to distinguish hunting from bullfighting, on the grounds that the latter is characterized by a reciprocity while the former is not, and although he allows himself to be impressed by "the frightening mystery of blood" in which blood is seen as sullying whatever it spills on, he allows that there is one exception to this, to wit "when it spurts from the nape of a bull that has been lanced well (*picado*) and spills down both sides of the animal. In the sun, the crimson of the brilliant liquid takes on a refulgence that turns it into a jewel. This exception, the only one that I know of, is as strange as the rule that it breaks."

This piety challenges us not to lose the propensity for strangeness, for what Keats calls the negative capability of "being in uncertainties, Mysteries, doubts, without irritable reaching after fact & reason."[12] But we had better not send reason off on permanent sabbatical leave. It is a question of balance and a question of judgment, where judgment is not to be confused with a judgment in the sense of a verdict. In my judgment Ortega errs on the side of giving himself and advocating for his readers a vacation from the human condition, a vacation so vacated of reason as to be atavistic. His reason for remaining paralyzed by the mystery of the relationship between the human being and the animal being, including the animal being whose mystery the human being senses in himself, is tilted so much in favor of the human being that his apparently deep ecology may after all be a shallow one, that is to say, one in which care for the nonhuman has become no more than a means of caring for the human. Awestruck by the charm of animals we should be, but we should not be struck dumb in regard to their own needs.

Responsive responsibility

Scruton too recognizes the wonder and charm of animals. We have seen that he also admits that we have duties to animals, for instance a duty to preserve animal species. But, following Kant, he advances an argument, not obviously consistent with that admission and certainly inconsistent in itself, to the effect that we can have direct moral obligations only to beings that can have obligations to us. From the fact that animals are not moral beings he seems to infer that they are not appropriate subjects of moral regard. "If they *were* moral beings, then Kant's categorical imperative would apply to them: it would be wrong to kill them, capture them, confine them, harm them, or curtail their freedom." But many of the people who live in my valley section think it *is* wrong to do many or all of these things except under certain circumstances such as would constitute allowable exceptions also in our treatment of human beings. Not to see this is not to see that Kant's categorical imperative is a less comprehensive account of the nature of morality than human inhabitants of our post-Enlightenment valley sections tend to think, and that it is time to move back or forward a section or more. Even if the formal moral law or its categorically imperative version straddles the entire valley or series of valleys, the maxims to which it applies do not. And if the application of the maxims to the circumstances of each section or neighborhood is to be ethical rather than merely legalistic, it must be effected not simply with responsibility as defined by the law and the maxim, but also with responsiveness to the singular inhabitants, with tact. Tact is the aesthetic aspect of ethics, but in a sense of aesthetic that implies not that the subject of our ethical response be regarded as an object, an *objet d'art,* to be passively enjoyed, but that he, she, or it be approached in the way an artist relates to the work being made. Ethical behavior is also in this sense aesthetic behavior. Responsiveness to the singularity of the work of art under way, meaning by singularity not its numerical singleness but its uniqueness, is matched by the responsiveness to the singularity of the recipient of our ethical regard. Furthermore, it is our responsibility to make ourselves responsive in this way. Only then do we open ourselves to the eventuality that the maxims to which we appeal as guidelines or rules of thumb may call to be adjusted, to be made more just, from time to time, from place to place, in one valley section or another. This crossing of responsibility with responsiveness and the interdependence between compassion and justice in wisdom (combining the love of wisdom and the wisdom of love, crossing philosophy with sophophily) may be illuminated by reference to what, following Derrida, I carefully call "something like the middle voice."[13]

Again, something like the middle voice

Another cloud of philosophy is condensed into the grammar of the remarkable syntactical cooperation of the speculative genitivity of representation that, on the one hand, is effected "objectively" and transitively by the representer and, on the other hand, is made "subjectively" by what is thus "objectively" represented or is expressive of it, so that the latter's objecthood is re-presented as something like a self-expressive subjecthood which is sensed to be this double genitivity's center of gravity. In this droplet of grammar, I fancy, is a glimpse of the *volte-face* in which the human being's running unto its death (Heidegger) is shocked to find itself overtaken (Levinas) and haunted (Derrida) by a sense of the mortality and fragility of other beings, human or unhuman, such that we who represent these beings are haunted by a sense that they represent themselves, as if our looking at them were simultaneously their looking to us, as if they were addressing to us the words "Do not destroy me."

The doubleness of genitivity of the representation of representation exemplifies what I refer to as, adapting Derrida's words, "something like the middle voice." The middle voice is the grammatical voice, called by some theorists "medial diathesis," between the active and the passive.[14] The force of the double "objective" and "subjective" genitive distinguishes what is distinctive of the middle voice, though historically the middle voice of Greek and Sanskrit lapses either into the passive or into purely self-affective reflexivity such as occurs when, to borrow an illustration from Sartre, a child kisses its own shoulder. The latter degeneration is facilitated by the fact that a verb in the middle voice expresses an involvement and concern of the bearer of the subject of the verb. In my partly heuristic invocation of the notion this involvement of the subject of the verb need not signal a self-reflexivity. If the self-involvement is self-affective the affection need not be *ultimately* narcissistic. The affection can be an affection impressed upon me in my being addressed by another. It can be an affection calling for a response made not for my own sake, but for the sake of that other who, as Emmanuel Levinas says, obsesses me.[15] This ambiguity between *pour soi* and *pour l'autre* is implicit in the idea of "watching out for" someone.

The likeness among tonalities in which the middle voice can be heard is a family likeness. Another member of that family can be heard and sensed in a sentence from a letter written by Edward Thomas brought to my attention by Robert Macfarlane.

> I come home daily with pockets full of the smooth pebbles, often pear-
> shaped (flattish), rosy or primrose coloured and transparent nearly, & in

the fresh moistness wonderfully beautiful: others white & round or oval:
some split & with grain like chestnuts: not one but makes me think or
rather draws out a part of me beyond my thinking.[16]

In this sentence Thomas, who was a great walker, so to speak changes the
direction of his stride while one foot is raised in midair. The change records
a distinction between a Cartesian *cogitatio* exercised by the subject, albeit
one occasioned by the look of the stones, and a possibly simultaneous more
closely focused experience of the subject exercised on it by the stones. The
subject is subjected to a passion which, as Thomas says, draws out, that is to
say attracts (from *trahere*, to draw) a part of the self that is other than the
part that thinks. No longer objects of thought, the stones magnetize the self,
seduce it, fascinate it, possess it rather than being possessed by it, perhaps
drive it ever so slightly mad. Thomas experiences the stones as a source of
astonishment, the passion of which Descartes writes:

> When the first encounter with some object surprises us, and we judge
> it to be something new, or very different from what we knew previously
> or from what we took it to be, this means that we wonder at it and are
> astonished by it; and because that can happen before we have any idea
> whatsoever as to whether or not this object is agreeable to us, it seems to
> me that wonder is the first of all the passions; and it has no contrary, for if
> the object that presents itself has nothing in itself that surprises us, we are
> not moved at all and we contemplate it without passion.[17]

But passions are still thoughts, *pensées, cogitationes,* in the broadest sense
Descartes gives to these words. They are patent of being accusatives of consciousness, ideas, or impressions, the wordless sensations that Helen Keller
hesitates to call thoughts. Philip Larkin, because he is contrasting words and
thoughts, is able to give to thoughts Descartes's broadest sense when in his
"or rather" or rather "rather than" sentence he writes:

> Rather than words comes the thought of high windows.[18]

The task taken up in this book is to consider whether prior to or simultaneous with the accusatives of our representative thinking (states of awareness,
ideas, objective representations, representative objects, propositions that are
answers to questions) we are bearers of an answerability that consists in the
self's being a representative in the sense of being someone who is called to
stand *up for* the things our ideas stand *for.* Is it not this doubleness of representation that is figured in the doubleness of regard as having to do both
with looking and with looking to or concern? So that the Cartesian "I think"
and "I see" would be crossed with the "Here I am, Send me" of the Hebrew

hineni, and meaningfulness as signification (*Bedeutung*) would be in chiasmus with meaningfulness as importance or significance (*Bedeutsamkeit*). What, however, if bearers of significance, "significant others," are not only human beings but also the unhuman and the inhuman or *inhumain*? What, then, is the ground of that significance? My answer to this question is given in terms of an *écologie blanche,* a white or (in case that description is tainted with color prejudice) a blank ecology. It is blank because it is not grounded on descriptions or predicates but on non-predicative sheer existence.

Among the temptations to which is exposed any attempt to answer the question just posed (the question, What is the ground of that significance?) is the positing of either an anthropomorphism of the nonhuman animal or an animomorphism of the inanimate thing. (The seductiveness of a divinism either of the nonhuman or of the inanimate or of both is a topic of my *Margins of Religion.*) These temptations are connected with the risk run by verbs expressing the middle voice of being confused not only with reflexives but also with passives. Corresponding to every transitive verb, for instance the verb "to see" in "I see the stone," there is a passive equivalent, for instance "The stone is seen by me." However, in the guidance I take from what, following Derrida, I guardedly call "something like the middle voice" there is more than a conversion of a grammatical object of an active voiced verb into a grammatical subject of a verb in the passive voice. There occurs also a complication of locutionary forces. The sphere of the ontological and epistemological and semantic is intruded upon by the ethical or/and the "aesthethical" [*sic*] or/and the political or/and the religious. This happens when "I regard *x*" is converted into not simply the passive "*x* is regarded by me" interpreted in terms purely of vision, but into "*x* regards me" with "regards" understood not as "looks at" but as "concerns" or indeed "looks to." Something similar though not identical happens with "representation." "I represent *x*" with the verb understood as connoting a semantic function has "*x* is represented by me" understood still semantically as an equivalent. But it does not have as a semantic equivalent "*x* represents me." Although it may be true that I represent *x*, it may be at the same time false or nonsensical to say that *x* represents me. It may be false not only when to represent is understood as a picturing or other intentional mental act and *x* is an inanimate object, say a stone. It may be false also when to represent is understood as to stand for, which is something a stone is capable of doing and would be doing when, for example, it stands for Wellington in a crude model of the Battle of Waterloo assembled in the sand. In the second of these circumstances however it would be true that something inanimate or nonhuman represents something or someone. It can do this without animomorphism or anthropomorphism, that is to say without our having to pretend that it is capable of intentionality and meaning in the sense in which a person may be. It is sufficient if these circumstances involve someone who is capable of intentional meaning, someone who interprets the situation, who may or may not be the one represented in it. It is sufficient if that someone is an advocate, by which I mean someone with enough imagination for it to be as if the inanimate or nonhuman being in question were saying "Do not destroy me," or showing itself as unworthy of being destroyed.

Note, by the way, that when something shows *itself*, as distinguished from being shown by something else, what happens may belong, with the example from Edward Thomas, to the cluster of candidates that merit description as cases of "something like the middle voice." Another example is the *es denkt in mir*, "it thinks in me," of Lichtenberg (an author whom Wittgenstein admired). Here the "it" may be interpreted either "decadently" on analogy with the "one" of *das Man* as interpreted by Heidegger ("It is thought," "It is said," "One thinks," "One says") or it may be interpreted as a lofty and more "worthy" (*digne*) counterpart of that, or it may be interpreted as the fount of this distinction. In the Lichtenbergian expression what is contrasted with the subject's thinking is not other than thinking, for instance feeling, as we took it to be on our interpretation of Thomas's sentence, but a thinking conducted by someone or something other than the subject, "another thinking," *ein anderes Denken*, the other thinking double-genitively *of* being or happening (*Ereignis*) of which Heidegger would say that it is more divine than what is talked of in such sentences as those in which Saint Paul employs the "or rather" construction, for instance "But now, after that ye have known God, or rather [*dé*] are known of God . . ." (Galatians 4:9), where the passive voice of a transitive verb is substituted for the active. In Galatians 2:20 Paul has second thoughts twice: "I have been crucified with Christ; yet [*dé*] I live, and yet [*dé*] no longer I, but Christ liveth in me." The doctrine of gift and grace that calls for this syntax inspires the doubleness of the prayer "Lord, hear my prayer and let my cry come unto Thee." The key word here and in so many other instances of "something like the middle voice" is "let," the conditionality of which is explicit in "Father, if thou be willing, remove this cup from me; nevertheless not my will, but (let) thine, be done" (Luke 22:42). Here even Christ's prayer that the will of the Father be done asks that the Son's very willing be willed by the Father. The prayer understood as either the praying or as what is prayed is conditioned by permission. Compare the line in the *Book of Taliesin* (3.12): *Ren Nef ry'm awyr dywedi*, "Lord of Heaven, let (grant that) my prayer be permitted by You." This line reminds Robert Maynard Jones of lines of a poem by Michelangelo where the imperfect subjunctive of "to lend" allows for the grace or gift in question to be withheld or taken back.

> Ben sarian dolce le preghiere mie,
> se virtù mi prestassi da pregarte:
>
> Truly sweet would be my prayers
> if Thou would'st lend to me
> the grace by which I prayed to Thee:[19]

Wordsworth's translation has "give" instead of "lend." Maybe this confirms his remark in a letter to Sir George Beaumont of October 17, 1805, that "so much meaning has been put by Michael Angelo into so little room, and that meaning sometimes so excellent in itself, that I found the difficulty of translating him insurmountable." In the line from the *Book of Taliesin* the verb *awyr* is a deponent form, indeed according to one authority "the only form of the dep. remaining in all Brit. languages."[20] A deponent verb is one whose meaning is active but whose form is passive (like, interestingly in this context, Latin *loquor*, I speak). Like the middle voice, deponence is neither straightforwardly active nor straightforwardly passive. It disposes of or dispenses with its active forms and thereby makes way for a certain *disponibilité*, understanding by this word very much what Gabriel Marcel does and, we shall see again in a moment, very much what Keats understands by the phrase "negative capability."[21]

In the above-cited Welsh line *awyr* asks or pleads for permission to ask for permission, but without demanding it. This suggests that deponency and its kindred middle voice are the grammatical structures most appropriate for speaking to God or another being regarded as superior in power or worth.[22] As we have seen, Luther writes that "Faith is permitting ourselves to be seized by the things we do not see." We asked in chapter 7 how we are to construe this permitting ourselves to be seized, this *Sichgefangengegeben*. We may ask here whether such a permitting and therefore some such faith is called for with regard to things we do see, for instance a handful of smooth pebbles, but without yet giving them the regard that is their due. If, as Heidegger and Sartre remind us, being has not been given its due, let us take care that the attempt to put this right does not distract us from giving what is due to beings. Even such beings as pebbles.

Of his smooth pebbles Edward Thomas writes: "not one but makes me think or rather draws out a part of me beyond my thinking." The "or rather" of this sentence works rather like the "or rather" in the celebrated and celebrating sentence in the letter in which Keats writes of Negative Capability. What is negative about negative capability is that it is not a simple exertion of the subject's will to power over what is other than itself. It is not an "I can" in that sense. In a sense to which we shall return in our last chapter, it is "impossible." Its "negative" capacity is a capaciousness such as lets me be vulnerable to the trauma of what is other than me, to suffer it as something positive. Negative capability is a positive vulnerability. Having said that it is manifested "when man is capable of being in uncertainties, Mysteries, doubts, without any irritable reaching after fact & reason—," Keats goes on to say:

> Coleridge, for instance, would let go by a fine isolated verisimilitude caught from the Penetralium of mystery, from being incapable of remaining content with half knowledge. This pursued through Volumes would perhaps take us no further than this, that with a great poet the sense of Beauty overcomes every other consideration, or rather obliterates all consideration.[23]

"Obliterates all consideration," or rather keeps consideration—Edward Thomas's "thinking"—in touch with what is other than consideration, in touch, if you like, with what Keats here calls the sense of Beauty, provided we follow him in not antithetically opposing beauty to truth, and provided we follow the philosopher poet and poet philosopher David Wood in acknowledging that negative capability has an ethical or, perhaps we could say, "aesthethical" dimension.[24]

Keats's "or rather" sentences just cited are analogous to Derrida's sentence about a certain *différance* "announcing or rather [*plutôt* and *plus tôt*, earlier, as in *hrathe*, the OE root of the first syllable of 'rather'] recalling something like the middle voice." *Différance* (to which we shall return), like deconstruction (ditto), is something like the middle voice that postpones in the sense of both putting behind and putting ahead, deferring (such deferring as I expect the inventor of the conceit *différance* would have been amused to fancy taking place when he reflected on the fact that he was born not on the French national holiday of July 14, but a day later). The idea of being born is expressed by a deponent verb in Latin, and deponence in Latin is a sign of at least something like mediality in the Greek that announces it. Of course, grammatical genitivity in its various modes belongs to the family of Greek words having to do with birth.

On another interpretation of Thomas's sentence what is contrasted with the author's thinking could be the thinking of (subjective genitive, genitive of origin) this *es*, this it, whatever it might be. It might be the it of which Heidegger writes *es ereignet*, it happens, where the pronoun stands perhaps for what the verb noun *Sein* stands for, being as distinguished from a being. It might be a being, for instance a tree, as suggested in a sentence in a book

Edward Thomas would have loved written by the person who brought his sentence to my attention. Speaking of Dutch Elm Disease and deforestation, Robert Macfarlane writes:

> It is valuable and disturbing to know that grand oak trees can take three hundred years to grow, three hundred years to live and three hundred years to die. Such knowledge, seriously considered, changes the grain of the mind.
>
> Thought, like memory, inhabits external things as much as the inner regions of the human brain. When the physical correspondents of the thought disappear, then thought, or its possibility, is also lost. When woods and trees are [despite their "Do not destroy me"] destroyed—incidentally, deliberately—imagination and memory go with them. W. H. Auden knew this. "A culture," he wrote warningly in 1953, "is no better than its woods."[25]

Something like the middle voice too, or a different way of characterizing the examples of it just given, is subjective genitivity as this is exemplified in the title of this book's third chapter, "The Experience of Language." The middle voice is not so devoid of strangeness that its equivocality does not itself require to be spoken of in something like the middle voice. So equivocal is it that, tracking back to Ortega, I must express my delight in finding a footnote on the topic in *Meditations on Hunting* in which he points out that the notion of hunting itself is expressed in Latin by the verb *venor*, which is a deponent verb, a verb whose passive form nevertheless voices an activity, and whose deponence is something like the middle voice of Greek and of Sanskrit, a language of the Indian valleys we have been visiting.

> Since hunting is not just an action, but one of the most transitive actions one can imagine, how is it that Latin employs a passive form, or more exactly, a "middle voice"? The middle voice is that which announces an activity which affects the very subject that performs it; therefore a reflexive action. "To fall asleep," "to move oneself," would be then "middle voice." But, *venari*, could it have meant "to hunt oneself"? That way, the game would be its own hunter in the hunt. . . . Or perhaps *venor* means "I hunt partridges for myself"?[26]

It could mean this, but there are more revealing ways of analyzing the middle voice that hit off better the semiotics of the relationship where reason and feeling meet in the practical exercise of the ecological imagination.[27] For example, meditation on the middle voice could help to make sense of the experience of a reversal of aspect where the word *Weltanschauung* takes on the meaning that what we look at is imagined not only as were the roses of

T. S. Eliot's "Burnt Norton" that "Had the look of flowers that are looked at," but imagined as looking at or looking to us.

Ortega goes on to inform us that the Greek *thereuō*, "to hunt," is a normal verb, but that Plato and Aristotle use it in the middle voice. Alas, here for once Ortega calls off the hunt. As too must I, but not before passing on one more remark of Ortega's the implications of which for an aesthethics of the ecological imagination I wholeheartedly and whole-headedly welcome.

> There is greater confusion than ever with regard to the norms which ought to govern the relationships between men, to say nothing of those which could orient and regulate our treatment of the other realities present in our environment: the mineral, the vegetable, and the animal. There are people who believe in good faith that we have no obligations towards the rocks and therefore have tolerated advertisers' smearing with pitch or white lead the venerable rocks of the mountain ranges, on which over the millennia the rains have woven prodigious covering of lichen and fungi.[28]

This transports us again to the rocks and minerals at the source of Aloo Dastur's river. And it returns me to the mountains at the head of the valley where a ten-*øre* piece led me to think of Arne Naess, thanks to my being trusted to climb to a slightly higher section of the valley by our sirdar, Yong Tenzing. Chris Bonington, a recipient of the financial patronage of Arne Naess junior, describes Yong Tenzing as one of his best Sherpas.[29] Yong Tenzing is a Buddhist, hence not able to bring himself to kill any sentient creature. Therefore by returning to him we are reminded of an ecological pattern extremely different from that in which hunting, whether for food or for fun, is a norm, whether clear or confused. It behooves me to add, however, reminding ourselves of Dastur's reference to ecological pockets and overlaps, that while our sirdar saw to it that the vegetarian members of his party were well cared for, for the carnivore members of the party slaughtering duties were assigned to Hindus. This is not the first time in the course of these meditations on ecology and hunting that there has been occasion to remark on the anthropocentric ingenuity of humankind.

Other-wise than properties and relations

It is however on anthropomorphism that I wish to make my final remark in this chapter. It may be objected that I was guilty of anthropomorphism when I proposed that each and every existent as an existent might be regarded also as a face, that is to say, not just as a fact or a constituent of a fact but as facing me in the way another human being faces me when he or she addresses me, or in a way analogous to that. Objectors will deny that there is an analogy between the face of a human being and the face of an animal, let alone between the face of a human being and a tree or a stone. One might begin by asking these objectors whether they therefore find meaningless any analogy between the human being and God. This might lead them at least to keep open the question whether there might be an analogy between the two analogies, that between human beings and a divine being and that between human beings and beings that are neither human nor divine. However, analogy turns on predicates and relations. My proposal has to do with sheer existence, and it assumes that existence is neither a one-place nor a pluri-place predicate. It is not a relation. Nor is the face to face as this is understood by Levinas, whom I am following here up to a certain point, as he follows Kierkegaard up to a certain point, the point at which he turns inside out what the Dane calls the inwardness of subjective thinking.[30] The face to face is the non-predicative and non-relational condition of predication and relationality because it is the addressing of the other's regard toward me and mine toward the other. Here there is more than an analogy with the performance of a speech act, which is not to be confused with anything that is constatively said. Because the face to face is not a relation, it is not an internal or an external relation. Nor does it make sense to ask of it whether it is a part or a whole. Of course, problems about the internality and externality of relations and parts and wholes are raised once we ask what counts as an existent. It may well be too that questions as to *what* (*ti estin*) have to be answered before we can answer questions as to *that* (*hoti estin*). They remain questions for philosophy understood as the hunt for wisdom. But philosophy itself remains a question for sophophily, the practical wisdom of love. It begs the question to suppose that the charge of anthropomorphism immediately puts an end to the question whether we can be face to face, in our special sense of that phrase, with beings other than humans, as Levinas himself was reluctant to allow. At the very least we must put to the test whether we can become educated into seeing the question-begging nature of the charge of anthropomorphism by exposing our imagination to ways of thinking and feeling that may be more common in Buddhist, Jain, and other "valley sections" than our own.

"Our own"? These words call for a final parenthetical reflection by way of postscript and project. Mention was made in the introduction of the risk of treating the distinction between so-called Continental and so-called British or American Analytic philosophy as a reciprocally exclusive opposition. The mention just made of Buddhism and other Oriental modes of thought in conjunction with the reflections on the middle voice conducted in this chapter and elsewhere in this book raises the question as to the possible risk of another and more embracing oversimplification. According to Heidegger philosophy is a Western phenomenon. He may well be right, not least because "philosophy" and "phenomenon" are very Greek words. Yet his own "other thinking" was nourished by conversations with Oriental thinkers, for instance one from Japan who helped him to hear in the word *tao* inklings of notions he and his visitor shared. Analogously (but that is another very Greek word, one that has at its heart the notion of logic that began to matter for the argument of this book from the first paragraphs of its introduction), would it not be worth exploring what turns on the fact that both Greek and Sanskrit share the middle voice or something very much like it? Someone with a better knowledge of world languages and with more time than I have to learn them should resume the study of the historical and philosophical link between the West and the East marked by the fact that the middle voice or something like it is a feature shared at least by Sanskrit and Greek. This exploration would take its practitioners beyond the problem of communication between conceptual schemes addressed in our second chapter.[31] We might learn from it not merely that we inhabit a place in our "valley section" other than the one we think we do. We might learn that our valley is not the one we thought we inhabited, and that as well as the difficulty of not being able to find our feet with others considered in chapter 2 and again in the meditation on that variety of representation called appresentation in chapter 7, we are faced by the difficulty of not being able to find our feet with ourselves.

ELEVEN

Barbarism, Humanism, and Democratic Ecology

In the final sentence of his book *The New Ecological Order* Luc Ferry writes: "Between barbarism and humanism, it is now up to democratic ecology to decide."[1] He means by this that democratic ecology, as that has been described in his book, must decide between barbarism and humanism, and from what has been said in his book it follows, he maintains, that it is for humanism that democratic ecology must opt. Ecology would not be democratic unless it were an ecology centered on the *dēmos*. By *dēmos* he means humankind, the third of the three things mentioned in the subtitle of his book, which is *L'arbre, l'animal et l'homme*, "the tree, the animal, and man." From what I shall be saying about this book will follow, I hope, some understanding of how, as Liddell and Scott's lexicon reports, *dēmos* could have meant first "a country-district, tract of enclosed or cultivated land." This is a meaning that is overlapped by what according to the lexicon, as noted in chapter 10, was meant at first by the Greek root of the word "ethics," namely *ēthos*, connoting not only "the habits of man," but "habitat" or, in the plural, "the haunts of animals." This Greek overlap is carried forward by the Latin overlap that licenses us to interpret humanism in terms of the humane.

The chief aim of this chapter is to propose what might be called a Blank Ecology, *une écologie blanche*. That will be the topic of the third and final part of the chapter. In the second part I shall make some comments about the relationship between the ecofeminine and the ecomasculine. In the first part I treat of the relationship between suffering and linguisticality and freedom.

Suffering and linguisticality and freedom

When the last sections of his book are building to their conclusion Ferry treats utilitarian ecology as humanocentric. But in the earlier pages, when he is dealing with the views of Peter Singer, he is clear that a utilitarian ecology takes into account the sufferings of all sentient creatures, not human beings alone. In Ferry's scheme of things too nonhuman beings are taken into account, but they are taken into account on account of certain "analogies" between, for instance, animals and humans; nonhuman beings are taken into account because animals are, as we have just found Ortega too saying, "equivocal," belonging ambiguously to the nonhuman realm and, in some cases, to a quasi-human realm, most saliently through their capacity to suffer. One sometimes wonders whether he would say that animals suffer quasi-pain or an analogy of pain, lest by allowing that animals suffer plain pain, his case for humanocentrism might be weakened. But his case for humanocentrism is based on the contention that animals can have no rights. They can have no rights because they can have no freedom. Freedom is what distinguishes the human from the nonhuman animal. It is on account of this distinction that Ferry maintains, against Singer, that human beings belong to a different species from nonhuman animals.

Ferry's critique of the concept of animal rights begins with a historical survey of some of the cases brought to courts of law in the sixteenth and seventeenth centuries where animals are literally summoned to appear in order to defend themselves against charges of misdemeanor. We learn that great care was to be taken in the formulation of accusations against the animals arraigned that the accusations were very precisely specified in order to forestall a defense or appeal on grounds of misidentification. The charge was then publicly proclaimed to them, and they were required to appear in court at a certain time and place.[2] Suppose, in light of the point made by referring to these cases, a retreat is made to the concession that animals need human advocates—and Ferry does record that a human advocate was appointed when an animal failed to present itself on the due date at court, though provision was made for its taking exception to the person appointed. If this provision is thought to entail that the animals have the right to be represented by human advocates, it may be objected that a meta-right is as difficult to attribute to an animal as a right, so that the argument for animal rights is no further advanced by this concession.

Observe, however, that, as these sometimes amusing case-histories demonstrate, it is the question of *legal* rights that is at issue, especially those vested in ecclesiastical courts. Without any commitment to the belief that animals can speak for themselves, it is arguable that such rights are recognized in the sense of being deemed to obtain by the utterance of a certain form of words; it is arguable that such rights are thereby performatively or operatively created. Defenders of animal rights may prefer that such legal recognition or acknowledgment be a formalization of rights, natural or moral or both, that exist independently of legal formalization. But there is still room for a degree of performative deeming at the level of *moral* law, notwithstanding that relevant considerations to support that deeming are called for. Depending on circumstances, in particular on the level of moral education that obtains at the time, the moral stand taken in such deeming may be too far ahead of its time to be widely endorsed, but such endorsement is itself to some degree the performative adoption of a position that does not follow by logical, empirical, or moral necessity from premises. Although the ambiguity of the notion of affirmation may conceal this logical point, a performative stance such as may be expressed under the rubric "I hereby . . ." presupposes states of affairs such as may be affirmed constatively, but the performative utterance is not entailed by the constative ones. This distinction and the educative force of ethics are topics to which I shall return at a later stage of this chapter.

Anyone who questions the coherence of the notion of animal rights may object that rights presume interests and that it is not coherent to ascribe interests to animals. Ferry does not go down that route. His narration of stories about animals summoned to appear at courts of law to answer to magistrates is designed to ridicule the idea that animals can be equipped sufficiently or at all with the power of language and reasoning required for them to claim their rights. However, it is not his view that the intrinsic rights depend upon such a power. This power, he argues, has less significance than is sometimes attributed to it by defenders of animal rights. It has less significance, he holds, than it is credited with having by Singer.

Ferry charges Singer with making "an obvious error"[3] in supposing that the possession of language, reason, or intelligence is what Enlightenment thinkers like Kant and Rousseau hold to be the property that differentiates humans specifically from nonhuman animals, notwithstanding that nonhuman animals have in common with humans the capacity to suffer, albeit "analogously." Freedom is what these Enlightenment philosophers count to be the differentiating property between humans and animals. So, Ferry infers, in order to rebut the claims made by these philosophers that animals and humans belong to different species it is irrelevant to cite behavior in which animals display intelligence, reason, or linguistic ability.[4]

Is Singer's alleged error as obvious as Ferry maintains? Ferry himself notes that freedom is called by Kant practical reason. But more or less manifest in Kant and persuasive in its own terms is the argument that what we call theoretical reason presupposes practical reason understood as freedom. No theoretical belief is a theoretical belief unless it is taken to be held by a being who holds it on what it assumes to be good grounds, that is to say because it is thought that the belief ought to be held. The same independence of causal determination is a condition of the capacity for language; so that an "ought," perhaps even a moral "ought," is implied in the claiming of a theoretical truth. Hence, at least implicitly, Singer is not as careless in his reading of Kant and Rousseau as Ferry contends. Singer or anyone else who maintains that at least some nonhuman animals share with human animals capacities for language, reason, and intelligence is thereby maintaining that these nonhuman animals share freedom.

Furthermore, Ferry goes some way to conceding to Singer that no sharply specific difference between the human and the animal can be grounded on freedom. Yet, agreeing with Kant, Rousseau, and Singer in denying the Cartesian tenet that animals are machines, Ferry writes that the animal is not only the *analogon* of a human suffering being, it is also the *analogon* of a free being, a being with a freedom the status of which I am tempted to characterize as "difficult." The *analogon* of a free being, Ferry goes on to say, is a trace of the human suffering being.[5] Unlike the machine, the animal directs itself toward certain ends, one of these being the avoidance of pain. Over and above the capacity to suffer that animals and humans have in common and on which utilitarian ecology is based, animals are endowed with an equivocal freedom sufficiently analogous to the freedom of human beings to serve as a basis for the belief that animals are to be respected not only because not respecting them might induce lack of respect for human beings, but also because they have an intrinsic right to respect. Ferry says this in paragraphs that are cast in the mode of the history of ideas. The particular idea here in question is not one with which he agrees, as will become more and more evident as the book proceeds to its end. Here in the middle of the book he is explaining only how people may have come to have this idea. Because in giving that explanation he describes the *analogon* of freedom as a trace of or as the *analogon* of the capacity to suffer, we might have expected him to say that what is chiefly important in his explanation is the capacity to suffer, and that it is on the basis of this that animals come to be considered as bearers of intrinsic rights. Why does the capacity to suffer not suffice for them to be so considered? Why rest the case on the trace of this capacity rather than the capacity itself? The explanation for this is that Ferry is aiming to persuade his readers that our granting the animal an intrinsic right to respect turns on an analogy with a factor that, unlike the capacity to suffer, is intrinsically human. Ferry holds that our granting nonhuman or some nonhuman animals the intrinsic right to respect turns only on an *analogy* with a factor that is solely human. This factor is freedom. The animal enjoys only an analogy of that, and the analogy is too remote to call into question the specific difference between the naturality of the nonhuman animal and what Ferry describes as the human being's "antinatural" status. By "antinatural" he seems to mean not simply non-natural, nor only that the human being is the being that can rise above nature and make its own nature for itself in the manner described by Sartre. Ferry's Enlightenment heroes, who include Rousseau—though on closer inspection Rousseau is perhaps what Ferry would describe as an equivocal case—are vehemently critical of the Romantic, backward-looking, back-to-nature, near-Nazi rightist tradition to which, according to Ferry, one wing of the proponents of deep ecology belong. The glory of humankind according to the Enlightenment proclaimers of the Rights of Man, and according to their brother Luc Ferry, is *Liberté*. The paramountcy of freedom must be acknowledged in any ecology, he proclaims. Freedom is one of the prolegomena of any future ecology. Furthermore, because unequivocal first-class *Liberté* belongs as far as we can know only to human beings and because it is entailed by *Egalité* and *Fraternité*, the species of nonhuman animals cannot be moral equals with the human species, nor, despite Saint Francis of Assisi, can they be our brothers, or our sisters.

In this mention of prolegomena for any future ecology the reference to the future and the invocation of the triple slogan of the French revolutionaries should not be allowed to mislead us into thinking that Ferry's conception of a future ecology is revolutionary or utopian. It is reformist. And while it dissents from the integrism of rightist deep ecologism, it dissents also from the singularism of its leftist wing. Definitive of the rightest wing is a break with the rationalist universalism of the Republican ideal of the Rights of Man in favor of what Guattari calls a resingularization, an emphasis on the priority of difference over sameness, as insisted on by, for example, those who, having questioned the right to paramountcy of the Rights of *Man*, stress difference of gender and go on to underline the special contribution feminist thinking of one variety has to offer in our rethinking of ecology.

Ecofeminisms and ecomasculinisms

There is a variety of feminisms. There is a corresponding variety of ecofeminisms. These range from the ecofeminism—let us dub it *gaiafeminism*—according to which the feminine is somehow closer to the animal and the earth than is the masculine, through the ecofeminism that resists this line of thinking and insists instead on women's equality with men before universal law—let us label this *legalitarian ecofeminism*—to the ecofeminism for which this centralizing of the universal is still a centralizing of the masculine—let us call this *singularist ecofeminism*. Singularist ecofeminism readily, but not necessarily, combines with gaiafeminism. It resists combination with legalitarian ecofeminism. There are other varieties, among which mention will be made here only of the Spinozan variety of ecofeminism according to which the world is the body of God,[6] but this is an explicitly theological variety of gaiafeminism. It is a bold doctrine to propose in an age for which the very idea of God is for many an embarrassment. However, the idea of God may live on in other guises. It may live on in the guise of the notion of the universal principle or law. So no less bold than this feminist doctrine of the world as the body of God is the singularist feminist doctrine according to which what is required is a feminist critique of universalism.

But what sort of critique could there be that did not appeal to universal principles? Must not any critique be conducted in terms of the principle of contradiction? But if the principle of contradiction belongs to the system that one variety of ecofeminism judges to be masculinist and phallogocentric, this judgment would seem to be self-contradictory. Would that be fatal to it? Why should ecofeminism of this kind be worried by self-contradiction given that logical consistency is a desideratum of the kind of thinking it believes must be called into question? Yet it would seem that it should be concerned to avoid inconsistency by the standard of the principle of noncontradiction and the other principles of classical logic if the masculinist subscribers to that logic are among the people it aims to convert from that logic's alleged phallogocentism. I suggest that this anti-androcentricism could escape this dilemma by taking a leaf out of the book of Emmanuel Levinas, a philosopher whose analysis of ethicality it might consider to be extremely masculinist—though, as I shall show, what is most extremely masculinist is extremism itself understood as the desire for polar opposition.

Aware of the danger of subscribing to an Enlightenment idea of ethicality in the very process of advancing putatively noncontradictory propositions
against it, Emmanuel Levinas urges his readers to take note that at the very
moment the author affirms a proposition designed to conform with classical
logic, he is addressing and responding to a reader.[7] So that for the purposes
of argument and critique he can consistently appeal at least to the laws of
thought of classical logic in terms of which are constituted formal contradiction and the no-less-general principle of the negation of negation of dialectical logic for which noncontradiction is as much the end as it is for thinking
that appeals to classical logic. Levinas can affirm propositions that are in
principle formed with a view to avoiding formal or dialectical contradiction,
yet he can affirm at the same time a contra-diction that arises not within the
logical system classically or dialectically conceived, but between the dictions
that belong to such systems of things said and the non-systematic dictions
that are sayings in response to someone addressed with whom one is face to
face. These said and saying dictions would not be parallel to each other. The
saying would be a contra-diction that was at variance with the apparent pure
rationality of the laws of thought and the propositions formed according to
them. It would be at variance with that picture of rationality in that it would
have contra-dicted their pretensions to pure rationality by showing that that
systematic rationality was already disrupted by the non-systematic rationality of *ratio* understood as the relation or *rapport* of encounter in which a
person responds to another with an *a priori* "at your service," a relationship
in depth so to speak, without which the so-to-speak lateral relations of epistemology, ontology, and logic could not obtain.

In spite of Levinas's argument that ethicality is ultimately to be interpreted in terms of masculine pronouns, ecofeminists could conduct their
critique of androcentrism in a manner analogous to that in which Levinas
conducts his phenomenology of ethical experience. They could follow him by
riding on the vehicle of classical logocentrism in order to bring out how the
very heart of its apparently purely conceptual sameness is affected, touched,
contaminated by the alterity not only of another human being but also of
what is other than human or divine, though Levinas would refuse this extension. We may not be persuaded by Levinas's replies in advance to those
who will charge him with androcentrism. We may not think that his defense
is much strengthened by noting that in Deuteronomy 14:29, a text he so frequently cites, it is the orphan, the stranger, and the widow, not the widower,
for whom we are said to be responsible. On the contrary, the endorsement
of that text might be read as a further sign of the paternalistic, patronizing,
and androcentric character of his conception of ethicality. In the translation

he gives of this very text, what he calls the orphan is, on a strict reading, the child without a father, not the child without a mother. So, at least *prima facie*, Levinas's conception of ethicality is paternalistic and masculinist. That it is is underlined when he calls his conception of ethicality a humanism of the other man, *l'autre homme*, this last word being also the last word in the subtitle of the original edition of Ferry's book, though the subtitle and with it the English for that word are omitted from the published English translation.

I leave temporarily this matter of Levinas's apparent masculinism and turn back to his way of dodging the logical and methodological difficulty of appearing to undermine his own position in arguing for it. The way in which he does this, I am suggesting, offers a possible exit from the similar difficulty confronting that kind of ecofeminism according to which classical logic and philosophical methodology are masculinely marked. Like him, ecofeminists can have their Greek philosophical cake and eat it. Of course, they might not wish to describe their way through this aporia in the manner in which Levinas sometimes describes the way through his, namely as the exposure of a "Hebrew" ingredient in the "Greek," or of a non-ingredient, perhaps we should say, like the absence of leaven in the loaf.

In a passage from *Difficult Freedom* that Ferry cites with approval Levinas writes:

> The Jewish man discovers man before discovering landscapes and towns. He is at home in a society before being so in a house. He understands the world on the basis of the Other rather than the whole of being on the basis of the earth. . . . This freedom is not in the least bit pathological, or strained or heartrending. It puts in second place the values of rootedness and institutes other forms of fidelity and responsibility.[8]

Does this mean that Jewish man's understanding calls to be corrected if the "whole of being" (*l'ensemble de l'être*) is to be given its due? The Jewish man referred to in Levinas's paragraph here stands for man and, as the sentence that precedes this paragraph explains, Levinas is speaking of "the first relation man has with being." In this relation man is "free with regard to landscapes and architecture, all those heavy and sedentary things one is tempted to prefer to man." Is this existence unfree with regard to God? Levinas's paragraph is a paraphrase of part of Psalm 119, verse 19, which declares "A stranger (an exile) am I on earth." This reflects the events of the critical time at which it was probably composed, when the strict observance of the law by Jews returning from exile in Babylon came up against the laxity of those dwelling in the homeland. The psalm is a song of praise for the law. But what of our own critical time "after the death of God"? Levinas writes that his paragraph is "the literal teaching of the Bible in which the earth is not possessed individually, but belongs to God." If you can believe that, you will be bound to think of the whole of being differently from how you will think of it if you cannot subscribe to this belief. Levinas also writes that his paragraph is "not an analysis of the contemporary Jewish soul," meaning by contemporary the time shared by the citizens of the "modern states" referred to in the title of the section in which his paragraph occurs. Although those citizens include many for whom God and His teaching are dead, they include many, like Levinas himself, for whom they are still alive. Does this mean that there must be at least two ecologies, a theistic one and an atheistic one, a theistic and an atheistic faith?

A point of departure toward an answer to this question would be the answer to the more specific question whether what Levinas calls the existence of the human being in his first relation with the other human being is free or unfree with regard to God. His answer to this question is that the existence of the human being in his first relation with being is both free and unfree with regard to God in the sense that it is tied to the idea of God. But in expounding that idea Levinas refers to the Kabbalistic story of a God who withholds his own power over the world in order to allow the human being freedom to accept a co-responsibility. And even if for him the first relation with being is what he calls the face to face with another human being and this is an interpretation of humankind created in the image of God, he never tires of stressing that the human relation is first. In saying that it is the relation of all relations he means that even the relation of the human being to God is among the relations of which the human face to face is an anarchic, unprincipial, condition.

So it is not entirely disingenuous of Ferry to omit sentences referring to God from his citation of the passage from *Difficult Freedom,* a passage in which he sees in Levinas a fellow traveler in the ideology of his own version of "democratic ecology" inspired by the Enlightenment and its ideals of freedom, equality, and fraternity. This omission of Levinas's mention of God is excusable, Ferry might argue, on the grounds that Levinas himself insists that talk of God derives its sense from the encounter of one human being face to face with another. But Ferry effaces also the trace of the face to face which, Levinas maintains, justifies that freedom of the active will by making it secondary to a freedom of passive responsibility that makes all the difference between the Enlightenment rationalism of a democracy based on the law and a democracy in which the other human being is not only a case falling under a law, but also what, following Derrida, could be called an archi-exception to law, where an archi-exception does not suspend law or principle—for a law is in principle universal—but refuses to allow law to go untested by the griefs and fears of the person, every person in his or her singularity. To this extent at least Levinas is a fellow traveler with Guattari and Deleuze and the other advocates of "resingularization" whom Ferry would class as advocates of regression to the darkness and Disenlightenment of primitivist barbarism (a barbarism which is the reverse of what is called Enlightenment or Galilean barbarism by Michel Henry).

Levinas reminds us that although the God of the psalmist is one who glorifies the law, he is no less the God who is merciful. Levinas reminds us that "*Rakhmana*," the Aramaic name for God as the one who is merciful, is cognate with "*Rekhem*," the word for womb.[9] A certain feminine marking returns to Levinas's account of the whole of being, assuming (perhaps wrongly) that it ceases to be there when, following the discreet presence of the other in the woman in the home which he says is the first appearance of the face, the feminine pronouns are succeeded by masculine ones denoting indiscreetness, for example the *il* of *illeité*, he-ness, or perhaps, when *Illéité* is written with an upper-case initial, God-ness.

If Levinas's genealogy of ethics imitates the narrative of Genesis and the later books of the Hebrew Bible (though without being *rooted* in them!), we should not abandon the hope of discovering in his "Greek" writings at least a description of ethicality that does not depend on that biblical narrative. This does not prevent our appealing to the biblical story to help us understand the "Greek" philosophical one. Nor does it prevent our appealing to the Hebrew language for the same purpose. We do both of these when we note that "*Shekinah*," the Hebrew word for presence, has overtones or undertones of femininity, as this was interpreted by the rabbis on the one hand and the Kabbalists on the other.

Reporting a Kabbalist doctrine, Rabbi Hayyim of Volozhin, on whose book *Soul of Life* (*Nefesh Hahayyim*) Levinas draws from time to time, tells us that "*Shekinah*" means fixed residence. He cites sources that associate this especially with Jerusalem, the place here on earth where the Creator wished to have a residence.[10] The *Shekinah* contrasts therefore with the travelling associated with the Jew in, for instance, the essay "A Religion for Adults" from which the sentences Ferry cites from Levinas are taken. That essay demonstrates that God's desire to have a dwelling on earth is not in conflict with his being on the move. As illustrated by the Festival of Tabernacles (*Succot*) and the nomadic life of the Jew in the desert, God is taken from place to place with his people. Now if the desire for "heavy sedentary things" is an expression of her-ness in his-ness, it will be a manifestation too of the temptation to prefer these things over man. It will be evidence of the dangerous desire of which Levinas writes elsewhere in *Difficult Freedom*,[11] the desire of seeking to be fused with God, a fusion from which the square letters of the Torah are a protection, throwing man back on his responsibility to approach God simultaneously through the interpretation of the words of the law articulated in those letters and through his presence to other human beings who are also occupied with the interpretation and application of those words. "Is it not," Levinas asks, "these consciously willed and freely accepted links—with all the traditions that freedom entails—which constitute modern nations, defined by the decision to work in common much more than with the dark voices of heredity?"[12] This work of one human being with and for another is the human being's way of cooperating with the God that has withdrawn in order that the human being voice the judgment of God, where the judgment of God is what challenges the judgment of history and "the dark voices of heredity." Meanwhile the human being continues to explore and study "the traditions that freedom entails," for instance the tradition of *midrash* that is the tradition of questioning traditions, for instance the traditions heard in the word "*Shekinah.*"

Traditions, in the plural. Thus in yet another essay in *Difficult Freedom*, "Judaism and the Feminine," Levinas touches on a disagreement between the Kabbalah and the rabbis as to the *Shekinah*. Scholem notes that in rabbinical writings the *Shekinah* is identified with what in the Bible is called the "face" of God. God is His *Shekinah*. In the writings of the Kabbalah, for instance in *Bahir* and *Zohar,* the *Shekinah* is an aspect of God, "a quasi-independent feminine element within him," figured as mother, wife, or daughter and complementing what Scholem describes as "the universally human and masculine principle," a conjunctive phrase that has given rise to the spilling of much ink by feminists and by Levinas himself in responding to them.[13] To what they have said I shall add only one remark. Although part of the meaning of the *Shekinah* is given by the idea that God is called the merciful one, and the word for mercy is, as noted earlier, cognate with the word for womb, there is a tradition according to which the mercifulness of the feminine principle (if "principle" is not the wrong word here) is ambivalently related to the principle (and "principle" would not be the wrong word here) of woman as stern judge, the judicial presence of God as *Dayyan*. This ambivalence would be what Levinas calls alternation or oscillation, but the oscillation would be describable not only as one between, on the one hand, the virile rigor of the law with the cases falling under it marked by the pronoun "he" and, on the other hand, the allegedly masculinely marked "you" of the fully ethical face to face. The oscillation could be described equally well as one between the two aspects of the femininely marked *Shekinah* just distinguished. So that this presence of God would be no other than the judgment of God. Instead of or as well as speaking about *illéité* we could speak of *elléité*.

Now of illeity Levinas says that it is liable to confusion with the *il y a,* what we could call ilyaity. One piece of historical backing for this liability is reported in a striking statement made by Scholem. He writes, "the power of stern judgement in God is the source of evil as a metaphysical reality, that is to say, evil is brought about by the hypertrophy of this power."[14] In other words, it is brought about by the over-enlargement of that power at the expense of the quality of mercy. But there can also be a hypotrophy of that power. This happens when the law is lost sight of, and, as Levinas writes, "the feminine . . . reveals itself to be the source of all decline."[15] Then it is as if we might force the French language to permit us to speak of *ellyaité*, because although the *il* of the *il y a* is neuter, although the "there is" is impersonal and anonymous and therefore neither masculine nor feminine, we sink into the *il y a* via an unprincipled, louche femininity. And this femininity would not be a femininity conceived only Judaically if in the essay titled "Judaism and Femininity" a parallel move is made to that made in the essay titled "A Religion for Adults," where, it will be recalled, we discovered that the analysis of what Levinas first referred to as Jewish man was an analysis of the human being as such. We should now be entitled to say that the Judaic conception of femininity would be one of femininity as such, if there is such a thing, that is to say, if the femininity as such does not remain a masculinity as such, though with a suchness that is paradoxically beyond essence. Remember that in the first place, in the ecology in which everything in the garden was still lovely, and love as yet knew no discord, Adam was the name of a human being who had two aspects. We may have to speak not simply of the *côte* of Adam, Adam's rib, but of Adam's *cotés,* his two sides, as in the story of the androgynous being in Plato's *Symposium.* Except that where in the case of the being imagined by Aristophanes in Plato's dialogue Zeus turns the two "halves" around so that they face into and are confused into each other in erotic love, if a "facing" is to be traced back to the condition of Adam, as it is by Levinas, it is a facing that leaves the "halves" facing outward from each other as a sign of the fact that in their proximity a respectful distance is maintained between them. Their belonging together, their *appartenir,* is an *apart-tenir,* a holding apart, but not of simple parts. This is why of Adam's initial androgyny Levinas writes, "If woman completes man, she does not complete him as a part completes another into a whole but, as it were, as two totalities complete one another—which is, after all, the miracle of social relations."[16] That is to say, the way woman and man complete each other as two wholes is a clue to the way any two human beings of whichever or whatever sex complete each other. The completeness is not the completeness of a fully rounded whole, for, as has now emerged, each of the two participants in humanity, like the God in whose image humanity is created, experiences an alternation within itself between mercifulness and strict justice.

However, there is no denying that in the "religion for adults" that Levinas discerns in the narrative of Genesis and in his adaptation of that narrative to a genetic phenomenology of ethicality, the masculinely marked members of the family circle appear to be credited with more adulthood than the femininely marked members. This is noticeable in more than one instance, including in those pages of *Totality and Infinity* in which from the I enjoying itself in the limited *oikos* of its home, via the discreet presence in that home of the feminine other (who nevertheless in Levinas's account of woman in Judaism is declared to be "allied to all indiscretions" in the sense of immodesties),[17] the transition is made to the indiscreet presence in open society of the other for whom the goods of the earth previously taken into the home for private, discreet, and even secret enjoyment, are, along with one's self, to be offered to the other who is now distinguished masculinely and whose face is a face that demands and commands rather than a face that is kissed and caressed.

This preference in favor of masculinity—if loading anyone with the burden of responsibility can be described as doing it a favor—is displayed in the singling out of paternity and sonship in the account Levinas gives of the descendants of Adam "beyond the face" when humanity responds to the command to "go forth and multiply." Unkindest cut of all, yet a precursor of the modern man some feminists would welcome into the home, it is a man who is charged with the responsibility of rocking the cradle. This should not surprise us now that we have learned that in the tradition on which Levinas draws there is an ambivalence not only in the feminine aspect of Adam but in the masculine aspect as well. The gender and genre of so-called "human nature" is beyond nature understood as essence.

Scholem observes that the ambivalence and alternation of the *Shekinah* is related to exile. He cites from the Talmud Megillah 29a where it is stated that "In every exile into which the children of Israel went, the *Shekinah* was with them."[18] This is the implication of the already cited reference made by Levinas to the Festival of Tabernacles and the nomadism of the Jews. The idea is picked up again but amplified in the concluding paragraph of "Judaism and the Feminine," where we read that

> the biblical figure which haunts Israel on the paths of exile, the figure that it invokes at the end of the Sabbath, in the dusk where it will soon remain behind without help, the figure in whom is stored up for the Jews all the tenderness of the earth, the hand which caresses and rocks his children,

is no longer feminine. Neither wife nor sister nor mother guides it. It is
Elijah, who did not experience death, the most severe of the prophets,
precursor of the Messiah.[19]

It is a man who announces the Messiah and who embodies *toute la tendresse
de la terre*. Heralding the return of God, who, we have been told, is as merciful as he is just, the prophet returns us to the earth. Without however going
back on the fact that Jewish man "finds a meaning to the earth on the basis of
human society,"[20] we are reminded that woman does not have the prerogative
of tears.[21] We are reminded of this too by the fact that in Tibetan Buddhism,
where wisdom is the primary attribute of woman, compassion is the primary
attribute of man (though it must not be overlooked that the man as embodied in the Buddha or Bodhisattva in the embrace with his consort is already
ambivalent in gender). No more than the feminine–masculine ambivalence
we have been discovering in the Judaic context does this ambivalence in
Buddhism have to be regarded as sexual ambivalence. In the case of both of
these traditions what is treated is not biological sexuality but the quality of
humanity. And this word "humanity" must be understood in its own ambivalent sense as the name both of a kind and of the kindness or capacity for
compassion that is part of that kind's so-called nature. The gender and genre
of so-called human nature is beyond nature as essence. It is beyond essence
as hankered after by, for instance, Luc Ferry. And beyond nature as essence
is the topic of my final remarks, to which I now turn under the description
blank ecology or *l'écologie blanche*.

Blank or white ecology

The capacity for kindness or compassion is exercised with regard to beings
of a certain kind, for instance beings that can suffer pain. But suffering is not
necessarily the suffering of pain. Something suffers when it is deprived of a
good. But among a thing's goods is its existence. Independent of the thing's
nature, of the predicates, essential or otherwise, under which it falls, is its
existence. The thing's existence as such is one of the thing's goods, what it
would ask us to safeguard if it could speak, and if it cannot speak, it behooves
those that can speak to speak for it, to voice its claim on its behalf. That is to
say, contra Kant and contra Levinas, whether we hold with Ferry that what
characterizes the humanism of the Enlightenment is freedom or whether we
say that what characterizes that humanism is the capacity for speech, neither
the capacity for speech nor the freedom that this capacity entails is necessary
for something to qualify as an object of direct eco-ethical responsibility. Nor

is the capacity to suffer pain. Entities that lack a voice have a vote in a more democratic ecological order, even if that vote is cast by proxy. They qualify qua existents.

Or is the electoral qualification of existence only a sham? Is anything gained by the recognition that a thing's existence is a good for that thing? If the existence of one thing is a good for it, the existence of another thing is a good for that other thing, and in deciding for which of these it behooves us to speak, in deciding which of them we are called on not to deprive of existence, we have to take into account and compare their respective qualities and relations. We can ultimately decide the question of existence, the question of the that, only by asking the question of essence, the question of the what. For the question we are faced with is not only the question as to the good for this or that entity. We are faced also with the question of the good where all things are taken into account. So is not an insistence upon existence as such as fatuous as is dividing through by zero? If existence as such is a good, is it not nevertheless ethically vacuous?

I am talking here about existence as such. I am treating not only of existence now as against existence in the past or in the future. But I am treating of existence in the field of eco-ethical decision, that is to say where what we do can make a difference to the existence of something, where what we do can contribute to bringing about its nonexistence. Unless it makes sense to speak of our bringing about or contributing to bringing about the existence or nonexistence of a mathematical entity, mathematical existence will not be eco-ethically relevant. So although existence as such is our topic, our topic is not existence in no matter what universe of discourse. However, this does not mean that we can make the distinction between mathematical and non-mathematical existence only in terms of predicates and that we cannot therefore distinguish the predicativity of the *what* from the non-predicativity of the *that*, or, in traditional terms, essence from existence. But it is open to us to refrain from making this distinction. That is to say, we can deny Kant's denial that existence is a predicate. We can and should affirm with Frege that there are at least two ways of denying or rejecting. And we could read Kant as doing this too. On this reading he and Frege would both be underlining that there are first-order predicates and second-order predicates, where second-order predicates define the universe of discourse in which first-order predication can take place. They determine the distinction between sense and non-sense, not the distinction between truth and falsehood or correctness and incorrectness, where correctness and incorrectness include ethical or eco-ethical validity and invalidity. Hence even if our phrase "existence as such" presupposes predicates in terms of which what is meant by existence in an ethical context is distinguished from what is meant by existence in another context, for instance mathematics, this does not prevent our distinguishing the issue of the predicated whatness of a thing from the issue of whether an instance of it exists. However, justice demands that a qualification be made to the relatively simple distinction I have just been drawing between the conditions of sense and the conditions of truth or correctness. But before making this qualification I want to amplify what I have said about the relation between existence as such and temporality.

When I argue for the ethical relevance of existence as such, I am not restricting existence to existence in the present. Of course, as recognized a moment ago, the pastness, presence, and futureness of the existence of something are relevant to whether and how it is a subject of eco-ethical consideration. My responsibilities to particular beings that no longer exist are not as direct as are my responsibilities to beings that confront me now or will confront me in the near or less-near future. But if we think, as we normally do, that something can retain its identity through time, confusion is threatened if we treat the time-slice in which a thing exists as definitive of the identity of the thing, unless of course the thing is the time-slice itself. Likewise for the space-slice and spatio-temporal-slice occupied by a thing. That is to say, we must distinguish predicative expressions from token reflexives, expressions like "now," "then," "here." The parameters of the world in which we conduct ourselves as ethical agents are not the unmeasurable para-parameters of a Heraclitean view of the world, unmeasurable because the tape measure and every other standard is in a state of flux in such a world. Nor are the parameters of the world in which we conduct ourselves as ethical agents the also unmeasurable para-parameters of a Parmenidean view of the world, unmeasurable because uncountable, because counting takes time and time is taken away in the Parmenidean universe. While the Heraclitean view collapses predicates into token reflexives, the Parmenidean view deprives our universe of the discourse of token reflexives altogether.

If in the universe of Parmenides there are no token reflexives or bearers of token reflexives, there is no distinction or separation between the you and the me, this separation that is the starting point of Levinas's humanism of the other human being. An analogous distinction holds for an eco-ethics of the other being, whether human or nonhuman. But how in an ecological ethics could there be not only a distinction but a separation? There would seem to be a conflict between separation and ecology at least if an ecology is understood as a context of interconnected components. The difficulty would be compounded if ecologicality were so understood that the contexts too would be interconnected. Do we embrace and are we embraced by an ontologically monist or an ontologically pluralist ecology? Is our conception of an ecologicality of existents one that favors oneness and sameness, or does it give preference to difference? The answer to these questions is that this existentist (which does not mean existentialist) ecology upholds the claims of both sameness and difference. And it is both monist and pluralist. It is both of these because, in the wake of Levinas's ecology of the other human being, but opening itself to the nonhuman being as well, it distinguishes but does not separate the ontological from the ethical, placing them in a proto- (but by no means primitive) relationship of chiasmus that declines the logic of simple oppositive negation that is brought to bear in conceptual classification and specification, for instance the specification of the human and the animal and the feminine and the masculine.

Manifesting that wisdom that is associated, as we have seen, with womankind in the Buddhistic and Judaic traditions, Iris Murdoch writes, "It is always a significant question to ask a philosopher: what is he afraid of." If you asked Levinas what he was afraid of, he would have said: Father Parmenides. And so would I. This is one reason why I keep on going back to Levinas, although I am afraid of some of the other things he writes. He and I both suffer from ontological claustrophobia. But he shows me an avenue of escape. It is an avenue of escape which he shows us, albeit showing again his paternalist bias (but now putting that bias in a historical context), when he refers to the relationship we referred to earlier between a father and a son as a challenge to the claim to priority of Parmenidean identity. Not only Christologically is the son both one with the father and different. On Levinas's understanding of this relationship, the genetical is genethical. It is a relationship not of owning but of owing. On my understanding this relationship is eco-ethical as distinguished from ontological, but not as separated from the ontological, for on this understanding the ontological is ethical from the beginning or before the beginning. This is why, speaking ontotheologically, when God created the world and each thing in it, he found that they were good. This God sees the world from the point of view of everything in it, every existent. He therefore sees that for each singular existent its existence is a good. Reading Proposition VI of Part III of Spinoza's *Ethics* not as a plain ontological but as an onto-ethico-ecological one, each singular thing makes a *prima facie* claim to be allowed to persist in its existence.

These claims are *prima facie* in the sense that one claim may be stronger than another. Such a claim is *prima facie* also in the sense that the claim is the claim of a case to be regarded as we regard a face. This holds for the face of the world as a whole. But a whole is not necessarily a stifling totality. And how we regard the whole, what we consider as a whole, will turn on how we regard the sub-wholes and singulars within it. How we regard them will turn on manifold criteria that have to do with essential or nonessential predicates, not with bare existence. Existence is not a criterion. However, its not being a criterion, its being apart from qualities and relations, its very vacuity, is what gives it its power. For its power is its power to force us to pause and think, not to rush in with dogmatic assurance that our checklist of criteria is sacrosanct. Its eco-ethical power is one that points toward a sense of the religious that would bind us to unbinding. The ligature of this *religio* is loosened in the sense that fidelity to the law that defines relig*ions* is tested by fidelity to existence that precedes and exceeds law because in being pre- and postpredicative it defies definition. This has a surprising corollary, one that obliges me to revise what was said a few paragraphs ago about the distinction between conditions of sense and conditions of truth and correctness. My earlier remarks about this distinction were aimed at preserving the ethical and eco-ethical force of existence in such a way as would not entail that existence retained this ethical sense for the existence of, for example, mathematical entities. The suggestion was that predicates would be presupposed in distinguishing one universe of discourse, for example the mathematical, from another, without this meaning that predicates would be implied in speaking of the existence of things falling within a particular universe of discourse. That is to say, I attempted to preserve a sense of existence as such in a particular universe of discourse by distinguishing presupposition from entailment, implication, or meaning. To make the point in terms that bring us back to Levinas, I was aiming to challenge his limitation of the range of ethical responsibility to human beings. In order to make room for a truly democratic ecological ethicality I argued that the ethically relevant is not only human beings, but beings, existents, as such. I wanted to open the door of ethical considerability to animals, trees, and rocks. This led me to propose a distinction that promised to allow us to open the door in this way without thereby opening the door to the notion that we have ethical responsibility to, for example, numbers. Is this notion of ethical responsibility to numbers a nonsense? Maybe. But nonsense itself is historically and geographically relative. What fails to make sense at one time and place makes sense at another. This is one reason why ethics is and has to be educative. And this is why, for the existentist concept of the ethical and therefore eco-ethical that I have been projecting to be as extensive and democratic as justice demands, we may be ethically obliged, not to be silent, to *schweigen*, but, called to be advocates, to talk nonsense.

TWELVE

Where to Cut: *Boucherie* and *Delikatessen*

Concerns and procedures

Referring in *The Animal That Therefore I Am* to *The Middle Voice of Ecological Conscience,* Derrida says that he wishes to recommend the latter book especially because, sharing the author's concern, he will perhaps proceed a little differently.[1] My concern in that book and particularly in chapter 8 of this one is to raise consciousness. It is to raise consciousness, where it seems to me to need raising, to conscience, and to raise conscience, where it seems to me to need raising, to responsibility. By responsibility I mean ethical responsibility in a sense I take to be the sense proposed by Levinas, except that I wish to persuade my reader that such responsibility is a response not only to other human beings. It is called for also, I argue in that book and in chapters of the second part of this one, by beings that, in one common sense of the word, cannot *call,* beings that, perhaps in Heidegger's sense of the phrase or in a sense he would like to have given it, do not *have the word* or are not possessed of or by it: nonhuman sentient beings, even nonsentient beings. My concern is to bring out for those who, like Levinas,[2] are in any doubt, that such beings directly concern us ethically. *Ils nous regardent.* They are our concern ethically and directly, not, say, merely because concern for the welfare of animals is prudent in so far as they may be of benefit to humans, or for the reason given by Aquinas and Kant that an unthinking attitude toward animals is liable to induce an unthinking attitude toward human beings.

That Derrida shares this direct concern is confirmed by references made in *The Animal That Therefore I Am* and elsewhere, for instance in the dialogue with Elisabeth Roudinesco, to our maltreatment of animals in factory farming and medical research.[3] It is shared too by his interlocutor in that dialogue. Even so, she expresses certain reservations that tell us something about the concept of concern. Derrida asks her what she would do if she witnessed what goes on in industrial slaughterhouses. Her response is twofold. She responds first of all that she might well give up eating meat. That is, if I may put these words in her mouth, she might well have said, "*Il faut bien renoncer à manger de la viande,*" "One would do well to give up eating meat," "I had better become a vegetarian." But she also questions an assumption that is perhaps made by Derrida's question. You do not necessarily get to know (*connaître*) something better by seeing it, she says.[4] Knowing (*savoir*) is not looking at. Nor is such knowing listening to or hearing. And, she says, if she found herself living in a street where trucks transporting calves to the slaughterhouse passed her window every day she would move house. She does not say what she would do if she found herself living in a street where trucks passed along her street transporting not calves to the abattoir but human beings to Belsen. Instead, she reminds us that animal transportation contributes to the French gastronomic tradition that is a part of French culture! The exclamation mark is borrowed from her. She is not unaware that she is being mischievously provocative. Indeed, she succeeds in provoking Derrida into noting that the French gastronomic tradition may survive without having to depend on industrial methods of slaughter. Attitudes toward these are in fact changing, and practices are being gradually transformed in some quarters under pressure from individuals and institutions that share Derrida's concern and express it practically.

What is it to express a concern? I have just referred to one way of expressing concern for the welfare of animals. We may inform ourselves about what goes on in slaughterhouses. We can do this without visiting the slaughterhouses themselves. If, like Elisabeth Roudinesco, I suspect that the accuracy and objectivity of my knowledge (*savoir*) of the procedures followed in them may be diminished by the emotions provoked in me by my immediate acquaintance (*connaissance*) with them, I can put myself in a position to do something to improve those procedures by consulting people who have direct experience of them. Doing something may take the form of supporting the charity Compassion in World Farming, challenging the law, waving placards on the steps of the Ministry for Agriculture, writing letters to newspapers, or writing a book. Doing something may be as ineffectual as the gesture of not participating in a colloquium at Cerisy-la-Salle by way of private protest at the fact that the dispensers of the French gastronomical culture manifested so magnificently there tended to be uncomprehending of the vegetarianism of some of the participants. The counterproductivity of this abstention from participation hardly bears imagining when note is taken of the fact that the colloquium in question was the very one that gave rise to the book in which Derrida wrote that he shared my concern but that he would perhaps proceed a little differently.

How differently? And how does the concern differ from the procedure? One way in which Derrida shares my concern consists in the facts that my concern is a clue to my procedure and that my procedure follows a clue I had picked up from an earlier writing by him. The procedure followed in *The Middle Voice* is a development of a passing reference he had made in his essay on "*Différance*" to the way in which precisely this "*ance*" of *différance*, marking a grammatical voice that is neither simply active nor simply passive, is "announcing or rather [*plutôt* and *plus tôt,* earlier] recalling something like the middle voice."[5] Now we have just seen that concern may be expressed by participation in action (even when the action is that of deciding not to participate in a colloquium). It may be agency on the part of someone who concerns himself or herself in doing something. It may be a procedure or process, for example a legal process like the *procès verbal* of giving an account, taking a statement, or issuing a summons. But while concern may mean my involving myself in an operation, in an intervention, it may be at the same time my being *con-cerné,* regarded, *obsédé,* beseiged, obsessed, possessed, haunted, *hanté.* That is, it may be simultaneously self-affection and affection by another. And this ambiguity of the transitive and the intransitive is the logical device with which I proceed to work in *The Middle Voice of Ecological Conscience.*

The concern that Derrida said he shared with me and that I have said is shared too by Elisabeth Roudinesco is also shared by Matthew Calarco, whose book *Zoographies,* to which I am about to turn, is another that Derrida would certainly have recommended.[6] All four of us participate at least in the sympathy of compassion in world farming and in what is expressed more generally in Bentham's statement regarding "the rest of the animal creation" that "The question is not, Can they reason? nor Can they *talk?* but, Can they *suffer?*"[7] In his conversation with Elisabeth Roudinesco, Derrida writes "*sympathie*" in italics, and adds for good measure that he is keen on this word.[8] He is passionate about the pathos of a certain passion, as he has made plain *passim* and in particular in an essay of which part of the title is "Passions." Part of the meaning that means so much for him in this word and in the word "passivity" is that of passed-ness, an absolute passed-ness that is always *plus tôt,* always earlier. However, this absolute passed-ness is not antithetically opposed to a certain absolute future, any more than in the medial diathetic syntax of *différance* passivity and activity are polar opposites. While not being simply deed or performance, the absolute past and the absolute to-come of com-passion—absolute (from *solvo,* to separate) because they were never and never will be present or represented—are crossed with activity that is never *actus purus* but is in turn affected by the passivity that contributes to the non-neuter hybridity of *différance* and of what Derrida calls his procedure. Drawing on the forces of this word that link it both to a way of proceeding that someone might follow and to a process that is undergone, Derrida says he will be proceeding perhaps a little differently from me. When he says this he knows that he is speaking not simply of his methodology. He is signaling that any discursive method he is about to follow in his meditation of the question "But as for me, who am I?" and on the topic "The animal that therefore I am" will not follow solely his initiative. Procedure, *différance,* deconstruction happen largely of their own accord, and the best that French can do to express this non-doing is to have recourse to the reflexive forms of the verbs. *Il se procède, il se diffère, il se déconstruit* are pronounced in something like the middle voice. To proceed is to go ahead, but it is to do so in a manner that gives something its head. It gives it a hearing, as in a hearing in court of law, in a *procès verbal.* It makes allowances. It gives ear, yields place, makes concessions, cedes, all shades of meaning allowed by the Latin verb *"cedo,"* as in *"quasi locum dare et cedere,"* cited from Horace in Lewis's Latin dictionary. There too it is noted that when used with the dative the word may mean to yield to, retreat before, submit to, be overcome by. When these senses are kept in balance with the sense of moving ahead emphasized by the prefix *pro-* we get something like the middle voice, a chiasmus of the active and passive, where, however, the "something" is not just one thing, but allows for a plurality; as does "middle voice," which, when invoked by me in this book—for instance in the references in chapter 10 to double genitivity and to Edward Thomas's "or rather" rephrasal—is not a modality of verbs only; and as does "deconstruction," which is no more monolithic or monographic than is the *procédure* and the *se procéder* that Derrida says deconstruction enacts and is enacted by. But we are about to discover that he, with the assistance of the description of a certain procedure due to Nancy, embeds the auto-affection that the *se* of *se procéder* could be taken to point toward in a hetero-affection, with the result that the chiasmic combination of this self-reference and this other-reference form one more droplet of grammar in which a whole cloud of philosophy is distilled. We are about to learn that in this droplet is reflected the strange logical syntax of the interconnection of the human and the inhuman.

Procedures followed in one place by Derrida may be different from those followed in another. Variation is to be expected where the procedures are followed in analyses or quasi-analyses of different texts. But in so far as the varieties are versions of something like the middle voice, they will all be teasings-out of what is found (discovered or deemed) to be implicit and complicit in the particular texts. They will be articulations of the texts themselves, spellings-out of what their author writes, even if he or she would be surprised to discover what is said to follow from what he or she has written, rather as the authors whose names might be associated with positions described in the *Phenomenology of Spirit* might be surprised to learn what is found (discovered or deemed) to be implied in those positions under the descriptions Hegel gives of them. Found just by letting happen and by looking, as Hegel says, rather as Derrida says that just by letting happen and by looking it is found that foundation deconstructs itself. Rather as that third phenomenologist Wittgenstein urges (*PI* 66), "don't think, but look!"

So we would be surprised, as surprised perhaps as Matthew Calarco is, to come upon a place in a text by Derrida where the latter seems to be affirming a position that seems not to be something he has come upon by a procedure of looking, but a dogmatic pronouncement of his own.

How does Calarco register his surprise? Having reminded us of "the dogmatic prejudice that Derrida's work on the question of the distinction between the animal and the human is aimed at overcoming," he writes:

> And yet, . . . Derrida resolutely refuses to abandon the human–animal distinction. . . . I take Derrida's insistence on maintaining the human/ animal distinction to be one of the most dogmatic and puzzling moments in all of his writings. And I am measuring my words carefully here, for Derrida's writings (despite whatever shortcomings they might have) are rarely dogmatic.[9]

My first reaction (or response) on reading these sentences was to ask myself about the word "overcoming." The experience of reading the works of Derrida over many years, and reading them against a Hegelian background, has conditioned me not to expect any overcoming of a dogmatic prejudice by Derrida to take the form of a simple direct denial of that prejudice. So that if his treatment resulted in his affirmation of an opposite of that prejudice, I would not expect this to be the end of the story. I would expect him to go on and find a way of somehow reaffirming the affirmation he had been analyzing or quasi-analyzing. I say quasi-analyzing in case analysis is taken to be a process of regress upon elements. If Derridian deconstruction is a kind of vigilant analysis, it is not an analysis that works down to atomistic elements. Its bedrock is at most molecular, if we can suppose that the components of a molecule contaminate each other.

Even when the story is amplified by mention of this expectation that more remains to be said, we have still not reached the story's end. For if we stopped at this stage we would be liable to give the impression that we had reached a point of neutral indifference or of mutual implication. This would be to skate over the historical and political aspects of the deconstructive procedure. Reference was made above to a dialogue between Derrida and Roudinesco. That dialogue will remain relevant to what we shall be saying below, since it is from it that Calarco takes two of the passages he cites to illustrate what he sees as manifestations of Derrida's alleged dogmatism. The blurb on the jacket of the printed record of this dialogue describes it as a dialogue between a philosopher and a historian. But Derrida's philosophy has as historical a dimension as does Hegel's. Symptomatic of this is the title of the dialogue in question. *De quoi demain . . .* , "Of what, tomorrow," it asks, abbreviating the question Victor Hugo asks in one of the poems included in his *Chants du crépuscule:*

> An always masked spectre that follows alongside us.
> One which we call tomorrow.
> Oh! Tomorrow is the great thing!
> Of what, tomorrow, will it be made?

In his introduction to these poems Hugo writes: "Every today, in the field of ideas as in the field of things, in society as in the individual, is in a twilight state. Of what nature is this twilight, by what will it be followed?"[10] It is already a question of following and a question of being, as with the animal that therefore I am (*suis*) and/or follow (*suis*). And it is already a question of tomorrow and today. It is already, always already, *toujours, tout aujourd'hui,* a question of the absolute yesterday, of the "yes" before any question, *plus tôt,* earlier than it, but also the earliest, *le plus tôt.* This "yes" of the always already yesterday to what is to come is Derrida's rereading of the already and not yet, the *schon* and *noch nicht,* of his predecessor Hegel, and of the most matutinal *früher Spur,* the early trace whose track he follows through the writings of his predecessor Heidegger. This pursuit of Heidegger, as prosecuted in *Of Spirit,* is in part a pursuit of Heidegger's endeavor to avoid being misled by the specter or ghost of a Hegelian gloss of *Geist*—ghost or spirit. It is in part also, or rather at the same time and alongside, or rather in chiasmus, a retracing of Heidegger's game of hide-and-seek (*fort-da*) with a Christian construal of *Geist*.

So Derrida does not proceed in a vacuum. The subjects of his researches, he insists, do not fall from an empty sky. His choice of them or their choice of him is often motivated by a date or an anniversary, something that is a live issue for him and his prospective reader today. Thus the essay "Faith and Knowledge" begins with the questions "How to talk religion? Of religion? Singularly of religion, today [*aujourd'hui*]?" Another question that is especially urgent in this time of industrialized farming is the one heard or not heard in the sounds made by the calves from within the animal transport truck that passed along our street this morning on its way to the nearest slaughterhouse or to one unnecessarily far away. These questions overlap. As Derrida observes, on the one hand the practice of delicate eating known as vegetarianism is apt to assume the power of a religion. On the other hand the history of religious sacrifice is a history of animal sacrifice and it remains that even where sacrifice has become troped as, for example, the lamb of God.

In the final paragraphs of *Of Spirit*, which imagine a debate between Heidegger and Christian theologians regarding spirit, Derrida seems to suggest that the verdict must be a both/and. He draws our attention to a certain *Zusage*, a Heideggerian version of the *plus tôt* "yes" of which Heidegger hears rumors in the supposedly non-Christian and non-Platonic *geistlich-Geist* that Trakl interprets as ghost and flame and ash. The Heideggerian maintains that this original affirmation is a condition of possibility of any onto-theological metaphysical position and therefore of the position taken up by Christian theologians. But Derrida imagines the latter identifying Heidegger's alleged condition with their own. Although speaking in a suspiciously Hegelian accent, they reply, "That's the truth of what we have always said." They say "yes" to the always earlier "yes" that conditions what is always to come. Up to a certain point, therefore, *jusqu'à un certain point*—though the *point* is a certain forward-moving negation, a *pas*—something like a union between the Heideggerians and the Christian theologians is imagined by Derrida. What we do not find is the assertion of one position and the denial of a contrary one. Can the same be said of the dispute over the relation of human beings and animals treated earlier in *Of Spirit* and a number of other places by Derrida?

As I read Derrida's treatment of Heidegger's reflections on that relation, the pattern of argument anticipates that of the last paragraphs of *Of Spirit*. If Derrida is taking sides in the dispute over whether there is an abyssal distinction between animals and humans, he is taking both sides. He does not see himself to be denying Heidegger's contention that there is such a gulf between animals and humans. So this leaves it open for Derrida to affirm that there is such a gulf if he wishes to. And on Calarco's reading, this is what Derrida does. Moreover, on his reading Derrida does so dogmatically and in contradiction with what he concludes from his analyses of the texts of Heidegger that deal with the human/animal distinction. But what Derrida concludes, or rather what his analyses uncover, is not that there is or that there is not a rigorous distinction between animals and human beings, but that Heidegger's way of marking the distinction fails. It fails, for instance, to show that what demarcates humans from nonhuman animals is that the former but not the latter have access to the as-such of things. The lizard lying on the rock experiences the rock's smoothness and warmth, but it does not experience the rock's being-smooth, being-warm, or being-a-rock. More generally, the phenomenon appears to the animal, but not the phenomenon's phenomenality.[11] That is accessible only to a being who is there, *da*, a being that is possessed of or by *Dasein*.

Derrida seeks to bring out that Heidegger's lengthy analysis of *Dasein* cannot provide a criterion that will mark off humans from animals. This, to abbreviate what is indeed a detailed and complex investigation, is because according to Heidegger the existential structures in terms of which *Dasein* is to be construed depend upon each *Dasein*-al being's being toward its death. Now one way of being toward my death is a condition of my authenticity, while another way, for instance conceiving death as the indifferent fact that people, including myself, die, is an inauthentic mode of being. In order for this difference between the authentic and the inauthentic to be possible, it must be possible for *Dasein* to have access to the phenomenality of death. But death, according to Heidegger, is the possibility of an impossibility. If we accept that—and perhaps also if we prefer to say with Levinas that death is the impossibility of possibility—death as such cannot appear. Death as such is, as it were, a permanent appresentation. So, whether or not this means that there can be no phenomenological ontology of *Dasein*, it means that the proprium of *Dasein*-humanity cannot be having access to the as such of death.

Should we say instead that the proprium of *Dasein*-humanity is *not* having access to the as such of death? That might be a way of distinguishing the human in its finitude from the divine. But it could not be a way of distinguishing the human from the nonhuman animal if the latter is poor in world (*weltarm*) and *Dasein*-humanity is world-formative, world-construing, or world-constructive (*weltbildend*).

What alternative way does Derrida have in mind when, in Calarco's words, he displays his "insistence on maintaining the human–animal dis-

tinction"? A distinction must be made between two ways of taking this distinction. As Calarco recognizes, and as is confirmed by the report made
above of Derrida's unwrapping of Heidegger's way of maintaining the hu-
man/animal distinction, Derrida has in mind no single alternative way of
distinguishing the human from the nonhuman animal if this is understood
as a distinction between what is called "the animal" or "the Animal" and
what calls itself "the human being" or "the Human Being." Derrida's interest
is in bringing out the plurality of differences between and among animals
and humans, and in how these differences crisscross one another. "Every
time one puts an oppositional limit in question, far from concluding that
there is identity, we must on the contrary multiply attention to differences,
refine the analysis in a restructured field."[12] Deconstruction is a variety of
restructuration that seeks to do justice to the differences to which we are
blinded by normal classifications.

Mention and use

It is timely to add at this point that Derrida's interest lies also in bringing
out that there is a plurality of Heideggers. Derrida's "critique" of what Heidegger writes in certain places is sometimes the working out of a hint given or
taken (given-taken, in something like the middle voice) from what Heidegger
writes elsewhere. So his "critique" is sometimes ironic, which is why this
"mention" of it comes with quotation marks. Because an irony is a doublet,
any multiplication of it will be at least a triplet. And might it not be that such
a triple irony happens in at least some of those places which strike Calarco
as rare instances of dogmatism on the part of Derrida? If the sentences that
strike him as being dogmatic are indeed dogmatic, we must take care not to
mislocate this dogmatism. We must take care to observe that at least some
of these offending sentences are ones in which "mention" is made of expressions. I again put this word "mention" in quotation marks or scare quotes to
act as a reminder that Derrida has qualms over the distinction between use
and mention. These qualms are closely related to those he experiences over
Heidegger's practice of erasure, as when a diagonal cross is superimposed
on the word "being." They are related again to Derrida's hesitating to accept
the idea of metastatement on account of the credence it might seem to give
to the notion of a statement that masters the signified content of another
statement from above without being exposed to the lateral extensions into
other contexts to which the signifying vehicle is exposed. When Derrida is
dismissive of a distinction in the way Calarco deems to be dogmatic it is as

though the former is writing of what he calls the *animot,* that is to say of the composite word for animals, *animaux,* in their plurality and multiplicity rather than primarily of the animal as an alleged kind. It is of what those (let us collect them under the name *humainimots*) who *call* themselves humans *call* animals that Derrida is writing, with visible or invisible quotation marks. The thesis that Derrida seems to Calarco to endorse dogmatically is "the thesis of a limit or rupture or abyss between those who say 'we men,' 'I, as human,' and what this man among men who say 'we,' what he *calls* the animal or animals."[13]

Let us suppose for a moment that Derrida is here endorsing the thesis he mentions. It is just possible that if he appears dogmatic in doing so he only appears to be dogmatic because he has his tongue in his cheek, aping a dogmatism with which he charges Heidegger. Heidegger, he says, is being dogmatic when he writes "Apes, *for example* [Derrida's emphasis], have organs that can grasp, but they have no hand."[14] The paragraph concluded by this quotation from Heidegger begins with Derrida's saying "Here in effect occurs a sentence that at bottom seems to me Heidegger's most significant, symptomatic, and seriously dogmatic." How can these words not remind us of the ones reproduced earlier from Calarco, *viz:* "I take Derrida's insistence on maintaining the human–animal distinction to be one of the most dogmatic and puzzling moments in all of his writings"?

Leaving undecided whether Derrida is aping Heidegger here and whether Calarco is copycatting Derrida, that is to say, whether there are layers of irony in the relationships among the passages from these authors that we are comparing, let us be clear that what Calarco thinks Derrida is being dogmatic about is the distinction between humans and nonhuman animals even considered in the plurality of the differences between humans and nonhuman animals, the topic which Derrida says is the one that merits discussion in contrast with the distinction between the singularly universal Human and the singularly universal Animal considered as founded on a supposed single difference. When in the dialogue with Elisabeth Roudinesco, Derrida grants that the quest for a single difference is not a complete waste of time, he is acknowledging, I suggest, that such a quest is a spur to the discovery of the multiplicity and complexity of differences. What is a waste of time is discussion as to whether the view to be found most widely adhered to by philosophers and laymen is the view that a gulf is fixed between what they call the Animal and what they call the Human. That that is so is beyond dispute. The logic and the rhetoric at work here are similar to those at work when, referring amongst other interventions to the genetic manipulations practiced in the meat industry, Derrida comments:

> All that is all too well-known; we have no need to take it further. . . . No one can deny seriously any more, or for very long, that men do all they can in order to dissimulate this cruelty or to hide it from themselves; in order to organize on a global scale the forgetting or refusal to acknowledge this violence, which some would compare to the worst cases of genocide.[15]

The indisputability of the prevalence of the view that a gulf is fixed between what we call the Animal and what we call the Human leaves open the question whether that view is justified. Derrida believes that the answer to this question depends on how one construes that gulf. His findings are those expressed in the words of Donna Haraway cited by Calarco because the latter claims to hear in them a suggestion of an alternative, not only to the biologistic monism and the animal/human dualism based on a single differentia, to both of which Derrida objects, but also to the multiplism Derrida puts in their place:

> By the late twentieth century . . . the boundary between human and animal is thoroughly breached. The last beachheads of uniqueness have been polluted if not turned into immense amusement parks—language, tool use, social behaviour, mental events, nothing really convincingly settles the separation of human and animal. And many people no longer feel the need for such a separation.[16]

The term "uniqueness" is the key to my understanding of this extract in a way that agrees with Derrida's response to animal/human dualism grounded on a single differentia that, to borrow another key word from Haraway, *settles* the separation. Calarco focuses instead on the words "many people no longer feel the need for such a separation." I interpret the "such" as a reference to the unique ground on which people have sought to found the separation. He interprets the phrase as a hint in the direction of the *"we could simply let the human–animal distinction go* or, at the very least, not insist on maintaining it." And he sees this as an alternative to all the views of the human/animal distinction considered in his chapter on Derrida, including the one he takes Derrida to propose.

Bêtise

Are Calarco's and Derrida's alternatives mutually exclusive? The answer to this question depends on how we understand the notion of groundedness to which we have just made several references, and on how we understand Derrida's references to the abyssal. In the first chapter of *L'animal que donc je suis*

Derrida makes use of the phrase *ligne en abyme*. In common with the phrase *mise en abyme*, what is suggested is the idea of an infinite repetition, as of the series of reflections and reflections of reflections one gets of oneself when one stands between two mirrors, or an infinite repetition in the picture on the label of a sauce bottle of a cook holding this bottle with the label visible upon it. The idea is that of an absence of foundation, a lack of ground, an *Abgrund*. What interests Derrida is the idea of the dividedness of the line that separates rather than the idea of the separateness or otherwise of the human and the animal. "*Limitrophy* is therefore my subject," meaning by this not only the arrangements made on each side of a frontier for feeding those on each side of it ("trophy" derives from the Greek *trephō*, meaning to rear or cultivate), "but also what feeds the limit, generates it, raises it, and complicates it. Everything I'll say will consist certainly not in effacing the limit, but in multiplying its figures . . . dividing the line precisely by making it increase and multiply."[17] It is as good or bad as to have no ground if there are two grounds between which one oscillates or falls.[18]

When Derrida writes that this "is therefore my subject," in the "therefore" (*donc*) may be heard the "therefore" of "I think therefore I am," and in "my subject" may be heard a reference both to his topic, namely the auto-biographical animal, and to the author. He, Derrida, allows his reader the liberty of thinking that the author (as well as the reader) himself would be more asinine than any beast (*plus bête que les bêtes*) to deny the thesis that there is a gulf between those who say "I" or "we" and those they call animals. To deny this is to go against the way the words "I" and "we" function in "our" language and thinking, yet in so doing to make room on our side of the divide for a property or non-property or mode at least something like the one we claim to be restricted to the other side, namely what we may risk calling the stupidity that the French call *bêtise*. The riskiness of calling this *bêtise* stupidity is emphasized in *The Beast and the Sovereign*. There fine distinctions are made between the English "stupidity" and the French *stupidité*. There too the translation of *bêtise* as "asininity" is queried:

> [E]ven when one introduces the apparent animal reference to the ass or to asininity, in French or other languages, for example Arabic, one is saying something close, but being an ass and being *bête* are not the same thing: the ass is ignorant, either vacant or innocent, does not know what he ought to know, but *bêtise* is not a defect in the order of knowledge: this is why Deleuze was right to dissociate it from error.[19]

Turning from the question of the possibility of finding an apparently animal characteristic in the human to the possibility of finding an apparently human characteristic in the animal, Derrida asks us to "ask Abraham's ass or ram or the living beasts that Abraham offered to God: they know what is about to happen to them when men say 'Here I am' to God, then consent to sacrifice themselves, to sacrifice their sacrifice, or to forgive themselves." That is to say, we have already undertaken the discussion that, he says in the next sentence, is only worthy of being undertaken "once it is a matter of determining the number, form, sense, or structure, the foliated thickness, of this abyssal limit, these edges, the plural and repeatedly folded frontier."[20] The multifoldedness of the frontier between human beings and nonhuman animals is already in play when Derrida says (declining to be as frontal before the naked truth in his philosophy as Adam and Eve were before each other and before God according to the first book of the Bible and as Derrida himself was vis-à-vis his cat in his bathroom according to the story told in the first part of *The Animal That Therefore I Am*) that it would be, as the French say, *bêtise* to deny the entrenchedness of the distinction between human beings and nonhuman animals. If Derrida or any other speakers of French call that denial a *bêtise*, they are giving voice to the thought that human animals may share the character of nonhuman animals. On the other hand, the thought that nonhuman animals may share the character considered typical of human animals is what is being raised when Derrida asks us to ask Abraham's ass a question. Coming from both directions, Derrida is demonstrating how tricky it is to speak straightforwardly here. He is showing that the apparent clean cut of the butchery (*boucherie*) of a banal opposition is cut across, contra-dicted and bent (*abîmé*) by a common turn of speech, a word of mouth (*bouche*) where our speaking habits and our eating habits intersect, and where our eating habits are already an intersection of eating and religious sacrifice. For *boucherie* was the slaughter of a goat (*bouc*), of a scapegoat, and the notion of dividing into kinds, *Geschlechter*, is linked with the notion of slaughter, *Schlachten*. This notion figures in paragraphs on Socrates' double procedure of collection and division attributed to Socrates by Plato in the *Phaedrus*, other paragraphs of which dialogue, the ones on writing and pictorial representation, are deconstructed in early writings of Derrida. After describing the procedure of collecting particular cases under a general idea, Socrates goes on to speak of the "other procedure" that

> enables us to separate a general idea into its subordinate elements, by dividing it at the joints as nature directs and not attempting to break any limb in half, after the fashion of a bungling butcher. And this procedure was followed in my two disquisitions about madness. Just as from one body there proceed two sets of members called by the same name but distinguished as right and left, so when my discourses had formed the

WHERE TO CUT: *BOUCHERIE* AND *DELIKATESSEN* | 253

general conception of madness naturally constituting one class within us, the discourse whose task was to divide the left-hand portion did not resist division into smaller and smaller parts, until it found among them a kind of left-handed love which it justly derided. The other discourse led us to the right-hand side of madness where it discovered a love bearing the same name as the former, but divine, which it recommended to us as the author of our greatest blessings.[21]

This text, which never ceases to be a context for my construction of the imadgination, never ceases to be a context for Derrida's deconstruction of the notions of the natural, of the opposition between the sinister left that is left over from the divinely dexterous sovereign right, and of decision, which, he says, agreeing with Kiekegaard, is always mad. This context is one that is taken up into the Husserlian rigorous science of essences and idealities treated in the first part of this book, and, because of Husserl's emphasis upon reason and responsibility and freedom, his rigorous science never ceases to be another context of the Derridian "dialectic" of deconstruction of such oppositions as the one under investigation in this chapter between reason and responsibility and freedom, on the one hand, and, on the other hand (*pace* Heidegger), the beast.

> I choose phenomenological vocabulary and Husserlian conceptuality to describe this situation because one finds in it this motif of freedom and therefore the correlate of that responsible, free, and sovereign personality that is so often implied to explain to us (for example, as Lacan and Deleuze do close to us, but as has always been done) that cruel bestiality and *bêtise* are proper to man and cannot be attributed to so-called animal beasts.[22]

With regard to precisely this opposition between what is proper to man and what is proper to beasts, it may be objected that when Derrida asks us to "ask Abraham's ass or ram or the living beasts that Abraham offered to God . . ." he has transgressed the frontier that divides the territory of philosophy and scientific fact from a land of fantasy or literature. But transgression is Derrida's subject. His topic, albeit shifting, is the crossing and crossing out of frontiers rather than such full frontality as that with which he is viewed in his bathroom by his cat, or as that with which one might affirm or deny a proposition. We should remember that already Husserl had made fantasy, *Phantasie*, imagination, a phenomenologico-philosophical method. We should not forget either that in the later work of Heidegger originary poetry, *Dichtung*, is wedded to "another thinking," *ein anderes Denken*. And we need to recall that even when Derrida departs from what these philosophers say, he departs in both senses of the word. He takes hints from them. Remembering these things, and remembering the words "repeatedly folded frontier" cited above from Derrida, we are struck by the thought that perhaps such a manifoldness characterizes the frontier of what we earlier called the matter-of-factness of the proposition that the view to be found most widely adhered to by philosophers and laymen is that a gulf is fixed between what they call the Animal and what they call the Human. This would not mean that we have to let go the distinction between the factual and its others. It could mean, however, that we might need to analyze that distinction more carefully than we usually do. It could mean that we might need to do this if we say with Matthew Calarco that "we could simply let the human–animal distinction go or, at the very least, not insist on maintaining it."[23]

Does Derrida insist on maintaining this distinction? Would not doing that be approaching the distinction "frontally or antithetically," something he says he does not propose to do?[24] Would not doing that be to leave undisturbed the classical or dialectical logic of contradiction the sovereignty of which it is precisely his aim to disturb? Here we must distinguish two distinctions. There is the human/animal distinction, and there is the canonical way of justifying that distinction that Derrida says Heidegger, among others, subscribes to. It is the latter, the traditional way of attempting to justify the human/animal distinction, that Derrida says he does not intend to attack frontally or antithetically. However, if he refrains from doing that, would we not expect him to refrain also from attacking the former distinction itself frontally or antithetically? Is it not his intention and interest to demonstrate that the methodology of thesis and antithesis is too crude and that the logic of formal and dialectical contradiction or contrariety requires to be supplemented by a logic of supplementation, a graphology of the graft, *différance*? His procedure in demonstrating this cannot be simply to deny or oppose a classical or metaphysical opposition. That would leave standing the structure of such opposition, not de-structure it or de-con-struct it or, as Cambridge philosophers used to say, dissolve it. This hyphenation of the "de" and the "con" brings out that deconstruction is a *double* reading that at one level intervenes between the opposites distinguished in the double procedure of Platonic or Socratic division, destabilizing their equilibrium, and yet leaves everything as it is at the level of customary, institutionally accepted discourse in which properties or characteristics are predicated of things. And that is what has been done with *bêtise* in this section of this chapter—except for the point at which it was referred to also as a non-property, the point at which we reported Derrida's qualms over saying that the French *bêtise* means the same as the English "stupidity." He hesitates to draw this equivalence. This is because doing that would create the impression that he is primarily interested in likeness and difference of conceptual meaning, for instance between the concept of the animal in general as opposed to the concept of the human in general. That opposition does indeed provide the context of *The Animal That Therefore I Am* and of large parts of the seminars on *The Beast and the Sovereign*. But it is as a background that this conceptual opposition serves in those works. Their foregound is a nonconceptuality or quasi-conceptuality that upsets oppositionality as conceived in the so-called square of logical opposition and in the logic that has dominated philosophy since Plato and Aristotle.

In *The Beast and the Sovereign,* in a procedure corresponding to that of the first part of Plato's method of division and Aristotelian "induction," Derrida assembles a library of texts by Hobbes, La Fontaine, Flaubert, Carl Schmitt, Valéry, Lacan, Deleuze, D. H. Lawrence, Büchner, Celan, Agamben, and others, reading them painstakingly with the effect that his readers or listeners are liable to learn that the contrast between the molar concept of the beast or animal and the molar concept of the human is less secure than they assumed. Pivotal in this educative process are the noun *bêtise* and the adjective *bête* in an employment that is, paradoxically, reserved for "us" (French) human beings (French or Franco-Lithuanian; Levinas imagines the phrase *trop bête* being used of the dog Bobby who haunts our chapter 8). The words *bête* and *bêtise* are used of deeds, happenings, and accidents. When they are used of a deed they are commonly used to accuse the person responsible of a kind of lapse. But what kind of lapse? It is not a lapse into error. *Bêtise* is not a false judgment. Yet it is connected with *jus* and the forces of justice that are part and parcel of the notion of judgment. It is so connected by being connected with the notions of responsibility and of freedom of will that, according to, for example, the scene described by Descartes, leave open to the human being the possibility of affirming judgments that are not clearly supportable by the understanding or evidence. *Bêtise* is not a mistaken judgment, whether determinant or reflective. It is a more or less habitual or momentary obtuseness of judgment in the scope of the more-or-less over which ranges not theoretical or empirical knowledge or pure reason but the will, as Aquinas too would have said, equating the will with the heart and anticipating Pascal, who preached the reasons of the heart, that "we are as much automaton as mind," and that there is need for the seeker after wisdom and beatitude to *s'abêtir,* to allow himself or herself to succumb to a sort of beastitude. So that the force possessed by this word *bêtise* borrowed from the lexicon having to do with animals is dependent on the cluster of notions constitutive of the lexicon used in arriving at legal, juridical, ethical, and political verdicts, a realm classically associated with responsible human action. *Bêtise*, then, we might perhaps say provisionally (but with a provisionality that the catalogue of cases cited by Derrida suggests will never be transcended), is an unresponsiveness in responsibility, perhaps something like a lack of what Aristotle calls *phronēsis*, practical wisdom, one of the topics that will be touched on below in chapter 13.

Lacan and Deleuze

Before bringing to a close the present chapter in which one of the main topics has been the puzzlement a remark on the division between the animal and the human made by Derrida causes one of his readers to experience, mention must be made of the puzzlement that may be caused by the way Derrida's procedure applies its comments on *bêtise* to Lacan. Lacan places *bêtise* in the realm of what he calls the imaginary, where the imaginary is contrasted with the symbolic as nature is contrasted with convention and reaction is contrasted with response. Derrida does not dismiss this contrast. He does, however, question the confidence with which it is made by Lacan and the Cartesian tradition to which he considers Lacan belongs. Such confidence, he writes elsewhere, "is not only philosophically deconstructible, critiquable, doubtful, for thinking and knowledge, but is also the first relinquishment of the ethical (la première *démission éthique*)."[25] What has been Derrida's procedure so far? It has been to show that there is no one thing that is meant when the French use the expression *bêtise*, and that not one of the several proposed translations of that expression is synonymous with the French. But this much can be said of many terms for the use of which there are no necessary criteria, most famously among readers of Wittgenstein terms like "language" and "game" whose referents have only a family resemblance. Yet we are not tempted to conclude that the use of such terms is not responsible but reactive, coded, programmed, hard-wired, fixed, and mechanical in the manner of the signaling behavior practiced by animals according to the Cartesian or, as Derrida writes, Cartesian-Lacanian.[26] However, such cases of family resemblance would share with cases of reactive behavior the negative feature of not depending on the rigorous ideality demanded in, for example, Husserl's account of meaning and its expression referred to in earlier chapters of this book. It is this demand that Derrida is primarily concerned to solicit and to replace with one in which thresholds, for instance the threshold between the concepts of the human and the nonhuman animal, are discovered to be unsimple and unsolid. Husserl would have knowing *how* to use terms require ultimately knowing *what* one means. His theory of meaning is representationalist. It is theoretical in that it turns on *theōria*, viewing, acquaintance, *connaissance*, and, Derrida would say, autopsy, suggesting both that seeing of some kind is involved, and that it is the death of meaning. Meaning is kept alive by the exposure of the signifier to repetition in contexts outside any allegedly circumscribed semantic field. But if keeping meaning alive requires that we have a theoretical knowledge of all those contexts, meaning would be possible only in paradise, "the promise or memory of paradise . . . at once . . . of absolute felicity and of an inescapable catastrophe."[27] We should need to have at our command the epistemologico-semantic sovereignty of the absolute knowledge of God. This explains why the reference to a certain inhumanity in the title of this book is jointly theological and zoological. It explains too the title of the book that contains Derrida's seminars, *Séminaire: la bête and le souverain*, with respectively feminine and masculine articles, though the implications of that fact are not articulated in detail in its first volume. This first volume coins the expression "divinanimality" to mark the supplementary logic of the connecting/disconnecting hyphen between sovereignty and *bêtise* whose implications are worked out in that volume. I hereby constate and recall some of these.

"I hereby constate. . . ." Here is a formula that recalls Austin's realization that there is no simple cut between the constative and the performative. This is recalled in turn by Derrida when he notes that one *accuses* someone, oneself, or another, of being *bête*. *Katēgoria*, the Greek for accusation, is a word from which English gets "category." From it too comes Kant's term *Kategorie*, but his "categories of the understanding" are concepts, formal concepts that order the use of subordinate concepts in propositions about—"constating"— states of affairs that may become items of knowledge. However, when I say "I hereby constate that *p*" I do more or less than constate. I do not simply represent. In uttering those words, other things being more or less equal, I thereby bring about a state of affairs. I make the utterance true. Now although saying of someone that he is *bête* may appear to be reporting a state of affairs, Derrida's close readings of various texts in which these words are used fails to arrive at a representation of a state of affairs that anyone who uses them would have to have in mind. It is as if accusations of *bêtise* had some sort of "as if" as their condition that never amounted to a necessary, sufficient, or necessary and sufficient condition for making the accusations. It is as though, somewhat in the manner of negative theology, for each proposed condition one could only deny that it was what was meant. Derrida cites similar experiments on stupidity conducted by Avital Ronell.[28] Coming away empty-handed, she infers, though moving into one of the other languages she investigates: "there is no tome that would bear the title *Vom Wesen der*

Dummheit (On the Essence of Stupidity)...."[29] (There is one that bears the title *Vom Wesen und Ursprung der Dummheit.*)[30]

Notwithstanding this overdetermination or underdetermination, we are usually successful in our performances of the deeds we wish to do with words. Not least when they are performative in the Austinian sense, as when one says with Zola *J'accuse,* or with Derrida "I challenge you." Derrida invites his readers to imagine he is challenging them to describe the conditions that must necessarily obtain if they are to know, and to know with the kind of objectivity Husserl claimed for his allegedly rigorous phenomenological science of free ideal meaning,[31] what they are doing when they utter a certain performative pronouncement like "I swear I know what I mean when I accuse someone of being *bête.*" Penetrating three layers of performance ("I challenge . . . ," "I swear . . . ," "I accuse . . ."), Derrida asks them to imagine this, to use the "faculty" of *Phantasie* that Husserl holds to be the handmaiden of phenomenology. This "as if" of Derrida's challenge is a reflection of the fact that neither he in challenging his reader nor the reader in responding to the challenge can have the theoretical and perhaps ultimately philosophical comprehension Husserl's rigorous science demands. As just noted, a phenomenological theory of expressive meaning is ultimately in the position of negative theology which permits us only to deny predicates of God, never, at least on this side of the dark glass, to achieve positive comprehension of his nature. With God the Sovereign, so too with *bêtise.* Yet, remember, this French word belongs to the juridico-ethical and ultimately social and international contexts in which accusations call to be justified or shown to be unjust and in which political conflicts may be resolved. Yet again, on the evidence so far available to us in the record of the seminars on *The Beast and the Sovereign,* the micrological examination conducted there provides no sure criterion to found even the claim we have so far left unchallenged in this chapter, namely that "'*bêtise* is not animality' and that man alone is exposed to it."[32]

This last claim is endorsed by Deleuze and Lacan, but it is the target of another challenge by Derrida. So far it has looked as though he was following them in their support of this claim. But in the course of the sixth session of the seminars there takes place a *volte-face.* It may have seemed until now that all three of them are, so to speak (and the seminars are all about speaking or so-to-speak "speaking"), standing up for the animal by assuring for him or her or it at least a modicum of the freedom, rationality, and responsibility brought in as it were through the back door of *bêtise.* For even if in its accusatory employment it is applied only to human beings, this word is not unconnected with nonhuman animality. So one might suppose that, indirectly and by rebound, at least a residue of the dignity that rationality and free responsibility give the human being would be credited to nonhuman animals. This would be an inference based on resemblance. But this is not how in the sixth session Derrida sees the argument developing. There we discover that what is universally taken to be the essence of responsibility, freedom, and rationality becomes unavailable through the front door for human beings and therefore through the back door for the animal from whom, etymologically if not genetically, the human being borrows its *bêtise*. It is as if both the human and the nonhuman animal are left with no more to stand on than a ground that is an unground, a *terra* that is terrifyingly *incognita*, *infirma*, and *unheimlich*: an *Ungrund* or an *Urgrund*, we might say, thereby stepping into the territory to which we were close when we coined the word *humainimot*, preparing the way via the intermediacy of divino-humanity or humano-divinity, incarnation, and mediation for the encounter with Derrida's word "divinanimality." This is a coinage that should prepare the way for a meditation on what he, following Schelling and Heidegger, has to say about a certain point of indifference. Postponing that meditation, and for the time being turning my back on the *terra infirma* on to which it would require us to trespass, let me end this section by citing a couple of affirmations in which Derrida is as frontal as he lets himself be about why he avoids frontality.

Humainimot is not his word. If he were willing to use or mention it, it would not be in order to mark a resemblance between the nonhuman animal and the human. To be assured of that we need only recall that in *The Politics of Friendship*, *Specters of Marx*, and elsewhere he resists the assimilation of otherness to fraternity. The other is not my neighbor, my next, *mon semblable*. Although in his reading of D. H. Lawrence's poem "Snake" in *The Beast and the Sovereign* he points out that it is said of the snake that "he seemed to me again like a king," like a sovereign, he warns against reading in this line a transfer of sovereignty to the snake from the human being who, watching the snake at the waterhole, hurled a stick at the serpent and then, like Coleridge's ancient mariner, experienced bitter remorse. The line is to be read as an invitation to rethink the notion of sovereignty in a way that, notwithstanding Saint Francis, raises the dust for a metaphysics or ethics or politics of assimilation. Aware that he may appear to be seeking predicates grounding a resemblance between the nonhuman animal and the human in the style of an ethics that turns on resemblances between the human being and the chimpanzee, he gives notice explicitly that "I do not want to homogenize things and erase differences."[33] His concern and mine and ours may be to speak up for nonhuman animals whose sufferings we find stratagems to conceal from ourselves, but his procedure does not pass directly via the claim that they share with human beings the capacity to suffer. His procedure is to

question whether we are too precipitate in our thinking of the logic of what
it is to share—the logic and rhetoric of what in a Platonic and Aristotelian
context we call participation, predication, *methexis,* or *mimēsis.* The purpose
of this procedure is to refine our idea of sameness and therefore of difference:

> it is to refine differential concepts that I am emphasizing a nonpertinence
> of the concepts and logic that are employed to reserve the privilege of
> what one thinks one can define as *bestiality* and *bêtise* . . . to that properly
> human animality supposedly free, responsible, and not reactive or reac-
> tional, capable of telling the difference between good and evil, capable of
> doing evil for evil's sake, etc.[34]

The logic that is thus employed is typically the logic of essences defined in
terms of necessary and sufficient conditions present to consciousness, the
logic of sharply defined determinate terms that has been found wanting in
the chosen case of the word *bêtise* by being shown to be for practical purposes
usable without the possibility or need to produce a definition in terms of necessary and/or sufficient conditions, a need, incidentally that, like the positing
of absolute knowledge, is itself an example of what we could mean by *bête:*

> [O]ne can always *use* (and I mean use, utilize, or even exploit, implement,
> or actualize) the lexicon of *bêtise* in a more or less appropriate way, pro-
> ducing more or less the expected effects, *without knowing what one means.*
> Without being able to answer for it in a theoretically, philosophically, and
> semantically responsible way. It remains then for us to discover the mean-
> ing of "say" and "do," of "try to produce effects," "appropriate," and "ex-
> pected effects," and of "more or less" (approximately appropriate, approxi-
> mately expected) [and of "something like" (as in, for example, "something
> like the middle voice")] when one cannot say to what they are appropriate,
> to what signification *as such,* nor can one objectify the meaning *itself,* the
> meaning as such, of what is an act or operation of language, in a given
> pragmatic situation, with a determinate practical strategy.[35]

If this is a lesson we learn in the seminars on *The Beast and the Sovereign* by
looking at, doing a "phenomenology of language" on, the grammar of *bêtise,*
it is a lesson that has wider implications.

> What is one saying and doing when one is always doing something or
> saying something the very meaning of which remains largely indetermi-
> nate, plastic, malleable, relative, etc.?
>   I recognize that this difficulty can affect other words and, ultimately,
> all usages, all so-called idiomatic implementations of a lexicon, the whole
> of a language and of languages in general.[36]

The lesson that appears to be taught both in Wittgenstein's *Tractatus* and in
his *Philosophical Investigations* is that a word has meaning only in the context

of a sentence. However, if we are to apply that lesson we must read it in the contexts of the texts of Frege and Derrida before we say that the former was saying the same thing when he wrote that "only in the context of a sentence do words have meaning" and that the latter was saying the same thing when he wrote "il n'y pas de hors texte."

I hinted above that a general point Derrida is trying to make about sameness of meaning might be supported by what Wittgenstein says about family resemblance. I went on to note that Derrida is more interested in difference than in resemblance, conceding that you cannot be interested in the one without being interested in the other. I must now add that although Derrida shares with Wittgenstein, Austin, and a host of other Oxford and Cambridge philosophers an interest in meaning in general (how with his background in phenomenology could he not?), his intellectual career has, by his own confession, never ceased to be driven by problems to do with living and life (*bios*, *zōē*, *chaïm*, etc.) whether or not as lived in language. The later Wittgenstein described language as a form of life. However, closer than the later Wittgenstein to Derrida's outline of a biologic and zoologic conceived as an alternative to the kind of rigorous logic of linguistic animation formulated by Husserl and the earlier Wittgenstein is Nietzsche with his prefiguration not only of insights developed by Deleuze but also of Derrida's logic of supplementation and *différance* (with a participial letter *a* that announces temporality) for which "the living being is divisible and constituted by a multiplicity of agencies, forces, and intensities that are sometimes in tension or even in contradiction."[37]

Archi-zoography

The logic of supplementation allows that with its procedure of deconstruction the human/animal distinction has in a way been let go. It is let go in the way that in the essay on *différance* and other early essays by Derrida the usual distinction between speaking and writing, while left standing for the purposes of daily discourse, is spoiled—and the verb *abîmer* that is cognate with the noun *abyme* has this force of to spoil or to ruin or, as it was translated earlier, to bend. It is bent or otherwise spoiled by the eruption of archi-writing. What would the analogue or anagraph of archi-writing be in the case of the historical fact that "we," including, I suspect, Calarco, make the human/animal distinction which for the purposes of daily discourse remains as uncontroversial as the historical fact that "we," including, I suspect, Calarco, make the distinction between speaking and writing? Would the analogue or anagraph of archi-writing be *bêtise*, the quasi-asinine stupidity that has been found lurking on the side of the human animal or what we have dubbed the *humainimot* but which could be a trace of the stupor that accompanies wonder as blindingness accompanies the brightness of the sun? Or would the analogue or anagraph of archi-writing be inhumanity or unhumanity standing for what does not stand in the posture of the erect man who takes his whoness from the who of the grammatical subject?

To his friend Jean-Luc Nancy, who, speaking of the "Who?," has just put it to him that "You validate it by suppressing that which, a priori, would limit the question to humanity," Derrida responds: "Yes, I would not want to see the 'who' restricted to the grammar of what we call Western language, nor even limited by what we believe to be the very humanity of language."³⁸ A few moments earlier, adverting to a radical friendship that is possibly hinted at in Heidegger's reference to "the voice of the friend,"³⁹ and alluding to "a responsibility that is to be found at the root of all other responsibilities (moral, judicial, political), and of every categorical imperative," he has cautioned: "To say of this responsibility, and even of this friendship, that it is not 'human,' no more than it is 'divine,' does not simply come down to saying that it is inhuman." Even so, he continues, alluding to the Kantian discourse of worth (*Würde*) and the *dignitas* that for a human being consists in rigorously obeying no law but that which the rationality of rational beings gives them,⁴⁰ "it is perhaps more 'worthy' ('*digne*') of humanity to maintain a certain inhumanity, which is to say the rigor of a certain inhumanity." To be reminded by *différance* of the fragility of an ancient Cartesian metaphysical opposition or of its newer Heideggerian transformation is to learn why "The idea according to which man is the only speaking being . . . seems . . . at once indisplaceable and highly problematic." That is how it seems to Derrida.⁴¹ It seems highly problematic once it has been deconstructively analyzed along the lines sketched out earlier in the present chapter. It seems indisplaceable for the purposes of everyday discourse. But how are we to construe the relation between the everyday and the philosophical? Derrida is as reluctant to pass quickly over this question as we ought to be reluctant to pass quickly over the question whether when Bishop Berkeley responds to Locke's claim about material substance he, the Bishop, is doing no more than saying what ordinary people ordinarily mean, as Berkeley maintains. Recall too that everydayness seems to be an indisplaceable element of Heidegger's analysis of humanity-cum-*Dasein*. That is why Derrida would have difficulties with the thought of letting the human/animal distinction go. If that means legislating it out of existence, we should recall his avowal, of which Calarco himself reminds us, "I do not believe in the miracle of legislation."⁴² This does not mean that he does not believe in legislation. It means that he believes legislation should be well informed and responsive, not *bête*. Whether letting a distinction go is compared to allowing it to die or to killing it off, itself a distinction about which Derrida is unsure,[43] scientific rigor requires that the collection of scientific evidence be conducted in the context of attending to the historical presuppositions that come with the distinctions we seek to supersede. But, Calarco would urge me to add: and vice versa. And Derrida too would urge this addition. Referring to his differential analysis of the alleged binary opposition between the human and the animal, he says that "what I am proposing here should allow us to take into account scientific knowledge about the complexity of 'animal languages,' genetic coding, all forms of marking within which so-called human language, as original as it might be, does not allow us to 'cut' once and for all where we would like in general to cut. . . . We know less than ever where to cut. . . . Today less than ever."[44]

We know today less than ever where to cut between discovery and invention, invention of the other as mentioned in the question posed at the end of *Zoographies:* "Might not the challenge for philosophical thought today be to proceed altogether without the guardrails of the human–animal distinction and to invent new concepts and new practices along different paths?" Already invention is simultaneously active and passive. We reproduced above Calarco's citation from Donna Haraway's *Simians, Cyborgs, and Women,* subtitled *The Reinvention of Nature,* and his suggestion that she might be a guide toward one way of taking up this challenge. In *When Species Meet* Haraway introduces us to Barbara Smuts, a bioanthropologist who studied a large group of baboons in the valley of the Great Rift. "At the beginning of my study," Smuts reports, "the baboons and I did not see eye to eye."[45] As she approached as close to them as she could, they tried to get as far away as they could from her. So she pretended to be just a fixed part of the landscape—not a be-worlded and be-worlding human being, not a poorly-worlded animal, but a worldless chunk of stone. And it was as a chunk of stone that they treated her at first. So, gradually, she learned to respond to them in ways similar to the ways in which the baboons responded to one another. "As a result, instead of avoiding me when I got too close, they started giving me very deliberate dirty looks, which made me move away." Haraway comments:

> [I]f she was really interested in these baboons, Smuts had to enter into, not shun, a responsive relationship. . . . In other words, her idiom leaves the baboons in nature, where change involves only the time of evolution, and perhaps ecological crisis, and the human being in history, where all other sorts of time come into play. Here is where I think Derrida and Smuts need each other.

Here is where I think Derrida and Calarco need each other.

All the different procedures distinguished in this chapter need each other if their practitioners are, in the words of Leonard Lawlor, to stand the best chance of responding with least violence to the concern they share.[46] Whether it does that is the test of whether the human/animal distinction should be let go, assuming that is something we can do. Is it clear that this is something we can do? Must we not hang on to the distinction if we are to let it go? For even if we resolve to avoid making this distinction in what we say, must we not, in order to carry out this resolution, retain the distinction in what we think? Is not the attempt to cut it out a promising way of entrenching it in the memory, rather as bidding people to forget something is a good way of ensuring that they don't? It is as though agreeing to the request to let something go in the sense of not holding on to it is apt to turn into letting it go in the sense of allowing it to run free, like detaching a dog from its leash or a calf from a crate or a cat from a bathroom may be granting them a new lease of life.

So to say that "we could simply let the human/animal distinction go" is not to say something simple. That Calarco recognizes this is indicated by his going on to say "or, at the very least, not insist on maintaining it." This addition may be the effect of what Derrida calls a supplement. It gives us to remember that if letting the human/animal distinction go is an activity that we can perform, this ability is conditioned by the inability of the passivity of the happening that Derrida calls archi-writing. In the context of the question whether we could let go the question where to cut the human–animal relation we could, adapting Calarco's title, call this archi-writing archi-zoography, understanding by this the life that exceeds the distinction between what we call the animal and what we autobiographical humans call "we."

Both *The Animal That Therefore I Am* and *Zoographies* experiment with a thought of a future in which "we" includes all sentient beings. The titles of these two books prepare the reader not to expect much attention, if any, to be given in them to the distinction between the life of sentient beings and the life of nonsentient living beings, plants, a distinction to which only passing reference is made in Heidegger's pages on ways of being and worldhood and in Derrida's comments on those pages. *The Middle Voice of Ecological Conscience* experiments with a thought of the future in which "we" includes all beings in a proximity that maintains distance.

THIRTEEN

Passover

Hors d'oeuvre

Ce sacré pas du repas, this blessèd and blasted *pastoverness* of the *repast,* was something that made Derrida and me smile. The occasion was the colloquium "Victor Cousin, the Ideologists, and their Relations with Scottish Philosophy" that took place at the International Study Center of Sèvres in 1982 under the direction of Derrida on the French side, of myself on the Scottish side, and of Pierre Alexandre, who, as then co-director of the Center and formerly director of the French Institute in Scotland, was well placed to coordinate our energies. Professor Henri Gouhier honored us with his presence and his comments. In the course of the weekend participants visited the Victor Cousin Library at the Sorbonne. At the end of the colloquium Derrida invited us to a reception at the École Normale Supérieure. On the final evening several of us, including my colleagues and friends George Davie and Nelly Demé, had dinner together in a restaurant in the rue Descartes. But without Derrida. We had omitted to invite him! Not entirely without good reason. For my part, I had considered that he would surely prefer to get back immediately to his writing. Even so, we should at least have invited him! That is to say, I myself should have, I who was perhaps both not sensitive enough and too sensitive.

Entrée

Can one be too sensitive? Is it one's responsibility not to be too *sensible*? Is it one's responsibility not to be too responsive, too susceptible to another's susceptibilities? If so, would this perhaps be on account of the word "too," for one ought not to be too anything, even too good? According to Aristotle the practically wise person, the *phronimos,* should avoid the *too,* whether the too little or the too much (or the too whatsoever, not excluding the too moderate?). Whether excess or lack, the too is in both cases both *de trop* and too little, a surplus and a minus: always a defect, always a fault, always a shortcoming. So let us avoid for a moment the word "too," not only in order not to gainsay Aristotle, but because every statement of the form "one should not overdo *x*" is presumably tautological. As a tautology, it could not serve as a principle of action. A tautology entails only another tautology. Still avoiding the word "too," should one then say rather that one ought to *ménager* the susceptibilities of others, that is, to treat them with care and consideration, that one ought to be susceptible regarding them? Is showing consideration for the susceptibilities of others a way of behaving with moderation?

Ménager, to treat with consideration and care, is to spare, to be unprodigal, to economize. And for there to be a *ménage* there must be an *oikos.* *Ménager* is a way of managing, of handling and maneuvering. From the notion of *ménage* one passes via that of the household to that of the hand, to the *manus* and the maintenance of at once touching and being touched. Now in *Le toucher, Jean Luc Nancy* it is to Merleau-Ponty, among others, that Derrida refers us when he speaks of simultaneously touching and being touched, and it is in the work of Merleau-Ponty also that the idea of the just perceptive distance is to be found.[1] This idea itself is to be found in the Aristotelian idea of the just mean, the *juste milieu,* the *mesotēs.* Excess, shortage, and the just mean belong to belonging, being a part of, *appartenance,* and to holding apart from, *à-part-tenance.* But two dimensions belong to belonging. There is the dimension of excess and shortcoming with respect to the just mean, and there is the dimension of the agent with respect to the *phronimos.* The first of these relations implicates the agent and the *phronimos.* But the relation that implicates the agent does not imply the relation that implicates the *phronimos.* It is necessary for the relation that implicates the *phronimos* to be adapted to the psychological and circumstantial condition of the particular agent. How is this adaptation achieved? Not in the light of a second *phronimos,* then of a third, and so on infinitely, but in the chiaroscuro of a knowing mixed with an unknowing. We judge. And the justness of the judgment is not equivalent to the justice constituted in relation to laws. Justness as disposition, as a modality, and as *savoir-faire*, practical knowledge, is not to be confused with justice as a state of which one has theoretical knowledge, *connaissance*. The justness of practical knowledge cannot become identified with justice defined by law without thereby falling short of justness. For while justice thus conceived has to do with universal and public criteria, justness has to do with the particular and personal occasion. This is why it is my ethical responsibility not only to do justice. To do justice would be to do only the act prescribed by the law. Ethical responsibility demands that the act respond to the nuances of the occasion, to its *ēthos*. It demands that what we decide to do expresses the *esprit de finesse*. Ethical responsibility calls to be exercised only responsively.

According to this Aristotelian figuration responsibility would be also an ability. It would be an "I can." The first responsibility of responsibility would be to learn a certain skill, an *habileté*. This *habileté* would embrace an *habilité*, specifically a capacitation or fitness that qualifies someone to serve as an example because he or she embodies the *phronimos* as exemplar, an exemplar as logical and "pathetic" paradigm and as standard and *logos* for acts and reactions. Except that neither I nor this *type* that I carry in myself answers every question that arises. I cannot make use of it to calculate what I should do, and no one can make use of me as an axiom for such calculation. The *phronimos* is not a paradigm in the Platonic sense. He, she, it is always a flesh-and-blood person, like the sculptor whose producing and product incorporate the happy mean that is the beautiful, or like the physician who prescribes a treatment that expresses the happy medium that is health. Aristotle understands virtue as a state of health. This does not mean that Aristotle is a Nietzsche before his time. For while with Aristotle the health that defines virtue is identified as a just measure by reference to a mean, with Nietzsche health is not a state, so *a fortiori* not a middle state. It is a process of movement toward an extreme, an excession where what is exceeded is the human-all-too-human. This is a tropic excess, an excess that turns its back on a human-all-too-human "too," a too human mean, in order to seek a "too" that is humanly superlative, a human-superhuman extreme the science of which is a joyful science that is at the same time a joyful madness rather than a sober wisdom. The "science" of moral science is mad because where there is morality there is no mathematics. There is decision for which there exists no procedure or method. In the last analysis moral science is mad precisely because it is the end of counting, number, calculation, and measure: because it is the end of mathematical precision and the beginning of *précis*, of summary and of the enthymeme whose missing premises are contingent. This is once again a question of *tingere*, of touch, of tact, of the manual, of the *manus* and of the rule of thumb. It is a question of that kind of question where the responsibility of the response is never without crisis, never without the leap, never without irresponsibility.

Aristotle insists that to expect mathematical exactitude in the field of ethics would be as inappropriate as to be satisfied with persuasive reasoning in the field of mathematics. Yet he also affirms not only that there could be a science, an *epistēmē*, of ethics, but that ethics is an *epistēmē*, namely the practical knowledge or wisdom he calls *phronēsis*. We know that *phronēsis* is virtue understood as practical competence in behaving according to the just measure, with *justesse*. But it is simultaneously the theoretical science of this practical competence. The disposition that calls itself practical wisdom is at the same time a theoretical science.

Thinking perhaps of what wisdom means for Aristotle and Hegel, both friends of an ultimate notion of wisdom conceived as thinking thinking on itself, *noēsis noēseōs*, Derrida employs the word "wisdom," "*sagesse*," with precaution. He "dares" to make use of it, he once said. But, without using this word to name this extreme Aristotelian or Hegelian wisdom, he has used it in addressing a compliment to a friend. He is therefore a friend of this word, or at least he is not an enemy of it. He once said too that he would never make use of the expression "post-deconstructive wisdom."[2] What could the expression "post-deconstructive wisdom" signify, if it signifies anything? Let us begin again with the wisdom not of the higher human being or the god but of the average person endowed with the virtue of finding the just mean as described by Aristotle. The *phronimos* to which this average person appeals allows no exception. If, however, this average person allows no exception, this is not because of the rigor of a law, but because the *phronimos* functions as a guide in functioning as an example, hence without there being room to formulate a law or a rule. From this point of view Aristotle's ethics approaches nearer to the *Critique of Judgment* (or the latter approaches nearer to the former) than it does to the *Critique of Practical Reason*. And when, against those who accuse him of anarchism, Derrida repeats that he is not against law, his reply borrows the "Jewish" language of this second *Critique*. This is a basis upon which the possibility of speaking of an exception may be founded. Without rule or maxim or law there can be no exception. But it is not an exception thus conceived that is the most interesting exception invoked in Derrida's writings. An exception thus conceived is part of the group of concepts that includes also the concepts of equity and legal reform. It occupies part of the space of legality and equality. Infinitely more interesting than this exception is what Derrida calls the archi-exception. Archi-exceptionality is also infinitely more interesting than the exceptionality of an exceptional wisdom. The latter exceptionality is a wisdom of an uncommon degree. However, understood in

Aristotle's sense, such a wisdom would remain a manifestation of *mesotēs,* of what the Romans will call *mediocritas.* It would still be critique, judgment, and critique of the faculty of judgment. Of infinitely greater interest than these two kinds of exceptionality, of greater interest because outside the field of inter-est, archi-exceptionality manifests, without manifestation, an essence, an essence without essence, a hypo-critical essence. We have seen that judgment understood as *justesse,* as sensibility responding to the nuances of the particular situation, is distinguished from justice determined in the light of principles. The archi-exception is more principial still than the principle and still more *hypo* than *justesse* and justice thus understood. It is more "archi," to the point that one cannot call it "archi" without a certain hypocrisy, that is to say without affecting a virtue that is not there. The archi-anarchic exception is an absolute exception, but absolute in a sense quite other than that of absolute wisdom.

Absolute wisdom con-structs the knowing and the known, construes them together. The archi-exception absolves itself from knowledge. In the archi-exception deconstruction deconstrues itself. Except that simultaneously the "itself," the *se* of *se déconstruire,* deconstructs itself. Does this "itself," this "*se,*" allow itself to be compared with the "*es*" of the Heideggerian "*es gibt*" or with Levinas's accusative absolute? To look no further, this "itself" of self-deconstruction loses itself in the heritage of the Heideggerian "*es*" and of the Levinasian absolute accusative. This "itself" has a history, like history itself. Can one compare things without which there can be no "can," no "*je peux*"? Is it possible to compare the conditions of the possibility of possibility and comparison? When what is in question is the being of reason and the reason of being, the *raison d'être,* when it is about or around, *um,* being that *es geht,* that is to say when what it is a question of is being, or when what is in question in any theoretical or practical question is he or she who poses such questions, we can speak only of quasi-conditions, quasi-possibilities, and quasi-comparison. Here the quasi is the *als ob,* the *comme si* of a pretention to *comme*-parison, a hypocritical and hypo-critical pretention, so pre-original fault: fault by "default" in a sense something like that which this word has when it is used in speaking of computer software, but before all calculation, before all foundation, and before all con-struction. Therefore undeconstructible.

Derrida says of justice that it is undeconstructible or, rather, indeconstructible, as he would prefer us to say, as for what English calls either unhuman or inhuman his French obliges him to say "*inhumain, une* certaine inhumanité.*" How can he speak of a justice that is indeconstructible, given that he says that even deconstruction deconstructs itself? To say that deconstruction deconstructs itself is not to say that deconstruction can be passed by, *dépassée*, or passed over, or out-of-date, except in so far as its job is to be out of date and out of joint. Recall the already cited "itself." To say that deconstruction deconstructs itself is to say that deconstruction is never *dépassée*, for to deconstruct itself means without meaning to—*veut dire* without *vouloir*—to be supplemented always by the plus of the more, the *plus de l'en sus*, and by the no more of the less, the *(ne) plus du moins*. It is always too much and always too little. It is always *exotic*, unlike *mesotic* wisdom. And since indeconstructible justice quasi-conditions wisdom, there cannot be any post-deconstructive wisdom. With indeconstructible justice as point of departure the *esprit géométrique* of judiciary justice and the *esprit de finesse* of *justesse* become mutually hybridized. Prior to the simple letter of the law, prior to the simple sensibility of the particular judgment, and prior to all construction, with indeconstructible justice as point of departure, singularity and the particularity of the case cross each other. And if justice is blind, indeconstructible justice is blind plurally. To the blindness of the judiciary justice of the third party indeconstructible justice contributes a supplement of vigilance toward the second person and the excluded third. This supplementation takes place at the blind spot where this blindness of the judiciary justice of the third party and this vigilance provoke each other. This spot, this point, is the not, the *point,* of construction, its zero point, its *pas.* It is the "there" where construction cannot be comprehended, the "there" that obliges us to admit that there cannot be a purely theoretical science, least of all a purely theoretical science of the practical such as Aristotle envisages, that there cannot be any purely speculative philosophy, that there cannot be any love of wisdom without there being a wisdom of love. A *non-lieu,* a not taking place and il-legitimacy at the heart of a chiasmus where "he," "she," "it," and "you" are in syncopation with one another, where, as Deleuze would say, one stammers even when one is speaking one's own language, as if the latter were another language, the language of the other, and as if, as Derrida would say, my own language were always the language of the other. A non-coincidence, as Levinas would say, of the said and the saying in the Saying of Desire, that is to say, in sophophily. A non-coincidence in the archi-trace, as again Derrida would say. A non-containment of the *in* of which the interiority is exteriorized thanks to a "Here I am" that is uncitable, because quotation marks take my breath away, but where I am nevertheless cited and incited, summoned to make an appearance that is not simply an appearing *to* the other, an *apparaître,* but an appearing *before* the other, *coram,* a *comparaître,* though a *comparaître* without comparison, to answer for a culpability that is not a fault of commission or omission.

Plat de résistance

For want of inviting Derrida to that meal in the rue Descartes I gave him the gift of being giver, forgiver. Now, as is said by, among others, Aristotle, cited by Derrida, does not friendship consist less in being loved, that is to say in receiving, than in loving, that is to say in giving? Or would it be better neither to give nor to receive? Not even the solitary individual is capable of such an abstention. The human being is fated to harvest dilemmas of exchange that lack a judicial standard according to which they may be marshaled, measured, and resolved. That is why the human being may be defined as the animal that smiles. And that is why the *pas du repas*, the passing-over of the repast, was a reason for an exchange of smiles between Derrida and me. This *faux pas* of the *repas*, its false step and full stop, inertia, *point*, its not, was not among the gravest of privations. No serious suffering or death, no *trépas*, no fatal trespass ensued from this passing over. But beneath that smile, like Writing beneath Saying, is the Smile that defines the mortality of human life, that marks human finitude, its way of being finite, finished, over and done with, terminated, and of being at the same time infinite, unfinished, incomplete: infinite because finite, and finite, defined by finitude, because infinite. I avow that I wrote to Derrida that I was inviting him, and I would-or-will (*aurai(s)*) have invited him hereby, by these presents, to a repast at which he would-or-will (*aura(it)*) have eaten honey-dew and drunk the milk of Paradise.

> For he on honey-dew hath fed,
> And drunk the milk of Paradise.

These are the last lines of *Kubla Khan*, an in-finite poem, unfinished, because during the composition of it Coleridge was interrupted by a visitor, the infamous "person from Porlock." I once said to Derrida that because so large and scrupulous a body of work as his required him to spend so much of his time at his desk, I was always afraid that in writing to him I would be the person from Porlock.

By way of precaution, and in case what Austin calls the conditions of felicity of my performative speech act are not all fulfilled, I offered Derrida (I hereby, by these presents, as the lawyer's phrase goes, now offer to his specter), with a smile, this all too unscrupulous and at the same time too scrupulous and too sensitive composition. The best part of what I am writing here gives back what he gave, but following what he said one day regarding Levinas and like the *pas* of the *repas*, without total or totalizing reciprocity. Although what I am writing here may seem to come full circle, it does not provide a solution to our dilemma. It finds no synthesis. For, if there is a dilemma here, it is not what Cicero would call a *complexio* of two propositions, nor is it an equilibrium of revenues. Remembering that a *lemma* is a received profit, let us call what is at stake here a di-lemma, understanding this, on the one hand, as a complication of propositions and revenues, and on the other hand, as a receiving of what gives itself, of what gives itself in the two senses, "objective" and "subjective," of this genitive. This would be a complication of a possible symmetry and an impossible asymmetry. Therefore it would be no resolution and no response to the blessèd by-pastness of the repast, where the blessèd—the blasted, the bloody, the cursed, the damned, the *sacré*—is, doubly anathematized, where the *sacré* is already rather the holy, the *saint,* and where the problem is instead already a mystery. This "therefore" resonates in a syllogistic where the interiority of the "in" is affected by the exteriority of the other, and where, therefore, self-affection is affected by affection by the other, again in the two senses of this "of," and in the sense of "self" that can give the appearance that this self-giving is reciprocal, but where this appearance simultaneously hides and expresses, as does the smile, which is simultaneously physiognomic and non-physiognomic expression. One is tempted to say that the smile is more than physiognomic because it is tragic, provided tragedy is not understood in terms of formal contradiction. Otherwise tragic, the Smile beneath the physiognomic smile, but at the same time insinuating itself into it, is, like tragedy, a serious matter. Serious because serial. Serial because relating to the series, not in the sense of the set-theoretical class but in the sense Derrida gives us to understand when he explicates the complication of the said and the saying and the Saying that makes possible the distinction between the said and the saying, in the writings of Levinas.

Here I open a parenthesis in order to speak briefly about the open mouth of laughter and the comic. But the laugh as such is never evasion. Sometimes we laugh in order not to embarrass another or oneself. However, like the rose of Angelus Silesius, laughter as such is without why. We laugh simply for the sake of laughing, as we weep only for the sake of weeping, although it is often over the loss of a person or a thing that we shed tears, and shedding tears can bring relief to our grief. Since to weep is to cry, it is understandable why laughing is often accompanied by the shedding of tears, as the tragic is accompanied by the comic. Laughing and shedding tears have the same structure, a structure that is destructured, deconstructed, schizo-psychotic. Archi- and anarchi-hypocritical, laughing and weeping are sincerity itself. Laughter and weeping come to us *sponte sua*. They surprise us. Both bear the trace of surprise par excellence, of the excess that maddens the Aristotelian just mean. What makes this *mesotēs* of Aristotle possible and impossible is *thaumazō*, the self-astonishment in which (and it is Aristotle, among others, who says this) philosophy has its beginning—as does sophophily, which is perhaps where life has its beginning, at least the life of the adult. (Is the newborn child crying or laughing? And what about the call of the newborn animal, the animal that, we are told, remains for ever *infans*, the so-to-speak unautobiographical animal?)

Hobbes writes that laughter is a sudden glory (I am tempted to write "gl-ory" with a hyphen in memory of *Glas*). *Exaiphnēs*, all at once, laughter is a glad start (a gl-ad start), a beginning that startles us. If Hobbes is right, one looks down from on high, *de haut en bas*, when one covers oneself with glory, with *kudos*, as the Greek says, thinking perhaps for example of the glory gained in warfare. So think instead of the Hebrew word *kavod*, of which Levinas makes use when he glorifies glory. For him this word means the respect and reverence without which there is no peace, unless this is only the peace that signifies the end of a war. Although a somber note can be heard in respectful *kavod*—and indeed the Hebrew word can signify heaviness in a figurative sense—*kavod* understood as the condition of peace remains something that gives one joy. And joy, like moral conscience as described by Heidegger, does not come simply from inside one. It comes as it were from above me and therefore without authorizing me to boast or to look down on others with a sense of superiority. It is this sense of looking down on others that is at work when Hobbes says laughter is a sudden glory. And it is the Greek notion of glory to which he is appealing when he deems that laughter expresses a sentiment of superiority over someone, someone, for example, who has failed to "get" a joke. The man who laughs is enjoying a little victory, whether over someone else or over himself regarded retrospectively as lowlier before he experienced the sudden glory. The Hobbesian laughter can be a laughing *with*, but it is also always a laughing *at*.

It was a laughter purely *with* that broke out on the occasion of a certain other meal, a meal with Derrida and other friends that this time did not fail to take place. This meal took place at the Nashville airport after a colloquium at Vanderbilt where the discussions never strayed far from the question of the signature. We ate. We conversed. Then, all of a sudden, we burst into laughter, gloriously. For as, gradually, Derrida emptied his plate and as we emptied ours, there was uncovered across the middle of the plate the single world "Signature." Generally, so not without exception, in order to be able to laugh one has to open one's mouth. Likewise in order to be able to speak or to eat. Whereas no less generally, so not without exception, one smiles without parting one's lips, without opening one's mouth. Without opening my mouth I am speaking here of the smile that is not a lesser degree of laughter, not the lowest degree on the gelotic scale, not even a laughing-with (*syggelaō*) that is nearer the laughing-at of a certain smile, *un certain sourire,* the smile without agitation that is in question at this moment. The smile I am thinking of is a de-rised one, a smile without *ridere* and altogether without derision: a *subridere* or *surridere* or archi-smile, an *archi-sourire* that is in a certain sense silent, sygetic. Here is a silence that is communicated without anything being spoken, a silence of writing, a silence, Derrida would say, of archi-writing, *archi-écrire.* And it has to be said that the smile, the *sou(s)rire,* over the passed-over repast that motivated a smile between us was essentially epistolary, between us, *entre nous,* and between the lines . . . a postal and *à la carte postale* Smile, a smile over a meal and by mail: a mailsmile, *meidēma.* We are speaking of a letter and of the unspeaking of the letter *m* of *muō,* a Greek word that, without knowing how to say anything, means to close. One supposes, supposing that such a thing as derivation exists, that *muō* derives from *mu'* or from *mu`,* which is pronounced by closing one's lips and which is associated with the Sanskrit *mū.* The dictionary wonders if this last is linked to the Latin *ligāre,* to tie or to link, an eventuality that would open the question of whether this tying is not only the *ligāre* of *religāre,* nor only the *legere* of *relegere,* to collect together, but is tied also to the untying of the *lēgāre* of *relēgāre,* to send away, distance, isolate, so that religion would have something to do with mystery and the mystical, the appellations of which derive or de-rive (with a hyphen) from *muō.* Consequently, we could imagine something like a smile that would refer to the mystical force not directly of (the) law, whether ethical or political, but to the mystical force of these via simple politeness and decency such as that to which Derrida referred, I recall, during the colloquium on his reading of Husserl that was held in the pyramid in Memphis.

Dessert

Ce sacré pas du repas! Is there anything more *sacré* than a repast? Is there anything more blessèd or blessed than its *re-* and its *pas*? Without speaking of the scene at Cana or of the thanksgiving of the Eucharist, I am thinking of the collation of the colloquium at Cerisy on the work of Levinas where the author of the essay "Name of a Dog, or Natural Rights" and I exchanged thoughts on the subject of the animal, and, aware of the fact that we were infringing a protocol of etiquette, on the subject of the meat in what he referred to as his *bonne soupe.* By the way, readers of that essay should be aware of the fact that the first half of its title can approximate the exclamation "Nom de Dieu!," "Good God!," or "In God's Name!" So although Derrida was missing from the table in the rue Descartes, present at the table in the château at Cerisy were Levinas, a dog, and perhaps also God.

I have attended other Cerisy *décades,* which are called *décades* because they last about ten days. Among them were the one dedicated to Nietzsche in 1972 in the course of which Derrida posed "La question du style,"[3] the one that took place in 1980 titled *Les Fins de l'homme. À partir du travail de Jacques Derrida,*[4] and the one that took place in 1992 titled *Le passage des frontières. Autour du travail de Jacques Derrida.*[5] At each of these colloquia, and at other gatherings attended by Derrida and myself at the universities of Edinburgh, Alabama, Chicago, New York, Memphis, and Berkeley, both of us were guests (*hôtes*), without the opportunity to be plenary hosts (*hôtes*). That is how it was again at the colloquium in Perugia treating of, among other topics, classification, following which I found myself in a train that stopped at a station where I was able to read on a board immediately opposite my window the name ("only the name," as Edward Thomas writes in his poem "Adlestrop") of my destination: "Classe." Alas, I did not attend the Cerisy colloqium of 1997 titled "L'animal autobiographique: autour de Jacques Derrida." Why? Because although one eats very well at Cerisy—and it has been said that one must indeed eat and eat well, *il faut bien manger*—I could not bring myself to eat the other animal. The Cordon Bleu cooks at the château at Cerisy had difficulty comprehending the concept of vegetarianism. They were on the side of Abel, who made an animal offering to God, rather than of Cain, whose offering was despised by God because it was vegetarian. What an irony! For Derrida finds the concept of vegetarianism comprehensible enough for him to have been able to say one day to David Wood and myself, if I recall aright, that we came close to converting him to vegetarianism. In any case, in the course of the ten days during which he spoke for a total of ten hours about *bios* and *zoē* he said that ever since the beginning of his writing career the question of the animal had always been for him the most important and decisive. In order to support this declaration he outlined what he called a zoo-auto-bio-bibliography enumerating the animals that had been invited aboard the archi-ark of his writings. *Mes Chances.* What chances I missed when I decided not to make rendezvous at this colloquium where Derrida spoke of "L'animal que donc je suis (à suivre)," "The animal that therefore I am (to follow)," and when I omitted to invite him to follow us in the rue Descartes! What a chance I lost to talk with him face to face on the subject of the sacri-sacrificial *pas* of the *repas* where the *pas* is already the *re-* because it conceals its presumed derivation from *paître* (to graze) so well or so badly that, with knife and fork in your hands, you feed (*repaissez*) on what some time earlier was feeding in its place in the sun!

Derrida was readier than Levinas to mention in the same breath a certain pair of inadvertences, and to wonder whether it is possible that one of the two, the one that might seem to raise apparently banal questions of cuisine, had something to do with the other, the one concerning the holocaust, of which it would be monstrous to deny the ethical and political monstrosity. One wonders too whether such ethical or hyper-ethical inadvertences could spring from an inadvertence consisting in such impoliteness as the omission to invite someone to join you at table. Don't laugh. Let us at least avow to each other between ourselves that although such an omission was the occasion for an exchange of smiles between Derrida and myself, in the sudden glory of the glottal stop of the smile that is the sister of the sigh, the *sourire* that is the sister of the *soupir*, there is something of a subsaying, a *sous-dire*, and something of a hypogelotic subscript, a *souscrire*, that witnesses to another just mean, a just *mi-lieu* between proximity and distance where *kavod* traverses *kudos* and where, from the reciprocity of the smile between us regarding the *pas* of the *repas*, the meal's *non-lieu*, there springs, silently and suddenly, the recognition without cognition of Elias or of the other other who would have been forever outside reciprocity, the stranger who will have been forever the one that was never invited.

Elie, alias Elias, alias Elijah was Derrida's secret, sacred, blessed circumcision name, the name of the prophet for whom a place is always kept unoccupied in readiness for him at the table of the Passover. But while this may be regarded only as a biographical fact to do with Derrida, he would have wanted it to be regarded too as a trope for a thought that has to do with us all and with whatever may be other than us: the thought of a place of welcome reserved in the moral, political, and non-institutionally religious imagination of every one of us for every other existent, be it terrestrial, extraterrestrial, human, humanoid, animal, Elephant Man, animaloid, vegetable, mineral, or whatever—for every other existent as existent, wherever the cut and whatever its what, whotever, if it has one, its essence.

To put this last word "essence" in apposition to "what" and to contrast both of them with "existence" is to touch on a question that is as ancient as philosophy. It is to touch on the ambiguity of *to on* as between being and a being, hence upon the ambiguity of the word "being" as used to translate "*esse*" in Proposition 6 of Part 3 of Spinoza's *Ethics,* the proposition that according to Levinas leads philosophy away from the ethical, but which, I have been arguing, leads philosophy toward an ethicality that is less unjust than his ethics of the other human being: "Every thing, in so far as it is in itself, endeavours to persevere in its own being," "Unaquaeque, quantum in se est, in suo esse persevare conatur." Does "*esse*" refer to the whatness, the essence of each thing, or does it refer to each thing's thatness, its existence? Is it not evident that if a thing endeavors to persist in its whatness or nature it thereby endeavors to persist in its existence? Is this not of the essence of existence, provided in putting brackets around the brackets that Husserl puts around existence (which is what we have been doing in this book: reducing reduction), we can understand the essence of existence in a way that retains ethicality? Or would it be consistent with Spinoza's Proposition to propose also that the whatness of a thing might include a desire to destroy itself or be destroyed? Is the possibility of the consistency of this juxtaposition supported or undermined by his clause "in so far as it is in itself"? This clause appears to rule out a thing's will to destroy itself for the sake of the continued existence of other things. Such self-sacrificial motivation exceeds the limit set by the words "in so far as it is in itself." An analogous excession takes place in willing to put an end to one's existence in order to put an end to one's pain. Pain is a predicate. To invoke it is therefore to transcend sheer existence. Or is the only thing that can be in itself what Spinoza calls God or Nature? That Totalism is what Levinas seeks to forestall by insisting that the human being is a being that cannot be in itself, that is beyond being self-identical, that is otherwise than an item, than an *idem*. In refusing Spinoza's limiting clause Levinas refuses Spinoza's Proposition 6.

Against Levinas, or exceeding him, the chapters of the second part of this book, the part titled Table Talk, have argued toward a conclusion that is supported by Proposition 6 of Part 3 of the work Spinoza significantly called *Ethics*, not *Ontology* or *Being* or *Knowledge*. That Proposition supports the key idea of those chapters that existence is a good for each thing. It is a key idea throughout these chapters because it extends beyond other human beings the range of beings to which this human being that says "I" owes responsibility. In thus going beyond being to the good beyond being it goes beyond other human beings toward a greater justice that is nevertheless never great enough to justify my unalloyed enjoyment of my place in the sun. It is never great enough because my representation of myself by myself or by others never reaches a view *sub specie aeternitatis* of a whole in which my responsibilities have been or could be met. As a thing that cannot, in Spinoza's words, "be in itself," I am, as Levinas maintains, not a being that can simply persist in my being. Here the fact of persistence in a temporality that according to Heidegger is the meaning of being is superseded by the requirement of an endurance of the rigor of a certain unfulfillable responsibility in which temporality is irreparably out of joint. The rigor of this responsibility, the difficulty to be endured, is, as Derrida maintains, greater than Levinas acknowledges. This is because the scope of those to whom ethical responsibility is owed is not restricted to human beings. It reaches out to every existent as such that is other than the one who owes that responsibility.

As far as concerns the absolute ethicality of the relationship of my being faced by you, ethicality undefined by predicates and empirical social circumstances, I, who am more responsible than all other existents, am the one with least rights. Least because zero. I have not yet been considered as a bearer of rights. My rights have their source in the relations with the third party. Rights are to that degree political in a broad sense of the term that applies to my relations with members of my family and loved ones, that is to say with those others whom I find myself more at home addressing in the second person than describing in the third. The ethical and the political are crossed chiasmically. That is to say, they are related neither as opposites nor as apposites nor synthetically. This is because they have no common ground, any more than what is said—statements, questions, commands, etc.—has common ground with the saying of it to another. Because "participation" is out of joint there is no place here for semantic representation. Recalling what was discovered in the rapid analysis conducted at the end of our first chapter of Wittgenstein's theory of representation in the *Tractatus Logico-Philosophicus,* the crossing of what is said with the addressing of what is said to another is not something that can be said. This is because semantic representation is a matter of predication. It has to do primarily with the what, whereas address has to do primarily with the that, the addressed and addressing existent. And existence abstracted from essence or whatness is sufficient to demand the attention of an addressee. For (to say this one more time) its existence is already a good to the existent. Existence is not a predicate, but, because of its immediate connection with questions of goodness and badness and whot experiences these, it is immediately connected to questions of the political in the broad sense referred to above.

That connection is treated rather incidentally by Levinas. This is partly because, like Kant, he maintains that one can have direct moral obligations only to beings capable of language, though he stresses the singularity of the linguistic existent, whereas it is the universality and the power to universalize of the person that are stressed by Kant. Once sheer existence is seen to raise the question of the existent's good, whatever or whotever the existent, whether possessed of language or not, it is seen to raise the question of the political. (To speak with Plato of the good beyond being is to say with Aristotle that human being is political being.) Detached from predicates, existence is attached to law, though to a blank law, lawfulness unspecified in terms of predicates.

Law leavened by regard from and to the singular signifying human being is Levinas's response to Spinozan and Hegelian Totalism. But the catchment of law is infinitely broader and the demand for attention to the political is infinitely stronger in the white ecology that Derrida dubs incoming democracy. This is because the predicate of humanity that defines the scope of the ethico-political for Levinas does not define its scope for Derrida. It is because semantic theoretical representation is representation through predicates that its chiasm with address cannot be represented. Whatever difficulty this poses will remain a difficulty when the ethico-political has reached the stage at which predicates affirmed of individuals and institutions have to be taken into account. But, before this stage is reached, the non-predicate existence, through its being a good for the existent in question, is already a ground for representation understood in the practical ethico-political sense of standing-up-for which was distinguished from the semantic or linguistic sense of standing-for in this book's introduction and at the end of its first chapter. Distinguished from, but not separated from. The semantic, the topic of chapter 6, and the linguistic, a topic of most of the other chapters of part 1, are forms of the minimal agreement without which disagreement is not possible. A semantically unrepresentable condition of this agreement and disagreement is the disjointed version of presupposition we have called chiasmus, in which what is said is crossed with the saying that we have called address, and address in its turn is crossed by the said, the inherited historical assumptions and the anticipations of experience, not least of the experience of language treated in chapter 3, that are the context of any address. This double crossing is not a reciprocity. It is not a reciprocity, because it is not a symmetry. It is not a symmetry, because although the third-person and the first-person plural of political justice are answerable reciprocally to one another, they are answerable also to the second-person singular of ethical justice. To the latter I am more answerable than is anyone else. That answerability is part of my predicament, part of the aporetic lot I am called by other existents to endure. It is the improper part, the part that is apart from predicates, property, and propriety. It is a part of and, at the same dislocated time, apart from the political. At the heart of the chiasmus of the ethical and the political, this part is *par excellence* outwith semantico-linguistic representation and political representation in so far as both of these are invocations of third personality.

The "of" of this phrase "invocations of third personality" marks a subjective genitive, a so-called genitive of provenance or origin, but one that postpones origin because the invoked third personality invokes a second personality by which it is always being approached. "A whole cloud of philosophy condensed into a droplet of grammar." And a whole cloud of sophophily: a wisdom of love expressed through the representative democracy of an ecology so blank that it exceeds any democracy we can represent, any representative democracy in which decisions turn on predicates. But the excession is double. For while the blankness of blank ecology that turns solely on the non-predicate of existence guards against prejudicial exclusivity, ethico-political decision must take the risk of getting its hands dirty by proceeding to predicates. Political representation must pass through conceptual representation. It must therefore respond to the difficulties to which conceptual representation shows itself to be exposed by the reconstructive political procedure Derrida describes as prudent (pro-vident) deconstruction. In the chapter on the question "Where to cut," his procedure and mine, each motivated by a common concern that justice be done both to a certain humanity and to a certain inhumanity or unhumanity, are distinguished from each other. This does not mean, however, that they do not intersect. Derrida's hauntology is itself haunted by the sheer existents that inhabit my blank ecology, the sheer existents that are put between brackets by phenomenology. In this suspension of suspension, the pro-vidence of a deconstruction that goes beyond phenomenology phenomenologically is haunted from out of the future and the past by the supervenience of the not yet and the revenience of the no longer extant.

FOURTEEN

The Rigor of a Certain Inhumanity

A passing bell sounds in the word "rigor" used in the phrase borrowed from Derrida in the title of this book to perform a double service. On the one hand the title refers to the *rigor mortis* threatened by the rigidly rigorous pure science of representation that Husserl and the young Wittgenstein both sought as an ideal and feared as an instigator of crisis. On the other hand the title refers to a deepening of crisis, to what may be described as a hyperCritical crisis because it is a crisis provoked by a responsibility, spelled out in the second part of this book, to let the rigor of universalist Kantian humanism and Enlightenment defined as freedom (as considered in chapter 11) be contaminated by a singularity that is other than particularity and predication.

For Husserl, for the young Wittgenstein, and for Kant rigor is the strict purity of the principle or law. What happens, we have asked with Levinas, when this rigor of the law of universalist humanism is crossed by the address of singularist ethical alterhumanism? What happens, we have asked with Derrida, when the rigor of the law of universalist humanism and the rigor of alterhumanism are crossed by the address of singularist ethical inhumanism? Then rigor no longer signifies purity and crystalline essence, but the hardship of the "rough ground" to which Wittgenstein urged readers of his later work to go back and the aporia that must, according to Derrida, be endured.

In the first chapter of the second part of this study note was taken of Derrida's reference to the many places where Levinas maintains that we have to go phenomenologically beyond phenomenology, and to Derrida's endorsement of that assertion when he writes "That is what I am trying to do, also. I remain and want to remain a rationalist, a phenomenologist"[1] and "I would like to remain phenomenological in what I say against phenomenology."[2] Further endorsement is made when in passages treating of so-called impossible possibilities he writes of their impossibility or possibility as something that "appears" and is "experienced as" an impossibility or as a possibility dependent on its impossibility.[3] His going beyond phenomenology is not least but not only a going beyond the phenomenology of language investigated in the first part of this study. It is a going beyond a phenomenology of language, truth, and formal logic to a modal logic that threatens or promises to provoke a crisis in the very logicality of the phenomeno-logical. In this modal logic, instead of being simply the opposite of impossibility as it is in the modal logics alluded to toward the end of the introduction of this study, possibility presupposes an impossibility. This impossibility that is a condition underlying possibility is a condition of the possibility of being under an obligation. Put baldly, and assuming it is true that either I can do x or that I cannot do x, the "I can do x" that according to Kant is presupposed or implied by "I ought to do x" ("Ich kann, denn ich soll," "I can because I should"), presupposes a certain "I cannot do x." This joint assertion of "I can do x" and "I cannot do x" is by the standards of classical logic impossible. However, on closer inspection we learn that it is not directly this classical logical impossibility that Derrida has in mind when he writes of a certain impossibility that is presupposed or implied by the "I can." What he aims to bring to our attention is an un-possibility corresponding not to an unqualified "I cannot" but to what exceeds the opposition of "I can" and "I cannot" of Kantian free choice. This un-possibility is not the modality of what I either can or cannot do, where the "or" is exclusive. It is a modality that breaks with my powers in order to make room for what is not within the realm of my power or potentiality, somewhat as the outwardly directed intentionality attributed to all consciousness in the phenomenology of Husserl is interrupted by the inwardly directed intervention and invention of what in Levinas's quasi-phenomenology is provisionally called reversed intentionality. If the "I ought" of ethical obligation or responsibility presupposes "I can," it does so only if "I can" presupposes a non-ability on my part. My non-ability is the condition of decidability and of givability and of forgivability and of hospitality, assuming that decision and giving and forgiving and hospitality ever take place, and assuming that taking place ever takes place. We say "assuming," as Derrida says *s'il y en a,* to connote the "iffiness" and the "maybeness" of the non-knowledge as to whether these deeds ever take place. For although we have to distinguish un-possibility from classical modal impossibility, it still looks as though the un-possibility entails an impossibility. But since the impossibility of doing these deeds is a condition of their possibility, we do not know whether we can do them. We cannot even believe that we can. At best we can trust or have faith. Whether these deeds, for instance a decision, ever take place is undecidable. Both possible and impossible, decision is mad. Sanity seems to allow only pseudo-decision, pseudo-giving, pseudo-forgiving, etc., where the deeds allegedly done, the performative speech acts allegedly accomplished, and the events that supposedly take place are in principle calculable consequences of the potentialities residing in my nature and surroundings.

Full knowledge, if it were possible, of the psychological, psychoanalytic, historical, economic, etc., circumstances would render responsible decision impossible, because decision would then have been replaced by deduction and prediction. However, this impossibility is the logical opposite of possibility, not the impossibility we have called unpossibility, meaning by that what is outside the opposition of what I am able to do and what I am unable to do. Unpossibility, "un-canniness," in this sense is absolutely unconditional impossibility. So such unpossibility is not removed even when one is ignorant of some of the circumstances. That ignorance only makes the exercise of my freedom difficult. So too does the thought that a decision to try to help someone may prevent my helping someone else. But freedom itself and decision and responsibility worthy of those names are possible only if the ability of decidability and responsibility exceed my power, and exceed it not because I am not powerful enough, but because a condition of their possibility is an impotency or unpower on my part, a passion and passivity to which my action is a response. This is a response to another, whatever the other may be, an acquaintance outside the possibility of, in the terms of Bertrand Russell's distinction, my knowing by acquaintance (for example, knowing Jones) and my knowing by description (for example, knowing that Jones is a Welshman). In so far as knowing is a consciousness of what is known, of epistemic and semantic representation, it tempts the ego to consider that it is sovereign over the other, whereas it is only to another that addresses me that I can respond.

The journey made in this book has been one from semantic representation to ethico-political representation. It has been at the same time a journey from presentation, via appresentation to depresentation. Husserl had recourse to appresentation because his ideal of knowledge was the one he found wanting in his reflections on "knowledge of other minds" in the fifth of the *Cartesian Meditations,* the one whose shortcoming Wittgenstein would diagnose as a failure to recognize the truth "condensed into a droplet of grammar" distilled in the remark cited at the beginning of our introduction: "I can know what someone else is thinking, not what I am thinking. It is correct to say 'I know what you are thinking,' and wrong to say 'I know what I am thinking.'"

Representation both in the epistemologico-semantic sense and representation in the ethico-political sense do a violence to whatever they represent unless the identity of my first-person singular I is exposed to the wound of non-knowledge, vulnerable to the traumatism of what is other than a subject of rigorous science, exceeding strict knowledge as to whether that other is human, animal, divine, or whatever. This ignorance is the condition of the possibility of the responsibility not to ignore the stranger, the condition that I prescribe no condition, the condition that the stranger be welcomed as a stranger in its utter strangeness.

The rigor of a certain inhumanity is therefore a condition of possibility of the responsibility of rigorous human and other sciences. But there are at least two senses of inhumanity. There is the inhumanity of the system and there is the inhumanity that interrupts system. Jean-François Lyotard writes:

> The inhumanity of the system which is currently being consolidated under the name of development (among others) must not be confused with the infinitely secret one of which the soul is hostage. To believe, as happened to me, that the first can take over from the second, give it expression, is a mistake. The system rather has the consequence of causing the forgetting of what escapes it.[4]

The rigor of the infinitely secret inhumanity that escapes the inhumanity of the system is a condition of prudence, that is to say providence. For any decision, any cut (Latin *caedo,* with the roots SAC and SEC),[5] for instance the cut between the human, the animal, and the divine, or the cut between ethico-political practice and theoretical science, has consequences for myself and others. But, over and above the hypothetical imperatives of teleology, and cutting across the ends of man and systems of legal justice, that rigor is an impossible because unpossible condition of the possibility of ethical freedom, justice, and responsibility. It *is* ethical responsibility: the unrepresentable condition of both semantic and political representation and of the distinction between them which is undecidable not on account of any statistical uncalculability but because counting and accounting are haunted by a singular responsibility to each and every unique other, a responsibility that exceeds both ability and inability, not least the ability to describe it or identify it in words. It is that about which, *wovon,* one cannot speak because any speaking about, including the utterance of *this* sentence, presupposes it; as does this *this;* as does the first-person singular pronoun of the utterance "*I* am more responsible than anyone else," which is something someone else could say as soon as and already before I have said it, so that although Levinas says this, he knows that it exceeds the powers of an essentialist phenomenology of language as imagined by Husserl and of a logico-philosophical treatise as conceived by the younger Wittgenstein. This is not only because the word "more" betrays, fails to carry out, his intention to say something about a responsibility that is not comparative but absolute. It is because his intention is not to report a matter of fact, but to mark an ethical moment that is presupposed, always pre-supposed, yet never posed, never *gesezt,* never semantically represented in a proposition, in a *Satz.* À propos of this moment one is tempted to declare what Wittgenstein declares at the end of the *Tractatus Logico-Philosophicus*—a masterpiece which, like Spinoza's masterpiece (like too in being made up of numbered propositions) is also a *Tractatus Logico-Ethicus*—that that about which one cannot speak is that of which one ought not to speak. These words, while not requiring that an exception be made to Kant's principle that "ought" implies or presupposes "can," constitute a complication of that principle.

Wittgenstein's words constitute also an anticipation of Levinas's remark at the threshold of the Conclusions of *Totality and Infinity* that the problem whether eternity is a new structure of time or an extreme vigilance of the messianic consciousness is a problem that exceeds the framework of that book. This is a problem or aporia of which Derrida says, placing temporality in chiasmus with eternity in one word, that, without promise of reconciliation, it has to be *endured, endurée,* through the hard time and the rigor of what he refers to as messianism without messiah and as the desert in the desert. This rigor is more rigorous than the rough ground of language in its daily use to which the later Wittgenstein bids us return. As the absolute unposited presupposition constitutive-and-deconstitutive ("de-con-structive") of the distinction between the constative and the performative, the unpower that is the unpossible condition of responsibility is the unpossible condition of possibility of speech acts and what Austin was ready to call their phenomenology. For my acts of speech, my meaning, my intention, and the free will expressed in any deeds done by me with or without words (the free will that according to Luc Ferry is more important for the proponents of Enlightenment humanism than the capacity for language) are responsible only if, paradoxically, they do not flow from any "-ibility" or ability of mine. They are responsible only if they are an im-possible response to the claim of the other in me whose alterity de-con-structs (constitutes-and-deconstitutes) my self-conscious and voluntarist human identity, making way for the rigor of a certain inhumanity.

The inhumanity at issue in the first of the chapters of the second part of this book was the implication of the divine by the human, an issue treated at greater length in *Margins of Religion*. Among the questions at stake in the later chapters of this second part was that of the implication of the animal by the human and therefore the questions how these concepts are to be defined and how conceptuality is to be conceived. In the comments made in those chapters on the notion of a certain inhumanity referred to in the remark of Derrida's that serves as the title of this book, prominence is given to animality. This is because humanity understood as a concept allows and conceals so much inhumanity understood as a value in the ways we behave toward or think of (or more commonly *don't* think of) animals. The vegetable and the inorganic have not gone without notice at least in so far as they are covered by the references made throughout those chapters to existents as such. But Derrida's and my senses of the word "inhumanity" cover also a range of what in traditional logic would be counted as existents or terms or relations, except that these classical classifications hide the difficulty of identifying some of the factors and forces ranged over by the certain inhumanity alluded to. Some of these factors and forces belong to the cluster that Heidegger associates with technology. Some of them appertain to one of the very areas of technology, namely medical technology, in which, in experimentation practiced in this area, animals are exposed by humans to various degrees of inhumanity, albeit that this inhumanity may, by intent or incidentally, be of benefit to other sentient nonhuman animals as well as to humans.

A point of transition from the involvement of the animal in particular to the involvement of the inhuman in a wider sense occurs in Jean-Luc Nancy's *L'intrus*.[6] *L'intrus*, *The Intruder*, is Nancy's afterthoughts on a heart transplant operation he underwent. One of the complications of that surgical procedure was the introduction into his body of an immunoglobulin directed at combating what he refers to as the "human defenses" of the body that lead to rejection of the implant. He observes that the instructions accompanying the administered medication describe its use as "anti-human." This expression consolidates the sense of thrusting force borne by the term "intrusion" (*trudere*). Intruders barge in at a party. They are uninvited and unwelcome. They do not belong. Their presence is inappropriate. However, it is precisely what constitutes belonging, propriety, appropriateness, and property that Nancy's analyses render unclear. What they bring out is the "general law of intrusion" to the effect that "there has never been a *single* intrusion: as soon as one of them is produced it multiplies, it identifies itself in its renewed internal differences."[7] It multiples itself like the tribes of Israel or the cancer from which Nancy subsequently suffered, the cancer mentioned among the possible side-effects listed on the wrapper containing the immuno-suppressant ciclosporin to which his body had been introduced or by which his body had been intruded into in the transplant operation.

His body? His? It is as though any mainline teleology with which he might have been identified is subdivided into a scatter of side-effects. His body has become an appendix without text, or at best with a text to which is appended a subtext that is continually being overtaken by other subtexts each of which, as medical research turns up hitherto unknown treatments, is liable to be rendered as otiose in future evolution as the organ in the human body called the appendix seems to have been rendered in the course of past evolution from the time when, Darwin speculates, it served the digestive requirements of an original vegetarianism.

> What a strange me!
> It's not so much that I have been opened gaping wide in order to undergo a change of heart. It's rather that this gap cannot be closed. (Anyway, as every x-ray photo shows, the sternum is sewed up again with twisted lengths of wire.) I am open and shut. Here is an opening through which passes an incessant flux of strangeness: immuno-suppressant medicaments, other medicaments called on to combat certain so-called side-effects, effects no one knows how to combat (such as the degradation of the kidneys), repeated tests, one's whole existence subjected to new parameters, to a thoroughly clean sweep.

(For a considerable period during the operation his blood circulated in machinery situated outside his body.)

> Life scanned and transferred on to a multiplicity of screens each one registering different risks of death.
> Thus in all of these accumulated and contrasted ways do I become the one that is intruded upon. *C'est donc ainsi moi-même qui deviens mon intrus, de toutes ces manières accumulées et opposées.*[8]

In this last proposition, assisted by the impersonal phrase *C'est donc* with which it begins, *qui*, "that," retains a trace of impersonal objecthood despite the use of the first-personal *deviens* rather than third-personal *devient*. This proposition is repeated in the postscript to *L'intrus* appended five years after the publication of the main text and six months after the death of Derrida, for whose carcinomatous pancreas, Nancy notes, medical science had not yet discovered a transplantation technique.

"I myself," he writes: my *soi*, my *se*, my self, and even my Self, printed with an upper case initial, in the way some specialist papers on auto-immunology print the noun, as though they might be treating of what in philosophies of Self-realization is called the Real Self or of what is called the Atman, the real soul or spirit or breath (in German *atmen* is to breathe) in varieties of Oriental thinking. In one of those varieties this Self is called "the One without second." In the thinking of Nancy and Derrida the One without second gives way to the second without One. The self is always with (the) thou, a singular second-person singular that is not necessarily a person; that is necessarily not only a who, yet necessarily not only a what, but rather a whot in the sense that although the self's other may be an it, it imposes upon the self a burden of responsibility that we human beings commonly assume to be impossibly imposable on us by any being other than a human or humanoid being. It is this burden that the thinking (*penser*) of Nancy and Derrida seek to weigh (*peser*), to ponder.

The project in which Nancy and Derrida are engaged is that of widening the constituency of the others to whom I owe responsibility, doing this without overlooking that meeting this responsibility, although it is impossible or unpossible in the sense that it is not an exercise of my *possum*, of my "I can," is impossible too without the intrusion into this hetero-affection of some sort of auto-affective narcissism. This is an echo of attempts made by Paul Ricœur, Michel Haar, and others to correct what they regarded as a one-sidedness in the teaching of Levinas.[9] In a different context the project could be described as an attempt to read in both directions the injunction to love thy neighbor as thyself, the suggestion being that not only am I to understand my love of my neighbor according to my love of myself, but that I am to understand my love of myself according to my love of my neighbor. What I take Nancy and Derrida to be saying beyond that, and what I take myself to have been saying since *The Middle Voice of Ecological Conscience*, is that the direct ethico-political responsibility called for by the other responded to as a thou is owed not only to the human but also to the inhuman. The inhuman imposes a claim on me even if the claim can be voiced verbally only by human advocates. Perhaps in the book just mentioned and in chapter 8 of this one I should, as Simon Critchley hints in his entirely admirable book *Ethics—Politics—Subjectivity*, have been more willing than I seemed to be there to allow that Levinas could agree with me.[10] Although Levinas was unwilling to do so in face to face discussion with me on this subject, there is more than one Levinas. *Il n'y pas le Levinas.*

Il n'y a pas le . . . , *il n'y a pas la* . . . , for example, *il n'y a pas la déconstruction, il n'y a pas le narcissisme, il n'y a pas l'animal* (there are only animals), *il n'y a pas l'inhumain* (there is only "a certain inhumanity") are forms of words Derrida recognizes he has been in the habit of employing. However, in *Le toucher: Jean-Luc Nancy,* one of his commentaries-cum-reconstructions of the corpus of Nancy's writings, for instance the essays by Nancy assembled under the titles *Corpus* and *Une pensée finie,* Derrida observes that phrases following this pattern began in his own more recent writings to give way to the phrase *s'il y en a.* The former phrases are expressions of dissatisfaction with attributions of ultimacy to universals or particulars. They are therefore expressions of dissatisfaction also with the assumption that Socrates has the last word when he complains that the interlocutors who respond to his "What is such-and-such?" kind of questions by giving him empirical examples beg the question as to what the concept or essence is that they must know in order to be able to list their particulars. The expression *s'il y en a* raises the possibility that a certain impossibility is a condition of possibility of the Socratic distinction, an impossibility or unpossibility of the modality explained above and exemplified by hospitality, witness, giving, forgiving, invention, evention, inhumanity, and so on.

Implied in particular by what has been said above is that inhumanity is not a polar opposite of humanity. Humanity and inhumanity are appendices of each other, intrusions upon intrusions, as figured by Nancy in the construction: *se toucher toi.* What Derrida refers to as the syntactic anomalousness of this French construction translates into archaic English as something like "touching oneself thou-ly and touching thee myself-ly." Less archaically:

> When I speak to you, I touch you, and you touch me when I hear you, from no matter how far away, and even by telephone, by the memory of an inflection of the voice over the telephone, by letter also or e-mail. But it is certainly necessary that in order for me to be touched by you I must be able to touch myself. In the *se toucher toi,* the *se* is as indispensable as *toi.* A being not capable of touching itself could not submit itself (*se plier*) to what opens it out (*le déplie*) absolutely to every other that, as every other, inhabits my heart as a stranger. No anthropological limit here. That should hold *on the one hand* for all "animal" *life, and on the other hand consequently,* should make the life of the living in general a derived concept with regard to this possibility of the *se-toucher-toi.*[11]

In the *se-toucher-toi* resounds another impossibility/un-possibility, one that deepens the skin-deep impossibility of a fully self-affective synthetic *expeausition* (Nancy's neologism) of touching and being touched investigated by Husserl and Merleau-Ponty and reinvestigated by Derrida in *Le toucher.* It also goes a step further beyond the notion of deep conscience that Heidegger says is voiced by the friend that *Dasein* hears within itself and that at the same time comes from over and above *Dasein*. Over and above or below these antecedents and Levinas's humanism of the other human being is Nancy's interpretation of the thou that intrudes upon the ego, making auto-affection incomplete, calling for the free first-personal will to listen to the thou's directives, making the possibility of its "I can" conditional upon what for the I is an unpossibility. This is a logico-rhetorical modality of saying that conditions the logical modality of what is said. It is the impossible proto-relation between humanity on the one hand and, on the other hand, divinity, animality, or, more generally, inhumanity. The transitive construction is anomalously "in" the intransitive reflexive construction, and vice versa, each construction intruding chiasmically on the other in something like the deconstructive middle voice.

One of the rigors of inhumanity is the ex-actitude, the exorbitant passivity exacted by the challenge to hear or otherwise sense the it and the thou resounding through each other. But only if this challenge is faced can not only Being or the other human being but any singular existent whotsoever be given its or her or his due. And the existent can be given its or her or his due only if we can let the existent face us as though for the first time. This is the difficulty touched on by Derrida and Nancy under the description "the first kiss" or, more exactly, the *avant-premier baiser,* that is to say, the kiss before the first one.[12] The ante-primal kiss is before the primal kiss not chronologically, for the temporality engaged here is incalculable, as too is the unchronological futurity (*a-venir*) of what Derrida calls oncoming democracy, *démocratie à venir,* which is strictly not *la démocratie,* but a singular plurality. In the sense that verbs have aspects in some languages, for instance Greek, the *avant* and the *à venir* are inseparable quasi-transcendental aspects of temporality analogous to but prior to Kantian schemata, a priority indicated by the "quasi" which marks a modality of address or saying or ethico-political representing rather than a form of the semantically or epistemically represented message.

What Nancy calls intrusion is a differentiation of what Derrida calls *différance* and deconstruction. It both structures and destructures incorporation and corporeal appropriation, extending both a threat and a promise, both suffering and enjoyment, one in the other and the other in the one, so that, as noted earlier, secondness is prior to oneness. Although by secondness here is not meant secondness or secondariness as defined by Peirce and explained above in chapter 3, nevertheless it resembles Peirce's notion in so far as indexicality plays a vital role in his definition and in the notion of secondness introduced here in glossing Nancy and Derrida. It was noted above in chapter 6 that indication (*Anzeichen*) is a notion to which Derrida considers Husserl's phenomenology of language gives too little prominence.

In the paradigm of transplantation commented on by Nancy in which the heart of another, perhaps the heart of a woman, is intruded into his rib cage as though in symbolic memory of the rib that was extruded from Adam's chest, a comment is being made also on Paul's allusion at Romans 12:5 to our being members of one another. The paradigm of the heart bypass procedure, a procedure with which I happen to be more intimately familiar than I am with the procedure of heart transplantation, helps to explain the explanatory clause in the preceding verse of Romans "as we have many members in one body, and all members have not the same office. . . ." A different office is assigned to a blood vessel when it is extruded from the leg, cut into three bits, and grafted on to blood vessels in or near the heart. Both Nancy's intrusion and mine had further complications, his cancerous, cancer being as good or bad a paradigm as any other of a malign multiplication of sideways-creeping rhizomatic complication; my complication being a benign intrusion into the vicinity of the heart of a stent the inserting of which I was able to watch narcissistically on a television screen. Narcissistically, but with a variety of narcissism that would have been slightly different if the stent had been made not of bare metal, but, as a recent development of medical technology has made possible, of corn starch that one could imagine becoming in due course absorbed into the wall of the blood vessel, into the blood system, and perhaps into the tissue of the very eyes, my eyes, though arguably now less mine, less I, marginally inhuman, through which (and through a geodetic framework of wire similar to that described by Nancy) I watched what was taking place on the screen and in a somewhat alienated me.

If it be asked what the relevance of the introduction and intruduction of these relatively trivial empirical contingencies is to matters of logic and philosophy (though they are also matters of life and death), the answer lies precisely in the fact of their contingency. The point of cataloguing them is to bring out the necessity of such contingency for the modes and modalities of the standard and modal propositionally representational logics taught in the medieval *Trivium* and touched on above in the introduction, and by so doing to recognize that there are more things in heaven and on earth than are dreamed of in the philosophy in which those logics are housed. But the contingency of the sophophily that chiasmically intrudes on the empirical contingency distinguished from necessity in traditional philosophies is the contingency of the above-mentioned quasi-transcendental intangibility that underlies the failure of mutual touching described by Husserl and Merleau-Ponty. When I say that the sophophilal contingency, the one that falls within the wisdom of love, is deeper than the philosophical contingency, the one that falls within the love of wisdom, I am remembering that the dimension of depth is invisible and intangible when it is the dimension of the space across which there is a meeting of eyes.

If it be asked further why prominence is given to such artificial prosthetic intrusions, the answer must be that the distinction between the artificial and the natural is one of those of which the complexity is being stressed. Is food and drink a natural intrusion by contrast with Nancy's new heart and the exquisite gold lattice spring that was implanted near to my heart and looked for all the world like something unearthed from a burial site at Sutton Hoo or La Tène, possibly to be brought to light again by a remotely future re-excavation, unless by then that life-preserving trinket had become reconverted into its mineral elements and absorbed into grasses grazed by beasts? These eventualities remind us that there is a wide-open plurality of criteria by which to distinguish the natural from the artificial, some of them more natural or more artificial than others. Another reminder of this is the eventuality of which Nancy writes on the final page of the postscript to L'intrus. Noting in passing Derrida's lifelong concern with the logic of survival and living on, he refers to a double intrusion in his own experience between familiarity and strangeness. As he gets used to living as the recipient of the heart of a stranger—strange enough for him not to know whether it was the heart of a man or a woman—his visits to the hospital lose the familiarity they had when they were more frequent. But the sense of a more profound strangeness comes over him, a strangeness induced by his not being sure whether and on what grounds he has a right to be alive. Now, no longer protected by the assumption of immortality we all make for ourselves, but alert to the fact that he is a survivor, he is struck from time to time by the thought that instead of having an intruder inside him, he himself is the intruder. "Is not that the banal awareness of my pure and simple contingency? Is it to this simplicity that I am led back and exposed afresh by technical ingenuity?"

It is to this simplicity that he is led back by the inhuman. So the story he tells, although a story of real life, is also a parable for the way the inhuman and the deconstruction of the human which it effects, effects also and thereby an affirmation of the human. It does this in a manner graphically and phonologically represented by the affirmative *oui* pronounced in the *jouissance* avowed when in his next and final sentence he proclaims, "This thought gives a singular joy." Quite contingently too, and contingency is still our subject, the French equivalent of "yes" happens to be also the phonetic equivalent of the English "we," and this is also still our subject. In this Franco-Anglican cordial *entente* the first-person plural pronoun echoes the affirmative particle, as Echo repeats the words of Narcissus, who is our subject too, the subject of *me toucher toi* and *m'aimer toi*, touching and loving myself thyselfly, and touching and loving thyself myselfly, as, but with one more turn, Leviticus 19:18 and Matthew 19:19 say. Perhaps in process here is what Derrida and Nancy might call "a deconstruction of Judeo-Christianity." In that case the comedy would be a divine or at least religious one, one that must be endured until the fast-approaching end.

If the aforementioned "we" is represented from the point of view of a third person, it stands for a symmetrical being-with. However, for each party to that togetherness, each looking at and being looked at by the other, the rapport is dissymmetrical. To each of them the other party can come as a surprise. The other can come as a surprise to me too when it is an it regarded as a you that addresses a claim to me, if only through an advocate. The other comes as a shock, as a stranger, notwithstanding that some of that shock may be absorbed by familiarity. That there is something rather than nothing may strike us with astonishment. But that there is this or that singular existent is astonishing too. My realization that the goodness of its existence to it as sheer existent engages my responsibility is a realization that stops me in my self-preoccupied tracks. The non-predicative notion of its existence, as the presupposition of predicative qualification, is logically prior to temporal priority, temporal posteriority, and temporal presence. It is also ethico-politically prior. This is marked by the fact that the corporeal auto-immunities and their breakdown described in the story recounted above are writ large in the body politic and its international relations.[13] However, it is to repeat the moral of the final paragraph of Nancy's story that the final sentences of the final paragraph of this book must be concerned.

The lesson Nancy expresses in his final paragraph is, in his words, a simple and banal thought, a *pensée* that is worlds away from the spirit or, rather, spiritlessness of Pascal's wager. *Cette pensée donne une joie singulière.* This thought gives a singular joy. It does this by being the thought implied in the conversation between Nancy and Derrida and continued in this book that the "we" and the "who" must endure a democracy in which the freedom of a certain familiar liberal humanity is liberated to the service of each and every single, singular, and unique thing, a democracy in which each existent has a voice and a vote by dint of its sheer unqualified existence. This thought is a hard thought, a *pensée dure,* a thought of a rigor that must be endured because in this democracy in which each and every existent makes an initial claim on our ethical, political, and religious though not necessarily theistic attention, joy that exceeds enjoyment is complemented by the exacerbation of a certain unavoidable injustice.

NOTES

Introduction

1. Ludwig Wittgenstein, *Philosophical Investigations*, trans. G. E. M. Anscombe (Oxford: Blackwell, 1953), p. 222.

2. Edmund Husserl, *Cartesian Meditations: An Introduction to Phenomenology*, trans. Dorion Cairns (The Hague: Nijhoff, 1960).

3. John Llewelyn, *Margins of Religion: Between Kierkegaard and Derrida* (Bloomington: Indiana University Press, 2009).

1. Ideologies

1. Aristotle, *The Organon*, vol. 1, trans. Harold P. Cooke and Hugh Tredennick (London: Heinemann, Cambridge Mass, Harvard University Press, 1949), p. 115.

2. Gershom Scholem, *On the Kabbalah and Its Symbolism*, trans. Ralph Manheim (New York: Schocken, 1965), pp. 76–77.

3. John Locke, *Works*, 11th ed. (London: Otrige, 1812), vol. 4, p. 529.

4. Ibid., pp. 134–135.

5. Richard Aaron, *John Locke* (London: Oxford University Press, 1937), p. 88.

6. Locke, Draft B, §62, in Benjamin Rand, ed., *An Essay Concerning the Understanding, Knowledge, Opinion, and Assent* (Cambridge, Mass.: Harvard University Press, 1931); Peter H. Nidditch, ed., *Draft B of Locke's Essay Concerning Human Understanding* (Sheffield, U.K.: University of Sheffield Press, 1982).

7. Norman Kretzmann, "The Main Thesis of Locke's Semantic Theory," in I. C. Tipton, ed., *Locke on Human Understanding, Selected Essays* (Oxford: Oxford University Press, 1977).

8. Locke, *Works*, vol. 4, p. 354.

9. Ferdinand de Saussure, *A Course in General Linguistics*, trans. Wade Baskin (London: Fontana/Collins, 1974), p. 120.

10. For more discussion of *meinen* and *vouloir dire*, see chapter 6 below.

11. Martin Heidegger, *Being and Time*, trans. John Macquarrie and Edward Robinson (Oxford: Blackwell, 1967); trans. Joan Stambaugh (Albany: State University of New York Press, 1996). Page references in my text are those of the edition of *Sein und Zeit* given in the margins of the translation.

12. Chomsky's depth grammar is innate. In view of Locke's attack upon innate ideas in the first book of his *Essay*, one can well imagine what he would have said about Chomsky's self-styled "Cartesian linguistics." On both Chomsky's representative structures in the speaker's unconscious and on Locke's representative ideas in the speaker's consciousness the verdict pronounced by the later Wittgenstein would be the same: that they are superfluous excuses, *unnötige Ausreden* (*PI* 213), words that butter no parsnips. See in particular Noam Chomsky, *Rules and Representations* (Oxford: Blackwell, 1980). Cf. Simon Blackburn, *Spreading the Word: Groundings in the Philosophy of Language* (Oxford: Clarendon Press, 1984), pp. 27ff.

13. Ludwig Wittgenstein, *Tractatus Logico-Philosophicus*, trans. D. F. Pears and B. F. McGuiness (London: Routledge and Kegan Paul / New York: The Humanities Press, 1961).

14. Friedrich Waismann, *The Principles of Linguistic Philosophy*, R. Harré, ed. (London: Macmillan, New York: St Martin's Press, 1965), p. 313.

15. Wittgenstein, *Philosophical Investigations*, p. 40. Unless otherwise indicated references in the text abbreviated as *PI* are to paragraphs. Edmund Husserl, *Ideas: A General Introduction to Pure Phenomenology*, trans. W. R. Boyce Gibson (London: Allen and Unwin, 1931); *Ideas Pertaining to a Pure Phenomenology and to a Phenomenological Philosophy*, trans. F. Kersten (The Hague: Nijhoff, 1982), §49.

2. Worldviews

1. Ludwig Wittgenstein, *Philosophical Investigations*, trans. G. E. M. Anscombe (Oxford: Blackwell, 1953).

2. Martin Heidegger, "Die Zeit des Weltbildes," in *Holzwege* (Frankfurt am Main: Klostermann, 1972), p. 85; *The Question Concerning Technology and Other Essays*, trans. William Lovitt (New York: Harper and Row, 1977), p. 132.

3. Ibid., p. 97; p. 146; Protagoras, fragment B, 4, cited in Hermann Diels, *Fragmente der Vorsokratiker* (Berlin: Wiedemannsche Buchhandling, 1903). Since Heidegger cites this to help explain the part played by waiting (*Verweilen*) in the Greek way of belonging in the world, it may help to explain what he means when in the interview in *Der Spiegel* he says "Only a God [or a god] can save us."

4. Heidegger, ibid., p. 84; p. 131.

5. Ibid., p. 83; p. 131.

6. This might explain why Aristotle's emphasis upon the priority of theoretical wisdom in Book 10 of the *Nicomachean Ethics* is not inconsistent with the stress he puts on practical wisdom throughout the rest of that work. Perhaps saying, as it is sometimes said, that Book 10 is Plato's revenge underestimates the height of "the highest doing."

7. Donald Davidson, "On the Very Idea of a Conceptual Scheme," in *Inquiries into Truth and Interpretation* (Oxford: Clarendon Press, 1984).

8. Benjamin Lee Whorf, *Language, Thought, and Reality: Selected Writings of Benjamin Lee Whorf,* J. B. Carroll, ed. (Cambridge, Mass.: M.I.T and Wiley, 1956), pp. 212–214.

9. Martin Heidegger, "Wissenschaft und Besinnung," in *Vorträge und Aufsätze,* vol. 1 (Pfullingen, Germany: Neske, 1967), p. 45; "Science and Reflection," in *The Question Concerning Technology,* p. 164.

10. "C'est dans la boîte," I once heard a young photographer remark after "getting" one of the Bronze Age rock carvings of the Vallée des Merveilles in the Maritime Alps north of Nice.

11. Whorf, pp. 246–247.

12. Ibid., p. 158.

13. Ibid., p. 70.

14. Ibid., p. 90.

15. Ibid., p. 70.

16. Ibid., p. 253.

17. Ibid., p. 70.

18. Ibid., p. 89.

19. Ibid., p. 212.

20. Ibid., p. 70.

21. Immanuel Kant, *Prolegomena to Any Future Metaphysics That Will Be Able to Present Itself as a Science,* trans. P. G. Lucas (Manchester, U.K.: Manchester University Press, 1953), p. 85.

22. Whorf, p. 147.

23. Ibid., p. 153.

24. Ibid., p. 226.

25. Ibid., p. 215.

26. Ludwig Wittgenstein, *Tractatus Logico-Philosophicus,* trans. D. F. Pears and B. F. McGuiness (London: Routledge and Kegan Paul / New York: The Humanities Press, 1961).

27. Whorf, p. 66.

28. Ibid., p. 252.

29. Edward Sapir, "Conceptual Categories in Primitive Languages," *Science,* December 1931, p. 578.

30. Whorf, p. 218.

31. A. C. Graham, "'Being' in Classical Chinese," in John W. M. Verhaar, ed., *The Verb "Be" and its Synonyms: Philosophical and Grammatical Studies* (Dordrecht, The Netherlands: Reidel / New York: Humanities Press, 1967), pp. 8, 14.

32. Davidson, "On the Very Idea of a Conceptual Scheme," p. 187.

33. P. F. Strawson, *The Bounds of Sense* (London: Methuen, 1966), p. 15.

34. Richard Rorty, "World Well Lost," in *Consequences of Pragmatism (Essays 1972–1980)* (Brighton, U.K.: Harvester Press, 1982).

35. Davidson, "On the Very Idea of a Conceptual Scheme," p. 194.

36. R. G. Collingwood, *An Essay on Metaphysics* (Oxford: Clarendon, 1940).

37. Jacques Derrida, "Envoi," in *Psyché. Inventions de l'autre* (Paris: Galilée, 1987), pp. 109–143; "Sending: On Representation," trans. Peter and Mary Ann Caws, *Social Research* 49 (2), 1982, pp. 294–326.

38. Martin Heidegger, *Einführung in die Metaphysik* (Tübingen, Germany: Niemeyer, 1953), pp. 198-291; *An Introduction to Metaphysics*, trans. Ralph Manheim (New Haven, Conn.: Yale University Press, 1959), pp. 158-161; *Platons Lehre von der Wahrheit, mit einem Brief über den "Humanismus"* (Bern, Germany: Francke, 1954); *Wegmarken* (Frankfurt am Main: Klostermann, 1976); *Pathmarks*, William McNeill, ed. (Cambridge: Cambridge University Press, 1998); *Zur Sache des Denkens* (Tübingen, Germany: Niemeyer, 1969); "The End of Philosophy and the Task of Thinking," in *Basic Writings*, David Farrell Krell, ed. (London: Routledge, 1978); "Hegel and the Greeks," in *Wegmarken, Vier Seminare* (Frankfurt am Main: Klostermann, 1977), pp. 73-74, 133-134. See Robert Bernasconi, "Aletheia and the Concealment of Concealing," in his *The Question of Language in Heidegger's History of Being* (Atlantic Highlands, N.J.: Humanities Press / London: Macmillan, 1985), pp. 17-27, for a sharp assessment of the differences between Heidegger and Paul Friedländer over the various editions of the latter's *Platon*, including *Platon, Band I* (Berlin: de Gruyter, 1954, 1964); *Plato I, An Introduction*, 2nd ed., trans. Hans Meyerhoff (Princeton, N.J.: Princeton University Press, 1973).

39. Hans-Georg Gadamer, *Truth and Method* (London: Sheed and Ward, 1975), pp. 267ff.

40. Heidegger, *Zur Sache des Denkens*, p. 78; *Basic Writings*, p. 390.

41. Hans-Georg Gadamer, *Reason in the Age of Science*, trans. Frederick G. Lawrence (Cambridge, Mass.: MIT, 1981), pp. 63, 68; "Hegel and Heidegger," in *Hegel's Dialectic: Five Hermeneutical Studies*, trans. P. Christopher Smith (New Haven, Conn.: Yale University Press, 1976), p. 100.

42. The distinction between "can ... if" and "could ... if" made here mirrors that between ability and capacity made by S. L. Hurley, "Intelligibility, Imperialism, and Conceptual Scheme," in Peter A. French, Theodore E. Uehling, Jr., and Howard K. Wettstein, eds., *Midwest Studies in Philosophy*, vol. 12, *The Wittgenstein Legacy* (Notre Dame, Ind.: University of Notre Dame, 1992), pp. 89-108.

43. W. V. O. Quine, "Speaking of Objects," in *Ontological Relativity and Other Essays* (New York: Columbia University Press, 1969), p. 1, cited by Davidson, "On the Very Idea of a Conceptual Scheme," p. 191. Compare this "Ptolemaic" comment of Quine's about language with Husserl's and Merleau-Ponty's comments about the "Ptolemaic" world that adheres to us throughout our actual or imagined travels. See Edmund Husserl, "Grundlegende Untersuchung zum phänomenologischen Ursprung der Räumlichkeit der Natur (Umsturz der kopernischen Lehre)," in M. Farber, ed., *Essays in Memory of Edmund Husserl* (Cambridge, Mass.: Harvard University Press, 1940), p. 324; and Maurice Merleau-Ponty, *Notes de cours 1959-1961* (Paris: Gallimard, 1996), p. 127.

44. Jürgen Habermas, *Philosophical-Political Profiles*, trans. Frederick G. Lawrence (Cambridge, Mass.: MIT, 1985), p. 109. See also Maurice Merleau-Ponty, *Phénoménologie de la perception* (Paris: Gallimard, 1945), p. 456; *Phenomenology of Perception*, trans. Colin Smith (London: Routledge and Kegan Paul / New York: The Humanities Press, 1962), p. 398: "There is no other world possible in the sense in which mine is, not because mine is necessary as Spinoza thought, but because any 'other world' that I might try to conceive would set limits to this one, would be found on its boundaries, and would consequently merely fuse with it." Merleau-Ponty refers here to Edmund Husserl, *Logical Investigations*, trans. J. N. Findlay

(London: Routledge and Kegan Paul / New York: The Humanities Press, 1970), vol. 1, §36, on relativism and anthropologism.

45. Gadamer, *Truth and Method*, p. 430.

46. Ibid., p. 422. See John Llewelyn, *The Middle Voice of Ecological Conscience: A Chiasmic Reading of Responsibility in the Neighbourhood of Heidegger, Levinas, and Others* (London: Macmillan, New York: St. Martin's Press, 1991); "L'intentionnalité inverse," in Eliane Escoubas, ed., *Dossier: Art et phénoménologie, La part de l'oeil*, no. 7, 1991; *Seeing Through God: A Geophenomenology* (Bloomington: Indiana University Press, 2004).

3. The Experience of Language

1. Frank Kermode, *The Romantic Image* (New York: Random House, 1964), pp. 127–128, cited by Frank Lentricchia, *After the New Criticism* (Chicago: University of Chicago Press, 1980), p. 6.

2. Lentricchia, *After the New Criticism*, p. 5.

3. Lyle M. Eslinger, *Kingship of God in Crisis: A Close Reading of 1 Samuel 1–12* (Decatur, Ill.: Almond Press, 1985), p. 40.

4. Ibid., pp. 427–428.

5. Ibid., p. 428.

6. C. S. Peirce, *Collected Papers* (Cambridge, Mass.: Harvard University Press, 1931–1958), 2.303.

7. Ibid., 2.302.

8. Jacques Derrida, "Signature Événement Contexte," in *Marges de la philosophie* (Paris: Minuit, 1972), p. 375; "Signature Event Context," in *Margins of Philosophy*, trans. Alan Bass (Chicago: Chicago University Press, 1982), p. 315.

9. Jacques Derrida, *Glas* (Paris: Galilée 1974), 233b; *Glas*, trans. John P. Leavey, Jr., and Richard Rand (Lincoln: University of Nebraska, 1986), 208b.

10. Jacques Derrida, *De la grammatologie* (Paris: Minuit, 1967), p. 227; *Of Grammatology*, trans. Gayatri Chakravorty Spivak (Baltimore, Md.: The Johns Hopkins University Press, 1976), p. 158.

11. Liddell and Scott give as reference Philo 2, 154f.

12. Ferdinand de Saussure, *Course in General Linguistics*, trans. Wade Baskin (London: Fontana, 1974).

13. Umberto Eco, *The Limits of Interpretation* (Bloomington: Indiana University Press, 1994), p. 38.

14. Peirce, 2.304.

15. Umberto Eco, *A Theory of Semiotics* (Bloomington: Indiana University Press, 1976), pp. 115–116.

16. Peirce, 2.247.

17. Ibid., 2.304.

18. Ibid., 2.276.

19. Gottlob Frege, *Philosophical Writings*, trans. Peter Geach (Oxford: Blackwell, 1952), pp. 45–46.

20. Peirce, 2.306.

21. Ludwig Wittgenstein, *Philosophical Investigations*, trans. G. E. M. Anscombe (Oxford: Blackwell, 1953), pp. 201, 212.

22. Frank Kermode, *Pleasing Myself; From Beowolf to Philip Roth* (London: Allen Lane, The Penguin Press, 2001), p. 160.

23. Michel Foucault, *The Order of Things: An Archaeology of the Human Sciences* (London: Tavistock, 1970), p. xv.

24. Martin Heidegger, *Being and Time*, trans. John Macquarrie and Edward Robinson (Oxford: Blackwell, 1962); trans. Joan Stambaugh (Albany: State University of New York Press, 1996), p. 161.

25. Peirce, 2.302.

26. Ibid., 2.278.

27. Ibid., 2.276.

28. Why only mainly? Perhaps because iconicity is a distinguishable but not separable aspect of signification along with indexicality and symbolism.

29. Douglas Greenlee, *Peirce's Concept of Sign* (The Hague: Mouton, 1973), p. 95.

30. Umberto Eco, *The Limits of Interpretation*, p. 38.

31. Peirce, 2.276.

32. Ibid., 5.475.

33. Ibid., 5.179.

34. Ibid., 5. 427.

35. Ibid., 5.504.

36. Ibid., 5.491.

37. Eco, *The Limits of Interpretation*, p. 39.

38. Richard Rorty, *Essays on Heidegger and Others: Philosophical Papers*, vol. 2 (Cambridge: Cambridge University Press, 1991), p. 119.

39. Derrida, *De la grammatologie*, p. 227; *Of Grammatology*, p. 158.

40. Ibid., p. 108; p. 73.

41. See, for example, Edmund Husserl, *Ideas: General Introduction to Pure Phenomenology*, trans. W. R. Boyce Gibson (London: Allen and Unwin, 1931), §70, which infers that "the element which makes up the life of phenomenology as of all eidetic science is 'fiction'. . . ."

42. Derrida, *Glas*, p. 134. See also Jacques Derrida, *Khôra* (Paris: Galilée, 1993); John Sallis, *Chorology: On Beginning in Plato's* Timaeus (Bloomington: Indiana University Press, 1999); Charles E. Scott, *The Lives of Things* (Bloomington: Indiana University Press, 2002), pp. 36–53; Charles P. Bigger, *Between* Chora *and the Good: Metaphor's Metaphysical Neighborhood* (New York: Fordham University Press, 2005). To this short list of publications, all in their different ways dazzling, I would add mention of Sarah Broadie, *Nature and Divinity in Plato's* Timaeus (Cambridge: Cambridge University Press, 2011), and of Basil O'Neill's book on Plato currently in progress.

43. W. J. T. Mitchell, *Iconology: Image, Text, Ideology* (Chicago: University of Chicago Press, 1987), p. 46.

44. Ibid., p. 29.

45. Derrida, *Marges*, p. 392; *Margins*, p. 329.

46. David Stern, "Midrash and Indeterminacy," *Critical Inquiry* 15 (Autumn 1988): 145, 154. St. Augustine, *The Confessions of St. Augustine*, trans. John K. Ryan (New York: Doubleday, 1960), p. 358.

47. Philo, "Who is the Heir of Divine Things," in *Philo*, 10 vols., trans. F. H. Colson and G. H. Whitaker (London: Heinemann, 1932), vol. 4, pp. 348–349.

4. Phenomenology as Rigorous Science

1. Edmund Husserl, *Philosophy of Arithmetic: Psychological and Logical Investigations with Supplementary Texts from 1887–1901,* trans. Dallas Willard (Dordrecht, The Netherlands: Kluwer, 2001).

2. Franz Brentano, *Psychology from an Empirical Standpoint,* Oskar Kraus, ed., English edition ed. Linda L. McAlister, trans. Antos C. Ramcurello, D. B. Terrell, and Linda L. McAlister (London: Routledge and Kegan Paul, 1973), p. 88.

3. Walter Biemel, "The Development of Husserl's Philosophy," in R. O. Elveton, ed., *The Phenomenology of Husserl: Selected Critical Readings* (Chicago: Quadrangle, 1970), pp. 156–162.

4. Edmund Husserl, *The Phenomenology of Internal Time Consciousness,* ed. Martin Heidegger, trans. James S. Churchill (The Hague: Nijhoff, 1964), §25, pp. 77–78.

5. Ibid., §24, p. 76.

6. Ibid., §36, p. 100.

7. Françoise Dastur, *Husserl: Des mathématiques à l'histoire* (Paris: Presses Universitaires de France, 1995), p. 55.

8. Edmund Husserl, *Cartesian Meditations: An Introduction to Phenomenology,* trans. Dorion Cairns (The Hague: Nijhoff, 1960), §64, p. 157.

9. Edmund Husserl, *Logical Investigations,* 2 vols., trans. J. N. Findlay (London: Routledge and Kegan Paul, 1970), Investigation I, §15.

10. Jacques Derrida, introduction to and translation of Edmund Husserl, *L'origine de la géométrie* (Paris: Presses Universitaires de France, 1962); *Edmund Husserl's "Origin of Geometry": An Introduction,* trans. John P. Leavey (New York: Nicolas Hays, 1978); *La voix et le phénomène* (Paris: Presses Universitaires de France, 1967); *Speech and Phenomena and Other Essays on Husserl's Theory of Signs,* trans. David B. Allison (Evanston, Ill.: Northwestern University Press, 1977).

11. Edmund Husserl, *Formal and Transcendental Logic,* trans. Dorion Cairns (The Hague: Nijhoff, 1969), §96, p. 242.

12. Edmund Husserl, *Psychological and Transcendental Phenomenology and the Confrontation with Heidegger* (1927–1931), ed. and trans. Thomas Sheehan and Richard E. Palmer (Dordrecht, The Netherlands: Kluwer, 1997), p. 115.

13. Maurice Merleau-Ponty, *La phénoménologie de la perception* (Paris: Gallimard, 1945); *Phenomenology of Perception,* trans. Colin Smith (London: Routledge and Kegan Paul, 1962); *Le visible et l'invisible* (Paris: Gallimard, 1964); *The Visible and the Invisible,* trans. Alphonso Lingis (Evanston, Ill.: Northwestern University Press, 1968).

14. Husserl, *Psychological and Transcendental Phenomenology,* pp. 169–170.

15. Edmund Husserl, *Analyses Concerning Passive and Active Synthesis: Lectures on Transcendental Logic* (Dordrecht, The Netherlands: Kluwer, 2001), §42, p. 196.

16. Edmund Husserl, *The Crisis of European Science and Transcendental Phenomenology: An Introduction to Phenomenological Philosophy,* trans. David Carr (Evanston, Ill.: Northwestern University Press, 1970), §38, p. 147.

17. Husserl, *Cartesian Meditations,* §38, p. 79.

18. Edmund Husserl, *Ideas Pertaining to a Pure Phenomenology and to Phenomenological Philosophy*, vol. 2, *Studies in the Phenomenology of Constitution*, trans. R. Rojcewicz and A. Schuwer (The Hague: Kluwer, 1989), pp. 181f.; *Phenomenological Psychology: Lectures, Summer Semester 1925*, trans. John Scanlon (The Hague: Nijhoff, 1977), pp. 7ff.

19. Edmund Husserl, *Experience and Judgment: Investigations in a Genealogy of Logic*, trans. James S. Churchill and Karl Ameriks (London: Routledge and Kegan Paul, 1973), $10, p. 46.

20. Husserl, *Formal and Transcendental Logic*, $60, p. 160.

21. Edmund Husserl, *Ideas: A General Introduction to Pure Phenomenology*, trans. W. R. Boyce Gibson (London: Allen and Unwin, 1931), $19, p. 84.

22. Moritz Schlick, "Gibt es ein materiales Apriori?" in Wissenschaftlicher Jahresbericht der Philosophischen Gesellschaft an der Universität Wien für das Vereinsjahr 1930/31, in *Gesammelte Aufsätze 1926–1936* (Vienna: Gerold, 1938); "Is There a Factual A Priori?" in H. Feigl and W. Sellars, eds., *Readings in Philosophical Analysis* (New York: Appleton-Century-Crofts, 1949). For Husserl's initial response to Schlick see *Logical Investigations*, vol. 2, p. 663.

23. Husserl, *Ideas*.

24. Husserl, *Psychological and Transcendental Phenomenology*, p. 94.

25. Husserl, *Ideas*, $20, pp. 86–87.

26. Husserl, *Psychological and Transcendental Phenomenology*, p. 102.

27. Ibid., p. 179.

28. Jean-Paul Sartre, *The Transcendence of the Ego: An Existentialist Theory of Consciousness*, trans. Forrest Williams and Robert Kirkpatrick (New York: Hill and Wang, 1960), p. 36.

29. Ibid., p. 41.

30. Jean-Paul Sartre, "Intentionality: A Fundamental Idea of Husserl's Phenomenology," trans. Joseph P. Fell, in *The Journal of the British Society for Phenomenology* 1(2): 5. Originally published in the *Nouvelle Revue Française* 52, January 1939.

31. H. Spiegelberg, *The Phenomenological Movement: A Historical Introduction*, 2 vols. (The Hague: Nijhoff, 1971), vol. 1, p. 226. See also Roman Ingarden, *On the Motives which Led Husserl to Transcendental Idealism*, trans. Arnór Hannibalsson (The Hague, Nijhoff, 1975).

5. Pure Grammar

1. Ray Monk, *Ludwig Wittgenstein, The Duty of Genius* (London: Vintage, 1990), p. 245.

2. Edmund Husserl, *Formal and Transcendental Logic*, trans. Dorion Cairns (The Hague: Nijhoff, 1969), pp. 3–5.

3. Ibid., p. 331.

4. Edmund Husserl, *Erste Philosophie (1923–4), Erster Teil: Kritische Ideengeschichte*, in R. Boehm, ed., *Husserliana*, vol. 7 (The Hague: Nijhoff, 1956), p. 14.

5. Husserl, *Formal and Transcendental Logic*, p. 4.

6. Husserl, *Erste Philosophie*, p. 25.

7. Husserl, *Formal and Transcendental Logic*, p. 267.

8. Ibid., p. 227.

9. Ludwig Wittgenstein, *Philosophical Investigations*, trans. G. E. M. Anscombe (Oxford: Blackwell, 1953), 81.

10. Edmund Husserl, *Logical Investigations*, trans. J. N. Findlay (London: Routledge and Kegan Paul, 1970), Investigation VI, p. 828.

11. Ibid., Investigation VI, p. 670.

12. Husserl, *Formal and Transcendental Logic*, p. 31.

13. Immanuel Kant, *Critique of Pure Reason*, trans. Norman Kemp Smith (London: Macmillan, 1929), B 220–223.

14. Kant, *Critique of Pure Reason*, B viii.

15. Husserl, *Formal and Transcendental Logic*, p. 13.

16. Husserl, *Erste Philosophie*, p. 37.

17. Husserl, *Logical Investigations*, Investigation IV, p. 525.

18. Antoine Arnauld and Claude Lancelot, *General and Rational Grammar: The Port-Royal Logic*, ed. and trans. Jacques Rieux and Bernard E. Rollin (The Hague: Mouton, 1975), p. 27.

19. Husserl, *Logical Investigations*, Investigation IV, p. 526.

20. Ibid., p. 524.

21. Kant, *Prolegomena to any Future Metaphysics*.

22. The Littré dictionary observes that in legal contexts *autrui* is less general than *les autres*. The sense of the expression *l'autrui* is *le bien d'autrui* or *le droit d'autrui*, the other's good or right.

23. Emmanuel Levinas, *Dieu, la mort, et le temps* (Paris: Grasset, 1993), p. 82.

24. See John Llewelyn, "Approaches to Semioethics," in Hugh J. Silverman, ed., *Cultural Semiosis: Tracing the Signifier* (New York and London: Routledge, 1998), pp. 196–218; and *Appositions of Jacques Derrida and Emmanuel Levinas* (Bloomington: Indiana University Press, 2002), chapter 14.

25. Husserl, *Logical Investigations*, Investigation IV, p. 50.

26. Kant, *Critique of Pure Reason*, B 104–105.

27. Ibid., B 94.

28. Ibid., B 29.

29. See James Edie, *Speaking and Meaning: The Phenomenology of Language* (Bloomington: Indiana University Press, 1976), chapter 2; and Jerrold Katz, *Language and Other Abstract Objects* (Oxford: Blackwell, 1981), p. 189.

30. Husserl, *Formal and Transcendental Logic*, p. 188.

31. Ibid., §20.

32. Husserl, *Logical Investigations*, Investigation IV, pp. 523–524.

33. Husserl, *Formal and Transcendental Logic*, pp. 70–71.

34. Kant, *Critique of Pure Reason*, B 376–377.

35. Edmund Husserl, *Vorlesungen über Bedeutungslehre, Sommersemester 1908*, in Ursula Panzer, ed., *Husserliana*, vol. 26 (The Hague: Nijhoff, 1987).

36. Husserl, *Logical Investigations*, Investigation V, §40. See also Edmund Husserl, *Ideas: General Introduction to Pure Phenomenology*, trans. W. R. Boyce Gibson (London: Allen and Unwin, 1931), §§111–112.

37. Wittgenstein, *Philosophical Investigations*, p. 222.

38. L. E. J. Brouwer, "Historical Background, Principles, and Methods of Intuitionism," *South African Journal of Science*, Oct.–Nov. 1952, pp. 140–141.

39. L. E. J. Brouwer, "Consciousness, Philosophy, and Mathematics," *Proceedings of the Tenth International Congress of Philosophy*, vol. 1, Fascicule 2 (Amsterdam: North Holland Publishing Company, 1940), p. 1247.

40. Wittgenstein, *Philosophical Investigations*, p. 230.

41. Ibid., 371.

42. Ibid., 370.

43. John Austin, "Ifs and Cans," in *Philosophical Papers*, J. O. Urmson and G. J. Warnock, eds. (Oxford: Clarendon Press, 1961), pp.179–180.

44. Husserl, *Logical Investigations*, Investigation VI, §64.

45. See John Llewelyn, *The HypoCritical Imagination: Between Kant and Levinas* (London and New York: Routledge, 2000), chapter 6; "Imadgination," in Kenneth Maly, ed., *The Path of Archaic Thinking: Unfolding the Work of John Sallis* (Albany: State University of New York Press, 1995), pp. 75–88.

46. Wittgenstein, *Philosophical Investigations*, 219.

47. Ibid., 546.

6. Meanings and Translations

1. Jacques Derrida, *La voix et le phénomène: Introduction au problème du signe dans la phénoménologie de Husserl* (Paris: Presses Universitaires de France, 1967), p. 19; *Speech and Phenomena and Other Essays on Husserl's Theory of Signs*, trans. David B. Allison (Evanston, Ill.: Northwestern University Press, 1973), p. 19.

2. J. Claude Evans, *Strategies of Deconstruction: Derrida and the Myth of the Voice* (Minneapolis: University of Minnesota Press, 1991), p. 30.

3. Derrida, *La voix*, p. 18; *Speech*, p. 18.

4. Ibid.

5. Derrida, *La voix*, p. 30; *Speech*, p. 20.

6. Ibid.

7. Evans, *Strategies*, p. 32.

8. Derrida, "Form and Meaning," in *Speech and Phenomena*, p. 125.

9. Derrida, *La voix*, p. 6; *Speech*, p. 8.

10. Edmund Husserl, *Formale und transzendentale Logik: Versuch einer Kritik der logischen Vernunft*, in Paul Janssen, ed., *Husserliana*, vol. 17 (The Hague: Nijhoff, 1974); *Formal and Transcendental Logic*, trans. Dorian Cairns (The Hague: Nijhoff, 1969), §2.

11. Derrida, *La voix*, p. 6; *Speech*, p. 8. In the French the last two words are printed in italics.

12. Evans, *Strategies*, p. 31. The emphasis is Evans's.

13. Edmund Husserl, *Ideen zu einer reinen Phänomenologie und phänomenologischen Philosophie: Erstes Buch: Allgemeine Einführung in die Phänomenologie*, in Walter Biemel, ed., *Husserliana*, vol. 3 (The Hague: Nijhoff, 1950), p. 305; *Ideas*, trans. W. R. Boyce Gibson (London: Allen and Unwin, 1931), p. 349, slightly modified.

14. Jacques Derrida, *Le problème de la genèse dans la philosophie de Husserl* (Paris: Presses Universitaires de France, 1990), p. vii.

15. Evans, *Strategies*, p. 51.

16. Ibid., pp. 36–37.

17. Derrida, *La voix*, p. 33; *Speech*, p. 31; emphasis added.

18. Ibid., p. 28; p. 27.

19. Dorian Cairns, *Guide for Translating Husserl* (The Hague: Nijhoff, 1973). Edmund Husserl, *Recherches logiques*, trans. Hubert Elie, Arion L. Kelkel, and René Schérer (Paris: Presses Universitaires de France, 1959–1964). Edmund Husserl, *Logical Investigations*, trans. J. N. Findlay (London: Routledge and Kegan Paul, 1976). In this section I repeat some sentences from my "Approaches to Semioethics," in Hugh J. Silverman, ed., *Cultural Semiosis: Tracing the Signifier* (New York: Routledge, 1998).

20. Derrida, *La voix*, pp. 17–18; *Speech*, p. 17.

21. Emmanuel Levinas, *Autrement qu'être ou au-delà de l'essence* (The Hague: Nijhoff, 1978), p. 46; *Otherwise than Being or Beyond Essence*, trans. Alphonso Lingis (The Hague: Nijhoff, 1981), p. 191.

22. The hyphen is dropped in what follows except for the nominal form.

23. Jacques Derrida, *Positions*, trans. Alan Bass (Chicago: University of Chicago Press, 1991), p. 98.

24. Levinas, *Autrement qu'être*, p. 47; *Otherwise than Being*, p. 189.

25. Derrida, *La voix*, p. 18; *Speech*, p. 18.

26. Husserl, *Ideen I*, p. 312; *Ideas I*, p. 355.

27. Derrida, *Speech*, p. 116; *Marges de la philosophie* (Paris: Minuit, 1972), p. 196; *Margins of Philosophy*, trans. Alan Bass (Chicago: University of Chicago Press, 1982), p. 164, modifying Bass who has "of the noematic sense." Husserl, *Ideen I*, p. 305; *Ideas I*, p. 347.

28. In "The Meaning of a Word" John Austin (in J. O. Urmson and G. J. Warnock, eds., *Philosophical Papers* [Oxford: Clarendon Press, 1979], pp. 55–75) conducts what he would be ready to call phenomenology of language in order to show that sentences, but not words, have meaning. Supposing he is right, we can still make the distinction on which our present discussion turns, the distinction between the meaning of a sentence and what someone means in uttering it or a word. See Jacques Derrida, *Mémoires pour Paul de Man* (Paris: Galilée, 1988), pp. 114ff; *Memoires for Paul de Man*, trans. Cecile Lindsay, Jonathan Culler, and Eduardo Cadava (New York: Columbia University Press, 1986), pp. 112ff.

29. J. N. Mohanty, "On Husserl's Theory of Meaning," *The Southwestern Journal of Philosophy* 5 (1974): 229–244.

30. For instance "Language and Proximity," in Levinas, *En découvrant l'existence avec Husserl et Heidegger* (Paris: Vrin, 1982), pp. 217–236; *Collected Philosophical Papers*, trans. Alphonso Lingis (The Hague: Nijhoff, 1987), pp. 109–126.

31. Paul de Man appears to add his approval to the translation of *"Meinung"* by *"vouloir dire"* on pp. 768–769 of "Sign and Symbol in Hegel's *Aesthetics*," *Critical Inquiry* 8 (1982): 761–775. He reports there part of Hegel's argument for the universality and mediacy of indexical expressions like "this," "now," "here," and "I," hence for the incoherence of the assertion that immediate sensory awareness is the fullest knowledge there is. The incoherence of this assertion, the split in it that makes it split on itself like the assertion of universal skepticism, arises from its purporting to say something about an object or subject allegedly presented immediately by pronouns and other lexical expressions that can stand for any other objects and subjects, allowance made for the differences of gender and number which some of

the pronouns mark. There is a contradiction, he writes, between *sagen* and *meinen*, between to say and to mean, between *dire* and *vouloir dire*. That is, de Man takes *"vouloir dire,"* Hegel's *"sagen-wollen,"* to translate *"meinen."* Does this not blur a distinction that has to be made if we are to get the full picture of Hegel's argument? Does it not mask a distinction that is almost but not quite touched upon by de Man when he writes, quoting Hegel, first in translation, then in the original: "'Since language states only what is general, I cannot say what is only my opinion [. . . *so kann ich nicht sagen was ich nur meine*].' The German version is indispensable here since the English word 'opinion,' as in public opinion (*öffentliche Meinung*), does not have the connotation of 'meaning' that is present, to some degree, in the verb *meinen.*"

In the text I endorse the statement de Man makes in the second of these two sentences. Before one also endorses the Hegelian thesis he reports in the first it should be noted that he is talking about the *meinen* of what is asserted, commanded, asked, and so on, that is, of what Frege calls an *Annahme*, or a thought, and Husserl a *doxa*. So *"meinen"* in this sense is translatable or definable by *"vouloir dire."* And Hegel himself uses *"sagen wollen"* interchangeably with *"meinen"* in this sense. He says that to affirm the philosophical thesis of sensible certainty, namely that the reality of the purely sensory has absolute truth for consciousness, is to say the opposite of what one wants to say, "das Gegenteil von dem sagt, was sie sagen will." However, Hegel does not substitute *"sagen wollen"* for *"meinen"* where the accusative is not something someone wants to say but something referred to about which someone may want to say something.

This distinction is important if we are to understand how the Hegelian dissolution of sensible certainty illuminates and is illuminated by Levinas's curious note purporting to endorse the introduction of *"vouloir dire"* into Derrida's interpretation of Husserl's semiotics. For Levinas denies that *Meinung* is just *visée* on the grounds that nothing can be meant or intended in the sense of *gemeint* without being intended as (*gemeint als*) an *instance*. This denial amounts to an agreement with Hegel's denial of the thesis of sensible certainty. Neither Hegel nor Levinas is denying that there can be *visée*. Whether or not they are denying that there can be *Meinung* which is not *visée*, as the Ricœur translation of *Ideen* used by Derrida implies that Husserl would, Levinas seems to agree with Hegel that at least in the context of identification there cannot be *visée* which is not also *Meinung*. In that context, Hegel writes, speaking of those who hold that one can mean an absolutely singular "this" bit of paper: "but what they mean is not what they say. If they actually wanted to *say* and *meant* [*wanted to say* it], then this is impossible, because the sensuous This that is meant cannot be reached by language, which belongs to consciousness, i.e. to that which is inherently universal." What Hegel wants to say here is that because to say something is to use words that are *allgemein*, I cannot say something *gemeint* that is only and idiosyncratically mine, *mein*. He is not saying that something cannot be simply *gemeint*. *Meinung*, meaning here non-doxic *Meinung*, is not being ruled out. "They certainly mean, then, *this* bit of paper here on which I am writing—or rather have written—'this'." Nor, plainly, does Hegel rule out the doxic *Meinung* of the thesis of sensible certainty, for he writes that "those who put forward such an assertion also themselves say the direct opposite of what they mean (*meinen*)." G. W. F. Hegel, *Phänomenologie des Geistes* (Frankfurt am

Main: Suhrkamp, 1970), p. 91; *Phenomenology of Spirit,* trans. A. V. Miller (Oxford: Clarendon Press, 1977), pp. 65–66; *Phenomenology of Mind,* trans. J. B. Baillie (New York: Harper and Row, 1967), p. 159.

What exactly is Hegel ruling out? Neither Baillie nor Miller stresses in their translations a certain word that is stressed in the original. This can lead the reader not to notice that when Hegel stresses "this is impossible," the "this" (*dies*) could refer, other things being equal, either to *saying* what is meant (*gemeint*) or to *meaning* [*wanting to say*] what is meant. The distinction is not trivial. It can be impossible to say something yet possible to want to say it, for instance when one has the false belief that one can say, in the sense of assert (the *aussagen* of Encyclopaedia, §24), not only propositions but also a physical object. When Rilke writes "sagen: Haus, Brücke, Brunnen . . ." and when Mallarmé writes "Je dis: une fleur" they are not asserting or assuming that one can assert houses and flowers. Nor is anyone asserting houses and flowers even in asserting "I assert houses and flowers." So the piece of paper that someone may indeed mean is not something that one can say in the sense of assert. One could think one could assert it only if one were confusing logical categories. However, since such confusion is possible, this reason why one cannot assert a sensible This like a flower or a house is not a reason why one cannot want to assert it. And indeed Hegel allows that the proponent of sensible certainty may want to assert the sensible This that he means. However the reason Hegel gives to explain why this desire cannot be realized is not that what is assertorically said cannot, logically cannot, be a red flower but can be only *that* this flower is red. Since the proponent of sensible certainty would presumably agree that a flower instantiates a universal, Hegel's objection must concern more plausible claimants to pure sensory denotation like "this," "here," "now," and "I." His objection therefore is that the "divine nature of language" is such that universality extends even to these expressions and that one can mean and even point to a sensible This only *as* one among many (*Phänomenologie des Geistes,* p. 92; *Phenomenology of Spirit,* p. 66; *Phenomenology of Mind,* p. 160).

32. Jean-Luc Marion, *Réduction et donation: Recherches sur Husserl, Heidegger, et la phénoménologie* (Paris: Presses Universitaires de France, 1989), p. 35.

33. Edmund Husserl, *Logical Investigations,* trans. J. N. Findlay (London: Routledge and Kegan Paul: 1976), vol. 1, pp. 285–286.

34. Marion, *Réduction et donation,* p. 41.

35. A question mark that belongs to Derrida gets transferred here to Marion.

36. Derrida, *La voix,* p. 109; *Speech,* p. 97.

37. However, on "abracadabra" see John D. Caputo, "The Economy of Signs in Husserl and Derrida: From Uselessness to Full Employment," in John Sallis, ed., *Deconstruction and Philosophy* (Chicago: University of Chicago Press, 1987), esp. pp. 103–108. I would say that "abracadabra" usually does the job it is intended to do only when it is intended not to have meaning as a whole or in its parts, for instance the four parts "a" which outside this context might be cases of the indefinite article.

38. Marion, *Réduction,* p. 56.

39. Ibid., p. 47.

40. Ibid., pp. 57–58.

41. Martin Heidegger, *Seminare, Gesamtausgabe* 15 (Frankfurt am Main: Klostermann, 1986), p. 377; *Questions IV* (Paris: Gallimard, 1976), p. 314. The latter

gives the reference to but omits the quotation from Simplicius. Note that on p. 312 it translates Heidegger's "eine Anschauung . . . unmittelbar *auf* eine Kategorie *gerichtet*" by "une intuition *donnant* directement *sur* une catégorie," though note too that Heidegger's next sentence is "Mit dem Ausdruck kategoriale Anschauung gelingt es Husserl, das Kategoriale als *Gegebenes* zu denken." See also Heidegger, *Prolegomena zur Geschichte des Zeitbegriffs, Gesamtausgabe* 20 (Frankfurt am Main: Klostermann, 1979), pp. 77–78, 89, 91; *History of the Concept of Time: Prolegomena*, trans. Theodore Kisiel (Bloomington: Indiana University Press, 1985), pp. 57, 66, 67.

42. Marion, *Réduction*, p. 53.

43. Husserl, *Die Idee der Phänomenologie: fünf Vorlesungen* (The Hague: Nijhoff, 1950), p. 61.

44. Husserl, *Ideen I*, p. 52.

45. Ibid., p. 157.

46. See Derrida, *Le problème de la genèse*, esp. pp. 182–185; *Donner le temps*, I, *La fausse monnaie* (Paris: Galilée, 1991); *Given Time*, I, *Counterfeit Money*, trans. Peggy Kamuf (Chicago: The University of Chicago Press, 1992)—especially the note on, respectively, pp. 72–74 and pp. 50–52, occasioned by Marion's remarks in *Réduction et donation* on Husserl on *gebende Anschauung*. See also Jacques Derrida, "Donner la mort," in *L'Éthique du don* (Paris: Métailié-Transition, 1992); *The Gift of Death*, trans. David Wills (Chicago: University of Chicago Press, 1995).

Re-introduction

1. John Llewelyn, *The HypoCritical Imagination: Between Kant and Levinas* (London: Routledge, 2000).

2. John Rawls, *A Theory of Justice*, rev. ed. (Cambridge, Mass.: Harvard University Press, 1999).

3. Martin Luther, *Table Talk*, Theodore G. Tappert, ed. and trans. (Philadelphia: Fortress Press, 1967), p. 12.

7. Approaches to Quasi-theology via Appresentation

1. *The Crisis of European Sciences and Transcendental Phenomenology: An Introduction to Phenomenological Philosophy*, trans. David Carr (Evanston, Ill.: Northwestern University Press, 1970), §38, p. 144.

2. Ibid., §38, p. 146.

3. Edmund Husserl, *Ideas: General Introduction to Pure Phenomenology*, trans. W. R. Boyce Gibson (London: Allen and Unwin, 1931), pp. 238–239.

4. Jacques Derrida, Jean-Luc Marion, and Richard Kearney, "On the Gift," in John D. Caputo and Michael J. Scanlon, eds., *God, the Gift, and Postmodernism* (Bloomington: Indiana University Press, 1999), p. 75.

5. Ibid.

6. Derrida, Marion, & Kearney, "On the Gift," pp. 75–76.

7. Ibid., p. 66.

8. Marcel Mauss, "Essai sur le don," in *Sociologie et anthropologie* (Paris: Presses Universitaires de France, 1978).

9. Jacques Derrida, *Given Time* I.

10. Husserl, *Ideas*, §24, p. 92.

11. Ibid., §19, p. 83. The passage has already been cited in the last section of chapter 4, above.

12. Dominique Janicaud, *Le tournant théologique de la phénoménologie française* (Combas, France: Éditions de l'éclat, 1991); *Phenomenology and the "Theological Turn": The French Debate*, trans. Bernard G. Prusak, Jeffrey L. Kosky, and Thomas A. Carlson (New York: Fordham University Press, 2000).

13. Derrida, Marion, & Kearney, "On the Gift," p. 60.

14. Jean-Luc Marion, *Étant donné: Essai d'une phénoménologie de la donation* (Paris: Presses Universitaires de France, 1997), pp. 327, 329, note; *Being Given: Towards a Phenomenology of Givenness*, trans. Jeffrey L. Kosky (Stanford, Calif.: Stanford University Press, 2002), pp. 235, 367.

15. Jean-Luc Marion, *Le visible et le révélé* (Paris: Cerf, 2005), pp. 183–184. Jean-Luc Marion, *De surcroît: Études sur les phénomènes saturés* (Paris: Presses Universitaires de France, 2001), p. 33; *In Excess: Studies in Saturated Phenomena*, trans. Robyn Horner and Vincent Berraud (New York: Fordham University Press, 2002), p. 29.

16. Martin Luther, *Werke, Erlangen Ausgabe*, vol. 46, p. 287, cited in Martin Heidegger, "Phenomenology and Theology," in James G. Hart and John C. Maraldo, eds., *The Piety of Thinking, Essays by Martin Heidegger* (Bloomington: Indiana University Press, 1976), p. 10.

17. See John Llewelyn, *Margins of Religion: Between Kierkegaard and Derrida* (Bloomington: Indiana University Press, 2009).

18. See Jean-Louis Chrétien, *Saint Augustin et les actes de parole* (Paris: Presses Universitaires de France, 2002), pp. 199–209.

19. Derrida, Marion, & Kearney, "On the Gift," pp. 61–62.

20. Martin Heidegger, "Mein Weg in die Phänomenologie," in *Zur Sache des Denkens* (Tübingen, Germany: Niemeyer, 1969).

21. John Llewelyn, *The Middle Voice of Ecological Conscience: A Chiasmic Reading of Responsibility in the Neighbourhood of Levinas, Heidegger, and Others* (London: Macmillan, 1991). Janicaud once expressed surprise at my hearing in Levinas something like the middle voice.

22. Derrida, Marion, & Kearney, "On the Gift," pp. 69–70.

23. Paul Ricœur, "Emmanuel Lévinas, penseur du témoignage," in Jean-Christophe Aeschlimann, ed., *Répondre d'autrui: Emmanuel Lévinas* (Neuchâtel, France: Éditions de la Baconnière, 1989), p. 39. See also Paul Ricœur, *Soi-même comme un autre* (Paris: Seuil, 1990), pp. 387–393; *Oneself as Another*, trans. Kathleen Blamey (Chicago: University of Chicago Press, 1992), pp. 335–341.

24. Emmanuel Levinas, *Totalité et Infini: Essai sur l'Extériorité* (The Hague: Nijhoff, 1980), p. 62; *Totality and Infinity: An Essay on Exteriority*, trans. Alphonso Lingis (The Hague: Nijhoff, 1969), p. 89.

25. Ibid., p. 194; p. 218.

26. Austin had borrowed it from my late good friend and colleague Stanley Eveling.

27. Derrida, Marion, & Kearney, "On the Gift," p. 68.

28. Ludwig Wittgenstein, *Philosophical Investigations*, trans. G. E. M. Anscombe (Oxford: Blackwell, 1953), para. 564.

29. Janicaud, *Le tournant théologique*, p. 50; Janicaud et al., *Phenomenology and the "Theological Turn,"* p. 63.

30. Jean-Luc Marion, *Dieu sans l'être: Hors texte* (Paris: Fayard, 1982); *God without Being: Hors-Texte*, trans. Thomas A. Carlson (Chicago: University of Chicago Press, 1991).

31. Michel Henry, *La barbarie* (Paris: Grasset, 1987).

32. Michel Henry, *C'est Moi la Vérité: Pour une philosophie du christianisme* (Paris: Seuil, 1996), p. 51; *I am the Truth: Toward a Philosophy of Christianity*, trans. Susan Emanuel (Stanford, Calif.: Stanford University Press, 2002), p. 37.

33. Ibid., p. 41; p. 29.

34. Ibid., p. 318; p. 255.

35. Ibid., p. 68; p. 50. Martin Heidegger, *Being and Time*, trans. John Macquarrie and Edward Robinson (Oxford: Blackwell, 1967); trans. Joan Stambaugh (Albany: State University of New York Press, 1996), p. 75.

36. Michel Henry, *Paroles du Christ* (Paris: Seuil, 2002), p. 109.

37. Ibid., p. 108.

38. Henry, *C'est Moi la Vérité*, p. 329; *I am the Truth*, p. 262.

39. Jean François Courtine, ed., *Phénoménologie et théologie* (Paris: Criterion, 1992), pp. 156–157; Janicaud et al., *Phenomenology and the "Theological Turn,"* p. 238.

40. Ibid., p. 158; p. 240.

41. Ibid., pp. 158–159; p. 240.

42. Ibid., p. 160; p. 241.

43. Henry, *C'est Moi la Vérité*, p. 74; *I am the Truth*, p. 55.

44. Courtine, ed., *Phénoménologie et théologie*, p. 159; Janicaud et al., *Phenomenology and the "Theological Turn,"* p. 240.

45. Derrida, Marion, & Kearney, "On the Gift," p. 71.

46. Marion, *Étant donné, Being Given*, Book 5, §28.

47. Jacques Derrida, *"En ce moment même dans cet ouvrage me voici . . . ,"* in *Psyché: inventions de l'autre* (Paris: Galilée, 1987), pp. 189–192; "At This Very Moment in This Work Here I Am," trans. Ruben Berezdivin, in Robert Bernasconi and Simon Critchley, eds., *Re-Reading Levinas* (Bloomington: Indiana University Press, 1991), pp. 36–39.

48. Derrida, Marion, & Kearney, "On the Gift," p. 66.

8. *Who* Is My Neighbor?

1. Jeremy Bentham, *An Introduction to the Principles of Morals and Legislation* (Oxford: Clarendon Press, 1907), p. 311.

2. On the subject of shoes, see Emmanuel Levinas, *Du sacré au saint* (Paris: Editions de Minuit, 1977), pp. 117–118.

3. Immanuel Kant, *The Metaphysical Principles of Virtue* (Part 2 of *The Metaphysics of Morals*), trans. James Ellington (New York: Bobbs-Merrill, 1964), p. 105.

4. Ibid., p. 106.

5. Emmanuel Levinas, *L'au-delà du verset: lectures et discours talmudiques* (Paris: Minuit, 1982), p. 106; *Beyond the Verse: Talmudic Readings and Lectures*, trans. Gary D. Mole (London: Athlone, 1994), p. 85.

6. Emmanuel Levinas, "Dieu et la philosophie," in *De Dieu qui vient à l'idée* (Paris: Vrin, 1982), pp. 113–114; "God and Philosophy," in *Of God Who Comes to Mind*, trans. Bettina Bergo (Stanford, Calif.: Stanford University Press, 1998), pp. 68–69, and in *Emmanuel Levinas: Basic Philosophical Writings*, Adriaan T. Peperzak, Simon Critchley, and Robert Bernasconi, eds. (Bloomington: Indiana University Press, 1996), pp. 140–141.

7. Emmanuel Levinas, *Totalité et Infini: essai sur l'extériorité* (The Hague: Nijhoff, 1981), p. 51; *Totality and Infinity: An Essay on Exteriority*, trans. Alphonso Lingis (The Hague: Nijhoff, 1969), p. 79.

8. Ibid., pp. 115–116; p. 142.

9. Ibid., p. 269; p. 293.

10. Ibid., p. 51; p. 78.

11. Levinas, *De Dieu qui vient à l'idée*, p. 115; *Of God Who Comes to Mind*, p. 69; *Emmanuel Levinas: Basic Philosophical Writings*, p. 141.

12. Franz Rosenzweig, *The Star of Redemption*, trans. William H. Hallo (New York: Holt, Rinehart, and Winston, 1970).

13. Levinas, *Totalité et Infini*, p. 244; *Totality and Infinity*, p. 266.

14. Rosenzweig, *The Star of Redemption*, p. 214.

15. Ibid., p.163.

16. Emmanuel Levinas, *Noms propres* (Montpellier, France: Fata Morgana, 1976), p. 108; *Proper Names*, trans. Michael B. Smith (London: Athlone Press, 1996), p. 74. See also Emmanuel Levinas and Françoise Armengaud, "Entretien avec Emmanuel Levinas," *Revue de métaphysique et de morale* 90 (1985): 302.

17. The reply made to the question the author put to Levinas on this issue at the *décade* on Levinas's work at Cerisy in 1986 included reference to whether in the animal's eyes it is possible to read the command "Thou shalt not kill."

18. Immanuel Kant, *The Moral Law* [i.e., Kant's *Groundwork of the Metaphysic of Morals*], trans. H. J. Paton (London: Hutcheson, 1963), pp. 67, 90–91.

19. Alexander Broadie and Elizabeth M. Pybus, "Kant's Treatment of Animals," *Philosophy* 49 (1974): 376.

20. Levinas, *Totalité et Infini*, p. 236; *Totality and Infinity*, pp. 258–259.

21. Ibid., p. 240; p. 262.

22. Ibid., p. 10; p. 40.

23. Emmanuel Levinas, *Autrement qu'être ou au-delà de l'essence* (The Hague: Nijhoff, 1978), p. 152; *Otherwise than Being or Beyond Essence*, trans. Alphonso Lingis (The Hague: Nijhoff, 1981), p. 197.

24. Ibid., p.147; p. 116.

25. Levinas, *L'au-delà du verset*, p. 190; *Beyond the Verse*, p. 158.

26. Ibid., p. 194.

27. Levinas, *Autrement qu'être*, p. 86; *Otherwise than Being*, p. 191.

28. J. P. Hyatt, *Exodus* (*New Century Bible*) (London: Oliphant, 1971), p. 214.

29. See Catherine Chalier, "Torah, cosmos, et nature," *Les nouveaux cahiers* 79 (hiver [Winter] 1984–1985): 3–13.

30. Maurice Blanchot, *L'écriture du désastre* (Paris: Gallimard, 1980), p. 49.

31. Robert Bernasconi and David Wood, eds., *The Provocation of Levinas: Rethinking the Other* (London: Routledge, 1988), p. 172.

32. Ibid.

9. Who or What or Whot

1. Søren Kierkegaard, *Stages on Life's Way,* trans. Howard V. Hong and Edna H. Hong (Princeton, N.J.: Princeton University Press, 1998), p. 476.

2. Søren Kierkegaard, *The Concept of Anxiety,* trans. Reidar Thomte in collaboration with Albert B. Anderson (Princeton, N.J.: Princeton University Press, 1980), p. 13.

3. Emmanuel Levinas, *Totalité et Infini: essai sur l'extériorité* (The Hague: Nijhoff, 1980), p. 282; *Totality and Infinity: An Essay on Exteriority,* trans. Alphonso Lingis (The Hague: Nijhoff, 1969), p. 305.

4. Ibid., p. 171; p. 197.

5. Ibid., p. 282; p. 305.

6. Søren Kierkegaard, *Works of Love,* trans. Howard V. Hong and Edna H. Hong (Princeton, N.J.: Princeton University Press, 1995), p. 21.

7. Emmanuel Levinas, *De Dieu qui vient à l'idée* (Paris: Vrin, 1982), p. 144; *Of God Who Comes to Mind,* trans. Bettina Bergo (Stanford, Calif.: Stanford University Press, 1998), p. 91.

8. Kierkegaard, *Works of Love,* p. 58.

9. Ibid., p. 60.

10. Levinas, *Totalité et Infini,* p. 51; *Totality and Infinity,* p. 79.

11. Ibid., p. 194; p. 218.

12. Kierkegaard, *Works of Love,* pp. 120–121.

13. Søren Kierkegaard, *Fear and Trembling. Repetition,* trans. Howard V. Hong and Edna H. Hong (Princeton, N.J.: Princeton University Press, 1983), pp. 44–45.

14. Kierkegaard, *Works of Love,* p. 57.

15. Levinas, "Le dialogue," in *De Dieu qui vient à l'idée,* p. 230; "Dialogue," in *Of God Who Comes to Mind,* p. 151.

16. Levinas, *Totalité et Infini,* p. 52; *Totality and Infinity,* p. 79.

17. Kierkegaard, *Works of Love,* p. 90.

18. Ibid., p. 57.

19. Levinas, *Totalité et Infini,* p. 261; *Totality and Infinity,* pp. 284–285.

20. Levinas, "Le dialogue," in *De Dieu qui vient à l'idée,* p. 227; "Dialogue," in *Of God Who Comes to Mind,* p. 148.

21. Levinas, *Totalité et Infini,* p. 52; *Totality and Infinity,* p. 79.

22. Ibid., p. 52; p. 80.

23. Søren Kierkegaard, *Purity of Heart is to Will One Thing: Spiritual Preparation for the Office of Confession,* trans. Douglas Steere (London: Collins, 1966), p. 47; see also p. 161.

24. Levinas, *Totalité et Infini,* p. 52; *Totality and Infinity,* p. 80.

25. Ibid., p. 64; p. 35.

26. Levinas, "Dieu et la philosophie," in *De Dieu qui vient à l'idée,* p. 110, n9; "God and Philosophy," in *Of God Who Comes to Mind,* p. 199, n15.

27. Emmanuel Levinas, *L'au-delà du verset: lectures et discours talmudiques* (Paris: Minuit, 1982); *Beyond the Verse: Talmudic Readings and Lectures,* trans. Gary D. Mole (London: Athlone, 1994).

28. Levinas, *De Dieu qui vient à l'idée,* p. 13; *Of God Who Comes to Mind,* p. xv.

29. Levinas, *L'au-delà du verset,* p. 9; *Beyond the Verse,* p. xii.

30. *Søren Kierkegaard's Journals and Papers*, 7 vols., trans. Howard V. Hong and Edna H. Hong, assisted by Gregor Malantschuk (Bloomington: Indiana University Press, 1967–1978), IX A 118.

31. Levinas, *L'au-delà du verset*, p. 11; *Beyond the Verse*, p. xiv.

32. Levinas, *De Dieu qui vient à l'idée*, p. 11; *Of God Who Comes to Mind*, p. xiv.

33. Ibid., p. 230; pp. 150–151.

34. Emmanuel Levinas, *Humanisme de l'autre homme* (Montpellier, France: Fata Morgana, 1972), p. 63; *Humanism of the Other*, trans. Nidra Poller (Urbana: University of Illinois Press, 2006), p. 44.

35. Emmanuel Levinas, "Aimer la Thora plus que Dieu," in *Difficile liberté: essais sur le judaïsme* (Paris: Albin Michel, 1976), p. 192; "Loving the Torah More than God," in *Difficult Freedom: Essays on Judaism*, trans. Seán Hand (Baltimore, Md.: The Johns Hopkins University Press, 1990), p. 144.

36. *Zohar*, trans. H. Sperling, M. Simon, and P. Levertoff (London: Soncino Press, 1931–1934), vol. 2, 60a.

37. Kierkegaard, *Purity of Heart*, p. 163.

38. Levinas, *Totalité et Infini*, pp. 224–225; *Totality and Infinity*, pp. 246–247.

39. Søren Kierkegaard, *Concluding Unscientific Postscript to "Philosophical Fragments,"* 2 vols., trans. Howard V. Hong and Edna H. Hong (Princeton, N.J.: Princeton University Press, 1992), vol. 1, p. 560, note.

40. Ibid., pp. 558–559.

41. Jacques Derrida, *Voyous: Deux essais sur la raison* (Paris: Galilée, 2003), p. 81. *Rogues: Two Essays on Reason*, trans. Pascale-Anne Brault and Michael Naas (Stanford, Calif.: Stanford University Press, 2005), p. 53.

10. Ecosophy, Sophophily, and Philotheria

1. Arne Naess, *Ecology, Community, and Lifestyle: Outline of an Ecosophy*, trans. David Rothenberg (Cambridge: Cambridge University Press, 1989). See especially chapters 2, 3, and 4.

2. Martin Heidegger, "The Anaximander Fragment," in *Early Greek Thinking*, trans. David Farrell Krell and Frank A. Capuzzi (New York: Harper and Row, 1975), pp. 13–58.

3. Aloo J. Dastur, *Man and His Environment* (Bombay: The Popular Book Depot, 1954), pp. 8–9.

4. Ernst Haeckel, *Generelle Morphologie der Organismen* (Berlin: Reimer, 1866).

5. Emmanuel Levinas, *Totalité et infini: essai sur l'extériorité* (The Hague: Nijhoff, 1969); *Totality and Infinity: An Essay on Exteriority*, trans. Alphonso Lingis (The Hague: Nijhoff, 1980).

6. See also my *The Middle Voice of Ecological Conscience: A Chiasmic Reading of Responsibility in the Neighbourhood of Levinas, Heidegger, and Others* (London: Macmillan, 1991); *Seeing Through God: A Geophenomenology* (Bloomington: Indiana University Press, 2004); and *Margins of Religion: Between Kierkegaard and Derrida* (Bloomington: Indiana University Press, 2009).

7. José Ortega y Gasset, *Meditations on Hunting*, trans. Howard B. Westcott (New York: Scribner's, 1986). Roger Scruton, *On Hunting* (London: Yellow Jersey Press, 1999).

8. Leo Tolstoy, "The Hunt," *Resurgence*, no. 131 (1988): 30.

9. Scruton, *On Hunting*, p. xii.

10. Ibid., p. 153.

11. Ibid., p. 161.

12. John Keats, *The Letters of John Keats: A Selection*, ed. Robert Gittings (Oxford: Oxford University Press, 1970), p. 43, letter of Keats to his brothers dated December 21, 1817. See also John Llewelyn, *The Middle Voice of Ecological Conscience*, chapter 9, titled "The Feeling Intellect"; and David Wood, *The Step Back: Ethics and Politics after Deconstruction* (Albany: State University of New York Press, 2005), especially the introduction.

13. Jacques Derrida, "Différance," in *Marges de la philosophie* (Paris: Minuit, 1972), p. 9; "Différance," in *Margins of Philosophy*, trans. Alan Bass (Chicago: University of Chicago Press, 1982), p. 9.

14. Ibid.

15. Emmanuel Levinas, *Autrement qu'être ou au-delà de l'essence* (The Hague: Nijhoff, 1974), pp. 127-128, 140-144; *Otherwise Than Being or Beyond Essence*, trans. Alphonso Lingis (The Hague: Nijhoff, 1981), pp. 100-101, 110-113.

16. Edward Thomas, *Letters to George Bottomley*, ed. R. George Thomas (London: Oxford University Press, 1968), p. 157, letter of E. Thomas dated 7 February 1908, written at Minsmere. For this reference I thank Robert Macfarlane, who first brought my attention to Thomas's sentence in readings broadcast on BBC Radio 3 in the autumn of 2009 (later repeated) in the series titled *The Essay*.

17. René Descartes, *The Passions of the Soul*, Part Second, Article LIII, in *The Philosophical Works of Descartes*, vol. 1, trans. Elizabeth S. Haldane and G. R. T. Ross (Cambridge: Cambridge University Press, 1931), p. 358.

18. Philip Larkin, "High Windows," in *Collected Poems* (London: The Marvell Press, Faber and Faber, 1988), p. 165.

19. Robert Maynard Jones, *Cyfriniaeth Gymraeg* (Cardiff: University of Wales Press, 1994), pp. 28-29. Michelangelo Buonarroti, *Rime*, ed. Enzo Noè Girardi (Bari, Italy: Gius, Laterza & Figli, 1960), p. 292. Wordsworth's translation is "The prayers I make will then be sweet indeed / If Thou the spirit give by which I pray."

20. Henry Lewis and Holger Pedersen, *A Concise Comparative Celtic Grammar* (Göttingen, Germany: Vandenhoeck and Ruprecht, 1937), p. 306.

21. Gabriel Marcel, *The Mystery of Being*, vol. 1, *Reflection and Mystery*, trans. G. S. Fraser (London: The Harvill Press, 1951), p. 145.

22. Marged Haycock, ed., *Blodeugerdd Barddas o Ganu Crefyddol Cynnar* (Llandybïe, Wales: Dinefwr Press, 1994), p. 152-154.

23. John Keats, *Letters of John Keats*, ed. Robert Gittings (London: Oxford University Press, 1970), p. 43, letter of Keats to J. H. Reynolds, dated 22 November 1817.

24. David Wood, *The Step Back: Ethics and Politics after Deconstruction* (Albany: State University of New York Press, 2005), pp. 4-5.

25. Robert Macfarlane, *The Wild Places* (London: Granta, 2007), p. 100. The words in square brackets are added. Of this book and its author a reviewer in the *Independent* judged that "when Macfarlane moves into the realities of the landscape, he makes them sing . . . a deeply stirring book." That judgment is supported by the same author's *Mountains of the Mind: A History of a Fascination* (London: Granta, 2003).

26. Gasset, *Meditations on Hunting*, p. 83, note.

27. See John Llewelyn, *The HypoCritical Imagination: Between Kant and Levinas* (London: Routledge, 2000). See especially chapters 2, 3, and 15.

28. Gasset, *Meditations on Hunting*, p. 89.

29. Chris Bonington, *The Everest Years: A Climber's Life* (London: Hodder and Stoughton, 1986), p. 41. See p. 206 and elsewhere for references to Arne Naess junior and Arne Naess senior, "a professor of philosophy . . . the father figure of Norwegian mountaineering who had made many new routes in Norway and led the first Norwegian expedition to the Himalayas."

30. Søren Kierkegaard, *Concluding Unscientific Postscript*, trans. David F. Swenson and Walter Lowrie (Princeton, N.J.: Princeton University Press, 1941), book 2, part 2, chapter 2. See also T. L. S. Sprigge, *The God of Metaphysics* (Oxford: Clarendon Press, 2006), chapter 4.

31. One good point of departure for it would be Thomas McEvilley, *The Shape of Ancient Thought: Comparative Studies in Greek and Indian Philosophies* (New York: Allworth Press, 2002).

11. Barbarism, Humanism, and Democratic Ecology

1. Luc Ferry, *Le nouvel ordre écologique: l'arbre, l'animal et l'homme* (Paris: Grasset, 1992), p. 275; *The New Ecological Order*, trans. Carol Volk (Chicago: The University of Chicago Press, 1995), p. 151.

2. Ibid., pp. 16–17; xiv–xv.

3. Ibid., p. 89; p. 32.

4. Ibid., p. 99; p. 38.

5. Ibid., p. 111; p. 46.

6. Rosemary Radford Ruether, *Gaia and God: An Ecofeminist Theology of Earth Healing* (London: SCM, 1993).

7. Emmanuel Levinas, *Autrement qu'être ou au-delà de l'essence* (The Hague: Nijhoff, 1974), 215ff.; *Otherwise Than Being or Beyond Essence*, trans. Alphonso Lingis (The Hague: Nijhoff, 1981), pp. 169ff., cited by Ferry at *Le nouvel ordre écologique*, p. 63, but not in the English translation of this.

8. Emmanuel Levinas, "Une religion d'adultes," in *Difficile liberté: essais sur le judaïsme* (Paris: Albin Michel, 1976), p. 40; "A Religion for Adults," in *Difficult Freedom: Essays on Judaism*, trans. Seán Hand (Baltimore, Md.: The Johns Hopkins University Press, 1990), p. 22.

9. Emmanuel Levinas, *Du sacré au saint* (Paris: Minuit, 1977), p. 158; *Nine Talmudic Readings*, trans. A. Aronowicz (Bloomington: Indiana University Press, 1990), p. 183.

10. Rabbi Hayyim de Volozhyn, *L'âme de la vie: nefesh hahayyim* (Paris: Verdier, 1986), p. 114.

11. Levinas, "Aimer la Thora plus que Dieu," in *Difficile liberté*, pp. 189–193; "Loving the Torah More than God," in *Difficult Freedom*, pp. 142–145.

12. Levinas, *Difficile liberté*, p. 41; *Difficult Freedom*, p. 23.

13. Gershon Scholem, *On the Kabbalah and its Symbolism* (New York: Schocken Books, 1965), p. 105.

14. Scholem, *On the Kabbalah and its Symbolism*, p. 107.

15. Levinas, "Le judaïsme et le féminin," in *Difficile liberté*, p. 59; "Judaism and the Feminine," in *Difficult Freedom*, p. 37.

16. Ibid., p. 56; p. 35.

17. Ibid, p. 59; p. 37.

18. Scholem, *On the Kabbalah and its Symbolism*, p. 107.

19. Levinas, *Difficile liberté*, p. 60; *Difficult Freedom*, p. 38.

20. Ibid., p. 40; p. 22.

21. See Catherine Chalier's beautiful *Traité des larmes: Fragilité de Dieu, fragilité de l'âme* (Paris: Albin Michel, 2003).

12. Where to Cut: *Boucherie* and *Delikatessen*

1. Jacques Derrida, *L'animal que donc je suis*, ed. Marie-Louise Mallet (Paris: Galilée, 2006), pp. 148–149; *The Animal That Therefore I Am*, trans. David Wills (New York: Fordham University Press, 2008), p. 107. John Llewelyn, *The Middle Voice of Ecological Conscience: A Chiasmic Reading of Responsibility in the Neighbourhood of Levinas, Heidegger and Others* (London: Macmillan, 1991).

2. Levinas read enough of the book to be sufficiently disconcerted to ask Derrida for reassurance about it on the telephone, a device Levinas was not fond of using.

3. Jacques Derrida and Elisabeth Roudinesco, *De quoi demain . . . Dialogue* (Paris: Fayard-Galilée, 2001).

4. Derrida and Roudinesco, *De quoi demain*, p. 120.

5. Jacques Derrida, "La différance," in *Marges de la philosophie* (Paris: Minuit, 1972), p. 9; "Différance," in *Margins of Philosophy*, trans. Alan Bass (Chicago: The University of Chicago Press, 1982), p. 9.

6. Matthew Calarco, *Zoographies: The Question of the Animal from Heidegger to Derrida . . .* (New York: Columbia University Press, 2008).

7. Jeremy Bentham, *An Introduction to the Principles of Morals and Legislation* (Oxford: Clarendon Press, 1907), p. 311.

8. Derrida and Roudinesco, *De quoi demain*, p. 112.

9. Calarco, *Zoographies*, p. 145.

10. "Spectre toujours masqué qui nous suis côte à côte. / Et qu'on nomme demain ! / Oh ! Demain, c'est la grande chose ! / De quoi demain sera-t-il fait ?" Victor Hugo, "Napoléon II," in *Les Chants du crépuscule*, vol. 1 (Paris: Gallimard, Pléiade, 1964), pp. 811, 838. Remarkable, given Derrida's play on *je suis* as "I am" and "I follow," is that the original Pléiade text of these lines from Hugo's poem has *suis*, not *suit*, after the third-person pronoun.

11. Jacques Derrida, *Apories* (Paris: Galilée, 1996), p. 99; *Aporias*, trans. Thomas Dutoit (Stanford, Calif.: Stanford University Press, 1993), p. 53. Jacques Derrida, *De l'esprit: Heidegger et la question* (Paris: Galilée, 1987); *Of Spirit: Heidegger and the Question*, trans. Geoffrey Bennington and Rachel Bowlby (Chicago: The University of Chicago Press, 1989), chapter 10.

12. Jacques Derrida, *Séminaire: la bête et le souverain*, vol. 1 (2001–2002) (Paris: Galilée, 2008), p. 36; *The Beast and the Sovereign*, vol. 1 (Seminars of Jacques Derrida), trans. Geoffrey Bennington (Chicago: The University of Chicago Press, 2009), p. 16.

13. Derrida, *L'animal que donc je suis*, p. 52; *The Animal That Therefore I Am*, p. 30.

14. Jacques Derrida, "Geschlecht II: Heidegger's Hand," trans. John P. Leavey, Jr., in John Sallis, ed., *Deconstruction in Philosophy: The Texts of Jacques Derrida* (Chicago: The University of Chicago Press, 1987), p. 173.

15. Derrida, *The Animal That Therefore I Am*, pp. 25-26. For a description of both the techniques of the mass rearing and killing of animals and the techniques of human denial see Jonathan Safran Foer, *Eating Animals* (London: Penguin Books, 2009). On p. 108 of that book he too cites the passage I have cited.

16. Donna Haraway, *Simians, Cyborgs, and Women: The Reinvention of Nature* (New York: Routledge, 1991), pp. 151-152.

17. Derrida, *L'animal que donc je suis*, p. 51; *The Animal That Therefore I Am*, p. 29.

18. Derrida, *Séminaire: la bête et le souverain*, vol. 1, p. 443; *The Beast and the Sovereign*, vol. 1, p. 344.

19. Ibid., pp. 228-229; pp. 168-169.

20. Derrida, *L'animal que donc je suis*, p. 52; *The Animal That Therefore I Am*, p. 30.

21. Plato, *Phaedrus*, 265-266. Jacques Derrida, "Geschlecht II: Heidegger's Hand," p. 448; David Farrell Krell, *Intimations of Mortality: Time, Truth, and Finitude in Heidegger's Thinking of Being* (University Park: Pennsylvania State University Press, 1986), p. 165.

22. Derrida, *Séminaire: la bête et le souverain*, vol. 1, p. 242; *The Beast and the Sovereign*, vol. 1, p. 178.

23. Calarco, *Zoographies*, p. 140.

24. Derrida, *L'animal que donc je suis*, p. 51; *The Animal That Therefore I Am*, p. 29.

25. Jacques Derrida and Jean-Luc Nancy, "Responsabilité—du sens à venir," in Francis Guibal and Jean-Clet Martin, eds., *Sens en tous sens: Autour des traveaux de Jean-Luc Nancy* (Paris: Galilée, 2004), p. 196.

26. Derrida, *Séminaire: la bête et le souverain*, vol. 1, p. 255; *The Beast and the Sovereign*, vol. 1, p. 189.

27. Ibid, p. 403; p. 302.

28. Avital Ronell, *Stupidity* (Urbana: University of Illinois Press, 2002).

29. Ibid., p. 68.

30. Annie Kraus, *Vom Wesen und Ursprung der Dummheit* (Köln, Germany: Jakob Hegner, 1961).

31. Edmund Husserl, *Experience and Judgment: Investigations in a Genealogy of Logic*, trans. James S. Churchill (London: Routledge and Kegan Paul, 1973), §65.

32. Derrida, *Séminaire: la bête et le souverain*, vol. 1, p. 245; *The Beast and the Sovereign*, vol. 1, p. 181.

33. Ibid., p. 245; p. 180.

34. Ibid., p. 243; p. 179.

35. Ibid., pp. 224-225; p. 165. Words in square brackets added by JL.

36. Ibid., p. 226; p. 167.

37. Ibid., p. 246; p. 181.

38. Jacques Derrida and Jean-Luc Nancy, "'Eating Well,' or the Calculation of the Subject: An Interview with Jacques Derrida," in *Who Comes After the Subject?* ed. Eduardo Cadava, Peter O'Connor, and Jean-Luc Nancy (New York: Routledge, 1991), p. 111.

39. Martin Heidegger, *Being and Time,* trans. John Macquarrie and Edward Robinson (Oxford: Blackwell, 1967); trans. Joan Stambaugh (Albany: State University of New York Press, 1996), p. 163.

40. Immanuel Kant, *Fundamental Principles of the Metaphysics of Morals,* in *Kant's Critique of Pure Reason and Other Works on the Theory of Ethics,* trans. Thomas Kingsmill Abbott (London: Longmans, 1959), p. 53.

41. Cadava, O'Connor, & Nancy, *Who Comes After the Subject?* p. 116.

42. Derrida and Roudinesco, *De quoi demain,* p. 111. Calarco, *Zoographies,* p. 160.

43. Derrida and Roudinesco, *De quoi demain,* p. 112.

44. Derrida and Nancy, "Eating Well," in *Who Comes After the Subject?* pp. 116–117.

45. Donna J. Haraway, *When Species Meet* (Minneapolis: University of Minnesota Press, 2008), p. 23.

46. For a discerning and compassionate analysis of what it is to respond with least violence see Leonard Lawlor, *This Is Not Sufficient: An Essay on Animality and Human Nature in Derrida* (New York: Columbia University Press, 2007), another book Derrida would certainly have recommended.

13. Passover

1. Jacques Derrida, *Le toucher, Jean-Luc Nancy* (Paris: Galilée, 2000), pp. 209–243.

2. In a letter to the author.

3. Jacques Derrida, *Éperons: Les styles de Nietzsche* (Paris: Aubier-Flammarion, 1978); *Spurs: Nietzsche's Styles,* trans. Barbara Harlow (Chicago: University of Chicago Press, 1979).

4. Jean Lacoue-Labarthe and Jean-Luc Nancy, eds., *Les fins de l'homme. À partir du travail de Jacques Derrida* (Paris: Galilée, 1981).

5. Marie-Louise Mallet, ed., *Le passage des frontières. Autour du travail de Jacques Derrida* (Paris: Galilée, 1994).

14. The Rigor of a Certain Inhumanity

1. Jacques Derrida, Jean-Luc Marion, and Richard Kearney, "On the Gift," in John D. Caputo and Michael J. Scanlon, eds., *God, The Gift, and Postmodernism* (Bloomington: Indiana University Press, 1999), p. 75.

2. Ibid.

3. Jacques Derrida, "Une certaine possibilité impossible de dire l'événement," in Jacques Derrida, Gad Spisana, and Alexis Nouss, *Dire l'événement, est-ce possible?* Séminaire de Montréal, pour Jacques Derrida (Paris: L'Harmattan, 2001); "A Certain Impossible Possibility of Saying the Event," in W. J. T. Mitchell and Arnold I. Davidson, eds., *The Late Derrida* (Chicago: The University of Chicago Press, 2007).

4. Jean François Lyotard, *The Inhuman,* trans. Geoffrey Bennington and Rachel Bowlby (Cambridge: Polity Press, 1991), p. 2.

5. SEC is Derridean for "Signature Event Context." See the essay bearing that title in Jacques Derrida, *Margins of Philosophy,* trans. Alan Bass (Chicago: The University of Chicago Press, 1982).

6. Jean-Luc Nancy, *L'intrus* (Paris: Galilée, 2000).

7. Ibid., pp. 31-32. Emphasis added.

8. Ibid., pp. 35-36.

9. Paul Ricœur, *Soi-même comme un autre* (Paris: Seuil, 1990), pp. 387-393; *Oneself as Another,* trans. Kathleen Blamey (Chicago: University of Chicago Press, 1992), pp. 337-340. Michel Haar, "L'obsession de l'autre," in Catherine Chalier and Miguel Abensour, eds., *Emmanuel Lévinas* (Paris: l'Herne, 1991), pp. 444-453.

10. Simon Critchley, *Ethics—Politics—Subjectivity: Essays on Derrida, Levinas, and Contemporary French Thought* (London: Verso, 1999), p. 73, and p. 80, n54.

11. Jacques Derrida, *Le toucher, Jean-Luc Nancy* (Paris: Galilée, 2000), pp. 326-327.

12. See the delicate discussion in the chapter titled "The First Kiss: Tales of Innocence and Experience," in David Wood, *The Step Back: Ethics and Politics after Deconstruction* (Albany: State University of New York Press, 2005), pp. 73-84.

13. See, for example, Jacques Derrida, "Force of Law: 'The Mystical Foundation of Authority,'" trans. Mary Quaintance, in Drucilla Cornell, Michel Rosenfeld, and David Gray Carlson, eds., *Deconstruction and the Possibility of Justice* (New York: Cardozo Law Review, 1992); *Voyous* (Paris: Galilée, 2003); *Rogues: Two Essays on Reason,* trans. Pascale-Anne Brault and Michael Naas (Stanford, Calif.: Stanford University Press, 2005).

INDEX

John Llewelyn is former Reader in Philosophy at the University of Edinburgh. He is author of several books, including *Appositions of Jacques Derrida and Emmanuel Levinas* (Indiana University Press, 2002), *Seeing Through God* (Indiana University Press, 2004), and *Margins of Religion* (Indiana University Press, 2009).